Conflict Management in the Mediterranean and the Atlantic, 1000–1800

Legal History Library

VOLUME 39

Studies in the History of International Law

Series Editor

VOLUME 15

The titles published in this series are listed at *brill.com/shil*

Claude Gellée le Lorrain, *Port de mer avec soleil couchant* (1639), Musée du Louvre. Image Frédéric Cousinié. Le Lorrain's harbour scene is assumed to represent a diplomatic *tableau*. It could be a contemporary *théâtre des nations* taking place in an imaginary seaport, cluttered with Roman quotations, where a confrontation of the great powers of the time, France and Spain, is being staged. The painting was probably presented by Pope Urban VIII to the King of France in the course of the former's attempts to improve relations between the papacy and the French monarchy. The groups of individuals depicted in the front of the painting seem to express a multitude of relations, exchanges and common elements. While in the centre, two mariners are fighting, who seem to be part of the group directed by a Frenchman, a Spaniard, wearing glasses, appears to intervene, while yet another individual, perhaps an Italian, is about to draw his sword. On the left side of the painting, a musician, who is also a (possibly, French) soldier, is entertaining two women and a child. In-between these two groups, another Spaniard seems to enter a conversation with two men – a Frenchman, or alternatively someone from the Low Countries, and an 'oriental' merchant wearing a turban. It has been surmised that beyond the representation of interacting individuals representing different nations, the painting perhaps refers to specific episodes of diplomatic history. Beyond any particular circumstances, one may recognise in these ambiguities of human relations represented against the background of a seaport the variety of maritime conflicts and ways of conflict management in pre-modern times.

F. Cousinié, 'Les disputes du Soleil : Le Lorrain crypto-bamboche' in F. Cappelletti, A. Lemoine, C. Léribault eds., *Les Bas-fonds du Baroque. La Rome du vice et de la misère* (Paris, Petit-Palais, février-mars 2015) (Paris-Rome, Paris Musée des Beaux Arts, 2014) 67–81. F. Cousinié, 'Du réalisme pictural à la *Realpolitik*. Claude Gellée Le Lorrain, *Scène de port* de 1639' in Sybille Ebert-Schifferer, Annick Lemoine, Magali Théron, Mickaël Szanto eds., *L'Art d'après nature de Poussin à Lessing*, actes de colloque, Université de Provence-Université de Paris IV, 9–10 octobre, MuCEM de Marseille, *Arte dal Naturale*, Quaderni della biblioteca Hertziana (Rome, Campisato Editore, 2018) 223–244.

Conflict Management in the Mediterranean and the Atlantic, 1000–1800

Actors, Institutions and Strategies of Dispute Settlement

Edited by

Louis Sicking
Alain Wijffels

BRILL
NIJHOFF

LEIDEN | BOSTON

Cover illustration: Claude Gellée le Lorrain, *Port de mer avec soleil couchant* (1639), Musée du Louvre. Image Frédéric Cousinié.

The Library of Congress Cataloging-in-Publication Data is available online at http://catalog.loc.gov
LC record available at https://lccn.loc.gov/2020015819

Typeface for the Latin, Greek, and Cyrillic scripts: "Brill". See and download: brill.com/brill-typeface.

ISSN 1874-1793
ISBN 978-90-04-38063-9 (hardback)
ISBN 978-90-04-40799-2 (e-book)

This book is printed on acid-free paper and produced in a sustainable manner.

Contents

Acknowledgements

This book includes chapters derived from papers presented at two conferences co-organised by Louis Sicking. They were possible thanks to the Prix Descartes-Huygens 2016 awarded to him by the Académie des Sciences of the Institut de France and the international research project *Maritime Conflict Management in Atlantic Europe 1200–1600*, directed by him and financed by the Netherlands Organisation for Scientific Research (NWO), Vrije Universiteit Amsterdam, Leiden University, and the universities of Cantabria at Santander, La Laguna at Tenerife, La Rochelle and Nova Lisbon. Most of the papers were presented at the conference *Gestion des conflicts en Méditerranée et Atlantique, XIIIe–XVIIIe siècles: Acteurs, institutions et modes de règlement de différends*, organised at the premises of the École normale supérieure, 45 Rue d'Ulm, Paris in collaboration with Anne Wegener Sleeswijk, Wolfgang Kaiser and Evelyne Oliel Grausz (IHMC-Paris I Panthéon Sorbonne), 5–7 October 2017. Some of the other papers were previously presented at the international workshop *Conflicts and their Resolution in Atlantic Europe (13th–17th c.)* in collaboration with Eduardo Aznar Vallejo (IEMyR-Universidad de La Laguna) at the Universidad de La Laguna, Tenerife, Spain, 21–22 April 2017. The Institución Milá I Fontanals of the Consejo superior de investigaciones cientifícas in Barcelona offered hospitality which allowed to finalize the work for this volume. Alain Wijffels held the European Chair of European history at the Collège de France in 2017.

Tables

Abbreviations

ACCIMP	Archives de la Chambre de Commerce de Marseille
ACP	Archivo del Colegio del Patriarca
ADLC	Archives Diplomatiques, La Courneuve
AGS	Archivo General de Simancas
AH	Arquivo Histórico, Lisbon
AHDE	Anuario de Historia del Derecho Español
AHN	Archivo Histórico Nacional
AMB	Archivo Municipal de Bilbao
AML	Arquivo Municipal de Lisboa
AMV	Archivo Municipal de Valencia
ANF	Archives Nationales de France, Paris
APS	Archivo de Protocolos de Sevilla
ARChV	Archivo Real Chancillería de Valladolid
ARV	Archivo del Reino de Valencia
ASG	Archivio di Stato di Genova
BAA	Bank van Assurantien en Avarijen
BL	British Library, London
BN	Biblioteca Nacional, Madrid
BnF	Bibliothèque nationale de France, Paris
Bodl.	Bodleian Library, Oxford
BS	Basilica scholia
BT	Basilica text
CADN	Centre des Archives Diplomatiques de Nantes
CAJS	Katz Center for Advanced Judaic Studies, Philadelphia
CCR	*Calendar of the Close Rolls, preserved in the Public Record Office* [Lyte, H.C.M., *et al.* eds.], 47 vol. (London 1900–1963)
CHR	Chancelaria de D. Afonso V
CPR	*Calendar of the Patent Rolls, preserved in the Public Record Office* [Lyte, H.C.M., *et al.* (eds)], 53 vol. (London 1891–1916)
CRC	Consejo Real de Castilla
CUL Or	Cambridge University Library, Oriental Collection
DK	David Kaufmann Collection, Library of the Hungarian Academy of Sciences, Budapest
DLHA	Directie van den Levantschen Handel, Directie Amsterdam
DN	*Diplomatarium Norvegicum*
f.	folio
FPE	fundamental problem of exchange

GAV	Gavetas
IOM	Institute of Oriental Manuscripts of the Russian Academy of Sciences, St. Petersburg
LCM	*Libro del Consulado del Mar*
MAE	Ministère des Affaires Etrangères, France
Ms.	Manuscript
NA	Nationaal Archief, The Hague
NgL	*Norges gamle love*
PROME	Parliament Rolls of Medieval England
RE	Registro de Ejecutorias
r.	recto
RGS	Registro General del Sello
SAA	Stadsarchief Amsterdam
TNA	The National Archives, Kew, London
T-S	Taylor-Schechter Genizah Collection, Cambridge University, Cambridge
TT	Torre do Tombo, Lisbon
v.	verso
VOC	Dutch East-India Company
WIC	Dutch West-India Company

Notes on Contributors

Thierry Allain

is Senior Lecturer in Modern History in France, at the University Paul-Valéry Montpellier III. He is also member of the research center CRISES in Montpellier and associate member of the research center TELEMMe in Aix-en-Provence. His current research themes are maritime history and international relations in Europe in the early modern period. He works on the Dutch presence in the Mediterranean across the wider field of the decline of the Dutch Republic in the eighteenth century. He published a monograph, *Enkhuizen au XVIIIe siècle. Le déclin d'une ville maritime hollandaise au XVIIIe siècle* (2015), drawn from his doctorate, and co-authored a handbook on the Dutch Republic (2019). Amongst his articles is 'International treaties versus 'bonne prise' : the case of the Dutch merchant ship De Vriendschap in the Mediterranean in 1745', *Comparative Legal History* 5 no. 1 (2017).

Cátia Antunes

(PhD 2004, Leiden University) is Professor of History of Global Economic Networks: Merchants, Entrepreneurs and Empires at Leiden University. Her publications include *Globalisation in the Early Modern Period* (2004) and the (co-) edited volumes *Exploring the Dutch Empire. Agents, Networks and Institutions, 1600–2000* (2015) and *Beyond Empires. Global, Self-Organizing, Cross-Imperial Networks, 1500–1800* (2016) Her research has been generously supported by the European Research Council, the Netherlands Organization for Scientific Research (NWO) and the FP7 Program.

Eduardo Aznar Vallejo

is Professor of Medieval History at the University of La Laguna since 1989. He has been invited lecturer at European and Latin-American universities. He is Coordinator of the Research Group 'Castilla y el Mar en la Baja Edad Media' and member of the Research Group 'Derroteros Atlánticos' (University of La Laguna), Associated member of the International Research Network 'La Gobernanza de los puertos atlánticos, siglos XIV–XXI' and the Associação Ibérica de História Militar, Associated member of the Instituto de Estudios Medievales y Renacentistas of the University of La Laguna, Corresponding Member of the Royal Academy of History of Spain and Knight of the Ordre des Palmes Académiques of the French Republic. His research focusses on Late Medieval and Early Modern Maritime History (14th-16th centuries) in three main areas: Society and Power in Maritime Frontiers of Late Medieval Castile, European-Iberian Atlantic Expansion, and Conquest and Colonization of the Canary Islands.

Catarina Cotic Belloube

After completing a Master's degree on the Atlantic sugar trade between Portugal and Brazil in the late sixteenth century, Catarina Cotic Belloube started working on a doctoral thesis under the direction of Wolfgang Kaiser at the Université Paris 1 Panthéon-Sorbonne, within the Institut d'Histoire Moderne et Contemporaine (IHMC), where she also teaches undergraduate courses on both Modern Religious history and European political and social history. Her research focuses on the role of communal relations in the structuring of international trade through the study of the Portuguese merchant community in London in the second half of the seventeenth century. She is also associated to the project 'The Economic History of Jews in Modern History : archives, practices and mercantile networks' (Paris 1/Paris 7/EHESS/Rothschild Foundation Europe).

Kate Ekama

defended her PhD dissertation at Leiden University in 2018. Entitled *Courting Conflict: Managing Dutch East and West India Company disputes in the Dutch Republic* it addressed the underused archive of the High Court of Holland and Zeeland to illuminate questions of conflict management involving the VOC, WIC and States General. She also researches, publishes and teaches on the topic of slavery in the Indian Ocean World. In 2019 she joined the History Department at Stellenbosch University as a postdoctoral fellow. Her current research project focusses on the financial underpinnings of slavery in the Cape Colony.

Tiago Viúla de Faria

is Researcher in History at the Instituto de Estudos Medievais, NOVA University of Lisbon. His research is funded by national funds of Portugal through the FCT – Fundação para a Ciência e a Tecnologia, I.P., under the 'Norma Transitória' – DL57/2016/CP. Before, he was a scholar and fellow of the Casa de Velázquez, the École pratique des hautes études, of Towson University, and the University of Porto, and an associate lecturer of the University of Kent, UK. His main interests lie in diplomacy and external relations from the thirteenth to the fifteenth century with a focus on Portugal.

Ana Belem Fernández Castro

is a Postdoc Researcher in the framework of the project 'Mediterranean Reconfigurations: Intercultural Trade, Commercial Litigation and Legal Pluralism (15th-19th Centuries)' funded by the European Research Council. In 2015 she got her PhD on History and Civilization at the European University Institute in Florence. She is interested in topics related to commercial legal history, mercantile and legal institutions and legal pluralism in the Early Modern period, particularly in the case of the Spanish Empire.

Jessica Goldberg
is Associate Professor at the history department of the University of California, Los Angeles (UCLA), focusing on the medieval history of the Mediterranean basin, Christian Europe, and the Islamic world, specializing in economic and legal institutions and culture. Her first book, *Trade and Institutions in the Medieval Mediterranean: The Geniza Merchants and their Business World* (2012) explores the nature and geography of the medieval Islamic economy, the ways a group of merchants engaged with local and long-distance infrastructures and institutions of trade, and how notions of identity – religious, political, and geographic – affected the practices of business. Her research interests include the history of medieval trade, business, and industry, definitions of regions and regional identity in Late Antiquity and the Middle Ages, epistolographic culture, and the idea and practice of law in medieval societies.

Roberto J. González Zalacain
is a Lecturer in Medieval History at the University of La Laguna, Spain. His PhD in Medieval History (La Laguna) won the Research Prize for the best doctoral thesis in history awarded by the Spanish Parliament (2011). His research focuses on fifteenth and early sixteenth century maritime history, with a special focus on the Atlantic world; the history of violence and crime; history of the family and digital humanities and education. He is currently working on the analysis of the Castilian Kingdom's maritime borders. He has been involved in numerous research projects, and is a member of various research groups, both in Spain and Argentina. He is the author of several articles published both in Spanish and foreign journals and books.

Ian Peter Grohse
is Associate Professor of History at the Universitetet i Tromsø – Norges arktiske universitet. Grohse holds a PhD from Norges teknisk-naturvitenskapelige universitet in Trondheim, and a Master of Arts from the Humboldt-Universität zu Berlin. He has previously held posts as Associate Professor at the Høgskulen i Volda and Alexander-von-Humboldt Postdoctoral Fellow at the Wilhelms Westfälische-Universität Münster. Grohse has published on a range of topics relating to medieval Norway and the North Atlantic in the central and late Middle Ages. In addition to studies of Norse law, his publications include studies of Norway's foreign relations, kingship and mobility and immigration.

Thomas K. Heebøll-Holm
PhD. is Associate Professor in Medieval History at the Centre for Medieval Literature, University of Southern Denmark. His research interests include the history of piracy and maritime law in medieval Europe, Danish foreign relations and intellectual contacts with England and France in the High Middle Ages, and the history of emotions in medieval warfare. Among his principal publications are the monograph *Ports, Piracy and Maritime War* (2013), several articles concerning late medieval English and French piracy and naval institutions, and a number of forthcoming articles on the transition in medieval Denmark from Viking slave-raiding piracy and to a European feudal military and navy.

Laurence Jean-Marie
est maître de conférences, habilitée à diriger des recherches, à l'université de Caen Normandie. Elle est membre du laboratoire du CRAHAM – UMR 6273 (UNICAEN/CNRS). Ses axes de recherche principaux portent sur les relations entre Normandie et Angleterre, les sociétés portuaires et urbaines et spécialement les élites laïques, les gens de mer et activités maritimes, au cours des XIIe–XIVe siècle. Elle s'intéresse également aux pouvoirs urbains et aux pratiques de l'écrit en milieu urbain, notamment à partir des coutumiers des villes normandes.

Daphne Penna
studied law at the University of Athens in Greece where she completed her Masters in Legal History (2003). She wrote a dissertation at the University of Groningen on *The Byzantine Imperial Acts to Venice, Pisa and Genoa, 10th-12th Centuries. A Comparative Legal Study* (2012). She is currently Assistant Professor in the Legal History Department of the Law Faculty of the University of Groningen. Her interests lie in Roman and Byzantine law and especially in their influence on the European legal tradition. She teaches the following courses: *Seminar Byzantine Law* (in English), *The Legal Heritage of Europe* (in English), *Roman Law, Tutorials* (in Dutch) and *History of Codifications* (in Dutch and English).

Pierrick Pourchasse
est professeur d'histoire moderne à l'Université de Bretagne occidentale à Brest et chercheur au CRBC. Ses recherches portent sur le commerce maritime à l'époque moderne et l'histoire économique de la Scandinavie. Il est l'auteur de plusieurs ouvrages dont *Le commerce du Nord. Les échanges entre la France et l'Europe septentrionale au XVIIIe siècle* (2006), *Le commerce de la rogue* (2013) et d'environ 80 articles portant sur ces sujets.

Pierre Prétou
is Lecturer in Medieval History at La Rochelle University. He is a member of the research group LIENSs (Littoral, environnement et sociétés, UMR 7266, CNRS), currently delegated at CLAMOR (Centre pour Les humAnités nuMériques et l'histOiRe de la justice, UMS 3726, CNRS). He is the chief editor of *Criminocorpus*, a digital journal on the history of justice, crime and punishment.

Ana María Rivera Medina
is a Professor of Medieval History at the Universidad de Educación a Distancia (Spain) where she obtained a PhD in Medieval History (2010). She also holds a PhD in American Modern History (1987) from the University of Seville and is the author of several scientific publications. Her current fields of interest and work are Urban and Maritime History. She is currently a Senior Visiting Fellow for the ERC-funded AveTransRiskProject and member of Spanish and European research networks and groups, including *La Gobernanza de los puertos atlánticos, siglos XIV–XXI*, *Gis d'Histoire Maritime & Sciences de la Mer*, *Castilla y el mar en la Baja Edad Media*, CITCEM – Centro de Investigação Transdisciplinar 'Cultura, Espaço e Memória'.

Louis Sicking
is the Aemilius Papinianus Professor of History of Public International Law at Vrije Universiteit Amsterdam and Lecturer in Medieval and Early Modern History at the University of Leiden. He is director of the research project *Maritime Conflict Management in Atlantic Europe, 1200–1600*, financed by the Netherlands Organization for Scientific Research (NWO) and the universities of Cantabria, La Laguna, La Rochelle and Nova Lisbon. His books include *Neptune and the Netherlands* (2004), *Colonial Borderlands* (2008) and *La naissance d'une thalassocratie* (2015). His main research interests are maritime and colonial history and the history of diplomacy and international law.

Carlo Taviani
worked on political conflicts in Renaissance Italy and economic and financial history of Genoa. He has been fellow of the Folger Shakespeare Library, Villa I Tatti (The Harvard University Center for Italian Renaissance Studies), visiting scholar at Yale University and Chicago University. He has thought at the Università degli Studi di Teramo, the Università degli Studi di Trento and at the University of Cape Town. He is currently co-fellow of the German Historical Institute in Rome and of Villa I Tatti. His research focuses on the Genoese trade diaspora in the Atlantic and Africa (1450–1530) and institutional transplantation.

Dominique Valérian

Professeur d'histoire médiévale à l'Université Paris 1 Panthéon-Sorbonne, après l'avoir été à l'Université Lumière-Lyon 2 (2011–2017), Dominique Valérian est agrégé d'histoire, ancien membre de l'École française de Rome, et membre de l'UMR 8167 Orient & Méditerranée (équipe Islam médiéval). Spécialiste de l'Islam d'Occident et de la Méditerranée, il a consacré une grande partie de ses travaux à l'étude des relations entre chrétiens et musulmans en Méditerranée et des réseaux d'échanges. Sa thèse, *Bougie, port maghrébin (1067–1510)* a été publiée en 2016 par l'École française de Rome, et son habilitation, *Ports et réseaux d'échanges dans le Maghreb médiéval*, est sous presse à la Casa de Velázquez. Il a en outre co-dirigé *Espaces et réseaux en Méditerranée. VIe–XVIe siècle*, I, *La configuration des réseaux* (Paris, 2007) et II, *La formation des réseaux* (Paris, 2011), et *Les territoires de la Méditerranée. XIe–XVIe siècle* (Rennes, 2013). Il co-dirige actuellement le séminaire de recherche sur la Méditerranée médiévale à l'Université Paris 1.

Alain Wijffels

teaches legal history and comparative law. He lectures in Kortrijk, Leiden, Leuven, and Louvain-la-Neuve. He is also research fellow of the French CNRS. He holds degrees in philosophy, law, canon law, Roman law, criminology, Medieval history. He was awarded the degree of doctor of law at the University of Amsterdam, and the degrees of PhD and DLitt in Cambridge. His research has focused on comparative legal history in Europe, with an emphasis on the civil law tradition in the practice of higher courts and in public governance.

INTRODUCTION

Flotsam and Jetsam in the Historiography of Maritime Trade and Conflicts

Louis Sicking and Alain Wijffels

Medieval and early-modern long-distance trade was fraught with risks. Maritime long-distance trade entailed specific risks. Adverse human and natural factors could easily result in a commercial venture's partial or total loss. Such risks, especially when they materialized, often created conflicts of interests, which, in turn, could affect how the partially or entirely failed venture could be dealt with, but also how the various actors involved in the conflict of interest would deal with each other in future business ventures. Not surprisingly, historians have shown great interest in the various ways those actors have tried to manage and solve the ensuing disputes. Through the study of conflict management and resolution, much information can also be gained on the business practices themselves, and the different social groups who played, directly or indirectly, a part in their preparation, in carrying them out, and eventually in dealing with the anticipated or unanticipated effects of such enterprises. These social actors were manifold: apart from the merchants themselves, they include (and could at times be the same as the merchants) sailors, investors, holders of public offices, privateers, pirates...

Long-distance trade quickly developed the role of agents, already ubiquitous in ancient sources. Agents both facilitated and complicated long-distance commercial operations and relations. They often reflected, but also bridged, the cross-cultural hurdles which had to be overcome. Those cross-cultural hurdles were even enhanced when they implied different religions and political cultures. In the case of disputes, they also entailed different mechanisms for handling conflictual situations. Conflict management and resolution operated characteristically in a context of multi-governance and pluri-jurisdictional polities with concurrent social networks and institutions, as illustrated for eleventh- and twelfth-century Cairo in J. Goldberg's key-note address. Jewish merchants were able to bring their interests and cases before either Jewish or Islamic jurisdictions, though the rationale for preferring one or the other option could depend on the circumstances and the effects they sought.

 | DOI:10.1163/9789004407992_002

Although maritime commercial practices varied from one marine region to the other around the European world, and differences were exacerbated by particular laws, institutions, and jurisdictions which often anchored locally, international trade still developed in spite of all the cultural, religious and political barriers. Merchants who engaged in far-distance trade had nonetheless to anticipate, and if possible, calculate, the hazards of the seas, of hostile populations on their journey, but also of different legal systems and different ways of doing business. Merchants, rulers and their delegated authorities had to address the difficulties of transcending such difficulties which could impede trade. Agents had to be persuaded and enabled to make firm commitments without finding themselves deprived of remedies when other parties failed to comply with their obligations. Agents themselves were not above the fray and suspicion. Some degree of institutional connections proved in some cases (as that of the Royal Aragonese, the Catalan and the Valencian mercantile institutions) effective in detecting and sanctioning those who had cheated the system and made it possible to develop alternative arrangements for dealing with issues arising from the principal-agent relations.[1]

1 The Normative Power of Conflict and Violence in Pre-modern Maritime Conflicts

From the high Middle Ages, maritime trade and various forms of conflict developed hand in hand. Those who went out to sea, whether seafarers involved in transporting goods, merchants, or fishermen, were willing to take risks. In medieval terms, they would face 'aventure'.[2] The perils of the sea were manifold, but so were the perspectives for profit. The Vikings, designated as such by their enemies, were seeking both adventure and profit. In their eyes, trading and plundering were intrinsically associated.[3] In the medieval Atlantic and Baltic Europe, too, trade and robbery were two sides of the same coin. The commercial network known as the Hanse suppressed or used piracy, which was an endemic occurrence.[4] The same was true for the maritime entrepreneurs

1 Eggertsson (1990) 40–48. Greif (2000); Greif (2005); Greif (2008); Grafe and Gelderblom (2010) and S. Ogilvie (2011).
2 De Boer (2007) 49–68. Tranchant (2008) 9–45. Tranchant (2013) 7–14.
3 Fitzhugh (2000) 14. Blockmans and Hoppenbrouwers (2014) 101–102.
4 Rohmann (2017) 1–49. U. Kypta and T. Geelhaar (2013) 198.

of the medieval Mediterranean. According to the *Llibre del Consolat de Mar*, the skipper and merchants on board a merchant ship could collectively decide to attack an enemy ship and then divide the loot taken.[5] In the medieval maritime environment, economic and violent actors were often the same.[6] Originally, maritime violence and robbery did not necessarily entail an emotionally charged negative connotation. A common saying in the late-medieval Hanseatic world expressed the common view by stating: 'to rob is no shame, the best of the land do it'.[7] If the opportunity arose, anyone sailing on the seas would seize it and reap a profit.

For a long time (and still frequently nowadays), historians have relied on an overwrought opposition between peaceful traders and violent pirates in order to explain or understand the mechanisms of maritime enterprise. However, one should be weary of applying such a modern distinction, on which entire historiographical narratives have been built for pre-modern times.[8] Before the emergence of the modern state, the notion of a monopoly of violence hardly prevailed, and even when such a claim became part of the discourse of late-medieval and early-modern governments, it remained far from a reality. First and foremost, pre-modern societies were shaped by legal and normative pluralism. Modern categories such as peaceful trade and violent robbery prevent therefore an adequate understanding of pre-modern developments of maritime conflicts and maritime conflict management. Conflict management was inherent to maritime enterprise, and is a central theme of the present volume.[9] In this context, it is worth recalling that Frederic Lane, a historian of the Mediterranean world mostly known for his classic study *Venice. A Maritime Republic*, developed a model which makes it possible to integrate the use of violence among the options available to those involved in maritime commerce.[10] As Lane and others have shown, in order to understand maritime enterprise in pre-modern times, long-distance or international trade can only be fully understood when the use of violence is taken into account.

5 Sohmer Tai (2012) 842–843. Sohmer Tai (2007) 5 (accessed 13 March 2017). Coulon (2004) 202.

6 Heebøll-Holm, Höhn, and Rohmann (2019) 29.

7 Sicking (2018) 435.

8 See Sicking (2018) and Heebøll-Holm, Höhn and Rohmann (2019).

9 This is recognized in recent research not only by medieval historians, but also by early modern historians. See for example Parrott (2012) 35–40.

10 Lane (1979). See more recently Bullard, Epstein, Kohl and Stuard (2004) 88–119.

Besides the use of violence, many other coercive measures were used in maritime trade, including blockades, the closure or relocation of trading posts, or the taxation of competitors (all which have been recognized as key factors in the success of the Hanse in Northern Europe).[11] When it is recognized that peaceful trade and violence were inseparable features in pre-modern maritime operations, the importance of maritime conflict management becomes obvious, although conflicts did not arise from the use of violence alone. Maritime conflict management includes a variety of devices, such as conflict enforcement through naval warfare, privateering, piracy and blockades, conflict resolution, whether through formal judicial and administrative procedures, or through more informal, possibly private, channels, but also conflict avoidance (for example through negotiations and diplomacy).

2 From Conflict Resolution to Conflict Management

The history of conflict resolution has often been studied through the prism of diplomacy and the law of nations. More recently, the emphasis has shifted to the process of conflict resolution itself. This, in turn, has fostered a more detailed interest in the different actors and institutions involved, alongside in-depth case studies. Conflict management has a broader meaning than conflict resolution, as the concept includes alternative modes of dealing with conflicts which do not necessarily result in resolving the differences. Beyond classical issues such as naval warfare, piracy and privateering, medieval historians and historians exploring the worlds of the early modern Mediterranean and Atlantic have increasingly directed their attention to forms of conflict settlement and conflict avoidance, but also looked into the vast diversity of formal judicial procedures and informal or private mechanisms of settling disputes.[12]

Maritime conflicts have been a developing area of research on conflict management, but it is an area which requires still more attention, because the overall emphasis has been on state formation, and has therefore remained predominantly land-oriented. The present volume aims instead at focusing on the maritime perspective, following an approach centred on the actors and their disputes. How did victims of maritime conflicts claim compensation

11 See for example Höhn (2019) 143–144.

12 Some recent literature Cordes and Höhn (2018); Sicking (2017); Miranda and Wubs-Mrozewicz (2017).

or restitution? How and to what extent could they count on the support from authorities and polities? How did individual actors and public institutions negotiate disputes which transcended jurisdictional boundaries (for example, those involving reprisal and piracy)? What strategies were activated in order to achieve resolution of those conflicts, and how effective were those strategies?

3 The Mediterranean and the Atlantic: Contrasting and Common Features

The Mediterranean has sometimes been perceived as an 'interface' between opposite religious-normative systems, Christianity and Islam. Piracy was acceptable (or even encouraged) against sailors of the other faith, which had the effect of blurring the distinction between privateering (or *corso*) and piracy (D. Valérian). Along the Atlantic coast, by contrast, piracy began to be systematically criminalised from the late fourteenth century onwards in the policies of the French and English kings (P. Prétou, T. Heebøll-Holm).[13] Perhaps, as suggested by some authors, those policies should be seen in the context of the kings' increasing interests in asserting their claims on some form of jurisdiction over sea-territories. However, T. Heebøll-Holm points out that the English king's claims of 'sovereignty' over the sea could practically not be implemented, and have to be distinguished from the criminalisation of pirates through the device of high-treason applied to the king's own subjects, which may be seen as a strategy which aimed at reinforcing the king's authority and control over the realm's available maritime resources. Prétou argues that the criminalisation of pirates did not work to the advantage of merchants, an argument which undermines the conventional dichotomy between the peaceful trader and the violent pirate, which would then appear to have been a political-legal construct of royal authority bent on increasing its power. Whereas damage inflicted through plundering could earlier on have been discharged as if a matter of accounting, the pirate now risked capital punishment. In contrast, the Mediterranean *corso* remained a system which could be settled financially. Even so, even in the Atlantic regions, financial settlement of plundering remained an

13 This phenomenon has also been recognized for the Hanse. Hanseatic efforts to criminalize piracy may have preceded those of England and France. Sicking (2018) 451. Rohmann (2017) 12–14.

option. Much depended on the political and diplomatic circumstances. The diversity of maritime conflicts offered both the private and public actors a range of opportunities, but also imposed some restrictions. Faced with a dispute, merchants could request the support of their ruler, or of their opponents' ruler. Such requests often offered the authorities whose support was sought a chance to enhance their authority. That was the case when the authorities provided help to their own subjects (who, for example, had been forced to contribute with their ships to their king's war-fleet, L. Jean Marie), but also when the authorities gave assistance to foreign merchants. Broader political and diplomatic considerations could convince a ruler to help settling a dispute where foreign merchants were involved in his realm. Diplomatic alliances between kings were nonetheless no full-proof guarantee for a successful or efficient settlement of damage claims between their subjects (T. Viúla de Faria).

Conflicts of interests are an essential feature of public and private commercial governance. Merchants who start on a venture will need to negotiate. Public authorities are concerned about trade balance, but also about the broader effects of trade on their domestic economy and social welfare, since a high rate of employment may secure a degree of social peace. Domestic peace and peace in foreign affairs can nonetheless prove elusive, and all social and political actors will therefore find it prudent to incorporate a calculation of such risks when planning commercial ventures and policies. Moreover, some conflicts of interests tend to be structural, inherent to particular trade relations. In addition, there is always the risk of the bargain turning wrong, or some external factor interfering with the planned enterprise. All risks had somehow to be accounted for in the calculation of costs. Some risks could be prevented or minimised, though not all could be insured against. Conflicts belonged to the risks of any venture and could occur in various ways. Conflict calculation was a day-to-day ingredient in trade planning, whether by individual merchants, firms and joint-ventures, or policy makers. Conflict resolution, which could take different forms, was one way to control and thus limit the risks, but it stood at the tail end of a whole panoply of devices of conflict management, which was often a more realistic approach to deal with conflicts of interests for which there was no quick or obvious outcome (J. Goldberg). Not all the devices of conflict management and resolution were judicial or even governed by legal considerations. During the later Middle Ages and the transition to early-modern times, judicial proceedings, whether state-controlled or not, as a form of conflict management were often (in contrast to the meaning given nowadays to the phrase) a newly available option of 'alternative dispute resolution' which presupposed the possibility of establishing a stable model of *trias forensis* acceptable to all those interest groups who had a stake in containing the strife.

Such general developments have received fresh attention from historians and legal historians in recent decades. The accumulation of evidence may by now suggest more general considerations about the techniques and features of conflict management and resolution in former times, but the dialectics of such historical research require that the particular features of a specific period, region or social group and their impact on conflict management patterns continue to be studied in their own right. The nowadays well-established comparative approach is one way to bridge the constantly shifting gap between specific findings and generalizations. The present volume reflects such an approach. Its original vantage-point is to bring together two experiences which in the past have often been viewed separately. The one is that of maritime (mostly commercial) relations in the Mediterranean and the other in the Atlantic, connecting countries and communities which happened to have coastlines on either one or both seas. Until recently, students of the maritime dimension have mainly studied either the Mediterranean or the Atlantic region, producing separate historiographies.[14] These two areas were of course not unconnected. Indeed, a great deal of maritime trade since the Middle Ages between Northern and Southern Europe (and Northern Africa and the Middle East) depended on the fluid and intensive intercourse that characterised the connexion between the Mediterranean and the Atlantic worlds. However strongly intertwined the two worlds could be, they nevertheless retained distinctive features, because of their respective geographical environment, political forces and dynamics, climate and weather conditions, and many other factors. Anyone who has sailed in the Mediterranean and along the Atlantic coast through the Channel to the North Sea, will have realised that the maritime conditions are not quite the same everywhere. Inspired by global history there is now a growing interest in questions regarding the connections between different seascapes.[15] The present volume aims to contribute to

14 These historiographies have also resulted in syntheses focusing on a particular seascape. For example Abulafia (2011), North (2011) and Butel (1997).

15 For instance Aznar Vallejo and González Zalacain (2015), the conference *Insularities Connected. Bridging Seascapes, from the Mediterranean to the Indian Ocean and Beyond* organised by Antonis Hadjikyriacou and Sakis Gekas at the Institute for Mediterranean studies, Rethymno, Crete, 10–12 June 2016 and the conference *Entre Mers – Outre-Mer: Spaces, Modes and Agents of Indo-Mediterranean Connectivity (3rd Century* BCE*–18th Century)* that was held at Heidelberg University in 2014 which resulted in Jaspert and Kolditz

connect the Mediterranean and the Atlantic from the perspective of conflict management; it brings together a range of scholars working on these two areas of research, allowing for a comparative and long-term perspective. This may reveal connections between the different seascapes and shed a useful light on the multiplicity and complexity of the paths chosen for the management of disputes.

The collected essays thus reflect the successive stages at which conflict management was required. At each stage, they also illustrate how public authorities and private merchants, whether individually or in some form of association, approached the issues.

4 Anticipation and Prevention of Conflicts

Among the strategies which appear from the earliest periods onwards, reconnaissance of the regions where trade was to take place played an important role. Information was required about the market overseas: What were the demands and what goods were being offered? What factors affected foreigners' trade: local usages, restrictions, taxes, recurrent warfare or unrest… Also, and here the contingency of potential conflicts appears, what mechanisms of protection were available to merchants who, through misfortune or disputes, were stranded or ill-treated in a foreign environment? In that context, several contributions illustrate how merchants tried to cope with the inevitable multinormativity they faced in the course of international commercial expeditions. Jewish merchants in eleventh and twelfth century Cairo 'were often eager to gain the greatest legal protections each kind of contract they entered into could offer – perhaps stronger evidence to their *ex ante* trust in the legal system's protective capacity than incidence of lawsuits or their resolution' (J. Goldberg). Young men who still had to learn the trade were sent abroad to understand the workings of foreign markets, their institutions, and were also, as in medieval Norway, encouraged to get a grasp of the various laws governing commercial operations (I.P. Grohse). Multi-normativity was probably always the common feature of maritime trade, whether in the Mediterranean or along the Atlantic. The regional diversity of normative systems remains a controversial issue. In contrast to earlier theories on overarching trans-regional maritime laws and on a general mercantile law, partly based on enactments or

(2018). See also the exihibition at Institut du monde arabe in Paris and the Mucem in Marseille and the catalogue *Aventuriers* (2016).

compilations of laws applicable in the Byzantine empire, in Norway, along the Atlantic coasts (*Rôles d'Oléron*) or in parts of the Mediterranean (*Consolato del Mar*), most of the contributions in this volume prefer to emphasise the nowadays more fashionable theme of the diversity of particular customs and laws and the ensuing 'legal pluralism' (D. Penna, I.P. Grohse, E. Aznar Vallejo & R.J. González Zalacain).[16]

Byzantine legislation, largely based on older layers of Roman law, with regard to shipwrecks and salvage, proved difficult to implement in regions where local populations perceived their legitimate interests to be better secured by other customs. The imposition of harsher penalties by the imperial lawmaker reflects the difficulty of regulating such practices. Some influential groups, such as Italian merchants from Venice or Genoa, succeeded in obtaining a specific legal regime of protection, which the emperors would then, or so they promised, more strongly enforce (D. Penna). In the late Middle Ages, the rulers of Castile would be confronted with similar conflicts of interests and heterogeneous norms (E. Aznar Vallejo & R.J. González Zalacain). The professional groups and local communities involved were a complex network of partly overlapping, partly diverging, interests, whose particular norms contributed to the overall complex normativity characteristic of maritime trade (A.M. Rivera Medina). Conventions made between rulers as part of the high politics of international relations, such as the treaties pledging amicable relations between the English and Portuguese Crowns, were only part of the equation in private merchants' and public authorities' calculations: during the recurrent hostilities during the Hundred Years' war, such treaties and diplomatic ties between the kings of England and Portugal proved often at best an unreliable default line for arguing compensation if they had failed to protect Portuguese merchants against acts of piracy or official interventions. Despite the formal framework of the treaties, merchants therefore constantly faced a diversity of risks and ensuing conflicts. For some, of course, risk assessment also entailed a commercial assessment of the opportunities wars and war-bound disturbances offered (T. Viúla de Faria).

Private and public interests could clash, but also overlap and coincide. Medieval kings who required naval capacities in wartime would seize private vessels, but their actions would have to balance the advantages of such seizures with the need to keep trade going until the war broke out and even during wartime (L. Jean-Marie, T. Viúla de Faria): in such cases, from the vantage-point of

16 This corresponds with the conclusions of Cordes (2017) 69–85 and Frankot (2012).

the merchants, the calculation of profit and risk became highly speculative (T. Heebøll-Holm). The manipulation of foreign policy in connection with warfare did not end with medieval times, as exemplified by the Dutch handling of the relatively brief and non-momentous war with Algiers in 1755–1757, an example which moreover shows that the merchant community itself could be divided, owing to internal rivalries (T. Allain). Therefore, in many contributions, it becomes obvious that it is not possible to recognise a clear-cut divide between private and public interests: a late-seventeenth century case in which the Portuguese Jewish merchant community in London successfully challenged the surveyor of the customs' attempts to crack down on illicit trade and tax evasion may be an indication that considerations in favour of maintaining the edge over foreign (here specifically, Dutch) competitors could set off the ordinary due process of law (C. Cotic Belloube).

Even piracy, one of the major factors of risk calculation for sea-merchants over the centuries, may not have been a topic of consistently straightforward public policy. Several contributions emphasise how the central authorities' fight against piracy has been instrumental in asserting the sovereign's supremacy both with regard to sea territory and to coastal communities which had traditionally enjoyed a degree of self-government (D. Valérian, T. Heebøll-Holm, P. Prétou). However, even the development of privateering, entailing a political and legal distinction which in theory should have entrenched even further the specific definition of the pirate, did not remove the 'fluid boundary of (il)legality' (C. Antunes & K. Ekama). For powerful companies such as the Dutch East and West Indian companies, privateering was both a threat and a commercial opportunity (*ibidem*), but, with the development of insurance techniques, even lesser merchants could somehow afford to view privateering as a calculated risk (P. Pourchasse).

Although multi-normativity continued to prevail throughout early-modern times, some progress towards common norms started to develop. Particularly in the Mediterranean, where the Northern and Southern coasts were divided by a deep religious and cultural fault-line, an inchoative system of common rules may be seen to have evolved: in the struggle against piracy, by state practice expressed through the progressive accumulation of treaties (D. Valérian), or by converging, yet distinct, practices in consular representation arrangements between Ottoman and Christian rulers.

Maritime trade, as the contributions in this volume make clear, took place against a backdrop of both war and peace. There is no clear border-line on the continuum of peaceful commercial ventures and aggressive forms of predatory expeditions. Conflicts were part of the risk assessment and the calculation of costs. Conflicts were hazards as much to be anticipated as accidents, storms, acts of God. Any preliminary consideration of dispute resolution or management needs to take into account how conflicts were part of the considerations and planning before any commercial venture set out.

5 The Diversity of Conflicts

A conventional distinction would be to differentiate between private conflicts and conflicts which affect peace and order, hence threaten public policy. As with the distinction between the Atlantic seas and the Mediterranean, those are not hermetically separate categories, they are interconnected and cover a grey area where both meet: for example, when conflicts of private interests acquire such dimensions that they start spilling over into the macro-economic interests of a state, they become inevitably issues of public policy, even if the conflicts themselves remain peaceful. The two terms should be seen as the 'poles' on a spectrum. On the one side, private conflicts which remained within a (often, contractual) trade relationship, but could nevertheless affect a (limited) number of merchants joined in a formal or informal association. In order to remain private, disputes of this kind should be handled, when a settlement is sought, relatively peacefully, i.e. should not be marked by actions *vi et armis*. Moreover, as suggested, they should remain confined to private interests, without affecting public interests such as necessary and strategic exports or imports of a state, or diplomatic relations. Conflicts became public as soon as public authorities started taking actively an interest in them, other than providing a framework for their settlement. Public conflicts, in other words, affected the policies of political governance. Such conflicts could occur within the domestic space of a polity, but in the case of maritime trade, also on and beyond the high seas.

The present volume offers examples of a wide variety of such conflicts. On board of ships, the commanding officer and the crew were to some extent bound by common interests, but these could also diverge in case of breaches of the discipline and other violations of conventional social norms. The joint liability for losses in some cases was obviously a recurrent cause of disputes (D. Penna, I.P. Grohse, E. Aznar Vallejo & R.J. González Zalacain), in one particular case discussed in this volume even of mutiny (C. Antunes & K. Ekama). Inevitably, also, the internal relations within commercial networks, for example between principals and their agents, could lead to conflicts exacerbated by distance and delays of communication (*ibidem*). Interference of the authorities in the existing networks of merchant communities encompassing rival nations abroad would cause tensions opposing such a community and the authorities responsible for the policies and those in charge of their implementation (C. Cotic Belloube). Barring circumstances which could lead to violence or other disturbances of the peace, the various networks of transporters and mariners, merchants and agents, both at home and abroad, were on the whole interdependent and shared therefore a common interest in avoiding or settling peacefully their disputes and escape the public eye's scrutiny and control. An intermediate situation was that of the ports where a consul was established. The latter often had a position combining commercial interests of his own and official duties, acting in addition as a mediator or intermediary between disputing parties, both private and institutional (T. Allain). Merchants forming a distinctive group or a particular nation abroad would be to some extent joined by common interests vis-à-vis the local and sovereign authorities where they were operating, and in relation with other foreign merchants, but such common interests did not preclude internal strife, whether in their outpost or on the home front (C. Taviani). Other networks involving merchants and other stakeholders in maritime trade were lobbying groups, whose actions could alternatively facilitate smooth relations or generate fresh disputes, not least because of the temptation or risk of corruption their interaction with office holders entailed (C. Cotic Belloube).

The more violent maritime operations, such as piracy and privateering, generated a use of force which authorities were at times keen to channel to their own advantage, but because of the threat they more often than not presented to their own merchant communities and to the sovereign's authority, they were subject to a pendulum of contradictory policies, which at times would support and incite their actions, at other times make a display of repression towards their perpetrators. Peace may have been a virtue and purpose of good governance, but the rulers' willingness to act in good governance seldom excluded warfare as a legitimate means of pursuing their policies. Toleration of piracy or active encouragement of privateering fitted on the scale of foreign policies which allowed for an intermediary range of policies between ensuring effectively peaceful relations and actual war (C. Antunes &. K. Ekama, T. Allain). Acts of piracy, often a regular occupation of coastal communities (A.M. Rivera Medina, T. Heebøll-Holm), operating both on the Atlantic and in the Mediterranean (P. Prétou), would only more forcefully be fought against if they were perceived to harm the polity's prominent interests, supposing the polity's rulers held a sufficient position of power to extend their authority on the high seas (A.M. Rivera Medina, T. Heebøll-Holm, T. Viúla de Faria, P. Prétou), a situation which was only to a limited extent achieved before the eighteenth century, and even then often required some joint diplomatic resolutions (T. Allain). *Lis lites generat*, was a saying sometimes heard with regard to litigation. Although the usual cliché about non-judicial or specialist commercial adjudicating bodies consists in pointing out the advantages, especially for merchants, of a swift and relatively less costly dispute resolution, examples are also occasionally to be found where the protracting of legal proceedings itself could enter the calculation of profits, by speculating on the accumulation of accrued compensation due (P. Pourchasse). Already in the Middle Ages, when the rulers' capacity to control the high seas was mostly limited, merchants had to take into consideration a diversity of strategies – some legal, some beyond the scope of the law – which might have helped them to seek compensation or cut their losses. The position was often different for investors or large-scale entrepreneurs who could diversify their ventures and for individuals, who would find themselves entangled in endless efforts to seek redress, without any certain prospect of recovering their claims or even their freedom (T. Viúla de Faria).

Historiography on the early-modern state has often emphasised how that early-modern state's development established itself by claiming successfully a 'monopoly of violence'. It is doubtful whether on the open seas, such a monopoly had been achieved by the end of early-modern times. From medieval times, recurrent (but intermittent) efforts were made in order to secure at least some of that authority in particular maritime areas, but maritime trade continued to navigate until the end of the Ancien Régime in waters which proved too elusive for the states' powers of the era. Control remained marginal and imperfect. An alternative typology of conflictual relations in that context might be based on the relative distinction between conflicts within the province of the state's power and jurisdiction, and at the other end those which were beyond the reach of the state's coercive sway.

6 Managing and Settling Conflicts

Conflict management in the context of maritime trade offers an exceedingly wide range of strategies. At one end of the scale, discreet negotiations between private merchants could result in finding a temporary or more permanent way out of a conflict of interests, while at the other end, public authorities would apply the full force of criminal law to mete out punishment – and depending on the type of conflict, that punishment could even extend to other states: in early-modern international law, it was common to envisage war as a form of adjudication, handing out justice, since international courts above the sovereign states were not available.

Before the late Middle Ages, the logistics of maritime trade did not always make it possible to appeal to adequate judicial assistance and control. Merchants were therefore often bound to seek a negotiated way out of disputes. Such low-profile forms of dispute management are rarely documented and escape to a large extent historical investigation (J. Goldberg). Among mariners, usages are better known when they were consigned to writing. Thus, Norwegian customs reveal that the pattern of communal justice was extended to conflicts arising at or beyond the sea, where the skipper's administration of justice may at times have been replaced by a more collective form of justice among crewmen through 'an assembly of oarsmen' acting 'as prosecutors and jurors' (I.P. Grohse). Notarial instruments, when they can be properly contextualised, offer occasionally some insight in non-judicial settlements (C. Taviani), for example by recording an arbitration (A. Belem Fernández Castro). Arbitration itself covers a wide range of forms of conflict management, whether informal or, when (semi-)official agents such as consuls intervened, in a more formal context (E. Aznar Vallejo & R.J. González Zalacain). Legal pluralism remained a feature in all jurisdictions until the end of early-modern times. The diversity of particular laws was in general sustained by a corresponding jurisdictional diversity. The studies both in the Mediterranean space and along the Atlantic show that conflicts related to maritime trade could be dealt with by ordinary, non-specialised courts, but sometimes more specialised commercial or maritime courts (prize courts, admiralty courts, merchants' courts ...) were available. Medieval Cairo was a commercial centre where several jurisdictional systems coexisted. An individual merchant's status, both within his particular (ethnical, religious, local...) community and in relation to merchants outside his community, however influential or prominent he was, ultimately depended on efficient interaction within the business network of his own community. Thus, the evidence from the Cairo Geniza on business practices involving Jewish merchants and on dispute management between them points out that preliminary steps towards litigation and actual procedural steps before a Rabbinic court may also have been strategies tending to involve, beyond the specific litigants, the wider community of merchants of those networks, who would therefore all be affected by litigation and its adverse publicity, and would therefore have indirectly a stake in the way the dispute was settled. Such considerations may have had an inhibitive or pacifying effect on full-scale formal proceedings, which could prove detrimental not only to the litigating merchants, but to the merchant communities to which they belonged (J. Goldberg). Another example, that of merchants from Valencia involved in long-distance trade, suggests that the variety and complementarity of available adjudicating institutions may have had a favourable effect on the effective ways of managing end resolving merchants' disputes (A. Belem Fernández Castro). That, of course, applied to civil disputes, where compensation for damage was usually the central issue (P. Prétou, P. Pourchasse). Statute law on shipwrecks and salvage in the Byzantine empire included both civil sanctions, but also incentives, in particular for finders (D. Penna). The development of reprisals in the Middle Ages, which in maritime relations lived on in different guises throughout the early-modern period, became at times more associated with violent forms of state-controlled or -approved self-justice (L. Jean-Marie). The banned use of force, resulting in piracy, invited the implementation of harsher state justice, *viz.* through criminal procedures (D. Valérian, T. Heebøll-Holm, P. Prétou) and, ultimately, when state actors were involved, war (T. Allain).

•••

Case-studies are notoriously tricky for teasing out general conclusions. Some general findings may, notwithstanding, be drawn from the different essays in the present volume. Several authors insist on the great diversity of conflicts and methods of dealing with conflicts. Although such an observation may seem trivial, it should be linked with the argument put forward by Regina Grafe, who suggested that the success of long-distance trade cannot be attributed to a single institution or to better institutions, but should rather be explained through the mechanisms of institutional variation and complementarity. That hypothesis seems confirmed in the case of sixteenth-century Valencia (Belem Fernández Castro). The emergence of new institutions with adjudicating powers in maritime conflicts from the later Middle Age onwards may provide further evidence which will enable future research to test the hypothesis.

Bibliography

Abulafia, D., *The Great Sea. A Human History of the Mediterranean* (London etc. 2011)

Aventuriers des Mers, VIIe–XVIIe siècle. De Sindbad à Marco Polo. Méditerranée - Océan indien (St. Egidio: Institut du monde arabe, Paris and Mucem, Marseille 2016).

Aznar Vallejo, E., and R.J. González Zalacain eds., *De mar a mar. Los puertos castellanos en la Baja Edad Media* (La Laguna 2015).

Blockmans, W., and P. Hoppenbrouwers, *Introduction to Medieval Europe, 300–1500* (London and New York 2014).

Boer, D.E.H. de, 'Looking for security. Merchant networks and risk reduction strategies' in: H. Brand ed., *The German Hanse in Past & Present Europe. A Medieval League as a model for modern interregional cooperation?* (Groningen 2007) 49–68.

Bullard, M.M., S.R. Epstein, B.G. Kohl and S.M. Stuard, 'Where History and Theory Interact: Frederic C. Lane on the Emergence of Capitalism', *Speculum. A Journal of Medieval Studies* 79 no. 1 (2004) 88–119.

Butel, P., *Histoire de l'Atlantique de l'Antiquité à nos jours* (Mesnil-sur-l'Estrée 1997).

Cordes, A., 'Lex Maritima? Local, Regional and Universal Maritime Law in the Middle Ages' in W.P. Blockmans, M. Krom and J. Wubs-Mrozewicz eds. *The Routledge Handbook of Maritime Trade around Europe, 1300–1600* (London and New York 2017) 69–85.

Cordes, A., and Ph. Höhn, 'Extra-Legal and Legal Conflict Management among Long-Distance Traders (1250–1650)' in H. Pihlajamäki, M.D. Dubber and M. Godfrey eds., *The Oxford Handbook of European Legal History* (Oxford 2018).

Coulon, M.D., *Barcelone et le grand commerce d'orient au Moyen Age. Un siecle de relations avec l'Egypte et la Syrie-Palestine (ca. 1330-ca. 1430)* (Madrid and Barcelona 2004).

Eggertsson, T., *Economic behaviour and institutions* (Cambridge 1990).

Fitzhugh, W.W., 'Puffins, Ringed Pins, and Runestones. The Viking Passage to America' in: W.W. Fitzhugh and E.I. Ward eds., *Vikings. The North Atlantic Saga* (Washington 2000) 11–25.

Frankot, E., *'Of Laws of Ships and Shipmen'. Medieval Maritime Law and its Practics in Urban Northern Europe* (Edinburgh 2012).

Grafe, R., and O. Gelderblom, 'The Rise and Fall of the Merchant Guilds: Re-thinking the Comparative Study of Commercial Institutions in Premodern Europe', *Journal of Interdisciplinary History* 40 no. 4 (2010) 477–511.

Greif, A., 'The fundamental problem of exchange: A research agenda in Historical Institutional Analysis', *European Review of Economic History* 4 (2000) 251–284.

Greif, A., 'Commitment, Coercion and Markets: The Nature and Dynamics of Institutions Supporting Exchange' in C. Ménard and M. Shirley, *Handbook of New Institutional Economics* (Dordrecht 2005) 727–786.

Greif, A., 'Coercion and Exchange: How Did Markets Evolve?' (2008). Available at SSRN: https://ssrn.com/abstract=1304204 or http://dx.doi.org/10.2139/ssrn.1304204 (September 2019).

Heebøll-Holm, Th., Ph. Höhn, and G. Rohmann, 'Introduction', in Th. Heebøll-Holm, Ph. Höhn and G. Rohmann eds., *Merchants, Pirates, and Smugglers. Criminalization,*

Economics and the Transformation of the Maritime World (1200–1600) (Frankfurt and New York 2019) 9–30.

Höhn, Ph., 'Pirate Places, Merchant Spaces? Distribution and Criminalization in the Late Medieval Baltic Sea' in Th. Heebøll-Holm, Ph. Höhn and G. Rohmann eds., *Merchants, Pirates, and Smugglers. Criminalization, Economics and the Transformation of the Maritime World (1200–1600)* (Frankfurt and New York 2019) 127–144.

Jaspert, N., and S. Kolditz eds, *Entre mers – Outre-mer: Spaces, Modes and Agents of Indo-Mediterranean Connectivity* (Heidelberg 2018).

Kypta, U., and T. Geelhaar, 'Marins, marchands, hommes du conseil. À propos des gens de mer dans les villes hanséatiques : les exemples de Lübeck et de Stralsund' in É. Guerber and G. Bouëdec eds., *Gens de mer. Ports et cités aux époques ancienne, médiévale et moderne* (Rennes 2013) 177–204.

Lane, F.C., *Profits from Power. Readings in Protection Rent and Violence-Controlling Enterprises* (Albany 1979).

Miranda, F., and J. Wubs-Mrozewicz eds., *Merchants and Commercial Conflicts in Europe, 1250–1600*, special issue of *Continuity and Change. A Journal of Social Structure, Law and Demography in Past Societies* 32 no 1 (2017).

North, M., *Geschichte der Ostsee. Handel und Kulturen* (Munich 2011).

Ogilvie, S., *Institutions and European Trade: Merchant Guilds, 1000–1800* (Cambridge 2011).

Parrott, P., *The Business of War. Military Enterprise and Military Revolution in Early Modern Europe* (Cambridge 2012).

Rohmann, G., 'Jenseits von Piraterie und Kaperfahrt: für einen Paradigmenwechsel in der Geschichte der Gewalt im maritimen Spätmittelalter', *Historische Zeitschrift* 304 (2017) 1–49.

Sicking, L., ed., *Maritime Conflict Management, Diplomacy and International Law, 1100–1800*, special issue of *Comparative Legal History* 5 no. 1 (2017).

Sicking, L., 'The Pirate and the Admiral. Europeanisation and Globalisation of Maritime Conflict Management', *Journal of the history of International Law* 20 (2018) 429–470.

Sohmer Tai, E., 'Marking Water: Piracy and Property in the Pre-Modern West' in J.M. Bentley, R. Bridenthal and K. Wigen eds., *Seascapes: Maritime Histories, Littoral Cultures, and Transoceanic Exchanges*, eds. (Honolulu: University of Hawaii Press, 2007).

http://webdoc.sub.gwdg.de/ebook/p/2005/history_cooperative/www.historycooperative.org/proceedings/seascapes/tai.html.

Sohmer Tai, E., 'The Legal Status of Piracy in Medieval Europe', *History Compass* 10 no.11 (2012) 838–851.

Tranchant, M., 'La "culture" du risque chez les populations usagères des mers et littoraux du Ponant (XIe–XVIe siècles): Première approche d'une histoire à constuire', *Revue d'histoire maritime* 9 (2008) 9–45.

Tranchant, M., 'Introduction. Pluriactivité et mutualisation des risques maritimes par les sociétés littorales: problématique et éléments de définition', *Annales de Bretagne et des pays de l'ouest* 120 no. 2 (2013) 7–14.

CHAPTER 1

The Courts, the Qadi, and the 'People': Resolving Mercantile Disputes in the Medieval Islamic Mediterranean

Jessica Goldberg

The Cairo Geniza contains very few records of lawsuits between Jewish merchants in the eleventh and twelfth centuries. And by very few, I mean there is only solid evidence of five such full-blown mercantile lawsuits coming before the Jewish court in the period 990–1150. Such a small number of cases is perhaps surprising – letters, the main source of information we have from merchants represented in the Geniza, are replete with disputes in need of resolution. It is all the more interesting because we know that Jews in major cities and some smaller towns throughout Fatimid and Ayyubid Egypt and Syria maintained local communal courts that oversaw, ratified, and recorded transactions, agreements, and arguments among Jews (they did not handle cross-confessional cases): sales, gifts, loans, commercial contracts and disputes, and those related to marriage, divorce, and inheritance. Indeed, the plurality of materials from the documentary Geniza are legal.

I want to unpack the possible meanings of the paucity of mercantile lawsuits in the light of recent scholarship from a number of fields. Such research helps to better contextualize this fact, and then use this context to help reassess explanations other scholars have offered as to the small volume of suits. I will then propose some alternative explanations where I try and place mercantile dispute processing into the context of both the commercial practice and recent research in medieval Islamic law.[1]

1 At the suggestion of the editors, this piece represents a lightly revised version of the plenary talk for the conference, with limited citations and a selected bibliography. I am grateful to Louis Sicking for helping me be part of the proceedings, and to Eve Krakowski, Marina Rustow and Oded Zinger for their help with the content. Their willingness to share their research in progress, and to discuss both theory and practice of law in the Geniza, have enriched my understanding of the subject at every turn.

 | DOI:10.1163/9789004407992_003

1 The Geniza, and its Legal and Mercantile Materials

I have now mentioned two terms of art: the *Cairo Geniza*, and the *documentary Geniza*. An explanation is in order. Between the eleventh and the nineteenth centuries, Jews attached to the oldest synagogue of Fustat, Egypt (the commercial sister-city of the royal Cairo, founded by the Fatimids in 969 and in the eleventh and twelfth centuries still largely a court enclave), like Jews as well as Muslims elsewhere in the Middle East, intermittently practiced *geniza*, a ritual disposal of worn-out and useless religious texts. The synagogue (now called Ben Ezra) holds a special place in the heart of historians because the community it served used a small chamber in the building as a permanent *geniza*, rather than a box or some other form of temporary storage that would periodically be buried. The collection of writings (on paper and parchment, handwritten or printed) that accumulated over nine centuries, now known as the 'Cairo Geniza', was discovered by European and American scholars in the late nineteenth century. Egypt's semi-colonial status, the complex question of the 'ownership' of the materials, and scholarly and collecting practices of the day means contents of the Cairo Geniza are now scattered across some seventy libraries and private collections in Europe and the United States.

Forms of *geniza* practice varied not only within and among communities, but also over time, with some periods during which the Ben Ezra Geniza was in use seeing significant deposits of non-sacred material. Most of the Geniza papers – about 380,000 folio pages in all – are fragments of literary manuscripts, largely on religious subjects. But somewhere between fifteen- and thirty-thousand pieces of paper contain what is usually termed *documentary material*; that is, they are everyday writings, texts written not to convey ideas to an anonymous and long-lasting audience but to communicate with specific recipients for immediate practical purposes. The largest and best-studied cluster of these everyday writings – perhaps as many as thirty thousand texts – dates back to the Fatimid and Ayyubid era (969–1250).[2] These kinds of everyday

2 The difference between *fragment*, *document*, and *text* helps explain these numbers. A *fragment* is an individual piece of paper extant in the Geniza. A *document* is a coherent piece of written composition – a letter, an entry in a legal register, a petition. A *text* is any part of a document found on any particular piece of paper. Since paper was valuable in the classical period under discussion, it was often re-used. Thus a piece of paper may contain more than one document. Equally, some documents were lengthy, using more than one sheet of paper (if they were not the kind of document that required a long scroll or *rotulus*). Finally, in their time in the Geniza storeroom, many sheets of paper were torn, meaning that even something like a letter, generally written on only one sheet of paper, might need to be reassembled virtually, some several pieces of paper, perhaps housed on different continents.

writings, from this era of dense deposit, are called the *documentary Geniza.* It is one of the largest groups of everyday writing to have survived from the medieval Islamic world, and perhaps the single densest and most diverse. It contains at least fifteen sub-corpora of identifiable types of writing with more than a hundred exemplars (and for a handful, thousands of exemplars) – records of court hearings, marriage contracts, pre-nuptial agreements and deeds of divorce, contracts and deeds involving property and commerce, learned answers to legal questions, magical amulets and recipes, commercial correspondence, family correspondence, communal correspondence, medical prescriptions, commercial accounts, accounts of communal property and charitable aid management, private petitions from the poor, petitions to state authorities and records of the Fatimid and Ayyubid governments.[3]

Many of the documentary Geniza's diverse sub-corpora of documentary types, moreover, are closely interconnected and illuminate some of the same people, practices, places, events, and institutions from multiple angles. For example (and not unrelated to my discussion), scholars have identified around two thousand documents produced by or for merchants who participated in the great markets for wholesaling primary production and manufacturing across the eastern Mediterranean and western Indian Ocean. The largest group is letters exchanged among merchants and business accounts, but it also comprises business ephemera (drafts and preparatory material for letters, shipping notes, office lists, orders of payment) and various materials pertaining to family affairs, communal activities, or scholarly pursuits, as well as a small smattering of legal materials (contracts, powers of attorney, settlements, lawsuits, wills – in no case more than a half-dozen). As many of these men formed a loose but identifiable group of individuals and families, we can trace their activities across several generations, from around the year 990 to the mid-twelfth century.

The relatively small number of scholars capable of handling the linguistic and paleographic challenges of the material, and the dispersal of the materials, long delayed progress in assessing the corpus in its entirety. But in the past decade and a half, an increasing pace of digitization has helped a growing number of specialists make more sense of contents, leading to a greater awareness not only that legal documents (court hearings, deeds, contracts, settlements,

3 The broad range of document types that provide an almost unimaginable treasure trove for social historians. Individually, these documents are often surprisingly detailed and varied as well as relatively well preserved, especially compared to pre-Islamic papyri. The corpus as a whole offers some of the best evidence we possess not only of the social, cultural, and economic history of Jews in the medieval Islamic world but also of the social and economic history of the pre-Ottoman Middle East in general.

quittances, and wills) are the plurality, but that more than half the materials of the documentary Geniza touch on the workings of the economy, the state, and the law. Of the legal documents themselves, most are records of hearings of the Rabbinic court. Not all of the court's business was lawsuits, nor even most of it: people also went to the Rabbinic court to have all sorts of agreements properly witnessed (one might best conceive of a combination notary office and court). But there are hundreds of records of lawsuits – meaning that the five lawsuits among living merchants makes them account for an exiguous part of the court's business. There is thus an apparent disjuncture – a set of materials full of people going to court, and almost as full of merchant materials, but with modest overlap between the two.

2 Contracts and Contract Enforcement: Jewish Law in a Muslim Milieu

Two different understandings of contract creation and enforcement among these Jews have been offered that could explain what seems to be an underrepresentation of lawsuits among merchants. S.D. Goitein proposed that Jewish merchants would have gone to Muslim courts, whose records are not extant; Avner Greif proposed that the courts were economically useless and contract enforcement was achieved without recourse to it. Both men's work has great value in recognizing important problems of mercantile practice and evidence, but I will suggest reasons why neither model really accords with the larger world of Geniza evidence that is currently emerging, and then present the legal, normative, and evidentiary context that I think better explains the nature of dispute resolution for the merchants.

S.D. Goitein, who pioneered the study of these merchants and their business methods in the 1950s and 1960s, proposed something like a divide between the public and private lives of Jews in the Islamicate Mediterranean. In matters of family, marriage, and religious devotion, he believed we should expect Jews to follow particularistic Jewish practices, developing norms out of their ancient written tradition. In the ecumenical marketplaces, neighborhoods, and even public spaces of the large courtyard houses that Jews often shared with Muslims or Christians, however, Jews could not have been that much different from their neighbors. In the particular case of merchants, he thought that they went to Muslim notaries to register their contracts so that they could be used in the markets. If, as he suggests, their contracts were written to conform to Islamic rather than Jewish law, the solution could be that merchants went to Muslim courts to settle their disputes even when the disputes were between fellow Jews. Such materials would not have ended up in the Geniza, which generally does not contain any legal evidence from the Muslim courts.

Could Goitein be right, that the relative absence of litigation is an illusion of source bias? In general, the Geniza records attest broadly to the possibility of 'forum shopping' by litigants; that is, it was possible, even in a dispute between two Jews, to bring a case before a Muslim judge.[4] Both the Fatimids and Ayyubids ruled their empires according to a model of judiciary established by the Abbasids, which permitted religious courts run by and for non-Muslims to operate alongside Islamic judges (qadis). These courts operated in the shadow of the state's own system of legal tribunals, through which any subject, whether Muslim or non-Muslim, could present appeals (*maẓālim*, literally '[complaints against] abuses') directly to the government. In the slow evolution of the relationship between state and court in the Islamic Mediterranean, the first state-appointed qadi in Egypt was installed in the 770s by the Abbasid caliph al-Manṣūr; a century later, ibn Ṭūlūn began accepting *maẓālim* petitions directly from his subjects – a key part of his assertion of independence, despite being nominally the Abbasid governor. The Fatimids absorbed and expanded both institutions, allowing qāḍīs of diverse legal affiliation to operate under the authority of a formally Isma'īlī chief judge (*qāḍī al-quḍāt*) while also responding to complaints and requests filed through an elaborated system of *maẓālim* petitions.

As my colleague Oded Zinger has shown, in certain kinds of cases litigants in Jewish courts would threaten to take a case to Muslim court. This was a particularly common strategy for women in inheritance disputes (daughters have universally enshrined rights to a share of the property in Islamic law but not in Jewish), but is also quite frequent in marriage disputes. Jewish litigants sometimes brought cases to the Muslim court by common agreement, and some business contracts (though none among the merchants we are considering) state that cases of dispute will be brought before the Muslim authorities if they fail to find an agreement in the Jewish court.

There is in addition scattered evidence from the Geniza more generally of Jews acquiring 'Arabic legal documents' (presumably from Muslim courts) for agreements with fellow Jews: of fathers having property deeds drawn up by the Muslim courts in order to pass property to their daughters, or of partners in a

4 Not only was this possible between a Jewish and Muslim court, one could also choose between qadi or *maẓālim* court, but most often, it was Muslim litigants who strategically choose from among different qadis.

shop bringing their Arabic partnership deed to the Jewish court in order to dissolve the partnership.

There are also a few bits of evidence that seem at first to support the idea that these Jewish merchants made agreements in Muslim forums. First, we find several incidents recounted in letters in which merchants called upon a qadi to intervene in a commercial dispute. Second, there is the evidence of a pair of contracts read into evidence in the Rabbinic court in the settlement of a case in which a merchant died en route to Sicily, and the elders of the community of Tripoli took possession of the goods he was carrying. The first contract attested that the goods were held in partnership between the deceased, a Sicilian, and his partner in Cairo. The goods were also labeled as belonging to the deceased. The second contract, contradicting the first, asserted that the goods were entirely the property of the merchant in Cairo. The court testimony records that the first contract had been written in order to evade excessive customs' duties then being imposed on 'foreigners' goods (indeed, some mercantile letters show that this ruse became so general that the Sicilian authorities escalated and charged the due on all goods, and then as suddenly gave up the scheme).

But on closer examination, none of these materials actually provides good evidence that Jewish merchants registered their agreements with Muslim notaries or took their disputes to Muslim courts to settle them. Certainly, the first contract regarding goods had been made to show Muslim authorities. Unfortunately, we do not possess the original contracts, only the records in Judeo-Arabic that they were read into evidence (as in many modern courts, documents must be read into evidence in order to become part of the suit – we have records of more contacts in this form than we have originals).[5] But nothing about the first contract actually suggests it was drawn up by Muslim notary – it does not follow the language of Islamic formularies.[6] Rather, it was composed according to norms we are just now beginning to recognize as a Jewish scribal legalese that emerged in the eleventh century, just like the second contract. Equally, the incidents in which a qadi is brought into a dispute between Jewish merchants, it is in order to take an executive action to sequester goods in dispute, not to actually rule on the merits of the case. Though an outsider might think that use of the Hebrew script would have made Jewish legal documents

5 Like many kinds of legal documents that might have an important afterlife for an individual or family, most originals were not deposited in the Geniza.

6 In the absence of a large number of contemporary contract edited from the papyri collections, it is not clear whether Muslims in Egypt would have adhered closely to such formularies at the time.

useless to non-Jews, Geniza evidence shows that individuals of the time were under no such illusions – when they wanted to keep something secret, they would write key terms (such as illicit items of trade or even terms for the officials they were afraid of) in the Hebrew language.

Rather, several strands of evidence suggest that Jewish merchants considered the Jewish courts the natural forum for pursuing lawsuits if they arose. The evidence of the extant lawsuits shows, naturally, the possibility of pursuing a commercial case in the Jewish courts. Though in principle they cannot tell us anything about the frequency of going to the Muslim courts as a court of first resort, it is interesting and important to note that in none of the cases do the litigants threaten to appeal to the Muslim court. (In the case with the longest paper trail in the Geniza, the court itself has the litigants promise not to pursue the matter in the Muslim courts, though the case had dragged on for months).

But rather better evidence for merchant practice is found in the letters. Though there are no mentions, interestingly, of active lawsuits in these, there are a substantial number of discussions of recourse to legal measures – of taking oaths, raising the possibility of issuing a power of attorney, discussion of sending powers of attorney, actual inclusion of powers of attorney, discussions of the consequences of issuing a power of attorney, threats (always made to third parties, never directly to one's opponent) to sue, appeals to legal experts for issuance of opinions, and many discussions of 'the people' that is, the community of merchants, attempting to resolve matters. Such mentions occur in more than ten percent of letters. And wherever the evidence is not ambiguous (as, alas, in the nature of letters, it very often is), the evidence points to the Jewish courts and Jewish legal experts when the dispute is among Jewish merchants. Thus, for instance, when we hear that a power of attorney was issued in Fustat against a merchant in Qayrawan, the merchant in Qayrawan goes to the Jewish judge to get assurance that the case will go his way if it proceeds, letting us know that the forum is the Jewish court. Similarly, in several cases where legal opinions are sought from experts, they are Jewish experts.

More in-depth study of the legal materials of the Geniza, as well as more research into the day-to-day nature of Jewish leadership in local communities at first deepen the mystery of why anyone would go to a Jewish court, and then helps explain why we might expect Jewish merchants to handle their affairs largely within the ambit or shadow of the Jewish court. First, as first discussed by my colleague Marina Rustow and then confirmed by several recent Ph.D. dissertations, we must understand the Jewish court not as part of a Jewish communal sphere that acted autonomously from the Islamic state and legal system (a very old vision of Jewish autonomy that the most recent generation of Geniza scholars has been at great pains to lay to rest), but as deeply embedded within it. Indeed, Jewish courts were considered a part of the state's judicial system and Jewish judges would, like qadis, receive deeds of appointment from the Muslim authorities.

By the same token, a great deal of research has also uncovered the rather severe limits on the enforcement capacity of the courts. That is, for most of the period documented in the Geniza, its officials lacked any real coercive power.[7] A few Geniza documents from the early eleventh century mention rabbinic judges sentencing Jews to flogging for specifically religious offences (e.g., keeping a shop open on the Sabbath), but none make clear whether the floggings were to be administered by agents of the Jewish community or of the state, or indeed whether they actually occurred at all.[8] After this, references to corporal punishments imposed directly by court officials disappear from the Geniza record; Jewish litigants appear to have been physically punished only by turning them over to the state for judgment. Short of this, rabbinic courts had three means of suasion at their disposal: they could require litigants to swear oaths of varying religious weight, fine them for legal infractions or for breach of contract, or excommunicate them, a form of social ban that theoretically prevented them from interacting with other Jews. The documents also suggest that only the Muslim or *maẓālim* courts could imprison defendants for failure to appear (and did so imprison Jewish defendants).

The impositions of the Jewish court are not necessarily trivial sanctions. But surviving documents suggest that in practice, all three were limited coercive tools. Fear of lying under oath might encourage a litigant's cooperation when he was in the courtroom, but could not ensure that he would show up there in the first place, nor obey officials' orders after he left. The fines stipulated in Geniza documents can be remarkably large, but this mattered little if there was no way to force litigants to pay them; in fact, all available evidence indicates that they were routinely renegotiated and rarely, if ever, paid in full.

7 I should note that *qāḍīs* did not maintain their own police force either, and were subordinate both to the *qāḍī al-quḍāt* and to state officials. *Qāḍīs* nonetheless possessed far greater executive power than did the *bet din*, not only because some controlled armed guards, but also because they possessed much closer ties to state officials and often worked together with them to administer physical punishments and to confiscate goods.

8 Taylor-Schechter Genizah Collection, Cambridge University, Cambridge (hereafter T-S) 8J7.18 (written by Efrayim b. Shemarya, about a Sabbath-violating shopkeeper), T-S 18J1 r. 6 (1028, Cairo, about a ritual slaughterer accused of malpractice), T-S 13J33 r. 4 (about a cantor accused of slandering a communal official).

Excommunication, the most severe punishment that the court could apply, bore theoretically drastic personal and economic consequences. But it was nearly impossible to implement perfectly – Geniza evidence for people isolated by the ban is remarkably thin on the ground – a shortcoming that meant it was thus best imposed infrequently, lest its overuse damage court officials' own credibility.

Jewish courts thus lacked effective means to enforce judgments or the terms of contracts that they had issued, or even to compel litigants to appear before them in the first place. Yet the same record that reveals this fact also demonstrates that they remained robust and well-patronized institutions throughout the Fatimid and Ayyubid periods. Even without any tangible mechanisms forcing them to do so, many Jews went to considerable expense to negotiate interpersonal conflicts and document their transactions in rabbinic court. But, as my colleague Eve Krakowski astutely analyzes and documents in her work, Geniza scholars have also misunderstood some of the complex cultural constructions of law in Islamicate societies in their thinking about the possibilities of forum shopping and the limits of practical enforcement capacity as limiting the appeal of courts. A central source of Rabbinic courts power was their claim to specialized *legal knowledge* of a kind that carried cultural weight throughout Fatimid and Ayyubid Egypt, and beyond – among not only Jews and other *dhimmīs*, but also the Muslims who ruled over them.

As Krakowski explains, the Islamic societies that emerged out of the Abbasid empire (750–945) shared certain common social and political assumptions, among them a notion of social order embodied by law. Religious law (*sharīʿa*) meant normative rules derived from written prescriptive texts that dictated both ritual and social behavior, to be administered in religious courts that commanded both sacred and civil respect. But such ideas did not just apply to Muslims: those following other legitimate religious traditions, *dhimmīs*, should possess their own characteristic bodies of religious law. This stance, as shown in the texts they wrote under the successor regimes from the tenth through fifteenth century, shaped Jewish and Christian leaders' own self-presentation. Jewish and Christian texts indeed show Muslim rulers must have valued *dhimmī* loyalty to their own legal tradition; accusing a fellow Jew or Christian of being untrue to their own law (engaging in *bidʿa*, the term in Islamic law for innovation) could be a successful strategy for gaining Islamic rulers' sympathies. Thus, though naïve piety has been rightly seen as an inadequate explanation for why *dhimmīs* should go to their own courts, in a milieu where the idea of religious law was both widely recognized and taken seriously, the practical legitimacy and power of the rabbinic courts could indeed be a serious matter for Jews.[9] Their own claims to standing as subjects worthy of state protection were bound up, at least in part, to their adherence to *dhimmī sharīʿa*.

Geniza research in the past two decades, moreover, has shown that Goitein's imagined separation of spheres – economic life lived according to Islamic norms, and family and marriage according to Jewish – signally fails to emerge in practice. Several recent studies of court production around family, gender and marriage has shown the degree to which Jewish families used the courts to ratify arrangements that conformed much more closely to Islamic law than that found in Talmudic texts, and also find the court working to avoid outcomes that were acceptable by Talmudic precept, like child marriage, but did not accord with Islamic norms of family in the Fatimid period.

If we turn then to the merchants in particular, their position in the community did everything to confirm that adherence to the Jewish legal arena would have been important to them, while at the same time making the Jewish courts the most practical place to rehearse disputes. Geniza merchants were usually among the leaders of their local Jewish community, part of the circles who supported the community financially and pursued prestige through scholarship both in youth and in adulthood. Many were not merely knowledgeable in law, but were experts nearly on par with the scholars – in one case at least, a scholar capable of writing *responsa* himself. In the Jewish courts, then, they were in a position of considerable power. The Jewish courts, in turn, were so eager to retain jurisdiction over this powerful segment of the community that they were willing to hear and settle cases even involving Muslim contracts and instruments that contained terms in direct contradiction to rabbinic law – the *qirāḍ* and *suftaja* – and to examine and certify the documents in Arabic that pertained to them.[10] Working within the Jewish legal system, merchants were sustaining their own prestige as leaders of a *dhimmī* community.

Appealing to the more powerful Muslim courts, moreover, represented an escalation that was costly and risky for both parties. It necessarily imposed expenses on both sides – payments to judges, fees, and perhaps legal experts (one letter describes the difficulties of finding a Muslim legal expert, *faqīh*, in an ownership dispute involving Muslims, Jews, and unidentifiable 'bales').[11] The Jewish merchant's knowledge of Islamic law was almost certainly less

9 There is some evidence indeed that state bureaucrats helped sustain the courts' authority over the Jewish population, even sending Jewish litigants who had agreed to a settlement in the Muslim court according to Islamic formulary back to the Jewish court to make sure such proceeding was done at the behest and with the agreement of rabbinic legal authority.

10 See, e.g., T-S 16.138.

11 T-S 16.179 r. 47–55.

wide-ranging, and he was a person both juridically and practically of less importance in such a forum.

This rather long excursus into an emergent picture of the Jewish legal system within the Islamic milieu will help, I hope, explain why I also believe an explanation for the lack of lawsuits widely accepted in economic history, that proposed by Avner Greif, does not really accord with the broader evidence the Geniza offers on dispute processing.

3 Contracts and Contract Enforcement: Economy, Society, and the State

Greif's argument began with the assertion that the Jewish legal system was unusable and thus went unused: citing evidence both of some particularly drawn-out inheritance disputes and the failure in another case of plaintiffs to receive payment for judgments in their favor, Greif claimed the futility of legal redress.[12] Greif then argued that rather than using any part of the legal system, the Jewish merchants of the Geniza instead represented a historical case of a self-enforcing system. He mapped out the theoretical possibility that a closed coalition of merchants could enforce agreements based on an internally known system of norms (provided a variety of other conditions required by the theory are met) without recourse to any external institutional framework. Rather than imagining, as Goitein had done, a long-gone heap of mercantile legal materials produced for Jewish litigants in Muslim courts, Greif's model of a self-enforcing coalition would explain the absence of lawsuits by arguing that the Geniza merchants' coalition was so effective that very little misbehavior occurred, obviating the need for lawsuits. Indeed, in a response to his critics, he pointed to the paucity of lawsuits as good prima facie evidence for his reputation-based coalition model.

I have argued elsewhere that Greif's theoretical model requires that the merchants' meet a number of criteria – including group closure, inheritance of reputation, evidence of ostracism and reprisal – for which there is little, if any evidence. I have also noted that he picks up on aspects of merchant agreements that do not fit parameters of the legal system. But in this context, Greif's work overlooks the extent to which merchants' preferences and behavior suggest that they were often eager to gain the greatest legal protections each kind of contract they entered into could offer – perhaps stronger evidence to their

12 It might be noted by legal historians that similar evidence can be produced in quantity by most functioning legal systems, including our own.

ex ante trust in the legal system's protective capacity than incidence of lawsuits or their resolution.[13] First, they made efforts to create contracts and to adhere to Jewish forms when possible. For instance, Jewish law expected partnership contracts to be written; though the court would rule on cases involving *mu'āmala* (unwritten partnership contract), it would only accept written evidence of contract stipulations.[14] Partnerships were very often formed to take advantage of two distant partners' positions to trade in their respective cities; the fact that they took the trouble to travel, as both principals had to be present in person, sometimes halfway across the Mediterranean, to legally secure a written contract surely shows a great devotion to legal norms.[15] If merchants did not expect to rely on the legal system's protection and thus need to follow its rules, we would expect to find them exclusively using the more convenient *mu'āmala*, but they did so rarely. They also trusted the protections of the Muslim legal system sufficiently to enter into partnerships with Muslims, and make Muslim merchants and brokers their agents.[16]

Equally, in Jewish law (as in Muslim), two vital contracts, that of sale and commercial agency, are solely oral or physical (or both).[17] Both could leave a paper trail: since sale and payment were separable, many sales would leave a residue of a debt in the market clerk's official records; port officials could record the ownership of arriving cargo, and into whose agency it was physically given. But of course, the primary legal evidence for such contracts would be witnessing. Indeed, merchants most show their devotion to securing legal protection for their contracts by the ubiquity of their attempts to secure legally valid testimony to their actions. Witnessing was systematic in public markets, but businessmen requested or surrounded themselves with witnesses in many other situations: valuations of unsold goods, testimony to the state of the

13 Both Greif and his critics Edwards and Ogilvie debate the meaning of both rates and success of lawsuits. But incidence of lawsuit can be read in different ways: as evidence for reliance on a legal system, as evidence for the failure of the threat of legal action to prevent cheating, as a first boundary or last resort for redress.

14 See Cambridge University Library, Oriental Collection (hereafter CUL Or) 1080J 290 for a lawsuit over a *mu'āmala*.

15 See, *e.g.* Institute of Oriental Manuscripts of the Russian Academy of Sciences, St. Petersburg (IOM).D-55.14 r. 28–29, v. 10–11.

16 A few examples: T-S 18J3.13 v. 5, T-S 8J 18.33 rt margin, Katz Center for Advanced Judaic Studies, Philadelphia (hereafter CAJS) 389 r. 30–31, v. 40, T-S 20.69, T-S 13J8.13, T-S 10J9.5, T-S 20.180, some were relationships of long duration.

17 There is also written instrument of agency, the power of attorney. The only transaction in commercial agency in which the Jewish court recognized a power of attorney might be used was in the collection of a debt – a situation in which the transfer of responsibility is not obvious.

market for a particular commodity, opening of bales lodged in a businessman's warehouse to verify contents, and witnessing to private sales made out those warehouses. Businessmen make specific reference to such witnesses and witnessing in over a third of their letters.[18] We thus find them certainly obtaining certificates attesting to transactions and quittances to completed contracts, but much more universally, making sure that their acts were witnessed. In fact, one of the most common requests we find in letters is one merchant being asked to read instructions from the sender to a third merchant, thereby making the recipient of the letter necessarily the witness, and turning written instructions into oral ones.

How, then, do I explain the low incidence of lawsuits? Well, first, there is the dodge (or reasonable hesitation, depending on your viewpoint) that Jeremy Edwards and Sheilagh Ogilvie proposed in their critique of Greif. Certainly, the incidence of lawsuits is low, but, in the absence of any comparable statistic from another merchant group, it is impossible to judge whether this particular rate of contract failure is unusually high, unusually low, or average. In this vein, I note the deformities of the evidence. First, there is the problem that the records of the rabbinic court encompass a far broader swathe of society than the correspondence of the Geniza. That is to say, the overwhelming majority of extant letters of any kind are sent among the relatively small number of the middling or upper-class individuals of this society. Though the Geniza is only beginning to reveal the degree to which different social groups in this society used literacy (though certainly people at every class used, whether willingly or not, some written documents), long-distance (or even medium-distance) correspondence tends to be the prerogative of the well-off. The records of the court capture a far wider swathe of society. As Dan Smail has discussed in his work *The Consumption of Justice*, many less-powerful people went to the courts in late-medieval Marseille because it offered, however imperfectly, a means of help to those without resources to get help themselves.[19] Thus, the relative statistic of a much smaller percentage of merchant cases at court in comparison to the substantial percentage of letters that are mercantile is partly explained by the demography of document production. Of course, we are still in no position at all to analyze the demographics of the Jewish community, aside from being able to document Jews across a very wide range circumstances of wealth and poverty.

18 For editions and translations of quittances and releases, see Ackerman-Lieberman, *Partnership Culture* volume 2. On this statistic, see Goldberg publications in the bibliography.

19 Oded Zinger's thoughtful studies (see bibliography) of what kinds of Jewish women went to court in Fatimid and Ayyubid Egypt helps underscore Smail's point.

In addition, there are some particular problems of the idiosyncratic nature of deposit practices. That is, not everyone in the Jewish community in the eleventh and twelfth centuries took *geniza* practice particularly seriously. Often, we find that our materials are dominated by the deposits of some key individuals who either were particularly scrupulous about *geniza* practice, or who left archives that an inheritor, perhaps long after their death, saw fit to deposit in the Geniza. In particular, the majority of mercantile material in the Geniza comes from the archives of just a handful of merchants (though the documents themselves make clear the existence of at least 150 identifiable Jewish merchants in the first half of the eleventh century, more than 400 in the second half, and at least 200 in the first part of the twelfth). So the disproportion between different kinds of documents may indeed be an illusion of deposit. But even with such hedging, I will still find it interesting that in a merchant community deeply aware of law, among whom some individuals were sometimes members of the court and legal experts, who took much time and effort to create a variety of legally valid documentation of their activities, and who actually talked about the possibility of legal action and legal disputes *regularly* in their letters, should those same merchants have so rarely ended up pursuing a lawsuit.

I suggest a few factors at work: the first one that mitigated the possibilities of dispute; the second one that shaped norms of what kinds of claims were thought court-actionable; a third that the procedure of pursuing a case helped reduce the chances of an actual lawsuit, and finally, some reasons ending up in court were more unappealing to merchants than perhaps to other kinds of litigants. Because our space is limited, and in some cases I have written far too much about these subjects, I will be somewhat summary about the first two. In framing the conundrum of the principal-agent problem in long-distance trade, economists paint a bleak theoretical problem: when a principal entrusts his goods to a distant agent, the agent can potentially use the distance to cheat (moral hazard). From shirking work to mis-reporting trades to embezzling goods, the agent can make use of delays or deficiencies in information, 'information asymmetries', to his profit.[20] Several strands of evidence show, however, that merchants took for granted the capacity of Islamic institutions of ports and markets to radically reduce the length of this list, and place rather strong limits on the potential losses that contract failure could present.

20 The long-distance principal-agent problem can properly be considered part of the general problem of contract enforcement, but one in which distance magnifies the possibilities of opportunistic behavior.

As I have already noted, market and port institutions provided both witnesses and records for some transactions and contracts.[21] But equally, merchants' methods of handling a problem of transport show that they trusted Islamic institutions of the market to protect them to an unexpected degree. The infrastructure of transport (as well as maritime law) meant someone had to oversee goods on board a boat or in a caravan; equally, when purses of money or letters were transported by ship, someone needed to carry them. Such tasks required almost nothing in the way of labor for anyone already traveling; at the same time, they seem to repose an enormous degree of trust in that person. Such tasks, interestingly, were essentially performed as a free service in the general merchant community, among both Muslims and Jews. Geniza merchants relied on fellow Jewish businessmen when possible: send this with 'one of our associates', they would ask, indifferent to which one. But a Muslim businessman would do, and in a pinch, a Muslim ship's captain might carry a purse, an individual sailor look after a bale. Such actions reveal both institutions and merchant beliefs: the institutions at the ports were sufficient guarantee that persons so entrusted could not simply walk off with their goods.[22] Letters suggest such trust was warranted: among a sea of troubles, no merchant ever records someone so entrusted absconding.

Indeed, both unloading of ships and major transactions were most often done in public space (ports, public markets, the warehouses of the 'agent of the merchants'), where both state officers and the local merchant community also provided substantial protection against 'information asymmetries'. Clerks recorded many transactions, payment agreements, and terms; they wrote up contracts; and they noted the state, nature, and labeling of shipments that were opened. But they were never alone: members of the Islamic merchant community witnessed these acts as well.[23] The system of registration and witnessing made it possible, for instance, for one merchant in Palermo to get a

21 Not only was it part of the ruler's duty to uphold the 'reputation' of the market, states had their own vested interest in these transactions, which both supplied tax revenue and parts of the government's own provisioning.

22 See David Kaufmann Collection, Library of the Hungarian Academy of Sciences, Budapest (herafter DK) 231 g-k r. 22, Bodleian Library, Oxford (hereafter Bodl.) MS Heb a3.13 r. 19, CAJS 414 among many others. Muslims carrying letters: T-S 13J28.9r 7, British Library, London (hereafter BL) Or 5542.9 upper margin 1–2. Asking that a businessman entrust goods to either a Jewish or Muslim businessman: T-S 13J26.9 r. 17–18, T-S 12.133 margin. Carrying money: T-S 8J21.2 r. 3–4, a merchant instructs the recipient to send it with 'whomever you deem suitable, Muslim or Jew'. Using a ship's captain to carry money: T-S AS 145.81r 6–7. Entrusting oversight and delivery of goods to a sailor, Bodl MS Heb a3.13 v. 11.

23 For deals gone wrong that give particular good details on the presence of witnesses, see CAJS 389 r. 13–21. 39–40, 63–69, T-S 20.122 r. passim, v. 1–12.

legal certificate on sales made by another, then send the evidence back to his associate in Alexandria (with whom he was in dispute) to prove his claim on the poor state of the market for some goods.[24] Registration was important enough that even businessmen quite attentive to their dignity would fight publicity over it: 'ibn al-Wasitī came to me when I was by the clerk and he said to him: 'record that they are to the debit of al-Wasitī'. I said to him, 'Don't record them on any name except that of their owners ... and a terrible fight broke out between us in front of a group of our associates'.[25]

States provided another prop against fraud: they set and publicized official market prices for important goods in the central markets when the bulk of a season's shipping arrived. Though actors in the market were not compelled to use the market price, sales before the market price was fixed, or that deviated too far from it, were voidable.[26] Information on transactions and prices was thus a public good; letters, often in multiple copies, traveled throughout the year: 45 percent contain some market price reports (but tellingly this percentage jumps to 85 percent if we look at letters traveling in market season between ports and central markets or between the central Mediterranean and Egypt). The setting of guideline 'official prices,' and the role of merchants in multiply disseminating this information both reduced information asymmetries in fact, and created trust that reported sales could not be too wildly inaccurate despite price volatility for many goods.

Perhaps the most surprising thing to emerge from the merchant letters is a second fact, that is, merchant norms regarding payments (Greif noted this conundrum as well). Sixty days was the standard term between sale and payment, with discounts given for immediate payment upon sale. But in a legal world where delayed payments in other circumstances formed a staple of the Rabbinic court's business, among merchants, delays in payment were not considered actionable, not even considered misconduct. Even more surprising, among merchants' who exhorted their colleagues to not let capital lie idle for a

---

24 Bodl Ms. Heb a3.13 r. 19–21.

25 T-S 10J 10.30 r. 9–21. Another such public fight is found Jewish Theological Seminary, New York (hereafter JTS) NS 1.79. Officially, registration was not of the sale, but of the resulting payment and credit obligations – sale and payment were separate transactions, often spaced months apart; registering such arrangements at the time of sale was thus crucial. T-S 10J6.1 contains more details on how clerks registered credits and debits resulting from sales and prior debt obligations.

26 Determining market price represented a significant investment on the part of the state – it involved the monitoring of shipping through a system of watchtowers (*ribāts*) as well as monitoring arriving goods. Market prices could only be indicative as fine distinctions of grade were made by buyers and seller. An incident in which the buyers claimed the rights to void a pre-market sale and the writer privately acknowledged it: CAJS 389 r. 63–69.

moment, there is no record of charges for late payment. Rather, a staple of merchants' letters is the tedious work of not only reminding one's correspondent directly that payment needs to be made, but, often more importantly, asking one's colleagues to intercede with the debtor, and getting their reports back (often in the form of 'he asks to be reminded of the matter when he is not busy'). A not untypical example has an exasperated merchant write to his colleague who had sold goods on his behalf and not yet sent the proceeds: 'Sir, it is a small account and has been hanging fire for two years. Is it not time for it to be done? I should not have thought this of you, being sure that you were taking care of all my business. Otherwise I should not have bothered you with something tiresome, having too much esteem for you. I think that if an unknown merchant had entrusted you he would have met with better treatment than this, since I know that it is your habit and in your nature to take care of people's needs. So I (can only) conclude: This is my luck and fate and you are not to blame'.[27] Thus, in a matter for which there *was* legally binding evidence, merchants relied instead on exhortation, pressure, and intercession. At a practical economic level, there were many reasons such norms made sense, but it had two consequences: first, it gave many merchants on-going stakes in each other's continued solvency, and second, it could turn the getting of payment into part of merchants' on-going struggles to assert and maintain their status and reputation, their '*jāh*', a word whose semantic field includes reputation and standing.

Merchants' sometimes protracted struggles to get paid, and the dynamics of involving other members of the community in negotiations, finally get us to the main mechanisms of dispute resolution, which in fact almost always involved ramified forms of *intercession*. In fact, I owe this insight into how to understand merchant dispute processing to my colleague Oded Zinger, who is in the midst of studying the place of intermediaries in access to both courts and the approach to Fatimid officials. What his work with letters across many classes and kinds of disputes reveals is that behind the legal records we have of disputes lies a stream of requests for someone who is neither party to the dispute in question, nor, interestingly, someone with official capacity to rule over it, to both hear the narrative, and then introduce it to someone who is part of the system of authority.

While in some ways such a method could be read as part and parcel of a deeply rooted patronage system, what is interesting in the case of merchants at least (whose relative statuses I am most aware of), is first, that the interceding party (or, often, parties) is not necessarily of higher status than the petitioner,

27 DK 230d.

nor always closer to the authority who might eventually be approached. Moreover, in the case of merchants, we find chains of intercession created with multiple links, not a single intermediary. Thus, in an example that shows the complexities of the process, we have a Palermo merchant 'Aṭā' b. Zikrī sitting in Alexandria, in a dispute with some other Sicilian merchants. He sends a legal query (an important step in the legal process) about the dispute. Seems simple enough as a beginning, although he sends it to Fustat, which might seem odd for a dispute among Sicilians. Not only that, he gives the query to an Egyptian merchant to carry (and no doubt read). But then he also sends a letter to another Sicilian merchant currently in Fustat. He instructs the second colleague, himself not a party to the dispute, to get the query from the first merchant (note, he could have sent the legal query enclosed in the letter but does not) and read also the enclosed account of the case and familiarize himself with the arguments. But, naturally, he is not to go directly to a legal expert but instead to 'Aṭā''s colleague Nahray b. Nissīm, a merchant of Fustat who is also a legal expert. 'Aṭā' notes, 'I know he does not answer legal queries, but read it to him anyway'. It is only at this stage, if no one has disapproved, that he is to go to the legal expert. He is not to give him the query, of course, but to present the case himself, 'I should like you to represent me as if I was there. Explain to him the arguments and tell him that the questioner is poor, miserable, dead, lost, and that he is presenting a (good) argument, and the (rabbi) will be assured a place in paradise'. And then, finally, 'If my master the rabbi hands down a verdict, as I said, see to it that this is witnessed by somebody whose signature is known in Sicily, (that is) if he will accept the evidence of the Sicilians in Fustat. (otherwise) have it witnessed by North Africans, by those who frequent Alexandria'. Thus, finally, do we understand that 'Aṭā' has attempted to involve a chain of five or six individuals unrelated to the case (indeed, he cautions his colleague to keep this secret from the Sicilians in town), simply in order to get a legal opinion in Fustat that might not, given the problems of witnessing, be of practical legal help when he returned to Palermo. Though we don't usually get chains this long, this practice of creating chains of intercession helps explain what used to be my favorite Geniza mystery: why one of the most important merchants of Fustat, almost always resident in the city, sent a letter from Alexandria to Fustat giving to a much less important merchant a power of attorney in order to sue his partner in a Fustat court.[28]

What we see in 'Aṭā''s case is that the processes of witnessing in the marketplaces and warehouses, of getting witnesses to one's orders, actions, transfers of responsibility, valuations of goods, sales, terms of payment that might

28 Both documents are edited in Mark R. Cohen (2013).

prevent the possibility of legal action, were balanced on the other side when disputes did arise by the gathering of adherents to one's narrative of events – a process that involved a constant testing of its efficacy and merits even as one attempted to pull more and more of the impartial community into the dispute. It was also, like the process of pressuring merchants to pay up, a marshalling of one's power of reputation and standing in the community, by attracting as many adherents as possible to one's side. In effect, then, Avner Greif had the right insight when he suggested that effectively, this made it true that it was often the merchant community, 'the people', (*al-nās*) that determined the merits and outcome of a dispute, as the chains of parties called upon weighed in as they were asked to intercede. Indeed, in a case Greif discusses, the same Nahray b. Nissīm who is appealed to in Fustat is told by a correspondent in Sicily that his own dispute there, and which also involved the sending of multiple streams of orders, narratives, and individuals with contrasting narratives, that the 'people' had decided some of his actions were not 'those of merchants' and that Nahray 'should be satisfied' his opponent agreed that some part of his claim would be accepted based on another merchant attesting to the arrangements described in a letter. But this suggestion was not made to Nahray because the community acted without law, but because an enormous accumulation of legal materials and legal maneuvering had already taken place.

In the larger world of the Rabbinic legal system revealed by the Cairo Geniza, lawsuits themselves follow the same logic of slow assemblage and negotiation, in which the competing narratives of the litigants are presented, but the court adjourns to acquire further legal opinions, to give litigants continual opportunities to agree to settlements, and to pressure litigants to avoid forcing the court to hand down a final judgment.[29]

S.D. Goitein claimed that it was a terrible blow to any merchant's reputation to go to law with an opponent. This was both true and untrue. A dignified Syrian merchant, faced with a claim that he had acted improperly, responded by saying that his business dealings were always correct, and concluded, 'I have been in business and concluded partnerships for sixty years, and never has anyone appointed an attorney against me, or brought me to court, and never have I owed a *habba* (1/72nd of a dinar) to anyone…'[30] That is, threats of legal action and beginnings of legal action were common, but getting to the stage of actually appearing in public court, even at the stage of registering a power of attorney, represented an extreme escalation. Even the power of attorney made

29 The medieval Islamic system of litigation operated in very similar ways. See the work of David Powers (in Bibliography) on al-Wansharīsī's compendium of legal opinions.

30 T-S AS147.4 r. 5–9.

a case truly public. And, since a power of attorney in Rabbinic court essentially empowered one's agent to collect a debt, it immediately cast doubt on the afflicted merchant's credit-worthiness. One merchant found that after such a complaint was made against him in Fustat, everyone in his hometown of Qayarawan delayed payments to him, and another creditor in Egypt, also concerned about his solvency, also took out a power of attorney against him – and that too was seen by everyone.[31] He immediately attempted a settlement.

But I think we must see that with the extensive and inevitable involvement of local merchant communities in helping to create the legal validity of merchant activity and the process its disputes, for a dispute to reach the stage of a lawsuit was to be avoided because it represented a failure, not only for the plaintiff and the defendant, but for the 'people', that is, the local merchant community. For the plaintiff, it meant his *jāh* was insufficient – insufficient to provoke compliance from his opponent, insufficient to gain him enough intercessors to pressure his opponent. It might also mean his business acumen was faulty in the first place, for having chosen the wrong partner or agent. For the defendant, not only was his probity called into question, his credit-worthiness, and hence his solvency, were often at stake. As for the local merchant community, not only had 'the people' failed to get the parties to settle, if insolvency actually ensued, they would be called upon to uphold the 'reputation' of the local market by assuring that foreign creditors were paid off before they would be able to make their own claims good.[32]

But we should not mistake all this maneuvering, intercession, and tendency to resolve matters before reaching a lawsuit as simply the process of peace-making in a small-scale community that had to live together; or a way for courts to avoid giving the judgments that might also reveal their lack of executive authority to enforce their decisions; or as evidence that merchants in particular did not bother to use a legal system that was too slow, cumbersome and ineffectual for their purposes. Rather, merchant materials in particular make clear that in most cases, early points on the path to a lawsuit proved an effective end to dispute processing. Other materials help clarify that Jewish courts acted in the shadow of 'authority' (either the *sulṭān's* men or, more ominously, just *sulṭān*),[33] not just the qadi courts, but the unnamable officials who

31 Bodl MS Heb a3.26, Bodl MS Heb 2.17.

32 An instance of local merchants being forced to do so is found in T-S 16.163 r. 23–28.

33 Though the English version of this word names a kind of Islamic ruler, the use of the title derives from the word for physical power or ability to impose, and thus came in the post-Abbasid world to refer to someone who held supreme political but not spiritual authority, unlike a caliph, who legitimately held both.

represented state power in its most imposing forms. And the slow, tenuous, many-step process of dispute processing, with its gathering in of many members of the community, and its many possible points to achieve resolution, must be seen against a backdrop of the ever-present threat that state power, with all its terrible speed and effectiveness, might be called in, and the nearer a case got to a lawsuit, the nearer too that threat became.

A Muslim qadi would have sufficient power, while the Jewish judge did not, to sequester goods during a lawsuit, which could help ensure the plaintiff's satisfaction, but at the same time impose financial penalties not only on the defendant, but on other members of the merchant community. Since the ownership of goods was sometimes unclear and sometimes shared, the financial hardship of such sequestration could affect many parties. In a quest to recover his property, an injured party who went to 'the authorities' thus risked permanently damaging his relationships with more colleagues than merely the defendant. Those who read the court's records tend to focus on the shame cast upon the Jewish community when its members revealed the legal problems within the community to the outside, the rhetoric of the court itself. Merchants' letters tell of more potent and individual woes: accusations of undermining Muslim institutions that left one facing the executioner's sword several times, imprisonment for non-appearance in a Muslim court (the imprisoned were required to pay the costs of their incarceration, risking torture if the guards were insufficiently paid and starvation if food were not provided), being forced to flee town, large shipments not given to one's opponent, but lost entirely in unplanned shipping. In a world of disarmed civilians, physical violations of one's person seem to have been particularly feared.[34]

Calling in *sulṭān* was not a weapon to which merchants resorted often – not only would one party have chosen retribution rather than recompense as a resolution of a dispute (no recorded instance of a Jewish merchant calling in the authorities ever resulted in getting any money back), but given the complex ownership of goods seized, and the webs of outstanding debt that (perhaps purposefully) tied merchants to one another' business, it was a weapon with often arbitrary and far-reaching consequences. And each step of the process of dispute settlement, rather than isolating the principals, pulled more and more people into cases, reminding them of their own necessary stakes in securing a peaceable and legal resolution, preferably within the bounds of their own courts' more limited and manageable authority.

34 E.g., CAJS 389 r. 389, T-S 20.122 r. passim, verso 1–12, T-S 13J17.11, T-S 10J6.1, T-S 16.179, T-S 13J17.11 r. 8–9. Also the query in Bodl MS Heb a 3.9.

Select Bibliography

Ackerman-Lieberman, Philip I., *A Partnership Culture: Jewish Economic and Social Life Seen through the Legal Documents of the Cairo Geniza* (Ph.D. Dissertation Princeton University 2007).

Ackerman-Lieberman, Philip I., 'Contractual Partnerships in the Geniza and the Relationship between Islamic Law and Practice', *Journal of the Economic and Social History of the Orient* 54 no. 5 (2011) 646–676. https://doi.org/10.1163/156852011X614000.

Ackerman-Lieberman, Philip I., 'Legal Pluralism among the Court Records of Medieval Egypt', *Bulletin d'études Orientales* 63 no. 1 (2015) 79–112.

Ackerman-Lieberman, Philip I., *The Business of Identity: Jews, Muslims, and Economic Life in Medieval Egypt* (Stanford 2014).

Cohen, Mark R., 'A Partnership Gone Bad: Business Relationships and the Evolving Law of the Cairo Geniza Period', *Journal of the Economic and Social History of the Orient* 56, no. 2 (2013) 218–263. https://doi.org/10.1163/15685209-12341301.

Cohen, Mark R., 'Geniza for Islamicists, Islamic Geniza, and the "New Cairo Geniza"', *Harvard Middle Eastern and Islamic Review* 7 (2006) 129–145.

Cohen, Mark R., 'Jews in the Mamlūk Environment: The Crisis of 1442 (a Geniza Study)', *Bulletin of the School of Oriental and African Studies* 47 no. 3 (1984) 425–448.

Cohen, Mark R. and Yedida K. Stillman, 'The Cairo Geniza and the Custom of the Geniza among Oriental Jewry – A Historical and Ethnographic Study' (in Hebrew), *Pe'amim* 24 (1985) 3–35.

Crone, Patricia, *God's Rule: Government and Islam* (New York 2004).

Edwards, Jeremy, and Sheilagh Ogilvie, 'Contract Enforcement, Institutions and Social Capital: The Maghribi Traders Reappraised', *Economic History Review* 65 no. 2 (2012) 421–444.

Goitein, S.D., *A Mediterranean Society; the Jewish Communities of the Arab World as Portrayed in the Documents of the Cairo Geniza*. 6 vols. (Berkeley 1967).

Goitein, S.D., 'The Commercial Mail Service in Medieval Islam', *Journal of the American Oriental Society* 84 no. 2 (1964) 118–123.

Goitein, S.D., *Letters of Medieval Jewish Traders* (Princeton 1973).

Goldberg, Jessica, *Trade and Institutions in the Medieval Mediterranean: The Geniza Merchants and Their Business World* (Cambridge 2012).

Goldberg, Jessica, 'Choosing and Enforcing Business Relationships in the Eleventh-Century Mediterranean: Reassessing the "Maghribī Traders"', *Past & Present* 216 no. 1 (2012) 3–40.

Goldberg, Jessica, 'The Use and Abuse of Commercial Letters from the Cairo Geniza', *Journal of Medieval History* 38 no. 2 (2012) 127–154.

Goldberg, Jessica, *The Geographies of Trade and Traders in the Eastern Mediterranean 1000–1150: A Geniza Study* (Ph.D. Dissertation Columbia University 2005).

Goldberg, Jessica, and Eve Krakowski eds., 'Documentary Geniza Research in the Twenty-first Century: A Handbook' *Jewish History* 33 nos. 1–3 (2019).

Greif, Avner, 'Contract Enforceability and Economic Institutions in Early Trade – the Maghribi Traders Coalition', *American Economic Review* 83 no. 3 (June 1993) 525–548.

Greif, Avner, *Institutions and the Path to the Modern Economy: Lessons from Medieval Trade*. Political Economy of Institutions and Decisions (Cambridge 2006).

Greif, Avner, 'The Maghribi Traders: A Reappraisal?', *The Economic History Review* 65, no. 2 (2012) 445–469.

Greif, Avner, 'Reputation and Coalitions in Medieval Trade – Evidence on the Maghribi Traders', *Journal of Economic History* 49 no. 4 (December 1989) 857–882.

Hoffman, Adina and Peter Cole, *Sacred Trash: The Lost and Found World of the Cairo Geniza*. (New York 2010).

Jefferson, Rebecca J.W., 'Sisters of Semitics: A Fresh Appreciation of the Scholarship of Agnes Smith Lewis and Margaret Dunlop Gibson', *Medieval Feminist Forum* 45 no. 1 (2009) 23–49.

Jefferson, Rebecca J.W., 'The Historical Significance of the Cambridge Genizah Inventory Project' in Nachum Dershowitz and Ephraim Nissan eds., *Language, Culture, Computation: Computing for the Humanities, Law, and Narratives: Essays Dedicated to Yaacov Choueka on the Occasion of His 75 Birthday* (Berlin 2014) 9–37.

Krakowski, Eve, *Coming of Age in Medieval Egypt: Female Adolescence, Jewish Law, and Ordinary Culture* (Princeton 2017).

Lange, Christian, *Justice, Punishment and the Medieval Muslim Imagination* (Cambridge 2008).

Leithy, T. el-, *Coptic Culture and Conversion in Medieval Cairo, 1293–1524 AD (Egypt)* (Ph.D diss., Princeton University 2004).

Mottahedeh, Roy, *Loyalty and Leadership in an Early Islamic Society*. (London and New York 2001).

Powers, David Stephan, *Law, Society, and Culture in the Maghrib, 1300–1500*. Cambridge Studies in Islamic Civilization (Cambridge and New York 2002).

Rapoport, Yossef. 'Legal Diversity in the Age of Taqlád: The Four Chief Qadis Under the Mamluks', *Islamic Law and Society* 10 no. 2 (2003) 210–228.

Reif, Stefan C., *A Jewish Archive from Old Cairo: The History of Cambridge University's Genizah Collection* (Richmond, Surrey, 2000).

Rustow, Marina, 'At the Limits of Communal Autonomy: Jewish Bids for Intervention from the Mamluk State', *Mamluk Studies Review* 13 no. 2 (2009) 133–159.

Rustow, Marina, *Heresy and the Politics of Community: The Jews of the Fatimid Caliphate*. 1st edition. (Ithaca 2008).

Rustow, Marina, 'The Legal Status of Ḏimmīs in the Fatimid East: A View from the Palace in Cairo' in Maribel Fierro and John Tolan eds., *The Legal Status of Ḏimmīs in the*

Islamic West (Second/Eighth-Ninth/Fifteenth Centuries) (Leiden and Boston 2013) 307–332.

Smail, Daniel Lord, *The Consumption of Justice: Emotions, Publicity and Legal Culture in Marseille, 1264–1423* (Ithaca 2003).

Tillier, Mathieu. 'Judicial Authority and Qāḍī s' Autonomy under the 'Abbāsids', *Al-Masãq* 26 no. 2 (2014) 119–131.

Udovitch, A.L., 'Formalism and Informalism in the Social and Economic Institutions of the Medieval Islamic World' in Amin Banani and Speros Vryonis eds., *Individualism and Conformity in Classical Islam* (Wiesbaden 1977) 61–81.

Udovitch, A.L., *Partnership and Profit in Medieval Islam*. Princeton Studies on the Near East (Princeton 1970).

Udovitch, A.L., 'The "Law Merchant" of the Medieval Islamic World' in Gustave E. von Grunebaum ed., *Logic in Classical Islamic Culture* (Wiesbaden 1970) 113–130.

Zinger, Oded, 'She Aims to Harass Him': Jewish Women in Muslim Legal Venues in Medieval Egypt', *AJS Review* 42 no. 1 (2018) 159–192.

Zinger, Oded, *Women, Gender and Law: Marital Disputes According to Documents of the Cairo Geniza* (PhD Princeton University 2014).

CHAPTER 2

Finders Keepers, Losers Weepers? Byzantine Shipwreck and Salvage in the Eleventh and Twelfth Centuries

Daphne Penna

1 Setting the Byzantine Scene

Travelling by sea in the medieval Mediterranean was associated with many risks and dangers. Journeys were long, heavy storms or pirates lurked and in a worst-case scenario the ship was wrecked. A shipwreck could give rise to disputes and conflicts amongst various parties. The main legal question concerned the ownership of these goods. Did the owner retain the right of ownership on the wrecked goods or, did the finder become owner of such goods? Was the finder entitled to a reward and if so, how was this reward estimated? And how was the situation complicated when the ship was of foreign origin? I will attempt in this paper to address these questions in Byzantine law and practice. Before examining the sources it is necessary to make a short introduction into Byzantine law, especially because the present volume on conflict management, consists of a wide spectrum of periods and areas. What do we actually mean when we speak of Byzantine law?

Byzantine law was born in the Eastern Roman empire, also known as Byzantine empire or Byzantium, an empire that lasted something more than a thousand years and covered a large part of South-Eastern Europe.[1] Most scholars agree that the Byzantine empire began around 325–330 AD, when emperor Constantine I founded the city of Constantinople and it collapsed in 1453 when the Ottomans occupied its capital. Yet, Byzantine influences in many fields - including the legal field- continued especially in the Southern-Eastern part of Europe. When explaining Byzantine law one has to go back to emperor Justinian because Byzantine law was born at the time of Justinian or better *because* of Justinian. As it is known, in the sixth century, the Byzantine emperor

1 For an introduction to the history of Byzantium, see for example, Herrin (2007), Cameron (2006) and Mango (2002).

 | DOI:10.1163/9789004407992_004

Justinian codified Roman law and produced an impressive legislation which was to have a tremendous influence in the formation of European private law later on in the Middle Ages. Justinian's legislation consisted of the following four parts: i. the *Codex*, ii. the *Digest*, iii. the *Institutes* and the *Novels*.[2] Despite the fact that Greek was the dominant language in Byzantium, Justinian promulgated most of his legislation in Latin. That was a problem at that time for the inhabitants of his empire because they could not understand it. That is why, shortly after Justinian promulgated his legislation, texts appeared in Greek summarizing, commenting upon and explaining his legislation. In fact, the law professors in this period developed a method to tackle the language problem when teaching the new legislation.[3] The transition from Latin into Greek in the sixth century marks traditionally the beginning of Byzantine law.[4] In short, Byzantine law is Roman law in Greek, or better, this is how it began. We come across shipwreck and salvage provisions in several Byzantine legal sources. In the first part of this paper I will examine these provisions from basic Byzantine legislation and legal collections, beginning from the Justinianic period up to the twelfth century. In the second part, I will focus on shipwreck and salvage provisions in some more 'practice-orientated' Byzantine sources, namely the treaties which Byzantium concluded with the Italian city-states in the eleventh and twelfth centuries.

2 Byzantine Legislation and Legal Collections

2.1 *Justinianic Legislation*

Justinian's legislation remained the bedrock of Byzantine legislation and that is why it is examined as first in this paper. Legal issues concerning the ownership of goods in case of a shipwreck were already regulated in Roman law, which had been codified by Justinian. A part of Justinian's legislation was the *Digest* or *Pandects*, which consisted of fragments of the classical Roman jurists who mostly had lived in the second and third century AD. According to Justinian's *Digest*, things being cast ashore from a shipwreck still belonged to their owner, as it is shown from the following fragment:

2 On the parts of Justinian's legislation, see, for example, Mousourakis (2015) 193–211.
3 See Scheltema (1970, repr. 2004).
4 See Stolte (2003–2004) 111–126 and more recently Stolte (2015) 355–373.

Digest 41,1,58 (Javolenus)

Quaecumque res ex mari extracta est, non ante eius incipit esse qui extraxit, quam dominus eam pro derelicto habere coepit.	Nothing salvaged from the sea becomes the property of the salvor until its owner has begun to treat it as abandoned.[5]

Only in the case that the owner treated the thing as abandoned it was possible for the salvor to become owner of the abandoned thing. In that case, the thing became a *res nullius*, that is, a thing with no owner and the salvor could become owner by taking the good in possession. In the latter case the salvor became owner by means of *occupatio*, which is an original way of acquiring ownership. In another part of Justinian's legislation, the *Codex*, which consists of imperial constitutions, it is clear that things deriving from a wreck were not claimed by the treasury because it was understood that they still belonged to their owners; the emperor emphasised that the treasury had no right at all to exploit this sad situation and profit from the wrecked goods:

Codex 11,6,1

Si quando naufragio navis expulsa fuerit ad litus vel si quando reliquam terram attigerit, ad dominos pertineat: fiscus meus sese non interponat. quod enim ius habet fisc in aliena calamitate, ut de re tam luctuosa compendium sectetur?	If at any time a ship has been pushed to the shore by a shipwreck, or if at any time it reaches the land left behind, it shall belong to the owners; my Treasury must not interpose itself. For what right does the Treasury have in another's calamity, that it gain a profit from so grievous a situation?[6]

Furthermore, many fragments in the *Digest* deal with thefts from a wrecked ship. The ninth title of the forty-seventh *Digest* book is entitled 'Fire, Collapse of buildings, shipwreck, raft, and ship taken by storm'. This title begins with the

5 The translations of all *Digest* fragments in this paper are from Watson (1985).

6 Frier (2016) vol. 3, 2657.

remedies that the *praetor*[7] provides in case of such a theft. Someone who stole goods from a shipwreck was liable to restore fourfold the value of the stolen goods within a year and after that, restore their value, as the following passage shows:

Digest 47,9,1 pr. (Ulpian)

Praetor ait: In eum, qui ex incendio ruina naufragio rate naue expugnata quid rapuisse recepisse dolo malo damniue quid in his rebus dedisse dicetur: in quadruplum in anno, quo primum de ea re experiundi potestas fuerit, post annum in simplum iudicium dabo.	The praetor says: 'If a man be said to have looted or wrongfully received anything from a fire, a building that has collapsed, *a wreck, or a stormed raft or ship* or to have inflicted any loss on such things, I will give against him an action for fourfold in the year when proceedings could first be taken on the matter and, after the year, for the value'.[8]

In the *Digest* part that follows after this fragment the *praetor*'s words were thoroughly discussed by the Roman jurists. They were concerned, for example, with the question on what does 'if anything from a shipwreck' mean? The jurists asked themselves whether this concerns an action at the time of the wreck or, after the wreck. They pointed out that 'wrongful intent' of the receiver is an important precondition for the action. It was also ordered that if someone maliciously concealed a wreck that had occurred and, as a result, help could not be sent to those who were in danger, he was to be punished under the *lex Cornelia*. The punishment under the *lex Cornelia* was the death penalty, provided the accused did not belong to the high class.[9] Moreover, it was added that people who stole from those who had suffered a shipwreck were also obliged to pay a fine to the state. Here is the corresponding passage:

7 The *praetor* was a Roman magistrate who was responsible for the Roman legal procedure. In short, he decided whether one could begin a legal proceeding or not.

8 For more references in the *Digest* and the *Code* on this matter see Ashburner (1909, repr. 1976) cclxxxviii.

9 D. 48,8,3,5: 'Legis Corneliae de sicariis et veneficis poena insulae deportatio est et omnium bonorum ademptio. sed solent hodie capite puniri, nisi honestiore loco positi fuerint, ut poenam legis sustineant: humiliores enim solent vel bestiis subici, altiores vero deportantur in insulam'. (The penalty of the *lex Cornelia* on murderers and poisoners is deportation to an island and the forfeiture of all property. However, nowadays capital punishment is customary, except for persons of a status too high to be subject to the [modern] statutory punishment; those of lower rank are usually either crucified or thrown to the beasts while their betters are deported to an island).

Digest 47,9,3,8 (Ulpian)

...item alio senatus consulto cavetur eos, quorum fraude aut consilio naufragi suppressi per vim fuissent, ne navi vel ibi periclitantibus opitulentur, legis Corneliae, quae de sicariis lata est, poenis adficiendos: eos autem, qui quid ex miserrima naufragorum fortuna rapuissent lucrative fuissent dolo malo, in quantum edicto praetoris actio daretur, tantum et fisco dare debere.	...again, by another senatus consultum, it is provided that those, by whose malice or design, knowledge of a wreck is forcibly suppressed so that no relief may reach the ship or those in peril thereon, shall be subject to the penalties ordained in the lex Cornelia de sicariis; but those who seize anything through the miserable plight of the shipwrecked and are designedly enriched will have to give also to the imperial treasury as much as the amount for which an action under the praetor's edict will be given against them.

In another *Digest* fragment Callistratus, one of the Roman jurists pointed out that: 'A wide variety of provisions has been made so that nothing should be snatched from wrecks or that no third party should interfere in the collecting of them'.[10] He then referred to a relevant law by emperor Hadrian:

Digest 47,9,7 (Callistratus):

Nam et divus Hadrianus edicto praecepit, ut hi, qui iuxta litora maris possident, scirent, si quando navis vel inficta vel fracta intra fines agri cuiusque fuerit, ne naufragia diripiant, in ipsos iudicia praesides his, qui res suas direptas queruntur, reddituros, ut quidquid probaverint ademptum sibi naufragio, id a possessoribus	For the defied Hadrian also by edict ordained that those holding property near the shore should know that if a ship be dashed against or break up within the boundaries of their lands, they are not to despoil the wreck, else governors will grant actions against them to those complaining that their property has been seized, so that if anything be proved to have been taken from the wreck, it may be recovered from the

10 D. 47,9,7.

Digest 47,9,7 (Callistratus) (cont.)

recipiant. de his autem, quos diripuisse probatum sit, praesidem ut de latronibus gravem sententiam dicere. ut facilior sit probatio huiusmodi admissi, permisit his et quidquid passos se huiusmodi queruntur, adire praefectos et ad eum testari reosque petere, ut pro modo culpae vel vincti vel sub fideiussoribus ad praesidem remittantur. a domino quoque possessionis, in qua id admissum dicatur, satis accipi, ne cognitioni desit, praecipitur.	landholder. But in the case of those proved to have looted, the governor is to inflict a grave penalty as on brigands. To facilitate proof in such cases, the emperor allows those who complain that they have suffered in such wise to approach the prefect and then to state their case and ask that the defendants, in proportion to their fault, either be bound or provide verbal guarantors and so be remitted to the governor. It is further provided that the owner of the land where this is said to have happened shall give security that he will be present for the hearing.

It is clear from this passage that the looting of wrecked goods had both civil and criminal consequences. The wrongdoers were not only obliged to pay compensation to the people who had suffered damage but they were also criminally punished by paying a penalty, as in the case of brigands. It is added that the defendants had to provide guarantors. This meant that if the defendant did not appear before court, the guarantor had to pay for him. It is further ordered that the owner of the land where the incident had occurred, should also give security that he will be present at the court. All these measures show that the emperor is trying to facilitate strongly the procedure of proof evidence for the people who had suffered looting of their wrecked goods.

2.2 *Byzantine Legislation from Ninth to Twelfth Centuries*

Justinianic legislation in respect to shipwreck and salvage was more or less repeated in later Byzantine legislation. As mentioned in the beginning, already at the time of Justinian because of the language problem, many Greek summaries and commentaries of the Latin Justinianic legislation appeared. By the end of the ninth century the situation was chaotic in respect to Greek legal collections. The emperors of that period, which belonged to the so-called Macedonian dynasty,[11] decided to put an end to this legal chaos and proceeded

11 The first emperor of this dynasty was Basil I (867–886) and the Macedonian emperors ruled from 867 up to 1056. For the legal culture of this period see Chitwood (2017).

to the 'purge of laws' (ἀνακάθαρσις τῶν νόμων), as they stated in their texts. The attempt to clear up the laws was part of a general cultural revival in many fields and is known as the Macedonian renaissance. The first results of this legal revival were two law books: the *Procheiros Nomos* and the *Eisagoge*.[12] In the *Procheiros Nomos* it was ordered that against a person who steals things from a shipwreck, a suit within a year can be raised for fourfold the value of the things, and after one year, for double the value of the things.[13] The same provision was included in the *Eisagoge* with the difference that after the first year, the suit was not for double the value of the things but just for the value.[14] In other words, the text of the *Eisagoge* repeats Roman law.[15]

The attempt of the Macedonian emperors to purge the laws was epitomised in the *Basilica*. The *Basilica* laws, 'τὰ Βασιλικὰ νόμιμα' (= the imperial laws) were promulgated around 900 during the reign of emperor Leo VI the Wise and reflected more or less Justinianic law in Greek. The idea behind the making of the *Basilica* was to create one law that would contain everything that derived from Justinianic legislation but then in Greek language. Instead of having several Greek summaries and commentaries of the Justinianic legislation, the *Basilica* compilers thought that it would have been better to have one text, which consisted of Greek summaries of the *Digest*, of Greek summaries of the *Codex* and summaries of the *Novels*.[16] After all, the compilers had all these Greek texts related to Justinianic legislation to their disposal and did not have to translate the Latin legislation of Justinian into Greek. The compilation of the *Basilica* was a long process and although we do not know all the details of its making, some information on how the *Basilica* laws were made can be found in other texts, for example, in the introductions of the *Procheiros Nomos* and the *Eisagoge*. In a later stage, scholia were added to the text of the *Basilica*.[17] The

12 Much has been written about the dating and the status of these law books. See the basic bibliography in Troianos (2017) 196–202.

13 *Procheiros Nomos* 39.25 in Zepos (1931, repr. 1962) 218: 'Κατὰ τοῦ ἁρπάσαντος πρᾶγμα ἀπὸ ἐμπρησμοῦ ἢ καταπτώσεως ἢ ναυαγίου, ἢ κατὰ τοῦ ὑποδεχομένου κατὰ δόλον τὰ τοιαῦτα πράγματα, ἐντὸς μὲν ἐνιαυτοῦ εἰς τὸ τετραπλάσιον δίδοται ἡ ἀγωγή, μετὰ δὲ τὸν ἐνιαυτὸν εἰς τὸ διπλάσιον'.

14 *Eisagoge* 40.28 in Zepos (1931, repr. 1962) 361: 'εἰς τὸ ἁπλοῦν'.

15 In particular the *Digest* fragment quoted earlier: *Digest* 47,9,1 pr. (Ulpian). Laiou has not taken into consideration that there is a difference between the *Procheiros Nomos* and the *Eisagoge* and therefore her conclusion that 'Byzantine law became stricter than Roman law' cannot stand. See Laiou (2001) 180, especially footnote 127. Troianos mentions this difference in Troianos (1992, repr. 2007) 521, n. 16.

16 The *Novels* were mostly in Greek. Little of the *Institutes* have been transmitted in the *Basilica*.

17 On the Basilica scholia and their distinction see Troianos (2017) 226–229. Last edition of the Basilica was made by Herman J. Scheltema, Douwe Holwerda and Nico van der Wal, Basilica: A (text) I–VIII, B (scholia), I–IX (Groningen, 1953–1988). Text and scholia have

Basilica laws were the last important legislation of the Byzantine empire and in respect to shipwreck and salvage issues, they repeat more or less Justinianic law.[18]

Emperor Leo VI the Wise promulgated many *Novels* and one of his *Novels* deals with shipwreck.[19] The emperor admits in this law that he is surprised that the death penalty is provided for people who steal and hide things from a shipwreck. He adds that this punishment is extremely heavy. The reference to a death penalty by Leo VI has caused some questions given that in the two earlier law books of the Middle Byzantine period, the *Procheiros Nomos* and the *Eisagoge* no death penalty is mentioned.[20] Leo VI points out that the crime of stealing things from a shipwreck is indeed a terrible one, but taking away the life of someone by establishing the death penalty for this crime, is utterly unfair; the emperor therefore orders that henceforth the wrongdoer will have to pay a fine of four times the value of the stolen things.[21] Towards the end of the twelfth century emperor Andronikos I Komnenos ordered the highest penalty for people who pillaged wrecked ships. He ordered that a person who pillaged a wrecked ship was to be hung from the mast of that ship. In other words, Andronikos returned to the *lex Cornelia* without making a distinction as to whether the person belonged to the high or low class.[22] This severe measure imposed by Andronikos proves that the problem of pillaging wrecked ships continued to exist, which is why the emperor tried to tackle the problem by imposing a very severe penalty.[23]

2.3 *The Rhodian Sea-Law and Salvage*

Except from the Byzantine imperial legislation there is a Byzantine legal collection that is definitely interesting for our subject. I refer to the *Rhodian*

---

been edited separately in this edition. This edition will be henceforth abbreviated as BT (Basilica text) and BS (Basilica scholia). Recently this edition has been published online by Brill, see http://referenceworks.brillonline.com/browse/basilica-online (date of access: 5 June 2018) accompanied by a comprehensive and updated introduction, *Praefatio* by B. Stolte and a complete bibliography by T. van Bochove.

18 B. 53,3,23 = D. 41,2,21 §§1. 2 jo. D. 16,3,18 (BT 2451/4–6) and B. 53,3,25 = D. 47,9,1pr. §§ 1.5. 2. 3 pr .§ 8 (BT 2451/9–12). On the *Rhodian Sea-Law* and its relation to the *Basilica* see further on.

19 Novel no 64. See Troianos (2007) 211. On this novel, see the article of Troianos (1992, repr. 2007) 515–526.

20 See the discussion in Troianos (1992, repr. 2007) 515–526.

21 The difference with the provisions of the *Procheiros Nomos* and the *Eisagoge* is that Leo VI does not diminish the penalty after the lapse of one year.

22 Reg. 1566; this act is not a novel, but an *entole*, an order.

23 See Laiou (2001) 183–184.

Sea-Law, a Byzantine collection of maritime law provisions which was compiled in the seventh or eighth century and has a rather complicated history of transmission.[24] To begin with, as the name *Rhodian Sea-Law* implies, this collection presumably derived from or was related somehow to an ancient text originating from the Greek island Rhodes. Rhodes was in antiquity a major sea power, as it is also proven by the fact that one of the seven wonders of the ancient world was to be found on that island.[25] As already mentioned, the *Digest* consists of fragments of the classical Roman jurists. The second title of the fourteenth book of Justinian's *Digest* is entitled 'The Rhodian law of jettison' (*De lege Rodia de iactu*) and deals with legal questions that arise from throwing cargo overboard in order to save the ship in case of bad weather. The Roman jurists discuss in the fragments of this *Digest* title provisions of the so-called 'Rhodian law of jettison'. We do not know whether these provisions were actually included as such in the ancient text deriving from Rhodes.

The *Digest* fragments dealing with 'The Rhodian law of jettison' have been transmitted in Greek in the *Basilica*, the laws that were promulgated around 900. As mentioned above, the *Basilica* repeated more or less Justinianic law but then in Greek. The relevant *Digest* fragments on this subject have been included in the fifty-third *Basilica* book. This particular *Basilica* book has not been preserved in the manuscripts but it has been reconstructed by the last editors of the *Basilica* on the basis of other works. What is interesting is that the Byzantine collection the *Rhodian Sea-Law* has been included as a whole[26] in the eighth title of the fifty-third *Basilica* book and this raises some questions. For example, since the *Digest* fragments about jettison have been transmitted in the *Basilica*, why did the compliers include also the jettison provisions of the *Rhodian Sea-Law* in the *Basilica*? Moreover, there is some discussion on whether the *Rhodian Sea-Law* has been inserted in the text of the *Basilica* as an eighth title or as a supplement.[27] In any case, the fact that the whole text of the

24 A critical edition of this legal collection accompanied by an English translation has been made by W. Ashburner, *The Rhodian Sea-Law*, Oxford 1909 (repr. Scientia Aalen 1976). For this Byzantine collection, see also Letsios (1996) and Rodolakis (2007), who provides a new critical edition of the *prooimion* of the *Rhodian Sea-Law* in pp. 115–117 and a new critical edition of the 53rd *Basilica* book in pp. 212–260, which includes the *Rhodian Sea-Law*, see further on.

25 According to the sources, the Colossus of Rhodes, a gigantic statue of God Helios was situated at the entrance of the harbour of Rhodes.

26 Without its *prooimion* however.

27 The last editors of the *Basilica* consider that the *Rhodian Sea-Law* has been included as a supplement in the *Basilica*; Rodolakis taking into account new evidence and with convincing arguments concludes that the *Rhodian Sea-Law* was in fact incorporated in the *Basilica* as the eighth title of the fifty-third *Basilica* book, see Rodolakis (2007) especially 175–204.

Rhodian Sea-Law is included in the *Basilica* proves the importance of this maritime law collection. Moreover, *Basilica* fragment B. 53,1,1 states that maritime issues or what happens at sea is regulated according to the *Rhodian Sea-Law*, when no other law contradicts the (*Rhodian-Sea*) law.[28] As Rodolakis rightly observes, the fact that this *Basilica* fragment B. 53,1,1 has been continuously repeated in more collections proves that there was a common belief that the *Rhodian Sea-Law* had become the standard 'maritime code'.[29]

In the Byzantine collection under the name *Rhodian Sea-Law* we find several and rather detailed provisions which deal with rewards of salving wrecked goods. In the *Basilica* text which transmits *Digest* fragments about maritime issues we do not come across such provisions dealing with rewards of finders of wrecked goods. This perhaps could be a reason why the *Rhodian Sea-law* was after all included as a whole in the *Basilica* exactly after the *Digest* fragments in Greek on maritime issues. In other words, the text of the *Rhodian Sea-Law* could have had a supplementary character to the *Digest* fragments on jettison and shipwreck.[30] The last three chapters of the *Rhodian Sea-Law* (45, 46 and 47) deal with rewards of finders of wrecked goods. Different criteria are set for the actual estimation of a finder's reward. In other words, the price of the reward is not always the same but it varies depending on several factors. First of all, a general provision for estimating the reward is fixed. According to chapter 45 of the *Rhodian Sea-Law*, he who brings a wrecked good safe to land receives as a reward an amount that corresponds to one fifth of the saved good:

...ἐὰν ἐν πελάγει πλοῖον στραφῇ ἢ διαφθαρῇ, ὁ ἀποσώζων τι ἐξ αὐτοῦ ἐπὶ τὴν γῆν λαμβανέτω ἀντὶ μισθοῦ οὗ ἀποσώζει τὸ πέμπτον μέρος.[31]	...if in the open sea a ship is overset or destroyed, let him who brings anything from it safe on to land receive instead of a fee, the fifth part of that which he saves.[32]

28 B. 53,1,1: 'Τὰ ναυτικὰ ἤγουν τὰ κατὰ θάλασσαν τῷ Ῥοδίῳ νόμῳ κρίνεται, ἐν οἷς αὐτῷ μὴ ἕτερος ἐναντιοῦται νόμος'.

29 Rodolakis (2007) 61.

30 See Ashburner (1909, repr. 1976) cxii.

31 Paragraph 45 of the *Rhodian Sea-Law,* Ashburner (1909, repr. 1976) 37 corresponds to *Basilica* 53,8β',45 Rodolakis (2007) 260.

32 The translation from Ashburner (1909, repr. 1976).

No distinction is made here to the person who helps, *i.e.* whether he is a sailor or not. In medieval maritime statutes we do come across special rewards provided for sailors who help in saving goods from the shipwreck. As Ashburner, the last editor of the *Rhodian Sea-Law* remarks, for example, according to the statute of St. Zeno, in Venice such sailors received three percent of the value of the goods that they had saved whereas in Pisa, according to the *constitutum usus*,[33] they received five percent.[34] Given that the above passage of the *Rhodian Sea-Law* does not specify whether or not the salvor ('ὁ ἀποσώζων') is one of the sailors, we can conclude that the term salvor could include anyone who helped.[35] In the following chapter of the collection, chapter 46, the same general reward estimation is provided. Here is the corresponding passage:

ἐὰν κάραβος ἀπὸ ἰδίου πλοίου τὰ σχοινία διαρρήξας ἀπόληται ἅμα καὶ τοῖς ἐμπλέουσιν ἐν αὐτῷ, ἐὰν οἱ πλέοντες ἀπόλωνται ἢ ἀποθάνωσι, τὸν μισθὸν τὸν ἐνιαυσιαῖον ἀποδιδότω ὁ ναύκληρος εἰς πλῆρες τοῦ ἐνιαυτοῦ τοῖς τούτων κληρονόμοις. ὁ δὲ τὸν κάραβον ἀποσώζων σὺν τῶν ἐφολκίων, καθὼς ἐν ἀληθείᾳ εὑρίσκει, πάντα ἀποδώσει, λαμβάνων οὗ ἀποσώζει τὸ πέμπτον μέρος.	A boat breaks the ropes and gets off from its ship and is lost with all hands. If those on board are lost or die, let the captain pay their annual wages for the full year to their heirs. He who saves the boat with its rudders will give them all back as he is truth finds them and receive the fifth part of what he saves.[36]

Yet, sometimes, the reward could be higher depending on other factors. The location of the wrecked good played a role in the actual estimation of the reward. For example, if the good was found in the sea or cast ashore. If the good was in the sea it also depended on the exact depth of where the good was found. The deeper it was found and saved, the higher the reward was, since it was more difficult to bring it out of the water. Relevant is the following fragment from chapter 47 of the *Rhodian Sea- Law*:

33 The *constitutum usus* was a collection of customs and regulated, amongst other things, matters of procedure and of commercial and maritime law. About this collection, see for example, Classen (1983) 82–89, Salvatori (2002) 13–32 and Storti Storchi (1998).

34 Ashburner refers to these provisions in Ashburner (1909, repr. 1976) cclxxxix.

35 See on this Ashburner (1909, repr. 1976) ccxc.

36 The translation from Ashburner (1909, repr. 1976).

ἐὰν χρυσίον ἢ ἀργύριον ἢ ἕτερόν τι ἐκ βυθοῦ ἐπάρθῇ ἀπὸ ὀργυιῶν ὀκτώ, λαμβανέτω ὁ ἀποσώζων τὸ τρίτον μέρος. ἀπὸ δὲ ὀργυιῶν δεκαπέντε, λαμβανέτω ὁ ἀποσώζων τὸ ἥμισυ διὰ τὸν κίνδυνον τοῦ βυθοῦ. τῶν δὲ ἐκριπτομένων ἀπὸ θαλάσσης εἰς γῆν καὶ εὑρισκομένων ἢ ἐπιφερομένων ἐπὶ πῆχυν ἕνα, λαμβανέτω ὁ ἀποσώζων δέκατον μέρος τῶν ἀποσωζωμένων.	If gold or silver or anything else is raised from the sea from a depth of eight fathoms, let the salvor receive one third. If it is raised from a depth of fifteen fathoms, let the salvor receive one-half by reason of the danger of the sea. Where things are cast from sea to land and found there or carried to within one cubit of the land, let the salvor receive one-tenth part of what is salved.

In some cases the provisions on salvage of goods are related to the contribution provisions. For example, in chapter 40 of the *Rhodian Sea-Law* we read:

ἐὰν πλοῖον συμβῇ ναυάγιον παθεῖν καὶ σωθῇ μέρος τοῦ γόμου καὶ τοῦ πλοίου, ἐὰν οἱ ἐπιβάται βαστάζωσι μεθ' ἑαυτῶν χρυσίον ἢ ἀργύριον ἢ ὁλοσηρικὰ ἢ μαργαρίτας, τὸ μὲν χρυσίον τὸ σωζόμενον δεκάτας παρέχετω, τὸ δὲ ἀργύριον πέμπτας ἐπιφερέτω· τὰ δὲ ὁλοσηρικά, ἐὰν ἄβροχα σωθῶσι, δεκάτας ἐπιφερέτωσαν, ὡς ὅμοια ὄντα τοῦ χρυσίου· εἰ δὲ βραχῶσι, κουφιζέσθωσαν τὴν ὑποτριβὴν καὶ τὴν ἀποβροχὴν καὶ οὕτως εἰς συμβολὴν ἐρχέσθωσαν. οἱ δὲ μαργαρῖται, καθὼς ἐκτιμηθῶσι, χρυσίου φόρτον τελείτωσαν τὴν ἀπώλειαν.	A ship is wrecked, and part of the cargo and the ship is saved. The passengers have on them gold or silver or whole silks or pearls. Let the gold that is saved provide a tenth, and the silver contribute a fifth. Let the whole silks, if they are saved dry, contribute a tenth, as being equal to gold. If they are wetted, let an allowance be made for the abrasion and the wetting, and let them come into contribution on that footing. Let the pearls according to their valuation contribute to the loss like a cargo of gold.

Another relevant position is to be found in chapter 41 of the *Rhodian Sea-Law*:

ἐὰν πλέωσιν ἐν πλοίῳ ἐπιβάται καὶ ἢ διαφθαρῇ ἢ ἀπόληται τὸ πλοῖον, τὰ δὲ τῶν ἐπιβατῶν σωθῇ, ἐπιφερέτωσαν οἱ ἐπιβάται εἰς τὴν ἀπώλειαν τοῦ πλοίου. ἐὰν δὲ ἐπιβάται	if there are passengers on board and the ship is injured or destroyed, but the goods of the passengers are saved, let the passengers make a payment towards the loss of the ship.

δύο ἢ τρεῖς ἀπολέσωσι τὸ χρυσίον αὐτῶν ἢ τὰ εἴδη, ἀπὸ πάντων λαμβανέτωσαν κατὰ τὴν δύναμιν πρὸς τὴν ἀπώλειαν ἅμα τῆς συμβολῆς τοῦ πλοίου.	If passengers two or three lose their gold or their goods, let them receive from all according to their capacity towards the loss together with the contribution of the ship.

According to Ashburner chapters 40 and 41[37] of the *Rhodian Sea-Law* do not deal with contribution. Ashburner suggests that the payments of the passengers to which these chapters refer to, should not be considered as contribution to the ship-owner, but as a sort of bribe in order to prevent the captain and the crew from plundering the goods.[38] Finally, in chapter 38 of the *Rhodian Sea-Law* we read that if a ship loaded with corn is caught in a gale and the cargo is lost, the captain and the sailors receive six percent of whatever is saved. Here is the corresponding passage:

ἐὰν πλοῖον πεφορτωμένον σῖτον ἐν ζάλῃ καταληφθῇ, ὁ ναύκληρος διφθέρας παρεχέτω καὶ οἱ ναῦται ἀντλείτωσαν. εἰ δὲ ἀμελήσωσι καὶ βραχῇ ὁ φόρτος ἐκ τῆς ἀντλίας, οἱ ναῦται ζημιούσθωσαν. εἰ δὲ ἀπὸ τῆς ζάλης ὁ φόρτος ἀδικηθῇ, ἐπιγινωσκέτωσαν τὴν ζημίαν ὅ τε ναύκληρος καὶ οἱ ναῦται ἅμα τῷ ἐμπόρῳ, τὰς δὲ ἓξ ἑκατοστὰς τῶν σωζομένων κομιζέσθω ὁ ναύκληρος ἅμα τοῦ πλοίου καὶ τοῖς ναύταις.	If a ship loaded with corn is caught in a gale, let the captain provide skins and the sailors work the pumps. If they are negligent and the cargo is wetted by the bilge, let the sailors pay the penalty. But if it is from the gale that the cargo is injured, let the captain and the sailors together with the merchant bear the loss; and let the captain together with the ship and the sailors receive the six-hundredths of each thing saved.

The *rationale* of all these provisions is the attempt to share the loss and establish a fair distribution of the damages amongst all parties. This *rationale* is characteristic of the *Rhodian Sea-Law*. It is also reflected in the principle of general average which derives from the so-called '*Rhodian law of jettison*' which the Roman jurists comment upon and implies the following: all parties in a sea venture will share the losses caused from a voluntary sacrifice of cargo to save the whole ship in an emergency. The legal principle of general average is still

37 As well as chapters 30, 31 and 37.

38 See Ashburner (1909, repr. 1976), cclviii–ccxciii, especially cclviii–cclxiii and ccxcii.

valid in modern legislation and this proves the significant influence of this ancient maritime collection.[39]

3 Byzantine Treaties with the Italians

3.1 *Preliminary Observations on the Material*

Until now I have referred to shipwreck and salvage provisions in Byzantine imperial legislation and Byzantine legal collections. It is worth taking a look into some sources that are more practice-orientated. I will use here some examples from the treaties which Byzantium concluded with the Italians in the eleventh and twelfth centuries. From the tenth century onwards the Byzantine emperors promulgated acts in favour of Venice, Pisa and Genoa granting important commercial privileges to the Italian city-states.[40] These documents were issued in the form of a privilege act, a so-called chrysobull.[41] Although these documents had the form of a privilege act they were in reality treaties between Byzantium and the Italian cities.[42] Italian embassies were sent to Constantinople to negotiate the Italian requests with the Byzantine side. Information on the negotiations is given not only in the chrysobulls but also in the Byzantine imperial letters that were sent to the Italian cities. From the Italian side a few letters of instructions have also been preserved by which the Italians instructed their envoys who were to travel to Constantinople on how to negotiate with the Byzantine emperor.[43] After the negotiations the emperor would grant his chrysobull which included what was agreed. All Byzantine imperial

39 See, for example, the Dutch civil code, book 8, article 610 and the German commercial code, § 588.

40 For a general overview of these documents from a commercial and political perspective, see Lilie (1984).

41 The word chrysobull (χρυσόβουλλον) derives from the Greek words 'χρυσός' (gold) and 'βούλλα' (seal) and it was used for documents bearing the Emperor's gold bulla.

42 On the use of the chrysobull as an act of foreign policy, see Dölger / Karayannopoulos (1968) 25 and 94 *et seq*. For the Byzantine documents concerning the Italian cities in particular, see also Heinemeyer (1957) 79–161.

43 There are six such letters of instructions preserved, which are as follows: i. to Amico de Murta between Oct. 1169 and April 1170 from Genoa, ii. to Grimaldo in 1174 from Genoa, iii. to Ottobono Dellacroce in 1201 from Genoa, iv. a letter to an envoy whose name is not mentioned according to Heinemeyer (1957) 109, footnote 146, v. to Uguccione di Lamberto Bono and Pietro Modano in 1197 from Pisa, vi. to Enrico Navigaioso and Andrea Donato, probably in 1197 from Venice. For the editions of these acts, see Heinemeyer (1957) 108–109. For ii. and iii. see also di Sant'Angelo (Rome, 1936–42) vol. II, 206–222, no 96 and vol. III, 194–199, no 77. For an analysis of these instructions, see Heinemeyer (1957) 108ff.

documents, i.e. chrysobulls and imperial letters were issued in Greek and were also translated into Latin by Byzantine officials.[44]

This material is interesting for our subject for two reasons. Firstly, because of the nature of these documents since, as explained above, these acts were in reality treaties between Byzantium and the Italians; they were not general laws but reflected the actual applicable law between both sides. These documents were after all, the result of negotiations between the Byzantine and the Italian side. A second reason which makes this material interesting for our topic is that they regulate situations of shipwreck and salvage of foreign ships, those of the Italians in the jurisdiction of the empire. Hence the study of the Byzantine imperial acts directed to Venice, Pisa and Genoa in the eleventh and twelfth centuries can give us information on the following questions: What happened when a foreign ship was wrecked within the Byzantine empire? Who was entitled to own these goods? Was it the original owners, the Italians in this case or the finders or the fisc? And do we come across any information on the finder's reward and its estimation in case of a wrecked ship?

3.2 *Shipwreck and Salvage Provisions*

One would expect that maritime legal issues, including shipwreck and salvage questions would have been regulated for all three Italian cities with the Byzantine side. The first preserved Byzantine privilege act in favour of Venice was issued in 992. Venice was the first Italian city to receive Byzantine privileges and was by far the most favoured one. It is therefore striking that no shipwreck or salvage provision has been included in the preserved Byzantine imperial acts addressed to Venice in this period especially because we find such provisions in the privilege charters that the Crusader kings promulgated in favour of Venice in roughly the same period. Laiou has suggested that the Byzantine chrysobulls do not include any salvage or shipwreck provisions 'presumably because the Venetians, treated as Byzantine subjects, were covered by Byzantine law'.[45] However, I do not agree with this opinion mainly because we see that the Byzantine emperors do regulate in their documents other legal issues which concern Venetians. For example, they regulate the situation in which a Venetian dies within the empire and has left no testament, or they settle issues of jurisdiction concerning Venetians. If the Venetians were indeed treated as

44 A copy of the original Greek act and its Latin translation was kept in Byzantine archives and another copy of the original Greek and its Latin translation was given to the Italians to take home. Unfortunately not all Byzantine imperial documents addressed to Italian cities have survived in both Greek and Latin.

45 See Laiou (2001) 181.

Byzantine subjects and were subject to Byzantine law, there would have been no reason for the emperor to regulate any legal issue at all concerning the Venetians. In short, I have not found a satisfactory answer to why shipwreck and salvage provisions are omitted from the Byzantine documents in favour of Venice in this period.[46]

The first Byzantine document directed to an Italian city that regulated issues of maritime law was the chrysobull of emperor Alexios I Komnenos to Pisa in 1111, which was also the first chrysobull granted to the Pisans.[47] The fact that the Pisans settled maritime legal issues already in the first privilege that they received from the Byzantines proves how important these issues were for the Pisans. After all, Pisa had a strong interest in the field of maritime law. Before 1160, the Pisans had already proceeded in a codification of norms regarding trade and navigation; this formed the so-called *constitutus usus* made by experts in law (*iurisperiti*).[48] This law book, together with the *constitutus legis*, which was another contemporary collection of norms of Roman and Lombard law, are considered sophisticated legislative texts.[49] It is, therefore, logical that Pisans were interested early on in regulating their maritime law issues with the Byzantine empire. By the chrysobull of 1111 Alexios I Komnenos assured the Pisans that if a Pisan ship was plundered within the empire and Byzantines removed Pisan goods from the ship, the emperor would take care to administer justice once proof was given.[50] Although a shipwreck is not specifically mentioned in this fragment, it does regulate the situation in which Byzantines remove goods from Pisan ships, which have been plundered within the Byzantine empire. This could include the situation, in which a Pisan ship because it had been captured and plundered was in the end wrecked, or part of it was destroyed and goods of that ship were eventually removed by Byzantine subjects. In any case, the emperor wants to reassure the Pisans that he will take action if their goods are removed by Byzantines from Pisan ships that have been plundered within the empire. A prerequisite for the emperor's help is that such a situation has to be proved. However, no details are given about this

46 See in detail, Penna (2012) 241–242.

47 For information of this document and a summary, see Dölger and Wirth (1995) 174, Regesten no 1255; the Regesten numbers will be henceforth abbreviated as Reg.

48 Salvatori (2002) 20. About this collection, see for example, Classen (1983) 82–89.

49 Salvatori (2002) 20.

50 'Εἰ κουρσευθῇ πλοῖον ὑμῶν ἐν τῇ χώρᾳ τῆς βασιλείας μου καὶ ἀπολεσθῶσι τὰ πράγματα ὑμῶν ἀφαιρεθέντα παρά τινων τῶν ὑπὸ τὴν βασιλείαν μου ὄντων, ἵνα ποιῇ ὑμῖν ἡ βασιλεία μου δίκαιον καὶ διόρθωσιν εἰς ἐνδεχόμενον καιρὸν μετὰ τὸ ἐλεγχθῆναι' in Müller (1879, repr. 1966) 44, lines 32–36, no XXXIV the Latin version 53, lines 25–30: 'Si depredata fuerit navis vestra in terra imperii nostri, et perditae fuerint res vestrae, ablatae ab aliquibus qui sub potentia imperii nostri sunt, faciet vobis clementia imperii nostri iusticiam et emendationem convenienti tempore, postquam probatum fuerit'.

procedure and the phraseology used in this fragment regarding the measures of the emperor is rather vague.[51]

In the chrysobull of Manuel I Komnenos to Genoa in 1169 shipwreck provisions were clearly included. It was ordered that if a Genoese ship was wrecked within the empire and goods were removed by someone, the lost goods would be recovered and regained after an imperial order.[52] One year later the Byzantine emperor Manuel I Komnenos promulgated a new chrysobull in favor of Genoa and included a similar provision.[53] By comparing these two provisions on shipwreck and salvage for Genoa to the earlier similar one to the Pisans, one observes in the case of Genoa a development in favor of Genoa. In the document in favor of Pisa the emperor is vaguer about the help he would provide to the Pisans. I conclude this from the phraseology used since the emperor speaks in that chrysobull in general of 'awarding justice' if a Pisan ship was plundered within the empire and Pisan goods were removed by Byzantines.[54] In the two chrysobulls in favor of Genoa however, it is clearly expressed that if a ship was wrecked or was in danger within the empire and goods were removed, the goods would have been recovered by imperial order. In the chrysobulls for Genoa there were stronger indications that a legal procedure would have followed since words as '*ἐκδίκησις πραγμάτων*' and '*vindicandi res*' were included, which mean claiming the things back.[55]

51 See on this further the comparison of this fragment with later chrysobulls to Genoa.

52 Reg. 1488. '...Et si aliqua navis Ianuensium a quacumque parte venerit, naufragium passa fuerit in Romaniam et contigerit de rebus eius auferri eis ab aliquo, fiet preceptum imperii eius vindicandi et recuperandi res amissas' in di Sant'Angelo (Rome, 1936–1942) vol. II, version Q, 112, lines 22–28, no. 50. Only a Latin translation has been preserved of this document in two versions; see in detail Dölger / Wirth (1995) 255–256.

53 '...καὶ ἐὰν πλοῖον Γενουιτικὸν ἀφ' οἱουδήτινος τόπου ἐρχόμενον εἰς 'Ρωμανίαν κινδυνεύσῃ καὶ συμβῇ τινὰ τῶν ἐν αὐτῷ πραγμάτων ἀφαιρεθῆναι ὑπό τινων, ἵνα γίνηται πρὸς ταῦτα τῆς βασιλείας μου ἐκδίκησις καὶ ἐπανάσωσις τῶν τοιούτων πραγμάτων' in Miklosich and Müller (1865, repr. 1968) vol. 3, 36, lines 2–6, no V and the Latin version in Bertolotto / Sanguinetti (1898) 432, lines 32–36, no IX: 'Et si navigium Genuense a quocumque loco veniens in Romaniam periclitetur et contingerit ut aliquid ex iis quae in ipso sunt ablatum fuerit a quocumque, fiat de his vindicta a maiestate mea et restauratio huiusmodi rerum'. This document (Reg. 1498) has been preserved as inserted in a later chrysobull of Isaac II Angelos in 1192 (Reg. 1609), preserved in both Greek and Latin versions.

54 Reg. 1255. We read in the Greek version 'ἵνα ποιῇ ὑμῖν ἡ βασιλεία μου δίκαιον καὶ διόρθωσιν' and in the Latin version 'faciet vobis clementia imperii nostri iusticiam et emendationem'.

55 The word 'ἐκδίκησις' (and 'vindicta' in Latin) is used here rather as claiming the things back, in the sense of a 'reivindicatio', a meaning that other Byzantine legal texts contain as well. In this respect, I do not agree with Laiou who writes '...the word *vindicta* in the text suggests punishment' in Laiou (2001) 182. See in detail Penna (2012) 250, with references to Byzantine sources.

In the chrysobull issued by Alexios I Komnenos in favour of Pisa in 1111 there is another interesting provision concerning salvage. It was also regulated that if a Pisan ship is wrecked within the empire, the Pisans can unconditionally keep the things that they themselves remove and save. If, however, Byzantines help them in rescuing their things, the Pisans can also keep these things under the condition that they will pay the Byzantines who helped them a reward according to the local custom, unless there is another agreement between the Pisans and the Byzantines, who helped them. Here is the corresponding passage:

Πλοῖον ὑμῶν εἰ ναυαγήσει ἐν τῇ ἐπικρατείᾳ τῆς βασιλείας μου, τὰ πράγματα ὑμῶν, ἃ ὑμεῖς ἐλευθεροῦτε καὶ ἐκβάλλετε σεσωσμένα, ἵνα ἔχητε ἀμερίμνως καὶ ἃ δὲ ἐκβάλλουσιν οἱ Ῥωμαίοι βοηθήσαντες, ἵνα ἔχητε κἀκεῖνα παρασχόντες κατὰ τὸν τύπον τοῦ τόπου πρὸς αὐτοὺς τὸν μισθὸν, εἰ μὴ ἴσως ἑκουσίως μέσον ὑμῶν κἀκείνων ἕτερόν τι συμφωνηθῇ.[56]

Navis vestra, si fracta fuerit infra potentiam imperii nostri, res vestras quas vos liberatis et extrahitis salvas habebitis sine dubio et illas autem quas Romei extrahent adiuvantes habebitis dantes eis mercedem secundum loci consuetudinem, nisi forte inter vos et eos aliquid aliud sponte pactum fuerit.[57]

If a ship of yours [of the Pisans] is shipwrecked within my empire, you can without any doubt keep the things that you yourselves have been able to safely recover from the ship; as for the things however, that the Byzantines will help to take out, you can keep these things also, provided that you give to them [the Byzantines] a reward as the regional custom requires, except if something else is willingly agreed between you and them.

We had already seen that there were Byzantine laws regulating issues of salvage of goods involved in a shipwreck. The *Rhodian Sea-Law*, which was also included in the *Basilica*, dealt with this issue and provided different rewards. What is interesting according to the chrysobull of 1111 to Pisa from a legal point of view, is that the emperor prefers to refer to local custom at this point in matters dealing with the salvage of goods in a shipwreck to regulating, for example,

56 Müller (1879, repr. 1966) 44, lines 37–43, no XXXIV.

57 Müller (1879, repr. 1966) 53, 31–37, no XXXIV.

a fixed amount within the whole empire for the salvor of the goods of a shipwreck. Local custom seems to play an important role in this particular field of law. Even if there had been a law regulating the reward of the salvor (in our case the *Rhodian Sea-Law*), it is the local custom that prevails at this point by imperial order. Local practice and customs did play an important role in medieval Mediterranean maritime law;[58] the emperor's preference for a local custom confirms that this was also the case in the Byzantine world.

It has been argued that the provision included in the first chrysobull for Pisa in 1111 by which it was mentioned that the Pisans were allowed to keep their wrecked goods if they had saved them themselves, implies that before it was issued, the Pisans could not keep their things if their ship was wrecked and that the goods from the wreckage of a foreign ship belonged to the Byzantine fisc.[59] It is interesting to note at this point that according to maritime statutes of the Middle Ages, lost goods from a wreck were not claimed by the fisc but remained the property of the owners while rewards were given to the finders.[60] Even in cases in which the owner was not found, a finder of a wrecked thing could become owner only after he had followed a special court proceeding.[61] According also to Byzantine legislation, as we saw earlier, the owner of the goods from a wrecked ship remained their owner. The question is, of course, whether this was to be applied to foreigners. The Byzantine legislator had not taken into consideration what was to happen to foreigners. This could explain why a provision concerning the ownership of the wrecked goods was included in the chrysobull in favour of the Pisans in 1111. Given that the Pisans were foreigners and that until then, no agreement had been made between Byzantium and Pisa in matters of shipwrecks, it is possible that if a Pisan ship were to be shipwrecked, the Byzantines could have been 'more eager' in looting the goods. Judging by the legal measures taken by different Byzantine emperors against pillaging, as mentioned in the first part of this paper, it is certainly possible that this was common practice. The Italians, in this case the Pisans and later the Genoese, needed a guarantee by the emperor that their wrecked goods would remain theirs. What better way to confirm such a guarantee than placing it down in a prestigious imperial chrysobull?

58 See Constable, *Jettison* (1994) especially 217 and Cordes (2017) especially 69–70 and 81, who points out the importance of local and regional legal concepts and proposes 'a general development model of geographic expansion, which can perhaps be described as 'from local to global'', on page 70.

59 Laiou (2001) 181.

60 See Ashburner (1909, repr. 1976) cclxxxix ff.

61 Ashburner (1909, repr. 1976) ccxci.

4 Conclusion

According to the Byzantine legal sources examined in the first part of this paper we can conclude that Byzantine legislation on shipwreck and salvage followed Roman law and regulated that wrecked goods remained property of the original owner. We have seen that there were many provisions dealing with the looting and stealing of wrecked goods and in some cases strict punishments were ordered, including the death penalty. The fact that Byzantine legislation was strict with those who stole from a shipwreck and that there were many provisions regulating such matters proves that the looting and pillaging of shipwrecks was something that often occurred in Byzantium and thus the emperors tried to tackle these problems by taking appropriate measures. In respect of salvage, the most interesting source is the *Rhodian Sea-Law*, a legal collection dating from the seventh of eighth century which was later incorporated in the last important Byzantine legislation, the *Basilica* (laws) promulgated around 900. In principal the *Basilica* reflected Justinianic law but in Greek. The fact that the whole text of the *Rhodian Sea-Law*[62] was included in the fifty-third *Basilica* book proves how important this maritime collection was. The *Rhodian Sea-Law* regulates rewards for people who help in recovering the wrecked goods. Although a general provision for estimating the reward was fixed in this maritime collection and corresponded to one fifth of the saved good, the actual estimation of the reward could vary depending on various criteria; for example, the depth in which the object was found etc.

In the second part of this paper I tried to investigate some Byzantine sources which were more practice-orientated. I used examples from the Byzantine imperial acts to the Italian city-states in the eleventh and twelfth centuries because these documents were the result of negotiations between both sides reflecting the actual applicable law in case. Three conclusions can be drawn from this material. First of all, it is concluded that customs played an important role in maritime issues. According to the chrysobull of Alexios I Komnenos to Pisa in 1111, it was customary to pay a reward to those who had helped saving the goods from a shipwreck and this reward was not a fixed amount but it varied from place to place. As we saw, the emperor in this document regulated the reward for Byzantines who had helped Pisans recover their wrecked goods. The Byzantine emperor preferred to refer to this custom to regulating a fixed amount as a reward, or to referring to the reward rules of an existing law, such as the *Rhodian Sea-Law*. This information proves that local custom played an important role in Byzantine shipwreck and salvage issues. It also corresponds

62 Except its *prooimion*.

to the general medieval Mediterranean practice in respect of maritime issues, which is characterised of the significant role of local practice and customs.

A second conclusion that can be drawn from the Byzantine imperial acts to the Italian city-states in the eleventh and twelfth centuries is that the danger of stealing from wrecked goods still existed in Byzantine practice in this period. Despite the fact that there were many Byzantine laws that protected the owners of wrecked goods and strongly punished theft and looting of these goods, the Italians considered such a scenario a real danger and that is why these provisions were eventually included in the chrysobulls in favour of Pisa and Genoa.[63] Let us not forget that the Italians were foreigners and there would have been questions regarding the applicable law. It was certainly better for them to assure the protection of their wrecked goods by the words of the emperor himself as inserted in these chrysobulls.

Finally, a third conclusion is that there is a gradual development of the actual help of the emperor toward the Italians. From a vague promise it becomes more concrete. This observation is based on the maritime provisions for the Pisans and the Genoese. As I have already mentioned no shipwreck or salvage provision is included in the acts directed to Venice and I have not been able to find a satisfactory reason for this. As the Pisans and Genoese receive more privileges from the Byzantine emperors, their demands -also in respect to shipwreck and salvage of their goods- are becoming stronger. Perhaps this development is somehow connected to other 'treaties' which were concluded by the Italians in this period. I am referring to the Crusader charters, the documents which were promulgated in favour of Venice, Pisa and Genoa by the Crusader kings of the new-established Crusader states. The subjects that the Crusader kings regulated in these charters were sometimes similar to the ones regulated by the Byzantine emperors for the Italians in the Byzantine chrysobulls. For example, shipwreck and salvage provisions were also included in the Crusader charters for the Italians. Was there some kind of interaction between the Crusader charters and the Byzantine documents at this point? Could the experience of the Italians with one side have influenced the negotiations with the other side? Are there similarities and differences in the regulation of similar legal problems for the Italians by the Byzantine emperors and by the Crusader kings? The comparison of the Byzantine documents to the Crusader charters addressed to the Italians in this period will certainly give us a better and more complete picture on the formation of maritime law in the Mediterranean in

63 No shipwreck or salvage provisions have been included in the chrysobulls in favor of Venice.

this period, which is a crucial period since it marks the rise of trade and commerce. But that is another subject.[64]

Bibliography

Ashburner, W., *The Rhodian Sea-Law* (Oxford 1909, repr. Scientia Aalen 1976).

Bertolotto, G. and A. Sanguinetti, *Nuova Seria di documenti sulle relationi di Genova coll' impero bizantino, Atti della Società di Ligure di storia patria 28* (Genoa 1898).

Cameron, A., *The Byzantines* (Oxford 2006).

Chitwood, Z., *Byzantine legal culture and Roman legal tradition, 867–1056* (Cambridge 2017).

Classen, P., *Studium und Geselschaft im Mittelalter*. Monumenta Germaniae Historica Schriften 29 (Stuttgart 1983).

Constable, O.R., 'The problem of jettison in medieval Mediterranean maritime law', *Journal of Medieval History* 20 (1994) 207–220.

Cordes, A., 'Lex Maritima? Local, regional and universal maritime law in the Middle Ages' in W. Blockmans, M. Krom and J. Wubs-Mrozewicz eds., *The Routledge Handbook of Maritime Trade around Europe 1300–1600* (Londen and New York 2017) 69–85.

Dölger, F., *Regesten der Kaiserurkunden des oströmishen Reiches von 565–1453* vol. 2, revised by Wirth, P. (Munich 1995).

Dölger, F. and J. Karayannopoulos, *Byzantinische Urkundenlehre. Erster Abschnitt: Die Kaiserurkunden* (1968).

Frier, B.W., S. Connolly et al. eds., *The Codex of Justinian, A New Annotated Translation, with Parallel Latin and Greek Text, based on a Translation by Justice Fred H. Bluhme*, 3 vols. (Cambridge 2016).

Heinemeyer, W., 'Die Verträge zwischen dem Oströmischen Reiche und den italienischen Städten Genua, Pisa und Venedig vom 10. bis 12. Jahrhundert', *Archiv für Diplomatik, Schriftgeschichte Siegel- und Wappenkunde 3* (1957) 79–161.

Herrin, J., *Byzantium, The Surprising Life of a Medieval Empire* (London 2007).

Laiou, A.E., 'Byzantine trade' in Angeliki E. Laiou and Roy Parviz Mottahedeh eds., *The Crusades from the perspective of Byzantium and the Muslim world* (Washington D.C. 2001) 157–192.

Letsios, D., *Νόμος Ροδίων Ναυτικός. Das Seegesetz der Rhodier* (Rhodos 1996).

Lilie, R.-J., *Handel und Politik zwischen dem byzantinischen Reich und den italienischen Kommunen Venedig, Pisa und Genua in der Epoche der Komnenen und der Angeloi 1081–1204* (Amsterdam 1984).

64 For a first approach of this topic see Penna (2018).

Mango, C. ed., *The Oxford History of Byzantium* (Oxford 2002).

Miklosich, F. and Müller, J., *Acta et Diplomata Graeca Medii Aevi*, 3 vols. (1865, reprinted 1968).

Mousourakis, G., *Roman Law and the Origins of the Civil Law tradition* (Auckland 2015).

Müller, G., *Documenti sulle relationi delle città Toscane coll' Oriente Christiano e coi Turchi fino all'anno 1531* (Florence 1879, reprinted 1966).

Penna, D., 'Similar problems, similar solutions? Byzantine chrysobulls and Crusader charters on legal issues regarding the Italian maritime republics' in D. Slootjes and M. Verhoeven eds., *Byzantium in Dialogue with the Mediterranean. History and Heritage* (Leiden and Boston 2019) 162–181.

Penna, D., *The Byzantine imperial acts to Venice, Pisa and Genoa, 10th–12th centuries, A Comparative Legal Study* (Groningen 2012).

Rodolakis, G., *Από το Νόμο Ροδίων στο 53ο βιβλίο των Βασιλικών*, in Greek [= From the *Rhodian Sea-Law* to the 53rd *Basilica* book] (Athens 2007).

Salvatori, E., 'Pisa in the Middle Ages: the dream and the reality of an empire' in *Empires and States in European Perspective* (2002) 13–32.

di Sant' Angelo, C.I. ed., *Codice Diplomatico della Repubblica di Genova, Fonti per la storia d' Italia*, 3 vols. (Rome 1936–1942).

Scheltema, H.J., *L'enseignement de droit des antécesseurs* (1970), repr. in N. van der Wal et al. eds., *H.J. Scheltema Opera Minora ad iuris historiam pertinentia* (Groningen 2004) A, 3, 58–110.

Scheltema, H.J., D. Holwerda and N. van der Wal, *Basilicorum Libri LX*, Series A: Textus librorum I–LX (8 vols.); Series B: Scholia in libros I–LX (9 vols.) (Groningen 1953–1988) http://referenceworks.brillonline.com/browse/basilica-online (date of access: 5 June 2018) accompanied by a comprehensive and updated introduction, *Praefatio* by B. Stolte and a complete bibliography by T.van Bochove.

Stolte, B.H., 'The Law of New Rome: Byzantine Law (Chapter 17)' in D. Johnston ed., *The Cambridge Companion to Roman Law* (2015) https://doi.org/10.1017/CCO9781139034401.023, 355–373.

Stolte, B.H., 'Is Byzantine Law Roman Law?' in *Acta Byzantina Fennica* 2 (2003–2004) 111–126.

Storti Storchi, Cl., *Intorno at Constituti Pisani della legge e dell' uso (secolo XII)* (1998).

Troianos, Sp., *Die Quellen des byzantinischen Rechts*, transl. by D. Simon, and S. Neye (Berlin 2017).

Troianos, Sp., *Οι Νεαρές Λέοντος ΣΤ' του Σοφού*, in Greek [= The Novels of Leo VI the Wise] (Athens 2007).

Troianos, Sp., 'Τα ναυάγια, η Νεαρά 64 Λέοντος του Σοφού και το κείμενο των Βασιλικών' in Greek [= Shipwrecks, Novel no 64 of Leo the Wise and the text of the Basilica] in

Πειραϊκή Νομολογία 14 (1992) 488–495 reprinted in Troianos, Sp., *Οι Νεαρές Λέοντος ΣΤ' του Σοφού*, in Greek [= The Novels of Leo VI the Wise] (Athens 2007) VII, 515–526.

Watson, A. ed., *The Digest of Justinian*, (transl. Mommsen, ed. maior), 4 vols (Philadelphia, 1985).

Zepos, J. and P. Zepos, *Ius Graecoromanum*, vol. II (Athens 1931, reprinted Scientia Aalen 1962).

CHAPTER 3

Bjarkeyjarréttr and *Farrmanna Logh*: Norse or European Laws of the Sea?

Ian Peter Grohse

1 Introduction

The earliest surviving example of Scandinavian maritime law stems from the elder *Bjarkeyjarréttr* (ON: 'birch-island law'),[1] a collection of articles supplementing the general laws of the Frostaþing province of central Norway.[2] Dated to at least the eleventh century, the *Bjarkeyjarréttr* regulated commercial affairs in the fledgling town of Nidaros (Trondheim) and provided securities for mariners and merchants travelling the waters along Norway's western seaboard.[3] Issues surrounding maritime voyages are addressed in nine articles comprising the so-called 'law of merchants' (*farrmanna logh*).[4] These paragraphs provide unparalleled insight into the organization and regulation of maritime ventures in early- and high-medieval Norway. Despite its familiarity to students of Scandinavian legal history, the *Bjarkeyjarréttr* is relatively unknown in the wider field of medieval maritime law.[5] This is remarkable given its exceptional provenance: even by conservative estimates, the written provisions of the *Bjarkeyjarréttr* likely antedate those of the *Rôles d'Oléron*, the most

1 Peter Andreas Munch believed that the name derived from the settlement of Bjarkøy in the northern Norwegian province of Hálogaland, Munch (1838) 5–6. Dagfinn Skre choses to translate it as 'Birka law', arguing that '[t]here is little doubt that the name refers to the Swedish Viking Age town [Birka]', Skre (2008) 88. See below.

2 *Den ældre Bylov eller Bjarköret*, in *NgL* 1 (1846) 301–336, §1–179; Hagland and Sandnes (1997).

3 Brattegard (1956); Meissner (1941) 310–457; Meissner (1950); Robberstad (1970) 356–372; Blom (1997) 75–92; Müller-Boysen (1997); Strauch (2011) 166–176, 112. See also, Knudsen (1967); Bugge (1912).

4 *Den ældre Bylov* (1846) 334–336, §169–177: *Her hæfiazc upp farrmanna logh*. Compared to the consolidated Town Law from 1276 (*Den nyere By-Lov eller Bjarkö-Ret* in *NgL* 2 (1848) 179–290), which contains multiple paragraphs concerning merchant contracts (252–267), *Bjarkeyjarréttr* contains relatively few rules pertaining specifically to trade. This should dissuade overemphasis of the laws commercial character, even if trade is addressed implicitly. I thank Prof. Øyrehagen Sunde for pointing out this contrast.

5 General surveys of medieval maritime trade and law often omit the *Bjarkeyjarréttr* entirely, see e.g. Cordes (2017) 11–35. As an exception, Frankot refers to the elder *Bjakeyjarréttr* in her study of maritime laws in Northern and Western Europe, but does not treat it as a central case for comparison, see Frankot (2012) 9.

 | DOI:10.1163/9789004407992_005

influential corpus of medieval maritime law, by nearly a century.[6] From this perspective, its 'law of merchants' is not only the oldest maritime law in Scandinavia, it is also among the oldest in Europe.[7]

The *Bjarkeyjarréttr* encapsulates the norms of a small yet exceptional seaborne society at the margins of Western Christendom. In articulating that point, the following seeks not only to widen the purview of research on medieval maritime customs, but also challenge conventional wisdom on the trajectory and totality of legal transmission. Studies of maritime history often work from the premise that shared customs for sailing, shipping, and trade, as well as the management of conflicts arising therefrom, facilitated positive interaction between mariners and merchants from different local, regional and national jurisdictions. Written laws based upon these customs, such as the *Rôles d'Oléron* of Western France or the *Waterrecht* of Wisby, then circulated to smaller or more peripheral maritime communities, providing common benchmarks for exchange throughout the North Sea and Baltic region.[8] However, recent studies have contested this view, demonstrating a greater plurality of merchant and maritime customs between different towns and regions.[9] In a similar vein, the following challenges assumptions about legal transmission along Europe's northern frontier. Impulses emanating from France, England and the Hanseatic sphere may have provided influential paradigms for maritime governance in western and northwestern Europe in the late-medieval and early-modern eras, but in the north, they were long preceded by regional traditions that were not secondary to those of Britain and Continental Europe.

2 Provenance and Purpose

The *Bjarkeyjarréttr*'s origins as a written instrument of law can be traced to the eleventh and twelfth centuries, but its pedigree lay in customs antedating the

6 Twiss (1871) 211–241; Ward (2009) 183–205, §1–24. The *Rôles* are traditionally dated to the early reign of Eleanor of Aquitaine (r. 1137–1204), but newer research suggests a later date. Runyan and Ward date the *Rôles* to roughly 1200 based on linguistic features, Runyan (1975) 98; Ward (2009) 20. Studies by Krieger and Frankot date it to the late-thirteenth century, Krieger (1970) 71; Frankot (2007) 159; (2011) 20. For discussion of the *Rôles'* dating and provenance, see also Heebøll-Holm (2013) 130.

7 The early development of Norse seafaring laws has not gone unnoticed, although few studies have been devoted to *Bjarkeyjarréttr* as a unique case, see e.g. Müller-Boysen (1990) 138–139; Frankot (2007) 158.

8 See e.g. Jahnke (2008) 65; Ward (2009) 20; Runyan (1975) 98; Wagner (1906) 97; Robinson, Fergus and Gordon (1985) 161. On the *Rôles* potential influence on other laws, e.g. Flemish *Vonnesse van Damme*, Scottish *Of lawis of scyppis*, Dutch *Ordinancie* and Wisby *Waterrecht*, see Frankot (2007); Frankot (2011).

9 Cordes (2001); Cordes (2003); Frankot (2011).

genesis of codified legislation. In retracing its development historians and philologists emphasise the law's mutability over time, accepting that its content and character in the earliest phases, prior to the twelfth century, remain somewhat elusive. It survives in late-medieval and early-modern transcripts based upon a common edition from the mid- or late-thirteenth century.[10] But much its content is older.[11] Whereas parts of the law were introduced or redacted during the reign of King Magnús Erlingsson (r. 1161–1184) in the 1160s and 1170s, others contain remnants of earlier regulations. This is witnessed by references to Nidaros' 'bishop', rather than archbishop, suggesting that some parts predated that town's elevation as the seat of the Norwegian metropolitan in 1152/53.[12] An earlier dating is also supported by a reference to the law in the *Þingasaga*, an early-thirteenth century narrative recounting a protracted legal dispute during the reign of King Eysteinn Magnússon (r. 1103–1123).[13] The principal litigant in that case, Sigurðr Hranason, is said to have invoked his right to judgment in accordance with the *Bjarkeyjarréttr*,[14] thereby distinguishing that collection of market and maritime laws from the general paragraphs of the Frostaþing provincial law.[15]

It is not clear when the *Bjarkeyjarréttr* was first committed to parchment. The earliest known reference to the law stems from surviving versions of an agreement between King Ólafr *digri* Haraldsson (r. 1015–1028/30) and the people of Iceland, wherein the former grants the latter certain rights in accordance

10 Hagland and Sandnes (1997) x. Two fragments, AM 315g. fol. and AM 60b, 4to, date to the middle ages, while several other stem from post-reformation manuscripts from Iceland, ibidem, 118–120. The oldest of these, AM 315g. fol., dates to the mid-thirteenth century (Seip (1955) 91) and contains the bulk of the so-called 'law of merchants' (*farmanna-lög*), Hagland and Sandnes (1997) xxii-xxiii; Blom (1997) 77. The general laws of the Frostaþing in central Norway have survived as a revision from the 1260s and in a fragmentary manuscript from the early-1220s, although they, 'without doubt, date to the 1160s', Vogt (2010) 73. The town of Nidaros, which was founded by King Ólafr Trygvasson (r. 995–1000) in AD 997, had existed for well over a century, and it is inconceivable that the centre thrived without specific regulation, Hagland and Sandnes (1997), xx.

11 Hagland and Sandnes (1997) ix. The more recent editions of the *Bjarkeyjarréttr* should not be conflated with the 'newer' *Bjarkeyjarréttr* (*hinn nye*), that being the consolidated urban code of King Magnúss Hákonarsonar from 1276, *Den nyere By-Lov* (1848) 179–290; Meissner (1950). The maritime laws of that work are collected in the so-called *Farmanna logh*, in *Den nyere By-Lov* (1848) 274–286, §1–23.

12 Hagland and Sandnes (1997) xi., (kap. 1, 3–4); Blom (1997) 76.

13 Storm (1877); Blom (1997) 81–82; Tveit (2015) 4–5.

14 Storm (1877) 34.

15 On the jurisdictional distinction between the urban space, wherein the *Bjarkeyjarréttr* prevails, and surrounding province, wherein the laws of the Frostaþing take precedence, see Hagland and Sandnes, xiv-xv. The boundaries between urban and provincial jurisdictions were neither hard nor fast, and there is considerable overlap between the laws the Frostaþing and the *Bjarkeyjarréttr*, see Blom (1997) 79–86.

with the *Bjarkeyjarréttr*.[16] However, it is unlikely that written articles existed in the early-eleventh century.[17] Rather, the agreement likely alludes a set of unwritten and broadly applicable customs for Norse marketplaces, or 'birch islands' (*bjarkeyr*) as they were commonly known throughout various regions of Viking Age Scandinavia.[18] Grethe Authén Blom suggested that the earliest written editions stemmed from a period of urbanization and increased market activity in Nidaros under King Ólafr *kyrri* Haraldsson (r. 1067–1093) in the late-eleventh century.[19]

The *Bjarkeyjarréttr* was not exclusive to Nidaros,[20] but applied 'in every fishing cove and in herring villages and on trading voyages' (*á fisknesi hveriu ok í sildveri ok í kaupförum*).[21] Its transferability was especially pertinent for those sailing to the coasts of Hálogaland in the north, where inhabitants frequently hosted merchants seeking trade in furs, ivories and fish,[22] and were receptive

16 *NgL* 1 (1846) 438: 'If brethren or another man comes to [Norway], he shall demand recollection at the assembly according to the *Bjarkeyjarréttr*' (*Ef næstabrøðre eðr nanare maðr kømr til þa scal hann æsta tacs at biarceyiar rétte til mótz*).

17 Hagland and Sandnes (1997) xi; Blom (1997) 62. The reference in question is abbreviated, obscuring whether it pertain to a single town or multiple towns. The agreement survives in two later transcriptions, and it is assumed its content was altered by later jurists. It was confirmed by Bishop Gissur of Skálholt (Iceland) in 1083, during the reign of King Ólafr *kyrri* (r. 1067–1093), Helle (1982) 93; Blom (1997) 369, n 17. Since the original terms were presumably altered, it is prudent to read the written agreements as expression of conditions in the late-eleventh century, Ibidem 93. See also Long (2017) 185.

18 More than a dozen islands or coastal settlements in Norway, Sweden and Finland bear that root name, some of which were prominent harbors and trading sites in the Viking age and early middle ages. For the origin of the name, see e.g. Wadstein (1914); Wadstein (1936); Wessén (1925); Wessén (1956) 657–658. As noted, Munch believed the name derived from Bjarkøy in Hálogaland, Munch (1838) 5–6, while Skre maintains that the name derives from the Viking Age town of Birka on Björkö, situated in Lake Märlaren (eastern Sweden), Skre (2008) 88. Blom argues that older, less comprehensive laws concerning trade and maritime activity existed as a 'customary law' (sedevanerett) long before the extant version was first composed, Blom (1997) 78.

19 Blom (1997) 78.

20 Ibidem, 76–77. The *Bjarkeyjarréttr* is commonly referred to as the earliest 'town law' (bylov) of Trondheim (Hagland and Sandnes (1997): i; Knudsen (1967); Lehmann (1911): (Stadtrecht), it did not isolate the town from the surrounding Frostaþing province of central Norway, in a jurisdictional sense. Residents and visitors were subject to the same general laws as provincial communities throughout central and northern Norway, Blom (1997) 79–86. Cf. Strauch (2011) 167, who questions whether it applied to other towns.

21 *Den ældre Bylov* (1846) §42.

22 Early sources, including the chieftain Othare's account of his enterprise in Hálogaland, Finnmǫrk and Bjarmaland on the Kola Peninsula from the late-ninth century, emphasize the importance of trade and taxation in those regions; furs, skins, down feathers and whalebone are among the principal commodities, see Munch (1874); Bugge (1923) 143–159. Growing demand for fish in the twelfth and thirteenth centuries, encouraged the

to legal impulses from the Frostaþing province.[23] Intensified market activity in Vágan on the Lofot Archipelago encouraged the production of a separate law, the *Vágabók*, the content of which has not survived but was likely based on the merchant laws of the *Bjarkeyjarréttr*.[24] Fundamental similarities between Vágan's laws and those of other coastal settlements in central and northern Norway presumably enabled merchants to seek justice on familiar terms.

Sailing to Bergen in western Norway brought crews beyond the jurisdictional boundaries of the Frostaþing province and into those of the Gulaþing, a separate legal environment with its own codices and courts.[25] Yet the basic legal conventions for inter-regional commerce may not have been so pronounced. Although the earliest market and maritime laws of the Gulaþing province have not survived, Knut Helle posited that the old maritime customs upon which the *Bjarkeyjarréttr* developed were similar to those practiced in Bergen and other coastal communities in western and southern Norway.[26] This may be inferred from the content of King Magnúss Hákonarson's (r. 1263-1280) national market law from 1276, a consolidated codex that superseded older regional regulations.[27] Although composed primarily on the basis of Bergen's earlier (lost) market regulations that law applied to all towns including Nidaros, throughout the Norwegian realm. While considerably more elaborate, the law's rules on maritime ventures contain some elements from the elder *Bjarkeyjarréttr*, including the bailing of vessels and the delegation of watch duties.[28] It is thus possible – though far from proven – that maritime laws within the realm of Norway prior to the mid-thirteenth century were also compatible and transcended regional jurisdictional frontiers.

Maritime ventures in foreign countries were more precarious as they demanded reverence for different and perhaps contradicting customs of the

establishment of regular trade networks running to Norway's principal market in Bergen, see Helle (1982) 355–364; Bertelsen (2000) 7; Hansen (1990); Bratrein and Niemi (1994) 158.

23 Regarded as an appendage of the Frostaþing province, Hálogaland practiced the laws the Frostaþing, including the supplementary laws of the *Bjarkeyjarréttr*. See Tveit (2015) 6–7. Hagland and Sandnes (1994) xxix. Generally on Hálogaland's relation to the Frostaþing province, see Tveit (2015); Hansen (2015).

24 The *Vágabók* is named in a diploma from 1291, wherein one the incumbent regents of Norway, Bjarni Erlingsson, forbids its use and implicitly demanded reverence of the new consolidated law codes (DN 3, no. 30). Scholars have debated the character of that 'book'. Seip proposed that it was a separate provincial law for Hálogaland, Seip (1934) 30, while Gustav Heber suggested it was a special set of ordinances pertaining to fish trade, Heber (1953) 101. More convincing is the theory that it was a local edition of the *Bjarkeyjarréttr*. See Bjørgo (1982) 50; Bertelsen (2009) 201–204; Tveit (2015), 7–8.

25 Eithun, Rindal and Ulset (1994) 7–12.

26 Helle (1982) 177, 494; Andersson (2003) 336.

27 *Det nyere By-Lov* (1848); Meissner (1950); Strauch (2011) 160–165.

28 *Den nyere By-Lov* (1848) §2, 23.

sea.[29] *Konungs skuggsjá*, a Norwegian didactic text from the mid-thirteenth century, encourages observance of the *Bjarkeyjarréttr* when sailing abroad,[30] yet also stresses respect for local laws and customs, advising merchants to learn them soon after arriving in a foreign port.[31] The author does not identify the foreign lands in question, but alludes to Anglo-Norwegian trade by underscoring the utility of 'valsk' (*valskr* = Romance languages, e.g. French), the language of England's Anglo-Norman officials and merchants.[32] Although diplomatic records from the period do not specify which laws were invoked in the management of conflicts between Norwegian and English merchants, it is likely that offenses against Norwegians in or near England were heard at town courts administered by the English king's officials.[33] In 1226 and 1227, for instance, King Henry III (r. 1216–1272) subpoenaed men from Norfolk for plundering the archbishop of Nidaros' ship and demanded that they be turned over to the correct local court for adjudication.[34] There is no evidence that the victims invoked their native laws in the prosecution of the offenders, suggesting that local conventions took precedence over those of the *Bjarkeyjarréttr*.[35] By

29 Frankot argues that merchants struggled less to decide which court to appeal to than which law to abide by. In cases of conflict, mariners and merchants typically sought justice at the courts nearest to the accident or site of controversy, Frankot (2007) 165.

30 *Kongespeilet* (1848) 6: 'If you wish to be a merchant, you will need no law more than the *Bjarkeyjarréttr*' (*er þú vilt kaupmaðr vera, þá þarstu engan rétt þér meir annan kunnan gera en Bjarkeyjar rétt*).

31 The allegorical teacher in that work regards no man perfect in knowledge unless he has thoroughly learned and mastered the customs of the place where he is sojourning, Ogilvie (2011) 371; Kadens (2015) on local laws.

32 *Kongespeilet* (1848) 6. Bagge (2000) xxxii-xxxiiii: It is suggested here that French would have facilitated trade with Northern France, the Netherlands and England. Diplomatic records confirm this impression, presenting England the principal trade destination for Norwegian exports throughout the central Middle Ages, see *DN* 19, div. The consolidated market law from 1276 is more specific about the potential arenas for trade, citing Denmark, Gautland and Sweden, Gotland and Samland (southern Baltic), England, Orkney, Shetland, the Faroes, Greenland, Iceland and Gardar (Russia), *Det nyere By-Lov* (1848) §6.

33 In 1225, King Henry III of England commanded his officials in King's Lynn to allow Norwegian merchants free access to the port so long as they paid their dues. He specified further that offenses against them should be reconciled without hast and without reaching the ear of the king (*DN* 19, no. 174). This implies that Norwegian merchants could seek justice in the local courts of king's Lynn, although it is unclear what laws should be employed in such a case.

34 *DN* 19, nos. 182, 183.

35 While foreign merchants in medieval Europe were occasional granted rights to govern internal affairs using their own laws, see Murray (2005) 223; Ogilvie (2011) 258–259, disputes between foreigners and local merchants were generally adjudicated by local magistrates using local laws, Kadens (2004) 61; Kadens (2015).

that same token, foreign merchants were likely subject to local courts and the rules of the *Bjarkeyjarréttr* when in Norway.[36] Whether or not those laws were compatible or derived from a similar source is a matter for debate (see below).

3 Content

The nine articles concerning maritime transport are commonly referred to as the book or law of merchants (*farrmanna*).[37] That designation is somewhat misleading, for the stipulations omit discussion of goods and trading practices, focusing instead on technical and organizational features of sailing. We may think of them alternatively as the 'laws of the sea' or 'laws of mariners', although it is crucial to recognize the lack of professional distinction between mariners and merchants in medieval Norway.[38] The themes addressed include the standards for a ship's seaworthiness,[39] the procedures for docking, launching and bailing ships,[40] and the delegation of on-board watch duties.[41] The most elaborate concern the prosecution of justice, particularly in cases arising at sea and in distant and foreign lands.[42]

The first paragraph outlines the function of witnesses in confirming contracts between the skipper (*styrimaðr*) and crew and providing testimony on other matters pertaining to a ship's readiness for departure.[43] Such contracts provided an initial framework of obligation and justice for the entire maritime venture.[44] The law also outlines penalties for crewmen who breach their contract, be it while at sea or waiting to depart.[45] In cases arising at sea or abroad, four 'oarsmen' (*ræiðu menn*) were to organise an impromptu court assembly 'like magistrates would in the town' (*sem giallkyri i caupannge*).[46] Remarkably,

36 Nedkvitne (2014) 297.

37 Seip (1959).

38 Bugge (1912) 2.

39 *Den ældre Bylov* (1846) §170.

40 Ibidem, §171, 177.

41 Ibidem, §176.

42 Ibidem, §171, 172, 173, 175.

43 Ibidem, §169. The Norse term ('steer-man') is roughly equivalent to 'skipper', although the authority granted to him appears to be someone limited compared to skippers in other legal traditions. The skipper was central to the popular levy (*leiðangr*), as kings appointed one to each naval vessel, see Robberstad (1972) 368–369.

44 *Den ældre Bylov* (1846) §171, 175.

45 Ibidem, §171, 175.

46 Ibidem, §172.

the law expressly discourages the skipper's intervention in these meetings, explaining that he should *only* intervene and initiate a case if one of the crewmen was dangerously unruly. Such cases should ideally be heard when the ship arrived in a port, preferably at the entrance to the quay.[47] If the ship was still at sea, the oarsmen should assemble and hear the case under the mast and sail. Once they had passed judgement and demanded a penalty, the sum should be divided, with half going to the skipper and half to the rest of the crew. The only exception was in the cases of murder, wherein the full sum should go to the king in the port they arrive, so long as he is a Christian ruler. If they fail to agree on a penalty by the time they sail into Nidaros, then the king there should take the full penalty.[48]

The *Bjarkeyjarréttr* also addresses the treatment of offenders. One paragraph outlines the procedures for the corporal punishment of thieves, something that should only take place on land and in Christian kingdoms.[49] There the crew should shave, tar and feather the accused before lining up and forcing him to run the gauntlet. Every crewman should participate in beating the accused with sticks and stones – but not so severely as to kill him – and was liable to a small monetary penalty for failing to participate. After this ordeal, the thief was absolved of his crime.[50] This is somewhat remarkable as it contradicts the norms for prosecuting thievery in mainland Norway, where crown officials should normally 'commission someone to kill him' (*fái mann til at drepa hann*) and where 'peasants are required to participate in the thief's execution' (*en böndr scylldir til at fylgia þiófi til dráps*).[51] The leniency toward mariners was

47 Ibidem, §173.

48 Ibidem. The law makes no explicit reference to Nidaros but specifies that the judgement or agreement should be established by the time the vessel reaches the town outfield (*tacmærkir*), which Hagland and Sandnes assume to be the area now known as Bymarka, an uncultivated woodland outside the town of Trondheim, see Hagland and Sandnes (1997) 102–103. While plausible, the paragraph also stipulates that certain fines for grave offenses 'belong to the king, there where [the vessel] lands undamaged and it is a Christian king who rules' (*þat a kononngr. Þar sem þæir briota bulca sinn at hæilu. oc er cristinn kononngr*), *Den ældre Bylov* (1846) § 173. This may indicate that the 'outfield' referred more generally to the boundaries of any Christian settlement.

49 Hagland and Sandnes (1997) 94, §144. The stipulation is *not* included in *NgL's* edition but has been added in Hagland and Sandnes's translation based on previously disordered manuscript fragments. Differentiation of Christian and non-Christian lands is not found in the national urban law of 1276, which lists several foreign lands and stipulates different penalties according to the proximity or distance of that law, *Den nyere By-Lov* (1848) §6. However, there is no mention of heathens or non-Christians.

50 Hagland and Sandnes (1997) 94. Müller-Boysen (1997) 96.

51 *NgL* 1 (1846) 252–253.

likely pragmatic: to kill a crewman would diminish manpower and jeopardize the welfare of the entire venture.

While most maritime conflicts in medieval Europe probably occurred in ports or eyeshot of coastlines, there was always potential for dispute on the high seas. Norwegians enjoyed a veritable monopoly on shipping in the North Atlantic and in parts of the North Sea, yet Norway's rulers never asserted claims of sovereignty over open waters.[52] Mariners departing western Norway were thus beyond the margins of spatial jurisdiction. Potential conflicts were most manageable when they emerged between members of the same crew. The *Bjarkeyjarréttr* regards ships as distinct juridical units while at sea, encouraging oarsmen to pass judgements through an assembly of oarsmen acting as prosecutors and jurors.[53] Sub-delegation of justice was a common feature of medieval maritime law (see below) and must have been most relevant for ships sailing long distances to markets under foreign jurisdictions. While this was less consequential for shipping along Norway's coastlines, where inhabitants and travellers abided by the same laws, it must have benefited crews traversing the North Sea and North Atlantic, where courts were either non-existent, remote or unreceptive to the articles of the *Bjarkeyjarréttr*.

4 Legal Peculiarities

International research has yet to fully appreciate the *Bjarkeyjarréttr*'s exceptionality within the wider compass of European maritime law. This may reflect a tendency of scholars to view historical developments, including legal developments, in outward trajectories, whereby customs and laws are believed to disseminate from dominant, central societies to dependent, peripheral ones.[54]

---

52 Norway's king in the mid-thirteenth century, Hákonar Hákonarson (r. 1217–1263), was known as king of the isles (*rex insularis*), see Imsen (2015). While the seas were important reference points and framed spatial lordship, kings did not claim authority over open waters, see Grohse (2017).

53 Helle (1982) 403. Müller-Boysen (1997) 91, 98–99

54 See Watson (1974) on 'legal transplants' in the process of legal development. The editors of a recent anthology on 'Western legal culture' argued that 'understanding legal developments requires more than simply focussing on the institutions and traditions of individual countries. We need a broader perspective that charts the transmission of legal concepts (and especially the tenets of Roman civil law in the *Corpus Iuris Civilis*) across legal, political and geographical boundaries', Dauchy et al. (2016) 2. Tveit has recently advanced this view with respect to Norwegian laws of inheritance, maintaining that there were notable transmissions of Roman and Germanic laws to Norway. See Tveit (2016). Cf. Hoff (2012).

To participate in international trade, societies with limited economic, technical or military capital are expected to adapt to the legal conventions of others with greater wealth and influence. Historians have proposed two directions of influence when explaining the *Bjarkeyjarréttr*'s origins, either from Norway to Western Europe or from Western Europe to Norway.

In the nineteenth century, a period of unmistakably nationalist historiography, Norwegian scholars were prone to view medieval Norway as a virile society from which many of Europe's cultural achievements, including maritime law, first emanated. In an essay dedicated to King Karl III Johan of Norway and Sweden (r. 1818–1844) in 1834, Peter Andreas Munch exalted Norway as an innovator of maritime legal traditions, arguing that they emerged from the country's own 'bosom', free of foreign influence.[55] 'In Norway', he continued, 'there existed a law of the sea, a native one, *αντονομν*, that was founded long before that commonly known as the Law of Wisby, which thrived in the ports of Denmark, Germany, Frisia, England and Sweden, and it is known that these used to practice that of their Mediterranean neighbours, commonly referred to as Consolato del Mare'.[56] *Bjarkeyjarréttr* was for Munch an ancient and uniquely Norwegian product that derived its name from Bjarkøy – the 'prize of Hålogaland' (*inclita Halogalandiæ*) – and provided the blueprint for later Scandinavian customs.[57] Similarly, Alexander Bugge advanced that Norse domination of the seas during the Viking Age facilitated the export of seafaring customs to Ireland, western France and Iberia, providing models for contracts between crewmembers witnessed in maritime laws such as the *Rôles d'Oléron* and *Costumes de la mar*.[58] Bugge built his assertion on the etymology of one term, *matelot* (matrose), which he argued was loaned directly from the Norse *mǫtunautr* (food fellow), 'a kind of comrade on board the ship'.[59] That the term matelot

55 Munch (1838) 5.

56 Ibidem: '*ut apud Norvegos exstiterit jus nauticum, patrium, αντονομν, diu antequam conditum sit jus illud recentius, vulgo Visbyense dictum, quod per Daniæ, Germaniæ, Frisiæ, Angliæ Sveciæque portus vigebat, et antequam innotuerit id, quo uti solebant maris mediterranei accolæ, vulgo dictum consolato del mare*'.

57 Ibidem, 5–6. This entomological explanation has been largely abandoned in more recent scholarship (op cit.).

58 Bugge (1912). Cf. Falk (1912) 3f.; Robberstad (1970) 356.

59 Bugge (1912) 7. Bugge elaborated the theory, arguing that the related concept of joint property (*félagi*), which he implied was a uniquely Norse feature of law, e.g. Ibidem 7f. Cf. Falk (2012) 8. In contrast to Roman law, maritime ventures in Western and Northern Europe built upon contracts between skippers and crew, something that, according to Twist, demonstrates that 'the slave had ceased to be a principal navigator', Twist (1871) 211. Bugge's assumption, that maritime contracts in France were specifically inspired by the Norse concept of *félagi* is ambitious and ultimately dubious.

appears in none of the early manuscripts of the *Rôles* – they refer to 'companions' (*compaignons*) – and has a broadly Germanic, and not necessarily Norse, root did not dissuade Bugge from assuming a Norse origin. That theory, however, was convincingly refuted by Kristian Nyrop.[60] As such, Bugge's proposition, that 'Norwegians who were settled in Ireland, and people in western France, had begun as early as AD 900 to develop fixed legal regulations', appears either exaggerated or wholly unrealistic.

More recent studies suggest a reverse trajectory: the *Bjarkeyjarréttr*'s maritime regulations are not features of unique Norse seafaring traditions, but rather products of foreign legal influence. Jan Ragnar Hagland and Jørn Sandnes proposed that Norwegian seafarers adapted their customs to those encountered in Western Europe, asserting that 'Western European maritime rules, codified in regions of France in the so-called *Rôles d'Oléron* (taking its name from the Île d'Oléron just outside La Rochelle), played a significant role in shaping Nordic maritime law'.[61] Similarly, Grethe Authén Blom pointed to Norwegians' history of far-flung maritime activity during the Viking Age and suggested that they derived their laws from the *Rôles* 'drainage basins' in Flanders or England around the turn of the first millennium.[62]

There are several caveats in accepting this theory of transplantation in the present case. First, it assumes that Western European customs and/or written laws were established before Norwegian ones. This is unlikely. Although older research dated the *Rôles* to the reign of Eleanor of Aquitaine,[63] newer studies suggests that they were first composed over a century later during the reign of King Edward I (r. 1272–1307).[64] And while those written laws were undoubtedly rooted in older customs, there is no compelling evidence that those customs antedated those illustrated in the *Bjarkeyjarréttr*. Second, historians have probably exaggerated the scale and frequency of commercial contact between Norway and France.[65] It is noteworthy that while the *Rôles* cite a number of

60 Nyrop (1919). Matelot is not known in French literature prior to the late-fourteenth century, Ibidem, 17. It is, according to Nyrop, inconceivable that the term was transferred to France by Norsemen in the ninth and tenth centuries, Bugge (1912) 5–8, yet remained dormant for four or five centuries, Nyrop (1919) 17. The term is quite universal, as is the concept of food fellow, Ibidem, 23, and can be traced to Middle Dutch, rather than Norse.

61 Hagland and Sandnes (1997) xvii.

62 Blom (1997) 78. This is, according to Blom, in contrast to later variants of German maritime law.

63 Op cit. n 6. Although less popular, the *Rôles* have also been dated to the eleventh century in e.g. *Collection de Lois Maritimes* (1828) 298–301.

64 Krieger (1970) 40–42, 71; Schweitzer (2006) 24; Frankot (2011) 12–13.

65 Bugge (1912) 4: Bugge cites the founding of Loire in the ninth century but emphasizes the more indirect – though supposedly influential – contact between Norsemen in Ireland,

regions for maritime activity, including in England, Flanders, Bordeaux, Brittany and Normandy and Scotland,[66] they are silent on contacts in Scandinavia.[67] It is conceivable that intense maritime activity in and around England and Ireland facilitated some diffusion of seafaring customs during the Viking Age; however, there is little basis for speculating on the nature of those customs or assuming that they provided the models for maritime governance encountered in the *Rôles*. Third, recent comparisons of European maritime laws reveal less direct transmission between central and peripheral societies than previously assumed. Edda Frankot's studies of Western and Northern Europe demonstrate that maritime laws in these regions featured a remarkable degree of heterogeneity.[68] The *Rôles*, she argues, had little discernible influence on laws in Hanseatic towns, at least in their early stages of development in the thirteenth and fourteenth centuries. It is, I maintain, unlikely that merchants in central Norway were more receptive to the *Rôles* or their prefatory customs than were their German counterparts.

In another publication, Blom proposed a broader and less geographically-specific diffusion of customs, claiming that the *Bjarkeyjarréttr* included elements derived from 'old European maritime law'.[69] Here, Blom alluded to what many believed to have been a supranational maritime trading culture in early-medieval Europe. Until recently, legal historians maintained that increased long-distance trade engendered the development of a common substantive merchant law, the so-called *lex mercatoria*, between the mid-eleventh and mid-twelfth centuries. That law supposedly transcended the jurisdictional boundaries of towns and kingdoms and took precedence over local rules in matters of trade and transport.[70] Newer studies by Emily Kadens and Albrecht

who engaged in trade, particularly wine trade, with Western France. 'Fixed rules' for this trade, he claimed, had developed by the tenth century. Further, he asserted that 'at least half of all French maritime terms are Nordic'. See also Bugge (1923) 64–89. Without discounting the intensity of Hiberno-Norse trade with France, one can doubt that this was the vehicle for acculturation between the laws of Norway and France. Furthermore, the claim on the dominance of Norse terms in French vocabulary is, according to Nyrop, 'a colossal exaggeration', Nyrop (1919) 24.

66 Ward (2009) §8, 11, 13, 17, 21.

67 In a similar vein, King Magnús Hárkonarson's consolidated urban law from 1276 notes a series of countries to which Norwegian traders ventured, including Denmark, Gautland and Sweden, Gotland and Samland (southern Baltic), England, Orkney, Shetland, the Faroes, Greenland, Iceland and Gardar (Russia), *Den nyere By-Lov* (1848) §6. France is not mentioned. See above, n 32, on Anglo-Norwegian trade.

68 Frankot (2007); Frankot (2011); Frankot (2012) Cf. Müller-Boysen (1997) 90.

69 Blom (1995) 251.

70 Ward (2009) 18: 'Both [the laws and customs of Oléron and the lex mercatoria] were seen as species of jus genrium available across frontiers'. The concept of the 'law merchant' in

Cordes, among others, dismiss this claim by highlighting the anachronism of the law merchant paradigm and demonstrating the tendency of merchants to negotiate contracts and conflicts according to the local laws of markets in which they traded.[71] This should not imply that commerce in medieval Europe was parochial. Even without a supranational, substantive merchant law, general and pragmatic norms for transportation and exchange and the ability of merchants to adapt to local laws and courts could support international outlooks. This is also illustrated in the Norse *Konungs skuggsjá*'s encouraging lesson on commerce: young men should seek prosperity in distant markets, and learn those markets' laws in the process.[72]

Nevertheless, Blom's assertion is equivocal enough to entertain. If the rules of the *Bjarkeyjarréttr* were rooted in a common Western European maritime culture, one should expect comparison with other laws to reveal more parallels than discrepancies. As the most ubiquitous source for study of maritime norms in Western Europe, the *Rôles* may serve as a fruitful case for comparison. Unsurprisingly, one finds several general similarities between the two sets of regulations, including the fundamental demand for delegating on-board duties and the issuance of contracts between skippers and crews.[73]

The differences are more striking. The *Rôles* are comparatively elaborate and touch upon a number of themes that go unaddressed in the *Bjarkeyjarréttr*, including the treatment of sick crewmen, the planning of meals, the delegation of wages, the bounding of ropes, and allowances to go ashore.[74] The *Bjarkeyjarréttr*'s most conspicuous omissions concern matters of wreckage, jettison

medieval Europe is supported in Berman (1983) 333; Trakman (1983) 7–21, especially 9–17; Benson (1989); Benson (1998).

71 See Kadens (2004), 39–65; Kadens (2012); Kadens (2015) 7; Cordes (2001); Cordes (2003). Kadens underscores the law merchant's infeasible chronology, which assumes an earlier development of a homogenous merchant law than is witnessed in the sources, Kadens (2004) 40–41. Some scholars have viewed these inconsistencies as evidence for the lack of common merchant laws, e.g. Ewart (1903); Baker (1979); Scherner (2001); Sachs (2006). Kadens nuances this view by arguing that *iura mercatorum*, a diverse collection of privileges and customs, both public and private, rather than a singular *lex mercatoria*, created norms for trade beyond local arenas, Kadens (2004) 42–43. Similarly, Cordes argues that general conventions and shared interests – rather than supranational law – could compel international trade, Cordes (2003).

72 *Kongespeilet* (1848) 6

73 Ward (2009) §1, 20; *Den ældre Bylov* (1846) § 171.

74 Ward (2009) §7, 10, 14, 21. While the eldest versions contain 24 paragraphs, newer editions from the fourteenth century contain a number of more elaborate stipulations on matter ranging from the organization of joint fishing ventures, the partition of 'great fish' (whales) and the punishment of foreign pilots and lords when charged with treachery. These later additions include a number of harsh penalties and greater internal hierarchy.

and salvage,[75] themes that are central to the *Rôles* and had resonance in a number of maritime legal traditions throughout western and northern Europe.[76] The absence thereof is perplexing. Shipwreck or the threat thereof was, according to Götz Landwehr, one of the 'certain inevitabilities present in nature and imposed by circumstances, which lead to the formation of identical rules as regards to content, regardless of geographical location or the state of legal culture at a particular time'.[77] Indeed, Norwegians were not unfamiliar with the themes of shipwreck and salvage.[78] Diplomatic sources from Norway in the mid-thirteenth century allude to certain rules of salvage,[79] and the matter is addressed at length in King Magnúss Hákonarson's consolidated urban law of 1276.[80] Nevertheless, we should not assume that such regulations would, as Landwehr professed, be 'identical' to those in other areas. Frankot's comparison of regulations from across Northern Europe reveals numerous variances between different laws, even between laws from the same general region.[81]

In a similar vein, very few of the themes treated in the *Bjarkeyjarréttr* are addressed in the *Rôles*. The former, for instance, discuss at length how crewmen should bail water from their boat as well as the procedures for keeping watch,[82] neither of which are mentioned in the latter. The *Bjarkeyjarréttr*'s also differentiates between maritime voyages in Christian and heathen regions,[83] issues upon which the *Rôles* are silent. Two of the ten paragraphs make this differentiation: fines collected in cases of manslaughter should be reserved for Christian kings, while thieves should only be punished in Christian lands. This *may* reflect the early provenance of the law. Committed to parchment at the threshold of a new era of religious practice in the eleventh century, it appears to demonstrate the uncertainties of Christian voyagers in the pagan strongholds lining the margins of northern Scandinavia.[84] As Norwegians also travelled

75 *Bjarkeyjarréttr* addresses damage to ships, although only the crew's obligation to take part in repairs *Den ældre Bylov* (1846) §174. In contrast to the *Rôles* (Ward (2009) §3, 8, 9), this clause does not address salvage.

76 Ward (2009) §3, 8, 9. See Ibidem 95–98; Frankot (2012) 27–52.

77 Landwehr (1985) 104; Frankot (2011) 27.

78 Musset (1976) 563–565; Raich (2016) 145.

79 *DN* 5, no. 1. See also Grohse (2015) 74.

80 *NgL* 2 (1848) 278, §8. See also, Frankot (2012) 47.

81 Frankot (2012).

82 *Den ældre Bylov* (1846) §176, 177.

83 Ibidem §176; Hagland and Sandnes (1997) 94, §144.

84 Op cit. n. 23. The period in question (c.1000–1280) witnessed a gradual northward expansion of the Christian faith and ecclesiastic structures, see generally Trædal (2008) 57–181. Royal efforts to Christianize the chieftains of Hálogaland took place during the reign of

eastward and beyond the Baltic, an area that would still have been regarded as heathen in the thirteenth century, this point alone admittedly does not prove its early origins.[85] However, it does seem to illustrate a unique trajectory in Norway's maritime ventures, with furs, ivories and fish compelling merchants and taxmen beyond the kingdom's northern frontiers and prompting contact with pagan communities of Finnmǫrk and the Kola Peninsula. This allusion to pagan lands, an unknown feature in other major European maritime laws, may thus testify to the *Bjarkeyjarréttr's* native origins.

While both laws sanction the fining, beating and expulsion of insubordinate or unruly crewmen, they differ in the procedures for enforcing discipline. The *Bjarkeyjarréttr* promote the collective shaming of thieves by calling for offenders to be tarred and feathered and beaten by all members of the crew in concert.[86] Disgrace is not an obvious feature of discipline in the *Rôles*, nor is castigation a collective affair. Shipmasters who were contradicted by subordinate mariners could demand a fine and strike the offender once with an open hand or fist, and although crewmen could defend themselves if the shipmaster used excessive force, they could never initiate an assault on the shipmaster, lest they be liable to a fine or the loss of a hand.[87] Apart from the obvious procedural dissimilarities, we may note a more subtle, yet fundamental difference between the enforcement of justice and, perhaps, the hierarchy of order on maritime ventures. The Norwegian law deemphasizes the role of skippers in adjudication whilst promoting collective justice. Oarsmen shouldered this burden by assuming the role of provisional 'magistrates' and adjudicating all cases apart from those involving incontrollable crewmen. Just as their cooperation in handing out sentences created horizontal bonds between crewmen, their collective execution of justice through the group shaming and beating of offenders strengthened their solidarity. Justice is more hierarchical in the *Rôles*. Although the shipmaster did not have unchecked authority and was liable to fines and punishment for maltreatment of crewmen, the *Rôles* emphasize his superiority in maintaining order: 'A shipmaster hires his sailors and must hold them in peace and be their judge if there is one who damages another' (*Un mestre lowe ses mariners et les deit tenir en pees / et estre lur juge, sil i a nul, qui*

King Óláfr Tryggvason in the late-tenth century, with the earliest churches being erected a century later, see Gabrielsen (1998); Bertelsen (2000) 8–9. Christianization was protracted in the Finnmǫrk, with early efforts to Christianize the indigenous population around the turn of the fourteenth century, see Norderval (2000) 15–16. Missionary efforts continued into the fifteenth century, Ibidem 16–17.

85 I also thank Prof. Øyrehagen Sunde for nuancing this point.

86 Hagland and Sandnes (1997) 94, §144.

87 Ward (2009) 197, §12.

endamage lautre par quei il).[88] The shipmaster's Norse counterpart 'has no authority to bring charges against anyone' (*a ænngan mann at sökia nema*) apart from in exceptional circumstances.[89]

5 Conclusion

The Norwegian *Bjarkeyjarréttr* is something of a footnote in the broader history of European maritime law. It is easily overshadowed by monumental works such as the *Rôles d'Oléron*, which left an indelible mark on the legal landscape of western and northern Europe and provided models for town laws and ordinances throughout the region in the late-medieval and early-modern eras. The *Bjarkeyjarréttr*, by contrast, had no obvious influence over merchants and mariners outside the Norse world and eventually receded from the European stage as quietly as it appeared. It was neither elaborate nor comprehensive enough to govern maritime ventures in an increasingly complex world of international commerce, and was, as such, superseded by a more modern codex and a series of detailed amendments in the late-thirteenth and fourteenth centuries. While it is not clear how closely subsequent laws adhered to, or deviated from, broader European norms, one may speculate, based on their more elaborate content and their context within the more integrated world of Northern European commerce, that they derived inspiration from laws emanating from commercial centres in France, England and the Hanseatic realm. But the case in focus is unique. Contrary to prior assertions, the *Bjarkeyjarréttr* was not the product of a burgeoning and integrated European maritime culture, but rather an artefact of distinctively Norse maritime traditions.

Norwegian historians have been surprisingly willing to dismiss or downplay the native origins of the *Bjarkeyjarréttr*'s maritime articles. This is perhaps rooted in an aim to bring Norway into the fold of European history, presenting that kingdom as a participant in the increasingly global world of medieval commerce and law. But it may be less the result of wishful thinking than an adherence to conventional wisdoms about the transmission of maritime customs, wisdoms that have come under increasing scrutiny in recent years. Today, scholars are less receptive to theories about the universality of maritime law, and more aware of regional peculiarities and legal pluralities. From this perspective, we may better understand how Norway, a land encompassing a miniscule population in the shadows of influential British and Continental

88 Ibidem, 197, §12 197, §12.

89 *Den ældre Bylov* (1846) §172.

kingdoms, could engender separate and distinct maritime customs. In attempting to understand this, one should consider the distinct nature of the society that fostered those rules. Norway was a seaborne realm like none other in medieval Europe. Sailing was elementary to communication, governance, defence, subsistence and trade, not only for a merchant elite, but for peasants and kings alike. Maritime travel was an important feature of many European societies, but it was both the fabric and attire of Norwegian culture. One need not accept Munch's romantic nationalism to appreciate that medieval Norway, as he maintained, had an intimate relationship with the sea and that those accessing it had a pressing interest in protection.[90] While undoubtedly susceptible to outside influences if and when expedient, particularly in overseas arenas, Norwegians were not dependent on foreign rules for sailing or the governance of sailing in the early Middle Ages.

Acknowledgements

I thank Assoc. Prof. Miriam Tveit and Prof. Jørn Øyrehagen Sunde for their thoughtful reading and constructive criticism of this paper, as well as Prof. Louis Sicking and Dr. Edda Frankot for their insights into other aspects of European maritime law(s).

Bibliography

Andersson, H., 'Urbanisation' in K. Helle ed., *Cambridge History of Scandinavia: Prehistory to 1520*, vol. 1 (Cambridge 2003) 312–344.

Bagge, S., 'Innledende essay' in A. Brøgger ed. and trans., *Kongespeilet* (Oslo 2000) i–lxxi.

Baker, J., 'The Law Merchant and the Common Law before 1700', *Cambridge Law Journal* 38 (1979) 295–322.

Benson, B., 'The Spontaneous Evolution of Commercial Law', *Southern Economic Journal* 55 (1989) 644–661.

Benson, B., 'Law Merchants' in P. Newman ed., *The New Palgrave Dictionary of Economics and the Law*, vol. 2 (London 1998) 500–508.

Berman, H., *Law and Revolution. The Formation of the Western Legal Tradition* (Cambridge, MA 1983).

Bertelsen, R., 'Nord-Norge og verden ved forrige tusenårsskifte', *Ottar* 229 (2000) 3–9.

90 Munch (1838) 3–5.

Bertelsen, R., 'Vágar, en kortlevd by eller et urbant fiskevær?' in J. Brendalsmo, F-E. Eliassen and T. Gansum eds., *Den urbane underskog, Strandsteder, utvekslingssteder og småbyer i vikingtid, middelalder og tidlig nytid* (Oslo 2009) 199–212.

Bjørgo, N., 'Vågastemne i mellomalderen' in S. Imsen and G. Sandvik eds., *Hamarspor, eit festskrift til Lars Hamre* (Oslo 1982) 45–60.

Blom, G., 'Trondheim vom Ende des 11. bis zum Ende des 13. Jahrhunderts' in E. Hoffmann and F. Lubowitz eds., *Die Stadt im westlichen Ostseeraum. Vorträge zur Stadtgründung und Stadterweiterung im Hohen Mittelalter* (Frankfurt am Main 1995) 240–262.

Blom, G., *Trondheims historie 997–1997, vol 1. Hellig Olavs by, middelalderen til 1537* (Oslo 1997).

Bratrein H. and E. Niemi, 'Inn i riket. Politisk og økonomisk integrasjon gjennom tusen år' in Drivenes, E-A., M. Hauan, H. Wold eds., *Nordnorsk kulturhistorie. Det gjenstridige landet*, vol. 1 (Oslo 1994) 146–209.

Brattegard, O., 'Bjärköarätt, Norge', in *Kulturhistorisk leksikon for nordisk middelalder fra vikingtid til reformasjonstid*, vol. 1 (Copenhagen 1956) 659–660.

Bugge, A., 'Paavirkning fra norrøn paa vestfransk sjøret i middelalderen', *Videnskapsselskapets forhandlinger for 1912*, no. 5 (1912) 1–15.

Bugge, A., *Den Norske sjøfarts historie. Fra de ældste tider til vore dage* (Christiania 1923).

Collection de Lois Maritimes antérieurs au XVIIIe siècle, vol. 1, ed. J. Pardessus (Paris 1828).

Cordes, A., 'Auf der Such nach der Rechtswirklichkeit der mittelalterlichen Lex mercatoria', *Zeitschrift der Savigny-Stiftung für Rechtsgeschichte, Germanistische Abteilung* 118 (2001) 168–184.

Cordes, A., 'The search for a medieval Lex mercatoria', *Oxford University Comparative Law Forum* (2003): http://ouclf.iuscomp.org/the-search-for-a-medieval-lex-mercatoria/.

Dauchy, S., et al., eds., *The Formation and Transmission of Western Legal Culture. 150 Books that Made the Law in the Age of Printing* (Cham 2016).

Diplomatarium Norvegicum [*DN*], vols. 1–23, eds. C. Lange et al. (Christiania/Oslo 1847–2011).

Eithun, B., M. Rindal and T. Ulset, *Den eldre Gulatingslova* (Oslo 1994).

Ewart, J., 'What is the Law Merchants?', *Columbia Law Review* 3 (1903) 135–154.

Falk, H. *Altnordisches Seewesen* (Heidelberg 1912).

Frankot, E., 'Medieval Maritime Law from Oléron to Wisby: jurisdictions in the law of the sea' in J. Pan-Montojo and F. Pedersen eds., *Communities in European History. Representations, Jurisdictions, Conflicts* (Pisa 2007) 151–172.

Frankot, E., *'Of Laws of Ships and Shipmen': Medieval Maritime Law and its Practice in Urban Northern Europe. Medieval Maritime Law and its Practice in Urban Northern Europe* (Edinburgh 2011).

Gabrielsen, T., *Kirkeoppkomsten i Nord-Norge*, Hovedfag thesis (Tromsø 1998).

Grohse, I., 'The Royal Origins of Norwegian Commercial Diplomacy. King Hákon IV Hákonarson and the Council of Lübeck, 1247–1250' in J. Solórzano Telechea, B. Arízaga Bolumburu and L. Sicking eds., *Diplomacia y comercio en la Europa Atlántica medieval* (Logroño 2015) 61–86.

Grohse, I., 'Between royal orbits: jurisdiction in the Northern British Isles ca 1100–1360', *Comparative Legal History* 5 no. 1 (2017) 16–35.

Hagland, J. and J. Sandnes eds. and trans., *Bjarkøyretten. Nidaros eldste bylov* (Oslo 1997).

Hansen, L., *Samisk fangstsamfunn og norsk høvdingeøkonomi* (Oslo 1990).

Hansen, L., 'The successive integration of Hålogaland and Finnmǫrk into the realm of the King of Norway' in S. Imsen ed., *Rex Insularum. The King of Norway and His 'Skattlands' as a Political System c. 1260–c. 1450* (Bergen 2015) 347–369.

Heber, G., 'Vaagebok', *Håløygminne* 3 (1953) 101–103.

Heebøll-Holm, T., *Ports, Piracy, and Maritime War. Piracy in the English Channel and the Atlantic, c. 1280–c.1330* (Leiden 2013).

Helle, K., *Bergen bys historie. Kongssette og kjøpstad til 1536* (Bergen, Oslo and Tromsø 1982).

Hoff, H., *Hafliði Másson und die Einflüsse des römischen Rechts in der Grágás* (Berlin 2012).

Jahnke, C., 'Hansisches und anderes Seerecht' in A. Cordes ed., *Hansisches und hansestädtisches Recht* (Trier 2008) 41–67.

Kadens, E., 'Order within Law, Variety within Custom. The Character of the Medieval Merchant Law', *Chicago Journal of International Law* 5 (2004) 39–65.

Kadens, E., 'The Myth of the Customary Law Merchants', *Texas Law Review* 90 (2012) 1153–1206.

Kadens, E., 'The Medieval Law Merchant: The Tyranny of a Construct', *Journal of Legal Analysis* 251 (2015) 251–289.

Knudsen, T., 'Nidaros bylov' in *Kulturhistorisk leksikon for nordisk middelalder fra vikingtid til reformasjonstid* 12 (1967) 299.

Kongespeilet (*Speculum Regale – Konungs-Skuggsjá*) eds. R. Keyser, P.A. Munch og C.R. Unger (Christiania 1848).

Krieger, K-F., *Ursprung und Wurzeln der Rôles d'Oléron* (Cologne and Vienna 1970).

Landrecht des Königs Magnus Håkonarson (*Germanenrechte NF, Nordgermanisches Recht* 2), ed. and trans. R. Meissner (Weimar 1941).

Landwehr, G., *Die Haverei in den mittelalterlichen deutschen Seerechtsquellen* (= *Berichte aus den Sitzungen der Joachim Jungius-Gesellschaft der Wissenschaften e.V. Hamburg* 3 no. 2) (Göttingen and Hamburg 1985).

Lehmann, K., 'Bjarkeyjarréttr' in *Reallexikon der germanischen Altertumskunde*, vol. 1. A-F (Strasbourg 1911–1913) 292.

Long, A-M., *Iceland's Relationship with Norway c.870–1100. Memory, History and Identity* (Leiden 2017).

Monumenta Juridica. The Black Book of the Admiralty, ed., T. Twiss (London 1871).

Murray, J., *Bruges, Cradle of Capitalism, 1280–1390* (Cambridge 2005).

Müller-Boysen, C., *Kaufmannsschutz und Handelsrecht im frümittelalterlichen Nordeuropa* (Neumünster 1990).

Müller-Boysen, C., '"Her hæfiazc upp farrmanna logh" Kaufmannsrecht im frühmittelalterlichen Nordeuropa' in Audun Dybdahl and Jørn Sandnes eds., Nordiske middelalderlover. Tekst og kontekst. Rapport fra seminar ved Senter for middelalderstudier 29.-30. nov. 1996 (Trondheim 1997) 87-102

Munch, P.A., *Jus Nauticum Recentius quod inter Norvegos olum valuit. Diem Natalem Augustissimi Regis Caroli Joannis ab Universitate Regia Fredericiana Die XXVI Januari MDCCCXXXVIII* (Christiania 1838).

Munch, P.A., Om Finmarkens politisk-commercielle Forhold til den norske Stat, in G. Storm ed., *Samlede Afhandlinger* (Christiania 1874) 274–297.

Musset, L. 'Les apports scandinaves dans le plus ancient droit normand' in *Droit privé et institutions regionals. Études historiques offertes à J. Yver* (Paris 1976) 559–575.

Nedkvitne, A., *The German Hansa and Bergen 1100–1600* (Cologne 2014).

Norderval, Ø., 'Fra hedendom til kristendom i Nord-Norge', *Ottar* 229 (2000) 20–26.

Norges gamle love indtil 1387, vol. 1 [*NgL* 1], ed. R. Keyser and P.A. Munch (Christiania 1846).

Norges gamle love indtil 1387, vol. 2 [*NgL* 2], ed. R. Keyser and P.A. Munch (Christiania 1848).

Nyrop, K., 'Et formentligt vikingeord', *Aarbøger for nordisk oldkyndighed og historie* (1919) 1–34.

Ogilvie, S., *Institutions and European Trade. Merchant Guilds, 1000–1800* (Cambridge 2011).

Ottar og Wulfstan. To rejsebeskrivelser fra vikingetiden, ed. and trans., N. Lund (Roskilde 1983).

Raich, S., 'Wreck of the Sea in Law and Practice in Eleventh- and Twelfth-Century England' in E. van Houts ed., *Anglo-Norman Studies. XXXVIII. Proceedings of the Battle Conference 2015* (Woodbridge 2016) 141–154.

Robberstad, K., 'Sjörätt' in *Kulturhistorisk leksikon for nordisk middelalder fra vikingtid til reformasjonstid*, vol. 15 (Copenhagen 1970) col. 356–372.

Robberstad, K., 'Styresmann. Noreg' in *Kulturhistorisk leksikon for nordisk middelalder fra vikingtid til reformasjonstid*, vol. 17 (Copenhagen 1972) 368–369.

Robinson, O., D. Fergus and W. Gordon, *European Legal History – Sources and Institutions* (London 1985).

Runyan, T., 'The Rolls of Oleron and the Admiralty Court in Fourteenth Century England', *American Journal of Legal History* 19 (1975) 95–111.

Sachs, S., 'From St. Ives to Cyberspace. The Modern Distortion of the Medieval "Law Merchants"', *American University International Law Review* 21 (2006) 685–812.

Scherner, K., 'Lex mercatoria – Realität, Geschichtsbild oder Vision?, *Zeitschrift der Savigny-Stiftung für Rechtsgeschichte: Germanistische Abteilung* 118 (2001) 148–167.

Schweitzer, J., *Schiffer und Schiffsmann in den Rôles d'Oléron und im Llibre del Consolat de Mar. Ein Vergleich zweier mittelalterlicher Seerechtsquellen* (Berlin 2006).

Seip, J., *Lagmann og lagting i senmiddelalderen og det 16de århundre* (Oslo 1934).

Seip, D., *Norsk språkhistorie til omkring 1370*, 2 ed. (Oslo 1955).

Seip, D., 'Farmannsloven' in *Kulturhistorisk leksikon for nordisk middelalder fra vikingtid til reformasjonstid*, vol. 4 (Copenhagen 1959) 169–170.

Skre, D., 'The Development of Urbanism in Scandinavia' in S. Brink and N. Price eds., *The Viking World* (2008) 85–149.

Stadtrecht des Königs Magnus Hakonarsson für Bergen. Bruchstücke des Birkinselrechts und Seefarerrecht der Jónsbók (Germanenrechte NF, Nordgermanisches Recht 3), ed. and trans. R. Meissner (Weimar 1950).

Storm, G., ed., *Sigurd Ranessöns Proces udgivet efter Haandskrifterne* (Christiania 1877).

Strauch, D., *Mittelalterliches Nordisches Recht Bis 1500. Eine Quellenkunde* (Göttingen 2011).

Trakman, L., *Law Merchant the Evolution of Commercial Law* (Littleton 1983).

Trædal, V., *Kirkesteder og kirkebygninger i Troms og Finnmark før 1800* (PhD Tromsø 2008).

Tveit, M., 'Integrasjon gjennom lovgivning? Rettsresepsjon i Hålogaland 1100–1500', *Heimen* 52 (2015) 134–147.

Tveit, M., *In Search of Legal Transmission. Inheritance and Compensation for Homicide in Medieval Secular Law*, PhD thesis (Tromsø 2016).

Vogt, H., *The Function of Kinship in Medieval Nordic Legislation* (Leiden 2010).

Wadstein, E., 'Birka och bjärköarätt', *Namn och Bygd. Tidskrift för nordisk ortnamneforskning* 2 (1914) 92–97.

Wadstein, E., 'Birka och bjårkoaråtť', *Namn och Bygd. Tidskrift för nordisk ortnamnsforskning* (1936) 1–10.

Wagner, R., *Handbuch des Seerechts* (Leipzig 1906).

Ward, R., *The World of the Medieval Shipmaster: Law, Business and the Sea, c.1340–c.1450* (Woodbridge 2009).

Watson, A. Legal Transplants: An Approach to Comparative Law (Edinburgh 1974).

Wessén, E., 'Birca och bjärkörätt', *Namn och Bygd. Tidskrift för nordisk ortnamneforskning* 11 (1923) 135–177.

Wessén, E., 'Till Birca-frågan', *Namn och Bygd. Tidskrift för nordisk ortnamneforskning* 13 (1925) 39–60.

CHAPITRE 4

Du conflit aux conflits : marchands et gens de mer lors de la rupture de trêve en 1224 entre les rois anglais et français

Laurence Jean-Marie

1 Introduction

Les mers du Ponant, et parmi elles la Manche, connaissent une fréquentation croissante au XIIIe siècle ; à cela des motifs économiques mais aussi politiques. Ce siècle voit sans conteste l'essor des activités commerciales dans cet espace, accentuant les phénomènes observables au XIIe siècle. En centrant le regard sur l'Angleterre, on peut constater que si les échanges avec le continent ne sont pas nouveaux, la mise en connexion se fait à plus large échelle. Ainsi, le XIIIe siècle est marqué par des relations plus intenses avec les côtes atlantiques de la France et au-delà d'elles. Des navires bayonnais, bordelais ou encore portugais circulent en Manche. C'est aussi l'évolution politique qui donne, en Angleterre, une place croissante à la mer. Le début du XIIIe siècle est marqué par une modification majeure de la configuration de l'espace dominé par les Plantagenêts. La perte de la Normandie en 1204 ne constitue pas une rupture des relations commerciales de l'Angleterre avec elle mais accroît les liens avec les autres territoires restés aux mains de Jean sans Terre. Pour les besoins du pouvoir, l'essentiel était jusqu'alors de traverser la Manche avec une courte navigation et une partie non négligeable des échanges commerciaux entre les territoires plantagenêts passait par cette voie[1]. Après 1204, il est nécessaire d'atteindre la côte atlantique pour mettre en connexion Angleterre et possessions du roi en France, à tout le moins pour des raisons politiques. On peut considérer qu'il y a une 'insularité' croissante du pouvoir Plantagenêt, sachant aussi que le pouvoir du roi capétien est désormais beaucoup plus proche des côtes anglaises. Certes, le Plantagenêt ne renonce pas à la Normandie mais il ne tente rien de ce côté, sauf à finalement s'assurer la maîtrise des îles que l'on peut qualifier commodément d'Anglo-Normandes et qui ont été un enjeu entre les deux rois dans les premières années XIIIe siècle. À la fin du règne de Jean sans Terre,

1 À ce sujet, voir Jean-Marie (2016b).

 | DOI:10.1163/9789004407992_006

l'avantage est du côté du Capétien avec l'intervention du prince Louis en Angleterre, même si elle se solde finalement par une défaite. Henri III, qui succède à son père en 1216, subit un nouvel échec avec la perte du Poitou et du port de la Rochelle en 1224[2]. Seule la Gascogne reste entre ses mains.

Les conflits qui opposent le roi de France et le roi d'Angleterre, qui se déclare encore duc de Normandie et d'Aquitaine, et comte d'Anjou, ont une dimension maritime majeure, non tant par des épisodes navals, que par leurs conséquences pour les marchands et les gens de mer et par l'implication de ces derniers[3]. En outre, le roi d'Angleterre doit pouvoir défendre ses possessions françaises, de plus en plus lointaines. Si, pour cette période, les aspects politiques d'un côté et économiques de l'autre, ont fait l'objet d'études, ce n'est guère sous l'angle de la fréquentation de la mer et des interactions entre le politique et l'économique. Plus largement, le XIIIe siècle, surtout à ses débuts, est le relatif parent pauvre de l'étude des circulations et des contentieux maritimes pour cet espace. Le sujet n'est pas aisé à aborder compte tenu de la disparité des sources, du fait qu'elles rendent compte d'une situation intermédiaire, antérieure à l'affirmation de l'État et largement à la définition d'un droit commercial et maritime.

Une période de guerre entre rois d'Angleterre et de France constitue un bon moment d'observation. Paradoxalement, c'est alors que les informations sont les plus fournies sur les échanges par voie maritime grâce aux lettres royales anglaises, patentes et closes, à un moment où justement ils sont perturbés. C'est alors que les conflits sont les plus visibles et susceptibles d'être soumis à analyse, tant par la multiplication des sources qui les mentionnent, que par la résurgence de contentieux antérieurs et l'apparition de nouveaux. Choix a donc été effectué de porter l'attention sur l'entrée dans la guerre en 1224. L'échec du renouvellement de la trêve puis l'avancée de Louis VIII en Poitou, suivie de la prise de La Rochelle au début août et de la menace sur la Gascogne où il prend pied pour quelques mois, ont été choisis pour mener l'analyse. Les décisions générales ou particulières du roi d'Angleterre montrent que marchands et gens de mer sont largement concernés par le conflit, qu'ils en soient victimes et acteurs ou qu'ils bénéficient de droits particuliers. Il faut ici tenir compte de la chronologie des évènements pour tenter de mettre au jour les logiques d'action. Cette situation complexe engendre ou réactive des contentieux dont il faut identifier les modes de gestion ou de résolution.

---

2 Né en 1207, il est alors mineur et sous la régence de Guillaume Le Maréchal puis d'un triumvirat à partir de 1219; Carpenter (1990) 14–15, 128.

3 Il faut toutefois mentionner la bataille de Sandwich en 1217; Carpenter (1990) 44–45.

2 L'entrée en guerre et ses implications commerciales et maritimes

La trêve avec Philippe Auguste, signée en septembre 1214 pour cinq ans, est renouvelée en 1220, pour une période de quatre ans[4]. Son expiration est prévue pour Pâques 1224, soit le 14 avril[5]. En décembre 1223, le pape écrit à Louis VIII pour lui demander de la prolonger. Un projet de trêve de 10 ans existe mais l'intervention du roi de France dans le sud-ouest de son royaume est une menace pour le roi d'Angleterre, compte tenu des ambitions de chacun d'entre eux sur le Poitou[6]. Ce dernier fait partie des fiefs confisqués à Jean sans Terre mais aucun des deux rois n'a réussi à s'y imposer. Dans le même temps, Henri III doit faire face à divers problèmes, telles la révolte de Foulques de Bréauté (avril 1224) puis la défection du baron poitevin Hugues de Lusignan (mai-juin)[7]. Le 28 avril 1224, Henri III adresse une lettre au roi Louis pour l'informer qu'il lui envoie ses fidèles, dont le maître de la milice du Temple d'Angleterre, afin de plaider pour un renouvellement de la trêve[8]. Les négociations n'aboutissent pas et la guerre s'ouvre le 5 mai 1224[9].

Des mesures précédemment prises dans les lettres émises par Henri III semblaient pourtant donner des gages en vue d'une prolongation de la trêve. Le 13 avril 1224, à la veille même de l'échéance de cette dernière, il avait donné conduit aux marchands, quelle que soit leur origine, de venir en Angleterre, puis le droit d'y rester et d'en repartir avec leurs marchandises, une fois les coutumes payées. Le conduit était valable jusqu'à 15 jours au-delà de la Saint-Jean-Baptiste, soit jusqu'au 9 juillet[10]. Deux jours plus tard, le 15 avril, il avait octroyé paix et sécurité à tous les marchands 'de potestate' du roi de France et à leurs marchandises dans les mêmes conditions[11]. De telles autorisations n'étaient pas nécessaires en temps de paix. En effet, si rien d'explicite ne figurait à ce sujet dans le texte concluant la trêve en septembre 1214[12], d'après les

4 Texte de la trêve de 1214: *Recueil des actes de Philippe Auguste*, 3, no. 1340 ; *Layettes du Trésor des chartes*, 1, no. 1083, 405 (lettre de Jean sans Terre donnant les termes de la trêve).

5 Carpenter (1990) 350.

6 Ibidem, 344.

7 Ibidem, 351, 355.

8 *Patent Rolls, 1216–1225*, 484.

9 Petit-Dutaillis (1894) 235 ; Powicke (1962) 88. Elle dure jusqu'au printemps 1227 ; Powicke (1962) 84.

10 *Patent Rolls (1216–1225)* 434.

11 Ibidem, 435.

12 *Recueil des actes de Philippe Auguste*, 3, no. 1340. Il n'y a rien non plus à ce propos dans le texte du traité de Lambeth de 1217 entre Henri III et le prince Louis (Smith (1979) 562–579) ni dans le texte prorogeant la trêve en 1220 (*Recueil des actes de Philippe Auguste*, 4, no. 1601, no. 1602, no. 1619). En revanche, les accords entre Louis VII puis Philippe Auguste

Annales de Dunstable, elle permettait que les marchands aillent et viennent librement[13]. Surtout, l'article 41 de la *Magna Carta*[14], affirmait la liberté de commerce entre l'Angleterre et le continent. La présence de cette règle dans la *Magna carta*, accordée en 1215 par Jean sans Terre aux barons anglais, témoigne bien de l'importance des enjeux des échanges commerciaux avec les terres continentales. L'article 41, dans le contexte de la guerre civile, est aussi à interpréter comme une concession aux Londoniens, soucieux de préserver leurs privilèges et de faciliter l'arrivée de marchands venus du continent afin de contribuer au dynamisme économique[15]. Il y est affirmé que si les marchands sont redevables des justes et anciennes coutumes, ils sont assurés de ne pas être soumis aux maltôtes, revendication des Londoniens.

Dans cet article, il est en revanche prévu qu'au déclenchement de la guerre, les marchands issus des terres ennemies doivent être retenus jusqu'à ce que la façon dont les marchands anglais sont traités dans ces dernières, soit connue. S'ils sont saufs, les marchands étrangers le seront également en Angleterre. Le roi de Norvège s'était d'ailleurs inquiété au cours de l'hiver 1223–1224, des menaces de guerre et espérait que l'alliance avec l'Angleterre allait continuer. Ce faisant, il s'alarmait du sort des marchands[16]. Le temps de la guerre, en dehors même des opérations militaires, peut ainsi avoir des conséquences immédiates sur les échanges commerciaux. Henri III, en délivrant des autorisations générales au moment où la trêve arrive à son terme, cherche peut-être à peser sur les négociations et à préserver les échanges. Il est également possible qu'il y ait là une part de stratégie car point n'est encore nécessaire de délivrer des autorisations alors que la trêve n'est pas achevée.

Des éléments supplémentaires doivent alors être pris en compte. Dès le 13 avril, soit avant la fin de la trêve et au moment où des autorisations de commerce étaient accordées, Henri III ordonnait aux barons des Cinque Ports de tenir prêts leurs navires pour aller dans les îles de Guernesey, Jersey, Aurigny et Sercq afin de les garder et défendre, selon ce que Philippe d'Aubigny, alors en charge de la garde des îles, demanderait[17]. Dix jours après la rupture, le 15 mai, Henri III informait les baillis et barons des Cinque Ports qu'en raison de la fin

et Henri II de 1177 et 1180 évoquent cette liberté de circulation (*Recueil des actes de Henri II*, 2, no. DVI, no. DL).

13 *Annales prioratus de Dunstaplia* 42.

14 Voir le texte de l'article sur le site du Magna Carta Project: http://magnacarta.cmp.uea.ac.uk/read/magna_carta_1215/Clause_41 ; voir également Carpenter (2015).

15 C'est l'analyse qui en est faite sur le site du Magna Carta Project.

16 *Royal and other historical letters*, I, CXCIII.

17 *Patent Rolls (1216–1225)* 435; à propos de ces îles, voir Everard, Holt (2004).

de la trêve, ils devaient retenir les navires de leurs ports dans ces derniers, en les préparant pour son service. En outre, il leur était ordonné d'interdire qu'un navire avec marchandises en sorte sans autorisation spéciale du roi et d'arrêter tous les navires et les hommes étrangers venant d'outremer[18]. Les mêmes lettres étaient envoyées aux baillis et 'probi homines' de nombreux ports[19]. Pour ceux d'Exeter, Bristol et Dartmouth, il était ajouté que les marchands, ou d'autres, ne devaient rien perdre de leurs biens[20]. Le roi s'adressait encore aux baillis et prud'hommes des Cinque Ports et à leurs membres[21], les informant de l'envoi de Philippe d'Aubigny afin d'organiser la préparation et le rassemblement des navires[22].

On peut considérer que ces ordres mettaient fin aux autorisations précédemment octroyées, et ce, en application des prescriptions de la *Magna Carta* puisque la trêve était rompue. Pourtant, le 14 juin une lettre d'Henri III signifiait à Savary de Mauléon, sénéchal de Poitou et de Gascogne, qu'il avait été convenu entre lui et le roi de France que tous les marchands de ses terres et des siennes pouvaient aller et venir avec leurs marchandises depuis Pâques jusqu'à 15 jours après la Saint-Jean-Baptiste, soit jusqu'au 9 juillet, comme prévu précédemment. Il devait les laisser aller en paix et si quelque chose leur avait été pris, le leur rendre[23]. Ainsi, malgré la fin de la trêve et les prolégomènes de la guerre, accord était conclu sur ce point. Il est possible qu'il concerne uniquement les ports du Poitou et de Gascogne car l'ordre est en contradiction avec les décisions prises pour l'Angleterre depuis la rupture de la trêve. Dans ses fiefs en France, la royauté anglaise n'est sans doute pas en mesure d'imposer les mêmes règles. On peut aussi s'interroger sur les motivations exactes des décisions du roi d'Angleterre au printemps 1224 et sur les objectifs poursuivis.

3 Gens de mer et marchands dans le conflit

Arrêter les navires dans les ports anglais peut donc être une conséquence de la rupture de la trêve et s'expliquer par les inquiétudes concernant le sort des

18 *Patent Rolls* (*1216–1225*) 483–484.

19 Portsmouth, Shoreham, Southampton, Safford, Poole, Exeter, Bristol, Dartmouth, Norwich, Yarmouth, Oreford, Dunwich, Ipswich, Lynn, Orwell, Little Yarmouth.

20 Concernant le vicomte de Cornouaille et de Devon, l'ordre de retenir les navires de leurs ports est remplacé par celui de retenir les navires arrivés dans les ports de la baillie.

21 Sandwich, Douvres, Romney, Ryes, Pagham, Winchelsea, Hythe, Hastings, Kingston-By-Sea et Pevensey

22 *Patent Rolls* (*1216–1225*) 484.

23 Ibidem, 443.

marchands anglais en France. Or, ces décisions atteignent aussi des pays non considérés comme ennemis et les activités d'échanges de l'Angleterre elle-même, alors que les liens commerciaux avec le continent sont essentiels à l'économie anglaise. De plus, dans une période où il est besoin de financer la guerre, cela diminue les rentrées des taxes portuaires. S'il y a volonté d'affaiblir les activités des ressortissants des pays ennemis, c'est par voie de conséquence celles des Anglais qui peuvent l'être, d'autant que leurs intérêts commerciaux sont liés et que navires et cargaisons peuvent être aux mains de ressortissants d'autorités différentes. Certes, mettre la main sur des marchandises peut constituer une compensation mais c'est aussi risquer des conflits dans le conflit et de s'aliéner la Norvège ou la Germanie qui ne sont pas en guerre. De plus, dans l'une des lettres, il est clairement affirmé que les marchands concernés par les arrestations de navires dans les ports, ne doivent pas être lésés. Il est encore possible de considérer que la présence d'hommes et de navires de pays ennemis dans les ports anglais représente une menace. Henri III craindrait à ce moment un débarquement en Angleterre. C'est peu probable car Louis VIII est occupé en Poitou. Si tel était le cas, l'objectif ne serait pas de parer au danger éventuel que représenteraient les navires étrangers dans les ports mais plutôt de priver le roi de France d'un potentiel.

Tout autant Henri III, qui se prépare à la guerre à la fin du printemps, cherche-t-il à disposer de forces navales. Elles sont nécessaires aux îles Anglo-Normandes, potentiellement menacées et utilisées comme point de départ d'opérations. Il faut en outre des hommes, de l'argent et du ravitaillement pour le Poitou. Dès le mois de mai, le roi projette d'envoyer hommes et navires à La Rochelle. Ils doivent être commandés par Richard de Nevill et, le 26 mai, 2000 marcs sont attribués pour l'expédition[24]. Mais Hugues de Lusignan trahit[25] et rien n'est finalement tenté à ce moment. Quoi qu'il en soit, les lettres d'Henri III précédemment citées font allusion aux navires que tel ou tel port anglais doit fournir. Pour les Cinque Ports, c'est, au moins en partie, un service dû[26]. Si le potentiel naval du roi est renforcé après 1204, il n'est pas suffisant. Les prescriptions du roi laissent donc entendre que besoin est de forces supplémentaires. Les lettres royales évoquées indiquent la possibilité de faire appel à des navires étrangers stationnant dans les ports anglais. Des lettres postérieures viennent le confirmer. Le 22 mai, Henri III demande aux baillis de Shoreham de libérer les marchandises des marchands de Rouen contenues dans le navire

24 *Rotuli litterarum clausarum*, I, 599–602 ; *Patent Rolls* (*1216–1225*) 441–442 ; Carpenter (1990) 355–356.

25 Petit-Dutaillis (1894) 238–239.

26 Voir notamment Murray (1935) et Rodger (1996).

qu'ils ont arrêté dans le port, mais de retenir le navire[27]. Le 2 juin, le roi enjoint aux baillis de Bristol qu'en dépit de son mandement d'arrêter les navires 'de potestate' du roi de France, ils permettent d'emporter les marchandises dans de petits navires jusqu'à 15 jours après la Saint-Jean-Baptiste (9 juillet) et qu'ils retiennent les grands navires dans le port afin qu'ils aillent à son service[28]. De même, il est ordonné aux baillis de Sandwich de laisser partir le navire d'un marchand de Dublin, qui a été arrêté en raison du précepte royal, s'il n'atteint pas une capacité de charge de six chevaux[29]. Ces ordres, pris après les décisions générales d'arrestation, montrent bien que ce sont les navires, et spécialement les grands, qui intéressent le roi. Les marchands peuvent en revanche aller librement avec leurs marchandises. Le 23 mai, sans que l'on puisse dire si cela concerne des navires arrêtés, est ordonné aux baillis de Ryes de faire venir cinq bons navires avec leurs marins à Portsmouth pour le service du roi[30]. Outre les navires, ce sont les équipages qui lui sont utiles, et leur rétribution est prévue. Le 21 mai, il est mandé aux baillis de Winchelsea qu'ils permettent au navire d'Étienne de Croy, qu'ils ont arrêté selon le précepte du roi, d'aller jusqu'à Portsmouth et que sept ou huit bons navires, avec leurs marins, viennent avec lui pour aller au service du roi[31]. Dans ce cas, il semble qu'Étienne de Croy, par ailleurs bénéficiaire à plusieurs reprises de sauf-conduits, mette son navire à disposition contre rémunération et que des responsabilités lui soient confiées. Le 10 juin, le roi s'adresse aux baillis de Portsmouth et aux marins qui sont rassemblés dans le port et les informe qu'il envoie Bartholomé de Kemesye, vicomte de Southampton, pour disposer des navires[32]. Il y a donc bien rassemblement d'une flotte. Le 25 juin, il est demandé au même vicomte qu'il utilise 20 marcs afin de rétribuer des marins à Portsmouth, qu'il retienne 15 des meilleurs navires et permette aux autres de partir[33]. Enfin, le 11 juillet, 30 livres sont attribuées au même pour le paiement des maîtres des 15 navires arrêtés à Portsmouth, en fonction du nombre de marins présents à bord et du temps pendant lequel ils seront en service[34]. Visiblement l'expédition tarde.

On peut en définitive poser la question des finalités de l'octroi par Henri III d'une autorisation générale de commerce, le 13 avril, soit avant la rupture de la trêve, et allant jusqu'au 9 juillet. Dès ce moment, le roi pouvait avoir à l'esprit la

27 *Rotuli litterarum clausarum*, I, 600.
28 *Patent Rolls* (*1216–1225*) 442.
29 *Rotuli litterarum clausarum*, I, 600.
30 Ibidem, 600.
31 Ibidem, 599.
32 *Patent Rolls* (*1216–1225*) 444.
33 *Rotuli litterarum clausarum*, I, 607.
34 Ibidem, 610.

nécessité de disposer de forces navales. La présence de navires étrangers dans les ports anglais était alors un atout. Il est difficile de mesurer quelle part tient la coercition, avec réquisition de navires, et il est possible que les maîtres et les équipages se soient mis assez facilement au service du roi contre rémunération. Des équipages peuvent être disposés à servir des intérêts politiques opposés à ceux du prince dont ils dépendent, sachant que certains sont probablement composites et que s'y côtoient différentes 'nationalités'. Les marchands, souvent distincts des maîtres et propriétaires de navires, récupèrent alors leurs marchandises.

Cette politique est également menée par Louis VIII. D'après les *Annales de Dunstable*[35], au moment de tenter de conquérir la Gascogne, en décembre 1224, le roi fait répandre le bruit qu'il a entamé des négociations avec les nobles d'Angleterre et qu'il compte faire valoir ses droits à la couronne. Il promet alors des gages très élevés aux marins et autres hommes de guerre, français et anglais, qui l'accompagneraient dans l'expédition. La situation s'est effectivement tendue après l'été. Entre juin et septembre, aucune décision générale n'est édictée par Henri III alors que le Poitou et La Rochelle sont tombés aux mains de Louis VIII. Mais, au début du mois de septembre, il est demandé aux baillis des ports de Lynn, Dunwich, Yarmouth et Ipswich de se saisir des marchands français et de leurs marchandises (6 septembre) arrivés dans leur baillie et, d'autre part, des Normands (8 septembre), et de les conduire là où le roi l'ordonnera. Dans le même temps, le roi mande au vicomte de Southampton, puis aux baillis des foires de Winchester, qu'ils fassent arrêter les Normands et les autres qui sont de la 'potestas' du roi de France[36]. Il ne s'agit plus ici de saisies dans les ports mais sur les lieux de foires et de la 'prise de corps'. Il est à noter que les Normands ne sont pas absolument considérés ici comme des marchands français, signe qu'ils peuvent être traités différemment et preuve que le roi d'Angleterre n'a pas abandonné toute revendication sur la Normandie. Ces mesures sont probablement à regarder comme des représailles après la perte de la Rochelle et la tentative de Louis VIII de pousser son avantage en Gascogne où seules les villes, et notamment Bordeaux, restent fidèles au Plantagenêt[37].

Pour autant, à ce moment comme dans les premiers mois après la rupture de la trêve, les relations commerciales entre France et Angleterre ne sont pas interrompues. Les mesures qui apparaissent répressives n'empêchent pas l'octroi d'autorisations de commerce, très ciblées et ponctuelles pour les unes, plus larges pour d'autres. Dès les premiers temps des arraisonnements et interdictions, le

---

35 *Annales prioratus de Dunstaplia* 92 ; Petit-Dutaillis (1894) 259.

36 *Rotuli litterarum clausarum*, I, 632.

37 Carpenter (1990), 374–378. En 1225, Henri III recouvre la Gascogne.

roi délivre des autorisations de navigation et de commerce, quasi absentes auparavant, preuve encore qu'elles ne sont pas nécessaires en temps de paix. À titre d'exemple, on peut citer la lettre du 21 mai dans laquelle Henri III s'adresse à l'ensemble des baillis des ports de mer et leur enjoint de laisser le navire de Josceus de Southampton, chargé de vin de l'archevêque de Canterbury et d'Hubert de Burgh, justicier du roi et l'un des membres du 'triumvirat', aller à Londres et revenir à Southampton et ce, rappelle-t-il, malgré le précepte demandant d'arrêter les navires arrivant dans les ports[38]. C'est dans le courant du mois de juin que les lettres royales se multiplient et elles deviennent très nombreuses à la fin du mois de juillet, alors qu'a lieu le siège de La Rochelle.

Sans être stéréotypé, le texte des lettres adressées aux baillis d'un port ou de l'ensemble des ports, comporte fréquemment les mêmes éléments. Les termes utilisés sont 'licence' ou 'conduit' et la lettre est parfois accompagnée de la mention 'de protectione'. La formulation ne permet pas de justifier l'emploi de termes différents, il n'est pas explicitement indiqué que le conduit correspondrait à une protection particulière accordée par le roi. Sont mentionnés les noms des bénéficiaires laissant entrevoir la distinction entre marchands, maîtres des navires et propriétaires. Un ou plusieurs navires sont parfois identifiés, avec ou sans mention de la nature de la cargaison. Le fait que des licences successives soient accordées le 24 septembre à un certain nombre d'individus peut suggérer que des navires circulent en convois ou bien qu'un même porteur est chargé d'aller les remettre à leurs bénéficiaires[39]. Fréquemment, il est précisé que l'autorisation s'applique à l'arrivée en Angleterre ou dans un port précis, et qu'elle comprend la possibilité de séjourner pour y effectuer des transactions commerciales, et de repartir. Peuvent être ajoutées des conditions limitatives. C'est le cas pour une licence du 18 juillet en faveur des maire et hommes de Dieppe permettant aux navires de la ville de venir en Angleterre avec leurs marchandises sous condition qu'ils ne remportent pas de marchandises, chez eux ou ailleurs, sans autorisation[40]. De façon générale, la durée de validité est déterminée par un *terminus ad quem* (Pâques, Saint-Michel, etc) correspondant à une période de quelques semaines ou plusieurs mois, voire plus. Ainsi, le 26 juillet les marchands de 'terra regis Dacie' (Danemark) bénéficient d'une licence de se rendre en Angleterre avec leurs marchandises pendant deux ans[41]. Ici, non seulement l'autorisation est de longue durée mais elle

38 *Patent Rolls* (*1216–1225*) 440.
39 Ibidem, 472.
40 Ibidem, 454.
41 Ibidem, 456.

s'applique à tous les marchands dépendants du roi de Danemark avec lequel Henri III n'est pas en conflit.

Il semble qu'il faille distinguer plusieurs motifs à l'octroi de ces autorisations. L'Angleterre ne saurait être coupée du continent. Les marchands et gens de mer anglais doivent poursuivre leurs activités. Or, compte tenu du zèle probable de certaines administrations portuaires, il est préférable qu'ils disposent de lettres attestant que le prince les autorise à naviguer, entrer dans les ports et se livrer au commerce. Les licences délivrées à des hommes de Southampton en octobre montrent bien qu'eux-mêmes sont susceptibles de se trouver dans une situation difficile d'autant que leurs activités peuvent être liées à celles d'hommes des territoires ennemis[42]. C'est pourquoi, ils ne peuvent emporter leurs marchandises outremer que s'ils sont à même d'apporter la preuve qu'elles sont les leurs, à un moment où le roi a demandé que soit saisies celles des marchands français. Dans l'adresse de nombre des lettres, figurent Geoffroi de Lucy et les barons des Cinque ports. On en déduit qu'elles ont aussi pour but d'éviter les arraisonnements en mer où patrouillent des navires sous leur commandement[43]. Les licences doivent permettre d'éviter des actes de piraterie ou l'expression des rivalités entre ports, donc d'anticiper des conflits en attestant la régularité de la situation. Les barons des Cinque Ports, eux-mêmes, obtiennent conduit pour se rendre en Poitou afin d'acheter notamment du sel et du vin[44]. Par ailleurs, il convient de ne pas envenimer les relations avec d'autres princes, rois de Danemark, de Norvège, duc de Saxe ou empereur, en autorisant les marchands de ces territoires à venir en Angleterre, parfois tous, tels les Danois[45]. C'est aussi une nécessité pour l'Angleterre de maintenir les échanges et les rentrées d'argent liées au prélèvement des taxes.

Enfin, il est probablement utile de récompenser ceux qui se sont mis au service du roi, fussent-ils issus de territoires réputés ennemis, tels les membres de la commune de Dieppe. Les attirer dans les ports peut en outre être un moyen de leur proposer rétribution en vue d'un service. C'est encore le témoignage que des liens commerciaux entre Angleterre et Normandie ont subsisté depuis 1204[46] mais peut-être aussi que des habitudes de service persistent. À cela s'ajoute le fait que l'aristocratie laïque et ecclésiastique anglo-normande

42 Ibidem, 452, 472, 477.

43 Il est commis à la garde de la côte anglaise ('maritima Anglie') le 29 août 1224 (*Patent Rolls* (*1216–1225*) 465) et les hommes des Cinque Ports apparaissent sous son autorité à ce sujet. En octobre, il reçoit la garde des îles (*Patent Rolls* (*1216–1225*) 465), charge auparavant exercée par Philippe d'Aubigny (*Patent Rolls* (*1216–1225*) 435).

44 *Patent Rolls* (*1216–1225*) 450–451.

45 Ibidem, 456, 459, 500.

46 Jean-Marie (2010), Jean-Marie (2017).

a encore des biens de part et d'autre de la Manche. C'est ainsi que peut être interprétée la licence accordée le 1er avril 1225 à onze marchands identifiés comme 'de terra Ricardi Mariscalli de Lodoro'[47], à savoir de Leure, 'ancêtre' du Havre, dont le seigneur est Richard Le Maréchal, deuxième fils de Guillaume Le Maréchal[48]. Il y a ici des éléments qui tiennent aux relations interpersonnelles et aux réseaux d'influence.

Il n'est pas aisé de déterminer la façon dont le système fonctionne et comment les lettres parviennent aux mains de leurs bénéficiaires. Par lettres patentes du 29 juin 1224, est accordé à différents individus, le droit de venir en Angleterre jusqu'à la Saint-Michel suivante, et ce, à la demande de plusieurs grands d'Angleterre, ecclésiastiques et laïcs. Il est ensuite mandé, par lettres closes, au connétable de Douvres qu'il permette au porteur des lettres patentes de les faire parvenir outremer et de ne pas gêner ceux qui pourraient venir en Angleterre (sous-entendu avec de telles lettres)[49]. Il est toutefois peu probable que la licence soit systématiquement envoyée à son bénéficiaire avant son voyage.

Quoi qu'il en soit, ceux qui ne disposent pas d'autorisation risquent sans doute gros, mais quand bien même ils en seraient destinataires, des problèmes peuvent surgir. En effet, décisions différenciées et règles non générales sont susceptibles de donner lieu à des interprétations erronées ou abusives des directives et de favoriser les pratiques iniques des agents royaux ou des hommes des ports, singulièrement ceux des Cinque Ports, très actifs. À cela s'ajoutent les revirements du roi liés aux évolutions du conflit et des relations diplomatiques.

4 Des conflits dans le conflit et leur gestion

Les gens de mer et marchands se trouvent plongés dans un conflit politique dont les tenants et aboutissants sont complexes et les dépassent en partie, même s'ils y ont part. Des contentieux se font jour dont les causes sont variées. Elles peuvent tenir au non-respect des prescriptions royales par les agents du pouvoir ou par les gens de mer et marchands eux-mêmes, telles de probables circulations sans licence. Les ordres et contre-ordres du roi favorisent vraisemblablement les erreurs. Enfin, l'exercice de représailles contre les marchands

47 Et non de la Loire.

48 *Patent Rolls* (*1216–1225*) 519–520.

49 *Patent Rolls* (*1216–1225*) 447–448.

ressortissants des territoires ennemis pose la question du droit de prise. Il faut alors trouver des solutions aux conflits, voire les prévenir.

Dans le texte des licences accordées par le roi, les injonctions explicites et répétitives aux agents royaux de ne pas causer de 'molestia', 'dampnum', 'injuria', 'inpedimentum' ou 'gravamen', ou encore les ordres de libérer navires et cargaisons, témoignent de conflits potentiels ou existants. Le roi peut ainsi faire droit aux plaintes de marchands qui s'estiment avoir été spoliés. Quelques exemples permettent d'illustrer ces situations. Au mois de juin 1224, plusieurs navires de Norvège, certains chargés de blé, ont la permission de quitter le port de Lynn[50]. Le 4 août, est ordonné qu'un marchand du duc de Norvège ('ducis Norwegie'), arrêté à Lynn en raison du précepte royal, puisse quitter le port sur son navire, avec biens et marchandises[51]. Le 15 juillet 1224, licence est accordée, jusqu'à la Saint-Michel suivante, à un marchand de Gand afin qu'il se rende dans les Cinque ports et les autres ports d'Angleterre pour retrouver le vin qui lui a été pris par les barons des Cinque Ports, à hauteur de l'*insula Berengarie*[52] et de Saint-Mathieu[53]. Cela témoigne bien de l'existence d'arraisonnements de navires en mer et du rôle des Cinque Ports en la matière. Ces exemples peuvent correspondre à des régularisations *a posteriori* de la situation des marchands mais les hommes des ports anglais ont pu passer outre les licences dont ces derniers bénéficiaient et ainsi susciter des contestations. Là encore se pose la question de la façon dont les autorisations parviennent à leurs bénéficiaires.

Le 21 octobre 1224, le roi ordonne que des marchands de Dieppe, arrêtés à Yarmouth, soient libérés et qu'il leur soit permis de retourner chez eux ('ad partes suas') avec biens et marchandises[54]. Il est ajouté que cela est valable jusqu'à la Purification Notre-Dame (soit jusqu'au 2 février 1225), précision étonnante pour ce type de lettre dont l'objet n'est pas d'octroyer une licence de commerce. Dans le rôle des lettres patentes, le texte est cancellé avec un renvoi à une entrée suivante dans laquelle une licence est justement accordée jusqu'à cette date. Le 18 juillet, soit trois mois auparavant, les Dieppois avaient déjà obtenu licence de venir en Angleterre jusqu'au même terme, avec réserve de la nécessité d'une autorisation pour remporter des marchandises, clause limitative qui est désormais supprimée. Pourtant, en septembre, on l'a vu, le roi avait donné l'ordre d'arrêter les marchands normands et leurs biens. Ces revirements sont malaisés à interpréter. Les décisions générales tiennent au contexte de

50 *Rotuli litterarum clausarum*, I, 606–607.

51 *Patent Rolls* (*1216–1225*) 459.

52 Ile de Béniguet (archipel de Molène) ?

53 La Pointe Saint-Mathieu à l'ouest de la Bretagne ; *Patent Rolls* (*1216–1225*) 452.

54 *Patent Rolls* (*1216–1225*) 476.

l'évolution du conflit avec le roi de France. Les contre-ordres ponctuels peuvent prendre en compte les récriminations de certains marchands et gens de mer, disposant de privilèges particuliers contredisant les ordres généraux, et auxquels le roi souhaite faire droit. Il est possible que les Dieppois bénéficient d'un traitement particulier lié à des habitudes de service qui ont perduré après 1204, car ces derniers, tout autant que des marchands, sont des gens de mer[55].

A l'arrière-plan de ces litiges, figure la question de la pratique de la prise puisque certaines saisies ont lieu en mer. Les sources mettent alors en évidence la définition de l'ennemi qui justifie la prise. Le 20 janvier 1225, une lettre informe les baillis anglais du fait que des vins appartenant aux hommes de la Rochelle ont été saisis dans le navire de Robert de Salern de Ryes et qu'ils ont ensuite été déposés dans le château de Douvres car, à ce moment, les hommes de la Rochelle étaient contre Henri et du côté du roi de France[56]. Après la perte du Poitou et de La Rochelle, les marchandises issues de territoires désignés comme ennemis sont l'objet de saisies, même si, comme dans ce cas, elles se trouvent dans le navire d'un Anglais. L'exercice de la prise est toutefois complexe. Un navire de Leure chargé de sel est arraisonné en vue de Guernesey[57]. Henri III demande, le 8 août 1225, qu'il soit libéré. En effet, bien qu'il ait été chargé en Poitou, aux mains des ennemis du roi, dit la lettre, il appartient à un bourgeois de Richard Le Maréchal à Leure (en Normandie). À la même date, il est ordonné que soient libérés les vins de deux marchands, l'un de Caen et l'autre de Winchelsea, arrêtés à Guernesey alors qu'ils avaient été chargés à Nantes, en territoire contre lequel le roi est en guerre et auquel appartient également le marchand de Caen, ajoute le texte. L'autorisation est accordée sur la foi du marchand de Winchelsea et de trois autres, probablement ses associés ou des hommes dignes de foi, que les vins arriveront et resteront à Winchelsea. On peut penser que c'est après appel de ces derniers au roi que la décision est prise. Ces exemples révèlent une forme de 'mondialisation' des échanges dans le sens où les parties prenantes sont multiples et qu'il est difficile de décréter des mesures générales sans atteindre les intérêts des Anglais ou de ceux qui ne sont pas en guerre contre eux. À cela s'ajoute le fait que l'aristocratie conserve des intérêts des deux côtés de la Manche et qu'il faut les préserver, comme l'atteste le cas de Richard Le Maréchal. À ce moment, en août, aucun ordre général d'arrestation des hommes et marchandises français et normands dans les ports anglais et sur les foires, n'est encore donné. En revanche, la définition de l'ennemi explique ces saisies en mer, sur lesquelles le

55 Jean-Marie (2010) ; Jean-Marie (2016a et b).

56 *Patent Rolls (1216–1225)* 504.

57 *Rotuli litterarum clausarum*, II, 48.

roi revient dans certains cas au moins. Reste à s'interroger sur le fait qu'elles soient réellement ordonnées.

L'existence de prises en temps de guerre est également attestée *a posteriori* par les décisions relatives à la répartition des fruits. Une rare endenture de 1212 montre que la décision de l'attribution revient au roi, au moins lorsque les saisies de navires et cargaisons sont effectuées par des galées royales[58]. Il est difficile de déterminer s'il s'agit d'une règle mais en 1217, le roi s'adresse aux barons des Cinque Ports à propos du même sujet[59]. Il leur envoie deux de leurs co-barons afin de vérifier qu'ils ont bien eu leur part après une saisie en mer et de déterminer ce qui lui reviendra. Cette lettre peut être interprétée de deux façons : ou bien une concession aux hommes de ces ports pour garantir leur fidélité alors qu'ils ont pris le parti du prince Louis dans la guerre, ou bien une affirmation du roi qui veut marquer que la décision de répartition lui revient. Le document atteste aussi qu'il n'existe pas de règles générales et notamment pas de fixation, à l'avance, des parts de chacun. Ces prises peuvent être un moyen de financer la guerre et en octroyer une part à ceux qui les ont effectuées, est de nature à les encourager[60]. Les mêmes pratiques existent du côté français mais on ne bénéficie pas de sources équivalentes pour les mettre nettement en évidence. Ainsi, une flotte anglaise venant apporter de l'argent à Richard de Cornouaille pendant son expédition en Gascogne à la fin de l'année 1225, est-elle retenue près de La Rochelle par le manque de vent ; averti par ses galées faisant croisière, Savary de Mauléon, servant désormais le roi de France et gardien de cette zone maritime ('custos partis maritimae'), ordonne aux Anglais de rentrer dans le port, sous peine de mort. Ces derniers refusent de se mettre à sa merci mais offrent une forte rançon. Savary se prépare alors à l'attaque lorsque le vent se lève et permet à la flotte ennemie de s'enfuir[61].

Toutefois, et c'est un élément majeur, il n'y a pas de traces, à cette période, de lettres de marque demandant expressément d'effectuer des prises même si, dès 1205, une lettre de Jean sans Terre accorde la moitié des prises potentielles à des équipages de galées à son service[62]. Les premières, avec partage des gains par moitié prévu à l'avance, ne semblent pas antérieures à la guerre contre la

58 Beryl, Formoy (1926).

59 *Documents relating to Law and Custom of the Sea*, 5–6 ; *Patent Rolls* (*1216–1225*) 88.

60 M. Mollat considère que c'est à partir du XIVe siècle qu'il y a une codification du droit de prise : Mollat (1975). Le roi a toujours réclamé une large part des prises et toutes les prises effectuées par les navires à son service ; Rodger (2004) 127–128 ; Nicolas, I (1847) 238–239 ; *Documents relating to Law and Custom of the Sea*, 5–8.

61 Petit-Dutaillis (1894) 258 ; *Annales prioratus de Dunstaplia* 98–99.

62 Hardy (1835) 51.

France en 1242–1243[63]. L'apparition de lettres de représailles permettant à ceux qui ont subi des actes de piraterie et n'ont pas obtenu dédommagement, de se rembourser par la force, est encore plus tardif et date de la fin du XIIIe siècle, d'après Marsden[64].

On pressent toutefois un enchaînement des faits avec prises et représailles. À cela se mêlent les revendications de ceux qui s'estiment injustement spoliés, mais il est malaisé de différencier ce qui relève de faits de guerre de ce qui a trait à d'autres conflits. En temps de guerre, à tout le moins, l'exercice de représailles est envisagé afin d'obtenir dédommagement. En décembre 1225, une lettre close adressée aux baillis de Sandwich indique que si les biens de divers individus, *a priori* Caennais, sont trouvés dans sa baillie, ils devront être confisqués jusqu'à ce que ces individus aient remboursé à un Anglais l'équivalent de ce qu'ils lui ont pris à Caen. Figure l'indication d'un montant de 20 marcs qui atteste que les pertes ont été estimées[65]. S'agit-il d'un conflit de nature commerciale ? On peut en douter compte tenu du contexte en 1225, mais le fait que quatre individus uniquement soient débiteurs interroge sur sa nature : s'il s'agissait d'une prise, on pourrait penser que tous les Caennais, voire les Normands, seraient redevables. Quoi qu'il en soit, la solution retenue ici est celle de la saisie et le règlement du contentieux peut être assimilé à des représailles. Il ne s'agit toutefois pas d'actions à mener en mer mais bien dans la baillie de Sandwich uniquement.

Des échanges antérieurs de lettres entre les rois jettent un éclairage sur ce sujet. La solution de tels contentieux peut en effet prendre du temps : certains sont pendants depuis la guerre précédente et ressurgissent à l'occasion de négociations pour le renouvellement d'une trêve. Les lettres y afférent renseignent sur les modalités de leur résolution. Des marchands français, considérant que leurs droits n'ont pas été respectés, paraissent s'être directement adressés à Philippe Auguste qui intervient auprès d'Hubert de Burgh, justicier d'Angleterre. Dans une première lettre, non datée, le roi de France demande de rétribuer ses bourgeois d'Amiens pour le blé qu'ils ont livré[66]. Il ajoute à son injonction que le justicier voudrait lui-même qu'il en fut ainsi fait pour les hommes du roi d'Angleterre. Dans une seconde, il s'inquiète de l'information fournie par son fils Louis à propos de deux de ses hommes de Calais, arrêtés et détenus par les hommes de Sandwich et de Shoreham. De plus, à Douvres, ce sont 20 navires, réfugiés dans le port en raison d'une tempête, qui ont été arrêtés et pour

63 Nicolas, I (1847) 239; *Patent Rolls* (*1232–1247*) 362.

64 Marsden (1909) 682. Voir aussi le chapitre de Thomas Heebøll-Holm dans ce volume.

65 *Rotuli litterarum clausarum*, II, 88.

66 *Royal and other historical letters*, I, CLXXXVI.

chacun desquels a été exigée une somme de 20 sous sterlings pour les laisser repartir. Le roi demande que le dommage soit réparé et il agite la menace d'en faire autant pour les Anglais en France[67]. Cette seconde missive est antérieure au 2 décembre 1220, date à laquelle Henri III s'adresse aux barons des Cinque Ports à propos de ces dommages causés aux hommes de Calais par les barons de Sandwich, Douvres, Winchelsea, Romney et Ryes[68]. Il leur enjoint de se réunir prochainement à Shepway avec le connétable de Douvres afin de considérer l'affaire et de faire justice selon les coutumes du royaume. Une délégation de Calaisiens doit également se rendre à cette convocation[69]. À partir de l'été 1219, ont eu lieu des négociations pour le renouvellement de la trêve qui aboutissent à un accord pour la proroger à dater de Pâques 1220[70]. Un tel moment est favorable à la résolution de contentieux vieux de plusieurs années. En effet, il est possible que les lettres de Philippe Auguste aient trait à l'intervention du prince Louis en Angleterre en 1216–1217 puisque c'est ce dernier qui attire l'attention de son père et que des navires de Calais ont été impliqués dans les actions du prince[71]. On ne sait si une solution est trouvée.

En 1224 encore, tous les litiges ne sont pas résolus[72]. Henri III aborde le sujet de façon plus générale avec la volonté de mettre en place une procédure permettant d'établir les faits et de déterminer un mode de résolution[73]. Dans une lettre patente du 25 mars, sans destinataire précis, il concède que soient désignés quatre procureurs (*attornati*), deux au nom du roi de France et deux au sien, afin qu'ils déterminent quels sont les dettes, dommages et pertes subis par les marchands et autres hommes du roi de France lors de la précédente guerre. Si au moins trois d'entre eux ne peuvent s'accorder, ils désigneront un cinquième, ce qui permettra de dégager une majorité. L'allusion à la guerre, vieille de plusieurs années, probablement encore celle de 1216–1217, atteste que les contentieux durent. Si en mars 1224, Henri III cherche à régler ces problèmes, c'est sans doute qu'il espère un renouvellement de la trêve et que ces sujets reviennent sur le devant de la scène.

L'ensemble de ces lettres témoignent qu'il n'y a pas de procédure ni d'instance de règlement de ce type de conflit. C'est au plus haut niveau que les solutions

---

67 Ibidem, CLXXXVII ; *Recueil des actes de Philippe Auguste*, 4, no. 1674.

68 *Patent Rolls* (*1216–1225*) 305–306.

69 *Recueil des actes de Philippe Auguste*, 4, no. 1674 (note).

70 Ibidem, 4, no. 1601, no. 1602, no. 1619.

71 Carpenter (1990) 23, 43.

72 Tous ne le sont pas encore en 1247 comme l'attestent les plaintes des marchands d'Arras et Gravelines enregistrées lors des enquêtes diligentées par le roi de France en 1247 ; *Enquêtes administratives du règne de Saint Louis*, 254 (5), 258 (42) ; Mollat (1982) 620–621.

73 *Patent Rolls* (*1216–1225*) 483.

sont négociées. Surtout, il n'y a pas de règles générales sur lesquelles s'appuyer et rien ne semble déterminé, au moment de l'établissement d'une trêve, concernant le règlement des contentieux encore en cours. Les intérêts des marchands et gens de mer sont donc soumis aux aléas des relations entre France et Angleterre. Ils peuvent pourtant avoir du poids. Les deux rois, dans leurs prétentions maritimes et en l'absence de véritable flotte, sont dépendants de leurs forces. Il est alors intéressant de noter que c'est lorsque la paix est menacée et donc que les rois ont potentiellement besoin de l'appui de navires, qu'ils se soucient de trouver des solutions aux litiges non résolus. En ce sens, la lettre d'Henri III du 25 mars 1224 peut également avoir pour objectif de contenter les marchands et les gens de mer susceptibles de poursuivre leurs activités en Angleterre, malgré l'échéance proche de la trêve, ou de mettre des navires à son service contre rémunération. Le fait de constituer une forme de jury mixte dédié à l'établissement des faits, peut être considéré comme un gage de bonne volonté[74].

5 Conclusion

Les conclusions sont évidemment partielles puisque l'attention a été portée sur un temps court. L'exploitation diachronique des multiples lettres du roi d'Angleterre ayant trait au sujet permettrait sans doute de mieux établir les choses et surtout de mettre en évidence des évolutions. Néanmoins, il est possible de tirer des enseignements de l'analyse de cette brève période.

Sans surprise, la guerre entre Angleterre et France intensifie les conflits et contentieux concernant les échanges maritimes. Mais ses prolégomènes sont aussi un moment où les princes prêtent attention à ceux qui ne sont pas résolus, parfois depuis des années. La multiplicité des lettres émises par Henri III montre des préoccupations majeures : défendre les possessions, disposer de moyens navals et faire pression sur l'ennemi, sans interrompre les liens commerciaux de l'Angleterre avec le continent. Gens de mer et marchands sont concernés à divers titres par l'affrontement entre les deux rois. On hésite à trouver une totale logique à l'action du roi d'Angleterre et de ceux qui le guident, preuve que les intérêts de la royauté sont contradictoires et que les décisions doivent être prises en fonction de l'évolution du rapport de force avec le roi de France. On pressent aussi des tensions avec les barons des Cinque Ports qui jouent un jeu parfois indépendant et outrepassent les ordres royaux, même s'ils sont un élément essentiel de la mise en œuvre des décisions du roi. Ils sont en outre en conflit avec d'autres ports anglais[75]. La question du respect

74 On le rencontre plus tard de façon institutionnalisée : Kowaleski (2007).
75 Kowaleski (2007) ; Brooks (1933).

effectif des licences octroyées est ainsi posée[76]. À l'inverse, l'attitude d'Henri III à l'égard de certains Normands laisse entrevoir des habitudes de service de ces derniers, voire des liens de fidélité étroits. Ce sont des éléments d'explication des revirements du roi et des ordres ponctuels de libération des navires et marchandises. Il s'agit bien de gérer les conflits au coup par coup plutôt que de mettre en place des procédures de résolution.

On soupçonne aussi que des conflits peuvent tenir à des oppositions entre ceux qui pratiquent le commerce, qui fréquentent la mer ou qui ont des intérêts en ce domaine : gens de mer, marchands et administrateurs des ports. Figurent dans les lettres, des indices d'associations, ponctuelles ou pérennes, de gens de mer et marchands qui peuvent appartenir à des entités politiques différentes. En outre, leurs intérêts sont parfois divergents. Les premiers disposent de navires et trouvent éventuellement profit à répondre aux offres de service du roi. Les liens entre sociétés portuaires de part et d'autre de la Manche, attestées avant 1204, sont susceptibles de perdurer[77]. Tout autant, il est possible que des maîtres de navires et des marins soient un temps associés dans une même affaire alors que, quelques temps plus tard, les mêmes sont engagés dans des entreprises opposées[78]. Ces facteurs multiples sont propres à générer des conflits et compliquent les décisions royales.

Plus largement, est posée la question de la nature et de l'exercice des pouvoirs royaux. Henri III se déclare encore duc de Normandie alors que les Normands sont identifiés comme étant sous la 'potestas' du roi de France. Le moment est ancré dans une période où la force des pouvoirs effectifs et des liens de fidélité est essentielle alors que le XIIIe siècle, certes peu entamé dans la chronologie de cette étude, a été considéré comme celui du début de la construction de 'l'État moderne'. Cette question a un réel intérêt concernant la gestion et le règlement des conflits opposant les ressortissants d'une 'potestas' à l'autre. Le pouvoir d'arrêter les navires dans les ports découle de la rupture de la trêve mais il n'est pas assuré, à la lecture des lettres, que le roi ait celui de réquisitionner les navires 'étrangers' pour son service. À tout le moins, maîtres et marins sont-ils rémunérés. Au-delà, le vocabulaire définissant l'étranger n'est pas réellement présent dans les lettres royales et, dans le même registre, les marchands et maîtres de navires anglais ne sont pas identifiés comme tels mais par leur port d'attache et les lettres royales ne les concernent pas dans leur globalité[79].

---

76 Au sujet de l'inefficacité possible des sauf-conduits au XVe siècle, voir Miranda (2017).

77 Jean-Marie (2016a et b).

78 Évoqué à propos des 'mixed crew' dans Kowaleski (2007).

79 A propos de la définition juridique de l'étranger, surtout à partir du XIVe siècle, voir Kim (2000).

Reste évidemment la question de la mer elle-même. Aucun droit 'international' ne s'y exerce. Les règles figurant dans la compilation dite 'Rôles d'Oléron', connue par des manuscrits de la fin du XIIIe ou du XIVe siècle, définissent d'abord des règles coutumières relatives à la vie à bord, la navigation, l'arrivée dans les ports ou encore les rapports entre maîtres et équipage ainsi que maîtres et marchands[80]. Aucune allusion à ce droit coutumier ne figure dans les lettres royales étudiées. Les règles établies lors des trêves concernent l'accès, évidemment par voie maritime, aux territoires des princes, et non la mer elle-même. On l'a dit, il n'y a pas d'ordre, conservé à tout le moins, d'effectuer des prises en mer. Elles existent, le partage des fruits en témoigne, et tiennent au fait que des navires, ceux qui les mènent ou les utilisent pour leurs marchandises, sont réputés ennemis. Ceux qui les effectuent en tirent profit tout autant qu'ils servent un pouvoir. De plus, la multiplicité des acteurs de ces navigations génère des contentieux sur lesquels les lettres royales se penchent au coup par coup tenant compte des intérêts du roi, qui peuvent être de préserver des réseaux de clientèle. Les difficultés générées par ces situations sont susceptibles d'expliquer les évolutions qui contribuent à la définition de règles, pour la résolution des conflits. Parmi elles, la *carta mercatoria* de 1303, si elle ne prend pas en compte la situation sur mer, vise toutefois, dans un contexte tendu, à assurer les relations commerciales entre Angleterre et continent[81].

Bibliographie

Sources éditées

Annales prioratus de Dunstaplia, Annales Monastici, III, Luard, H.R., éd. (Londres 1866).

Documents relating to Law and Custom of the Sea, Marsden, R.G., ed., I, 1205–1648 (Londres 1915).

Enquêtes administratives du règne de Saint Louis, Delisle, L., éd., Recueil des historiens des Gaules et de la France, 24 (Paris 1904).

Layettes du Trésor des chartes, Teulet, A., éd., I (Paris 1863).

Patent Rolls of the reign of Henry III preserved in the Public Record Office, AD 1216–1225, printed under the superintendence of The Deputy Keeper of the Records (Londres 1901).

Patent Rolls of the reign of Henry III preserved in the Public Record Office, AD 1225–1232, printed under the superintendence of The Deputy Keeper of the Records (Londres 1903).

80 Jean-Marie (2016a).

81 Sur ces sujets, voir notamment Miranda (2017) et la bibliographie citée dans l'article, de même que Heelboll-Holm (2013).

Recueil des actes de Henri II, roi d'Angleterre et duc de Normandie, concernant les provinces françaises et les affaires de France, Œuvre posthume de Delisle, L., Berger, E., ed., 2 (Paris 1920).

Recueil des actes de Philippe-Auguste, roi de France, Samaran, C., dir., 3, Monicat, J., Boussard, J., ed. (Paris 1966).

Recueil des actes de Philippe-Auguste, roi de France, Samaran, C., dir., 4, Nortier, M., ed. (Paris 1979).

Rotuli litterarum clausarum in turri Londinensi asservati, Hardy, T.D. ed., 2 vol., 1204–1224, 1224–1227, (Londres 1833–1844).

Rotuli litterarum patentium in Turri Londinensis asservati, 1201–1216, Hardy T.D. ed., (Londres 1835).

Royal and other historical letters illustrative of the reign of Henry III from the originals in the Public Record Office, I, 1216–1235, Shirley, W.W., ed. (Londres 1862).

Littérature

Beryl, E., et E.R. Formoy, 'A maritime indenture of 1212', *The English Historical Review* XLI (1926) 556–559.

Brooks, F.W., 'The Cinque Ports' Feud with Yarmouth in the Thirteenth Century', *Mariner's Mirror* 19 (1933) 27–51.

Carpenter, D., *Magna Carta* (Londres 2015).

Carpenter, D., *The Minority of Henry III* (Berkeley and Los Angeles 1990).

Everard, J.A. et J.C. Holt, *Jersey 1204: the forging of an island community* (Londres 2004).

Heelboll-Holm, J.K., *Ports, Piracy and Maritime War: Piracy in the English Channel and the Atlantic, c. 1280–1330*, (Leiden and Boston 2013).

Jean-Marie, L., 'Close relations? Some examples of trade links between England and the towns and ports of Lower Normandy in the thirteenth and early fourteenth centuries', *Anglo-Norman Studies* 32 (2010) 96–113.

Jean-Marie, L., 'Une aristocratie de la mer ? L'exemple de la famille anglo-normande des *Vituli* (XIIe–XIIIe siècles)', in Bates, D., Bauduin, P., ed., *Penser les mondes normands médiévaux (911–2011)* (Caen 2016a) 475–492.

Jean-Marie, L., *Le prince, la Normandie et la mer, milieu du XIIe siècle-1204* (mémoire inédit de l'habilitation à diriger des recherches, université de Caen 2016b).

Jean-Marie, L., 'Entre Paris et l'Angleterre : les activités commerciales des Rouennais au "siècle de saint Louis"', in J.-B. Auzel, J.-F. Moufflet, eds., *Saint Louis en Normandie (hommage à Jacques Le Goff)* (Saint-Lô 2017) 57–71.

Kim, K., *Aliens in Medieval Law: The Origins of Modern Citizenship* (Cambridge 2000).

Kowaleski, M., '"Alien" Encounters in the Maritime World of Medieval England', *Medieval Encounters* 13 (2007) 96–121.

Marsden, R.G., 'Early Prize Jurisdiction and Prize Law in England', *The English Historical Review* XXIV (1909) 675–697.

Miranda, F., 'Conflict management in western Europe: The case of the Portuguese merchants in England, Flanders and Normandy, 1250–1500', *Continuity and Change* 32-1 (2017) 11–36.

Mollat, M., 'De la piraterie sauvage à la course réglementée (XIVe–XVe siècle)', in Mélanges de l'École Française de Rome. Moyen Âge, Temps Modernes 87-1 (1975) 7–25.

Mollat, M., 'Philippe Auguste et la mer', *La France de Philippe Auguste. Le temps des mutations* (Paris 1982) 605–623.

Murray, K.M.E., *The Constitutional History of the Cinque Ports* (Manchester 1935).

Nicolas, N.H., *A history of the Royal Navy : from the earliest times to the wars of the French Revolution*, 2 vol. (Londres 1847).

Petit-Dutaillis, C., *Étude sur la vie et le règne de Louis VIII* (Paris 1894).

Powicke, F.M., *Thirteenth century, 1216–1307* (Oxford 2nde éd. 1962).

Rodger, N.A.M., 'The Naval Service of the Cinque Ports', *The English Historical Review* CXI (1996) 636–651.

Rodger, N.A.M., *The Safeguard of the Sea : a Naval History of Britain, 660–1649* (Londres 2004).

Smith, J.B., 'The Treaty of Lambeth, 1217', *The English Historical Review* XCIV (1979) 562–579.

CHAPTER 5

Maritime Conflicts and Their Resolution in Late Medieval Castile

Eduardo Aznar Vallejo and Roberto J. González Zalacain

1 Introduction

A combination of factors – some human, others having to do with nature – produced an abundance of conflict in Castilian seas during the Late Medieval period. On the one hand, the 'people of the sea' lived the sort of itinerant lifestyle that fostered rootlessness and alienation. On the other hand, the hostile and dangerous nature of their surroundings required two qualities that are propitious for conflict: determination and toughness. Depending on the cause, maritime disputes will be analyzed according to three categories: hazards at sea, human depredation and professional conflicts. The conclusion will include a discussion on the role of maritime societies in resolving such quarrels.

2 Maritime Conflicts in Late Medieval Castile

2.1 *Riscum Maris*

The forces of nature at sea entailed enormous risks to ships and goods and to trade in general. Of the disputes to ensue in the wake of a shipwreck, the first to arise concerned the ownership and rescue of the wreck, involving the ship's owners and nearby coastal dwellers or the authorities administering the territory.[1] In the thirteenth century the *Partidas* – laws established by King Alfonso X – obliged the return of spoils to a ship's rightful owners regardless of local custom or privilege.[2] These laws also condemned deliberate acts intended to cause a shipwreck: the efforts of covetous sailors or the pursuit of deception so that a ship would run aground. These practices, therefore, indeed happened and were probably boons for a seafaring population. Indeed, the later

1 See the chapters by Daphne Penna and Ian Peter Grohse elsewhere in this volume.

2 *Las Siete Partidas del rey Alfonso el Sabio* (1807) V, IX, 7, 10 and 11.

 | DOI:10.1163/9789004407992_007

Ordenamiento de Alcalá from 1348[3] and the rulings of the *Cortes de Toledo* in 1480[4] prohibited the application of local tariffs to ships that had taken refuge in ports.

Laws were categorical. But ownership rights were harder to ascertain when a shipwreck left no survivors and compensation was due to rescuers. Local rulings thus developed regarding *trovadura*, the accidental discovery of the goods of a wreck.[5] Evidently claims over shipwrecks were common, in particular during the beginning of the period and in cases involving foreign ships with Castilian destinations. A study of relations between Castile and England in the early fourteenth century reveals this tendency in the seven documented occupations of Castilian shipwrecks.[6] Spanish claims ensued because there were survivors in these instances, and the goods rescued could not be considered mere wreckage or 'spoils of the sea'. Interestingly, analogous arguments would be used, in other contexts, to justify such occupations.

To insulate themselves from the effects of these contingencies, Castilian merchants in Bruges obtained a special privilege in 1366 which ensured that any wreckage or spoils found in Flanders would not be confiscated or submitted to local appropriation. The merchants would have to provide compensation in the form of payments covering the expenses of rescuers, which were priced according to Bruges law.[7]

Merchants' claims were also often directed at longstanding privileges enjoyed by lords over the spoils of a shipwreck. All the cases we know of concern the ports under the lordship of the Duke of Medina Sidonia.[8] The ports of Cádiz and Rota, nevertheless, ceased to be subject to that jurisdiction when Enrique IV granted them, including the royal fifth and the shipwrecks, as payment to Rodrigo Ponce de León after he had loaned the monarchy money.[9]

Finally, another cause for a shipwreck could be the deliberate sinking of a ship during a battle,.[10] At times ships were deliberately wrecked so as to ensure their rescue. The *Partidas* established that the cost of damage caused by the

---

3 *Los códigos españoles* (1872).

4 *Cortes de Toledo in 1480* (1861) 151.

5 An example can be found in Ordinance 28 in Plencia (Erkoreka Gervasio 199: p. 590) and Ordinance 16 in Luarca (Suárez Álvarez 1975).

6 Egiluz Ortiz de Latierro (1978) appendix nos. 23, 24, 25, 26, 35, 37 and 51.

7 Gilliodts van Severen (1902) 57 and 62–63.

8 Archivo General de Simancas (AGS), Registro General del Sello (RGS), III no. 3616 (27 October 1484); and VI no. 461 (6 February 1489). See also the work of González Gallego (1974) appendix no. 39, 15-II-1432.

9 Archivo Histórico Nacional (AHN), Osuna, leg. 183, no. 4 a, b and c.

10 ags, RGS, 23 May 1500, f. 70.

cutting of masts before a storm had to be shared by the merchants.[11] When damage was fortuitous, however, the merchants bore no financial obligation, given that they usually only rented the ships. A similar policy was adopted when ships had run aground on beaches or had crashed against rocks. If these were accidents, the ship's owner had to pay the expenses; but if the merchant had sought to reach the shore so as to avoid getting lost, then the damage was his responsibility. The *Fuero de Layrón*, a Castilian version of the *Rôles d'Oleron*, specifies that merchants first had to consult the shipmaster regarding the necessity of cutting the mast or cutting the anchors loose.[12] Any damages incurred had to be assessed before goods were unloaded, and any compensation for delays on further shipments had to be covered.

Indeed, legal provisions varied depending on, among other things, what had been lost, what could be done to recover or complete the shipments, and who had to foot the bill. Such matters involved three parties: the owner, the shipmaster and the merchants. For example, if the ship was lost but the rigging had been spared destruction, the shipmaster could not then sell the rigging without the owner's consent. In cases where the ship was damaged but most of the goods on board had been saved, the owner could still charge for the expenses of the journey undertaken up to that point. If the damage could be quickly repaired, the trip could resume; but otherwise it was legal for the merchant to rent another ship, paid for with the rescued goods.

Damage to ships may have been caused by accident, sometimes resulting from collisions. In cases like these, the two ships involved and their cargo had to share responsibility for the damage done. If, however, the crash had been instigated by one of the two ships, then reparations were the sole responsibility of representatives of that ship. On other occasions, mooring in very tight spots caused problems. Rules established that the first ship had to request that the second move or otherwise face the full expense that could be incurred by potential damage. The anchors, also, had to be beaconed in order to avoid entanglements. Any damage to the cargo was also categorized depending on whether it had been due to natural causes, and whether the cargo had to be jettisoned to ensure the seaworthiness of the ship. In the first case, laws and freight contracts mandated certain technical requirements of the ships.[13] Nonetheless, when there was damage due to strictly natural causes (rain, salinity, humidity,

---

11 *Las Siete Partidas del rey Alfonso el Sabio* (1807) V, IX, 4 and 5.

12 The various versions of the law can be found in Serna Vallejo (2004). Even though they are almost indistinguishable, our reference has been the version found in Manuscript 716 at the Biblioteca Nacional (BN) Madrid. See also the laws 9, 3, 4, 15 and 16.

13 A thorough analysis can be found in Martínez Gijón (1983).

etc.), together with the effects of imperfect packaging, responsibility would be apportioned differently. Therefore, cargo normally travelled below deck, where it was secured using wooden frames, and stowed together using cork to avoid collisions between the crates. Another part of the cargo could go on deck, but would be placed there under *pañoles* – a cover which included light woods and textiles.

Under these circumstances, deterioration of the cargo was par for the course. The *Fuero de Layrón* established blame only if the cargo had in any way been diminished by the crew, in which case they were responsible unless the merchants themselves had allowed or prompted them to take such actions.[14] There was an interesting waiver, however, in cases when wine had been poured out during a storm: members of the crew could swear an oath that they had done so for the sake of the ship. If the *canteles* – consisting of a wooden frame and canvas used to block, brace and latch together cargo – were defective, merchants could demand compensation, though here again the crew could exonerate themselves through an oath. Maritime pilots, *prácticos*, were liable for any damage they caused, but this responsibility ended at the harbor entrance, since the loading and unloading of cargo were tasks allotted to the crew. Certain other types of damage were also considered accidents, like those occurring during the transfer of goods from the ship to small harbor boats. In those cases, merchants shared liability.[15]

The final problem that arose regarding the cargo was the *echazón*, the jettisoning of cargo for the saving of the ship or the general average. This practice involved the dumping of cargo to prevent the ship from sinking. As in the case of shipwrecks, the monarchy focused on guaranteeing the owners the property of any cargo that was rescued.[16] The cost of this operation was then established, the brunt borne by all concerned. The *Partidas* listed the merchants – including those that traded in high-end products such as jewels, currency or serfs (*siervos*) – among the injured parties.[17] Payment was due even if the ship eventually sank. The *Ordenamiento de Alcalá* and the *Ordenanzas de Montalvo* reiterated the rulings of the *Partidas*,[18] whereas the *Fuero de Layrón* would be more precise in this regard. In the latter text, the *echazón* necessitated consultation with the merchant, though the crew's opinion still predominated.[19] In addition, the assessment of damage when port was reached had to incorporate

14 Serna Vallejo (2004) leyes 10, 11 and 25.

15 *Las Siete Partidas del rey Alfonso el Sabio* (1807) V, IX, 8.

16 Ibidem, 7.

17 Ibidem, 3 and 6.

18 These laws will go from the *Ordenamiento de Alcalá* to the *Ordenanzas reales de Castilla*, Título XII, Ley 4. *Los códigos españoles* (1872) 472.

19 Serna Vallejo (2004) ley 8.

the value of the cargo lost and of the transport service, as well as the cost of the *quintaladas* – a special benefit given to designated seamen in trade – owed the crew.

2.2 *Riscum Gentium*

The *riscum maris*, though common and significant, paled in comparison to the risk posed by human actions. Men's violence might stem from privateering or piracy, two legal categories whose definitions were based on formal characteristics that were difficult to distinguish in practice. Privateers, officially, required royal authorization; their employment was aimed at infidels or countries the king was at war with or had economic claims upon. The actual application of causalities incurred was nonetheless far from simple. Infidel status could vary depending on whether a peace treaty existed, and the ship's nationality was often different from that of the merchants.[20] Piracy thus overcame these complications by openly and indiscriminately preying on other ships. These practices, which were common, prompted the elaboration of an extensive legal framework.

Above all, the monarchy sought to insure merchants and shippers specifically in order to avoid collective liability. Thus the *Ordenamiento de Alcalá* and the *Ordenanzas Reales* prohibited the seizure of any ships heading towards the kingdom's ports.[21] This policy was later reinforced through private and collective insurance. Royal policy then established measures of deterrence. At the end of the Middle Ages, the *Ordenamiento* maintained the laws of Alfonso XI, which ordered the construction of a fleet to police the seas – *para excusar los robos y represalias*.[22] Expeditions were mounted to fight piracy, most famously the effort led by Pero Niño in the Mediterranean[23] against Castilian pirates who were attacking national and foreign ships alike.[24] Finally, losses were also compensated. Among the possible damages incurred, there was frequently the theft of cargo, arms, armor and provisions; even members of the crew or a ship's passengers were often captured and held for ransom.

2.3 *Professional Disputes*

Ship captains and masters possessed obligations to the crew. There were also obligations that governed the relations between various parties: dockhands

20 See also the chapter by Dominique Valérian in this volume.

21 *Ordenamiento de Alcalá,* Título XXXII, Ley LI; *Ordenanzas Reales de Castilla*, Libro VI, Título XII, Ley II. *Los Códigos españoles* (1872) 481 and 472.

22 *Ordenanzas Reales de Castilla*, Libro VI, Título XII, Ley V (*Los Códigos españoles* 1872: 472–473).

23 See the chapter by Pierre Prétou in this volume.

24 *Las Siete Partidas del rey Alfonso el Sabio* (1807) V, IX, 1 and 2.

and shippers, or merchants and shippers and their financers. Within these contractual relationships, the *Partidas* were overly concerned with two issues: the relation between merchants and shippers, and the authority that shipmasters wielded over their crews.[25]

In the first case, the preparedness of the vessel – including its caulking and rigging and the storage of weapons and sufficient provisions – was the responsibility of the ship captains. They also were required to include a scribe and a suitable crew on board their ships. The captain's responsibility extended to damage due to any of the following causes: the crew's incompetence while sailing during *mare clausum* (11 November to 10 March), or travel through unsafe waters without merchant consent. Ship owners and captains wielded executive power over the crew, which allowed them to imprison or discipline crew members as they saw fit, barring permanent injury and death.

The *Fuero de Layrón* also regulated these issues. Ownership of a vessel resided clearly on land, and the shipmaster could not sell it without the owner's authorization; he could, however, pawn the rigging in order to maintain the crew, if the latter consented.[26] The *Fuero* also clarified the relations among the crew.[27] The shipmaster had to check with the crew regarding sailing conditions or otherwise be held liable for the payment of any damage to the ship and cargo if problems arose. In cases of shipwreck, the crew had to be given the means to return to port, usually by selling flotsam. The crew's freedom of movement depended on whether the ship was adequately moored. If it was anchored near a port or inlet, the sailors could not disembark without the master's permission. But if the ship was bound by four moorings on a wharf, the crew no longer needed such permission. Anyone wounded or sick had to be tended on board, unless they had disembarked without leave.

Discipline was treated in detail in the *Fuero*.[28] The shipmaster was the law among the crew and it was his responsibility to keep the peace. Any act of disrespect among or towards the crew was a threat to this peace; the crew, in turn, had to accept this authority in the form of disciplinary slapping or fisting. Self-defense was only legitimate in response to excessive punishment. The master possessed the authority to fire unruly sailors. If they expressed remorse and promised good conduct going forward, they could still finish out the job and get paid in full. In the case of absence, a substitute had to be paid by the shipmaster.

25 Ibidem, 1 and 2.

26 Serna Vallejo (2004) Law 1.

27 Ibidem, Laws 2–5, 7 and 8.

28 Ibidem, Laws 12 and 14.

The crew's economic benefits were also described in the *Fuero*.[29] The sailors had the option of securing an established *quintalada* – a payment based on benefits derived from trade, or left to the *fuero de la nave*, the customary practice of the ship. They also possessed the right to carry one barrel of water for every four crew members. If this barrel were dumped, it would be worth its content in wine. After the cargo was unloaded, the sailors had to be paid their salary, although it could be withheld if they slept on land. If the destination port changed, the crew's prior consent was necessary only if it was salaried, not paid according to the profits taken. When the crew disembarked at port, they could take with them their ration only of food, not of drink; and it was their obligation to return on time to carry out their tasks or be held liable for any damage incurred.

Sometimes gaps in the rules were covered by local or guild regulations, at least in northern Castile.[30] At times these ordinances echoed the *Fuero de Layrón*, as was the case for the municipal laws of Luarca. There, if the provisions of the crew had been depleted in a foreign port, the master had the right to meet with the sailors so that they could agree on what could be sold to acquire further provisions.[31] In other cases, the participation of the brotherhoods that the sailors belonged to was welcomed. Luarcan rules established that sailors who had been injured doing their jobs could be compensated via the alms received by the brotherhood. If a sailor died, his widow would receive a *quiñón* – a plot of land assigned to the dead sailor in the wake of his fatal accident.[32] In other cities, such as San Vicente de la Barquera and Deva, the compulsory hiring of retired sailors and orphans was considered a form of charity.[33] This corporative spirit is further evident in the statutes of Plencia, which established a *atoaje* – a towing fee – applicable by any member of the society. If a particular ship did not pay this fee, then service would not be provided by any other member.[34]

These regulations place a strong emphasis on the maintenance of agreements. We will provide two examples. In Luarca, the fine levied on a sailor who broke the terms of an arrangement was ten *maravedís*, one hundred if the violator was the shipmaster.[35] At Plencia the rules were more detailed. A master

29 Ibidem, Laws 18–21.

30 The differences between the Cantabrian and the Andalusian coast can be seen in Aznar Vallejo (2012).

31 Suárez Álvarez (1975) Law 9.

32 Ibidem, Law 13.

33 Erkoreka Gervasio (1991) 487–488.

34 Chapters 49 and 62. Erkoreka Gervasio (1991) 596 and 600.

35 Law 36. Erkoreka Gervasio (1991) 487–488. See also Solórzano Telechea (2011) 1036.

could not fire a sailor from his company between 11 November (the feast day of Saint Martin) and 2 February (the day celebrating Purification of Mary). Similarly, he could not agree to the hiring of a substitute crewmember from another ship, except in cases of lengthy voyages. Merchant sailing was rare in this era, and most sailors were committed to fishing crews. They could abandon such a commitment only if the alternative was a long-range merchant expedition, for example to Flanders, England, Andalusia, or any destination beyond the Cantabrian coast. In cases such as these, the sailor was liable for the expenses incurred by the master and was compelled to help find a substitute for him. The Biscayan port stressed the importance of prior agreements and forbade shipmasters from arrogating other vessels' freight. Towards the end of this period, regulations became increasingly restrictive, especially when dealing with ship procurement. The development of the 'acts of navigation' on behalf of the monarchy, and the protectionist policies of some mercantile corporations, warranted this tightening of the rules.

The first round of legislation sought to favour Castilian ships employed for trade, particularly the larger vessels. In 1397–98 Enrique III ordered that all Spanish merchants use Spanish boats when trading,[36] a directive that the Catholic Kings updated in 1500.[37] This law had a dual objective: at once an economic and a military measure, it prompted the development of a fleet suitable not only for trade but for war – and thus in 1501, the sale of these vessels to foreigners was forbidden.[38]

The second set of rules enhanced protectionist measures undertaken by trading ports. The laws of Bilbao, from 1489 onwards, made it mandatory for foreign traders to communicate their shipment agreements to the local authorities, which would provide local shippers an opportunity to bid for some of them. These same port officers administered the licensing of moored ships, on whose behalf various fees and damages had to be paid.[39] These regulations were extended when consulates were created. The oldest consulate, in Burgos, obtained in 1494 the royal prerogative of chartering ships for convoys that were

---

36 This rule was applied on 12 and 24 March 1397, to, it is presumed, the Cantabrian coast ports. On 7 February of the following year this same rule was applied in the Archbishopric of Seville. *Memorias de la Real Academia de la Historia* (1917) 144. Nonetheless, local concessions did exist. See, for example, Archivo Municipal de Bilbao, box 1, reg. 2, no. 37: Enrique III confirms a privilege granted by him to the towns of the Lordship of Biscay, which commanded that all trade from those ports had to be on board Biscayan ships (Arévalo, 24 March 1397).

37 Ley 174 de las Pragmáticas, Granada 3 September 1500. García Gallo and Pérez de la Canal (1973).

38 Ley 176 de las Pragmáticas, Granada 11 August 1501. García Gallo and Pérez de la Canal (1973).

39 Archivo Municipal de Bilbao, Box 14, reg. 4, no. 1.

allowed to assemble along the Cantabrian coast – *Marina de Castilla* and the Basque Country.[40] In response, Basque merchants protested and the king stepped in to mediate the dispute and arrange for negotiations.[41] After a prolonged stalemate in the talks, the monarchy resolved the conflict by allowing free shipping, although convoys still had to be formed.[42] Further adjustments followed, leading eventually to the creation of the consulate of Bilbao in 1511. Finally, the lack of regulatory development entailed that contracts were to be followed to the letter.

This dense mesh of relations resulted in complications based on the ownership and use of the ships themselves, especially when possession was divided or transferred. Owners shared the ship and its goods, including shipping benefits and mastery (*maestrazgo*), but were also together subject to many burdens. In any case there was a need for clear demarcations, including the possibility that one owner had preferential rights regarding any possible sale.[43] Transfer of ownership entailed certain obligations, and if these were not met, problems might well ensue.[44] Also, the prohibition on the sale of ships to foreigners, though not always enforced, limited available options.[45] Ownership status was also affected by specific actions taken by the parties involved. There are examples in which a ship was impounded because a shipmaster and the vessel's co-owner had engaged in piracy[46] or, in an analogous instance, because an agreement had been breached.[47]

Indeed, like any other form of property, vessels could be seized.[48] Authorities had the power to requisition ships for purposes of military defence or because royal laws had been broken. In the first case, the embargos were temporary, but the hardship they caused required compensation. Claims made in this regard were sometimes put forth by the very dock men who had moved the freight. A Genoese merchant accused a shipmaster of entering the port of Cadiz without permission, an action that had led to the confiscation of his cargo.[49] Similarly, the merchant guild of Burgos was able to lift the embargo on certain ships in Bilbao and Laredo, where cargo of wool and iron was waiting,

40 Ley 190 de las Pragmáticas: Medina del Campo, 21 July 1494 (García Gallo and Pérez de la Canal 1973).
41 Real Cédula. Madrid, 14 February 1495. Basas Fernández (1994) 157.
42 Real Cédula. Tarazona, 20 September 1495. Basas Fernández (1994) 157.
43 Examples in Lacueva Muñoz (2013) no. 1857 and 2054.
44 AGS, RGS 15 June 1478, f. 20.
45 AGS, RGS, 16 May 1488, f. 201.
46 AGS, Consejo Real de Castilla (CRC), leg. 82, no. 17 (1510).
47 AGS, RGS, 24 November 1478, f. 98.
48 Some examples are provided by Bono Huerta and Unguetti Bono (1986) 38-5, 150.
49 Bono Huerta and Unguetti Bono (1986) 85-25, 247.

because these goods were likely to become severely damaged.[50] At times, the authorities themselves would accept liability, and they even conferred with the shipmasters about compensation with regard to obligations they might have neglected,[51] or else granted them priority in port activities when they returned to trading.[52] Nonetheless, if state policy was contravened, confiscated goods might not be returned.[53]

Mastery rights were buyable,[54] although at times such transactions could be made 'graciously, out of love'.[55] They implied a special kind of trust, in particular when ownership resided with people not directly involved in the trading sector. Nonetheless, there is no lack of complaints regarding rental agreements, usually related to defaults on payment, which would be resolved through the agreement of guarantors.[56] On certain occasions there was fraud in these sorts of disputes. The secretary of the duke of Medina Sidonia, for example, claimed that the caravel captain Sebastián Rodríguez had concealed part of the gold shipment he had brought back from his voyage to the Gold Coast (Mina de Oro).[57] An added dimension here involves the claims made against owners because of the crews' actions, which usually entailed compensatory payment.[58]

Sharing the benefits or losses of a shipment also often generated conflict, if proportions and rights were not respected. Sources of contention included payment of the ship owner's profits and the wages due the crew, as well as the installment payments due the shipbuilder. The contributions of course varied, as did the importance of the claims.[59] Investments could be negotiated, thereby increasing the number of parties involved.[60]

Contracts between shippers and merchants frequently gave rise to disputes. The easiest resolution was to agree to give up the freight. There were usually regulations that attempted to ensure merchants that vessels would carry out

50 AGS, RGS, 13 November 1487, f. 23.

51 AGS, Patronato Real, leg. 52, docs. 49 and 54: Letter from the queen to the king of England requesting that certain shipmasters be protected from any consequences of their tardiness, since their departure had been delayed because of the fleet of the archduchess (1496).

52 AMB, Box 4, reg. 5, no. 212 – Box 18, reg. 1, no. 13: royal insurance to all shipmasters who lost business because their vessels had been loaned to the royal navy being mustered in Bilbao (15 July 1476).

53 AGS, RGS, 18 September 1498, f. 163.

54 Bono Huerta and Unguetti Bono (1986) 43-20, 161.

55 Lacueva Muñoz (2013) no. 2106.

56 An example can be found in Bono Huerta and Unguetti-Bono (1986) 22–24, 125.

57 AGS, RGS, 17 and 20 July 1490, f. 433 and 226.

58 AGS, RGS, 26 May 1480, f. 209; and 16 June 1480, f. 253.

59 The example provided is described in Lacueva Muñoz (2013) no. 2300.

60 See, again, the example in Lacueva Muñoz (2013) no. 3060.

their contracted orders, but when confronted with more favourable destinations or cargoes, shipmasters often breached the contracts, causing merchants great economic harm.[61]

Instances of another important type of claim occurred when merchants accused the captain of fraud – usually known as *baratería* – undertaken with or without the crew's collaboration. Such fraud, though taking many forms, was most obvious when the captain sold cargo for his own profit. But there were also cases when the shipmaster orchestrated an assault of the ship by pirates: Burgos merchants sued Martín Guía of Bilbao, for example, after French pirates raided his ship at Unaflor. What gave the game away was the selective seizure of cloth: only the cloth of the Castilian merchants had been stolen, not what had been freighted by Basques.[62] Suspicions often extended to shippers, particularly when the merchants were reluctant to pay for their services.

Dealings between shipmasters and crew were also often difficult. Shipmasters took umbrage when sailors abandoned their posts before the end of their terms of service, which often entailed additional problems and expense, because wages paid to substitutes had to be added to the money paid out beforehand to absconding crew members. Sailors, too, had their grievances: they sometimes complained that shipmasters had not paid them, despite their contractual obligation to do so.[63] Financing also caused problems, more often than not when insurers delayed payments that had come due.

3 Means Used to Resolve Conflicts

This review of the laws and the types of conflicts they had been enacted to resolve prompts an analysis of how maritime societies dealt with them. The conflicts of maritime trade were usually resolved using the mechanisms available

61 ARChV, Registro de Ejecutorias 84-22: litigation between Juanote de Urdayaga, from Belmonte de Usúrbil, and Lorenzo de Reszusta, master of the ship *Santa María*, who was from Deva. It dealt with the devolution of the 253 ducats which the former paid to hire a ship to Bordeaux and Flanders, a voyage which was never carried out. He also demanded reparations for this lost profit opportunity.

62 AGS, RGS, 16 September 1491, f. 207; 26 September 1491, f. 165, 166 and 167; and 26 November 1491, f. 111.

63 ARChV, RE, Box 211-6: Litigation between Antonio de Esquivel, from Vitoria, and Pedro Sánchez de Aldaba, Juan Ruiz de Liendo and their consorts, all from Laredo and Castro Urdiales. They had been hired to go fishing in Irish waters for a gold florin or its equivalent (20 December 1506). Also Box 199-5: Ramiro de Madariaga, a scribe from San Vicente de Abando, claimed a *castellano* of gold from one Martín de Gorgollo, from Bilbao, because he had not been paid for his service on the voyage that took Princess Juana to Flanders (17 June 1505).

in any Late Medieval controversy, albeit sometimes recurring to authorities exclusively devoted to seafaring matters. Otherwise, economic conflicts were resolved using ordinary courts whenever possible.

Lawsuits were presented before councils, which acted as local courts and made decisions based on the legislation described above. An alternative form of judgement could be made by special appointees sent by maritime institutions and given the power to deal with seafaring matters. This, apparently, happened often in Castilian Andalusia where, despite a lack of evidence, it was well known that the admiral of Seville held jurisdiction over many such matters. The admiralty, especially in Seville, had been growing in power; at times his power was stretched beyond his exclusive competence.[64] Occasionally a lawsuit reached the king himself, as with litigation between the citizens of Palos, Pero Franco and Alonso Gallego on one side, and the pilot Juan de Triana of Puerto de Santa María on the other, which ensued after Triana joined the French pirates who had raided the caravel on which he was serving.[65]

In Seville we also find the oldest examples of another type of maritime justice. After the city was granted its charter in 1250, a neighborhood was created for people involved with trade. This area had its own mayor, who possessed the power to oversee civil and criminal trials. This legal arrangement, necessarily focused on trade-related affairs, was created in response to constant demand. Other seaward cities were endowed with similar royally appointed institutions during the Later Middle Ages.

In the north, the Crown had also established judgeships solely based on maritime issues, although the preferred model there was to use the guilds, relying on an institutional framework which was well established and respected in northern Castile.[66]

Not all conflicts, however, were resolved through the decisions of judges. A parallel mechanism was the notarial protocol, a sub-judicial resource which usually required that both parties recognize the fairness and finality of the arbitration that each needed, ultimately, to accept. These practices were often employed to avoid protracted court procedures.

The Enrique Otte archive is of great value in understanding the maritime world of Lower Andalusia. It contains transcriptions of the notarial protocols of Seville, which have been made by Otte and several collaborators for decades.[67] His records include several mentions of these types of extrajudiciary

64 Aznar Vallejo (2014).

65 AGS, RGS, 1500-V-36. Palos, 25 May 1500. There is an extensive account in González Zalacain (2016).

66 Serna Vallejo (2009–2010).

67 They have been published in part by Lacueva Muñoz (2013).

arrangements for conflict resolution. Although the actual reason for a particular quarrel is not always known, such disputes always refer to some trade business. Ascertaining whether these conflicts concern the sea can be difficult, particularly given Seville's diverse economy.[68] When the litigators are foreign merchants, and the litigation occurs in the port city of Seville, matters pertaining to trade at sea are obviously implied. There are two cases in which the Genoese merchants Antono and Martin de Pinelo sued Diego de Orihuela because of hundreds of *maravedís*. They agreed to appoint as mediators Andrea de Odón, archdeacon of the Queen, and Diego's brother Gonzalo de Orihuela.[69] Trust is inescapably necessary in this type of litigation, since both parties have to agree to accept third-party arbitration. Often these arbiters needed to be socially prominent and well respected figures. It is surprising, but telling, that one of the mediators appointed in the case above was the brother of one of the parties in the dispute. Gonzalo de Orihuela was a person of great social standing, and unerringly trustworthy.

The next example, indeed, underlines this idea of social prestige. Jácome de Sorbanis, a Genoese merchant of Seville, had a legal conflict with Par Mirón Coa, also a Genoese merchant but from Sanlúcar de Barrameda. They agreed to accept the arbitration of two 'discreet and honourable' Genoese men from Seville, Juan Lomelín and Antonio Salvago. Three days of arbitration was agreed upon to resolve a conflict involving some cargo and an unspecified amount of money. As indicated above, such a means of conflict resolution in the world of maritime trade was similar to what was employed in other contexts,[70] albeit with some specific adaptation to the conditions of the merchant trade.

Arbitration was also used when hiring contracts were affected by one of the numerous problems regarding ship hiring described above. Sometimes the problems were not attributable to any of the parties – accidents, piracy – in which case the arbitration sought ways to split the compensation expenses between them. The owners and the merchant of a *cópano* – a small auxiliary vessel – that was stolen by Portuguese, for example, had each to make compensatory payments.[71] The same can be said of the other mechanism used, which is described below.

68 For details see González Zalacain (2016).

69 Lacueva Muñoz (2013) no. 871 and 1126.

70 For the study of the use of sub-judicial mechanisms in Castile, see González Zalacain (2013) 314–333.

71 Agreement between the fisherman Cristóbal Alfón, and Juana Ferrández, both neighbors of Carretería in Seville, with Pedro Ferrández Gaeta, a fisherman from the neighborhood of Triana. The former two men rented a *cópano* from the latter, but it was taken by people from Asilah – modern Morocco, then under Portuguese control. They designated arbiters (12 April 1475). Archivo de Protocolos de Sevilla (APS), Oficio V, leg. 3211 (old 5.5) f. 31r.

This other way of resolving conflict in an out-of-court manner did not really refer to events that had already occurred, but was rather a way of insuring, or establishing the liability, of the local authority, inasmuch as it had to guarantee the safety of the beneficiary. Of this type of broad security we only have certain royal charters as evidence, but it was probably a multi-level reality throughout the Middle Ages.

In the *Registro General del Sello* – the official records registry of Castile – there are more than 2,500 references to insurance and safeguard charters enacted in the last quarter of the fifteenth century. Of these, more than one hundred were granted to foreign merchants.[72] They provide a wealth of information regarding conflicts of the sort that have been discussed in this chapter. For example, in 1489 the kings granted insurance to the ships and merchandise arriving at the port of Moguer; this insurance had been requested by Pedro Portocarrero, the local lord, in compensation for damages caused by the men of the Duke of Medina Sidonia. Two years earlier, ships that had been mustered by Juan Boscan to explore the Mina de Oro in the Gulf of Guinea were provided a special privilege that protected their journey from whatever origin to the mustering site of Palos.

These examples describe situations of potential conflict in the maritime world of Lower Andalusia. At times, the monarchy attempted to right wrongs and impose royal authority but it was not always successful in doing so. Often, government action did not necessarily follow royal policy but rather accorded with judicial rulings, whose authority was not always willingly obeyed.

4 Conclusion

This paper has reviewed the multiple causes and forms taken by litigations involving maritime trade in Late Medieval Castile. The grounds for the various disputes could be prompted by natural or human factors. In this sense, legal conflict with regard to the sea was not too different from what it was in matters taking place on land, albeit the maritime context brought forth different implications. Nonetheless, issues of ownership or claims on payment were normally problematic. How these conflicts were resolved, like the causes behind them, were primarily based on medieval legality in general.

Another example can be found in the acknowledgement of the debt that the fisherman Pedro Ferrández de Gaeta owed María Rodríguez and Cristóbal Alfonso de Villalobos. The arbiters chosen, Diego Gutiérrez and Alfonso Sánchez Negrete, ordered the payment of 1.500 mrs in lieu of the lost *cópano*. It had to be paid by Christmas (decided 15 April 1475) APS, Oficio V, leg. 3211 (old 5.5) f. 35 v.

72 González Zalacain (2013) 66–82.

The existence of certain specific regulations relating to the sea, such as the *Fuero de Layrón*, demonstrates this sector's specific needs and shows how the usual legal mechanisms were not always applicable. The existence of courts geared solely towards the world of sea trade, particularly in places where this economic activity was predominant, bears witness to this demand.

Finally, the solution of legal conflicts outside the ordinary court system was not new to medieval law; arbitration and mediation were also used within the context of sea trade. This variegated system illustrates the complexities of a rich and evolving Castilian maritime world, whose network of laws and jurisdictions would become significantly denser only in the early decades of the sixteenth century. At that time, the growing impact of the colonization of the New World would require a substantial alteration of the network developed in the Later Middle Ages.

Acknowledgements

This paper is a result of the research projects *Solidaridad y/o exclusión en las fronteras marítimas. Castilla en la Baja Edad Media* (HAR 2013-48433-C2-2-P), funded by the Economic & Competitivity Minister of Spain, and *El mar como frontera. Transgresiones legales en el Atlántico bajomedieval* (PGC2018-095719-B-Ioo), funded by the Science, Innovation & Universities Ministry of Spain.

Bibliography

Printed Sources

Cortes de Toledo de 1480, in *Cortes de los antiguos reinos de León y Castilla* vol. IV (Madrid 1861) 151.

Las Siete Partidas del rey Alfonso el Sabio, cotejadas con varios códices antiguos (Madrid, Real Academia de la Historia 1807).

Los Códigos españoles concordados y anotados (Madrid 1872).

Memorias de la Real Academia de la Historia vol. V (Madrid 1917).

Secondary Literature

Aznar Vallejo, E., 'La regulación de los oficios del mar en Andalucía' in J. Solórzano Telechea, M. Bochaca and A. Aguiar Andrade eds., *Gentes de mar en la ciudad atlántica medieval* (Logroño 2012) 95–120.

Aznar Vallejo, E., 'Las rentas del Almirantazgo castellano. Entre la ley y la costumbre', *En la España Medieval* 37 (2014) 131–163.

Basas Fernández, M., *El consulado de Burgos en el siglo XVI* (Burgos 2nd facsimile edition 1994).

Bono Huerta, J. and C. Unguetti-Bono, *Los protocolos sevillanos de la época del Descubrimiento* (Seville 1986).

Egiluz Ortiz de Latierro, F., 'Veinticinco años de fricciones en el comercio marítimo cantábrico (1301–1325)', *Boletín de la Institución Sancho el Sabio* XXII (1978) 89–113.

Erkoreka Gervasi, J., *Análisis histórico-institucional de las cofradías de mareantes del País Vasco* (Vitoria 1991).

Ferrer i Mallol, Mª.T., *Corsarios castellanos y vascos en el Mediterráneo medieval* (Barcelona 2000).

García Gallo, A. and M.A. Pérez de la Canal, *El Libro de la Bulas y Pragmáticas de los Reyes Católicos* (Madrid facsimile edition 1973).

Gilliodts van Severen, L., ed., *Cartulaire de l'ancien consulat d'Espagne à Bruges* (Bruges 1902; 1973).

González Gallego, I., 'El Libro de los Privilegios de la Nación Genovesa', *Historia, Instituciones, Documentos* 1 (1974) 275–358.

González Zalacain, R.J., *La familia en Castilla en la Baja Edad Media: violencia y conflicto* (Madrid 2013).

González Zalacain, R.J., 'Violencia y conflicto en las sociedades portuarias de la baja Andalucía a fines de la Edad Media' in J.A. Solórzano Telechea, B. Arízaga Bolumburu and M. Bochaca eds., *Las sociedades portuarias de la Europa Atlántica en la Edad Media* (Logroño 2016) 365–399.

Lacueva Muñoz, J.J., *Regesto de documentos notariales relativos al comercio sevillano, recopilados por Enrique Otte*, Volume I (1441–1503) (Seville 2013).

Martínez Gijón, J., 'La práctica del fletamento de mercancías con las Indias (siglo XVI)', *Historia, Instituciones, Documentos* 10 (1983) 119–155.

Serna Vallejo, M., *Los Rôles d'Oléron. El 'coutumier' marítimo del Atlántico y del Báltico de época medieval y moderna* (Santander 2004).

Serna Vallejo, M., 'La autonomía jurídica en los mares. Derecho propio, jurisdicciones privilegiadas y autogobierno', *Ius fugit: Revista interdisciplinar de estudios histórico-jurídicos* 16 (2009–2010) 197–218.

Solórzano Telechea, J., 'Las ordenanzas de la Cofradía de Mareantes de San Vicente de la Barquera (1330–1537): un ejemplo temprano de institución para la acción colectiva en la Costa Cantábrica en la Edad Media', *Anuario de Historia del Derecho Español* 81 (2011) 1029–1050.

Suárez Álvarez, Mª.J., 'El "novilísimo gremio" de mareantes de Luarca', *Asturiensia Medievalia* 2 (1975) 239–258.

CHAPTER 6

Maritime Conflicts and Larceny in the Bay of Biscay from the Fourteenth to the Sixteenth Centuries

Ana María Rivera Medina

1 Introduction

With regard to the Middle Ages, the expression *passage d'outre-mer* evokes the particular maritime nature of long-distance transport, involving economic, technical, logistical, tactical and strategic aspects. All such endeavours took place in a notoriously hostile environment.[1] The harsh conditions endured by seamen, especially those engaged in transport and commerce, were coped with in a variety of ways; primarily, through the creation of specific procedures derived from custom, and later the development of a proper regulatory regime, the law of shipmen.[2] Thus, Hispanic maritime law originated in the Mediterranean and the North Atlantic,[3] including the Cantabrian Sea.[4]

In establishing management and control mechanisms, and by the rigid discipline applied in their execution, the legal instruments governing maritime transport focused on the vessel, the cargo, and the crew. However, political instability, war, the fluidity of maritime borders, widespread violence, and plain greed were all potent menaces that struck at the heart of the commercial system of international trade. In response to piracy and larceny, rulers instituted several legal codes to try to curb such informal and shadowy economic activity.

1 Mollat (1967) 345–359.

2 Serna Vallejo (2010) 197–218. The author argues that the autonomy of seamen is embodied at a time of insufficiently consolidated political structures, due to the lack of interest of authorities in maritime issues. The pillars of this autonomous structure are self-regulation and organisation.

3 On sources and bibliography of European commercial law: Pohlmann (1973) 801–834. Among authors who have analysed the Rôles in Spain: Iglesia Ferreirós, *et al.* (1969), 213–316; Iglesia Ferreirós (1986) 219–439, Iglesia Ferreirós (1997)109–142; García Sanz (1992) 289–302. Flores Díaz (1998) 78; Serna Vallejo (2000) 33; Serna Vallejo (2004).

4 Arias Bonet (1968); Gacto (1971); Martínez Gijón (1974); Porras Arboleda (2000) 18. Porras Arboleda (2001) 141. Porras Arboleda (2002); Porras Arboleda (2005) 231.

 | DOI:10.1163/9789004407992_008

In this sense, Biscayan seamen, subjected to the authority of the Castilian Crown, played an ambiguous role. They could be either victimizers or victims, and they could also serve as representatives of authorities who became involved in numerous incidents. These incidents became the focus of profuse legal procedures, records of which are held in national and local archives. Focusing precisely on these instances, this chapter analyses the regulations and methods implemented to grant security to maritime traffic from the fourteenth to the sixteenth centuries. I will attempt here to classify such conflicts through a consideration of the actions of the participants, the interests involved, the reactions of the injured parties, and the responses of the authorities.

More specifically, this classification will focus on extant testimonies regarding larceny in the mercantile routes towards the Northern European markets, highlighting in particular the interactions between Biscayans and the English in the Bay of Biscay and the English Channel, and their counterparts in the Mediterranean region.

2 Terms, Types, and Regulation of Maritime Conflict

Seas became ever more insecure in the period from the Late Middle Ages to the start of the sixteenth century. Traffic increased in both volume and value, and routes expanded. Marauders now had easy, tempting, and reliable prey to target; violence previously carried out in inland commercial circuits now shifted to the seas.[5] Piracy and privateering flourished, depredating the merchants in the English Channel.[6] Effective control of both phenomena became necessary and was developed over the course of the period. Nonetheless, the limits, scope, and implications of the different players involved remain nebulous.

It is known that in the various languages used in the Atlantic ports there existed two terms whose use differentiated piracy from privateering. For the former we encounter *piracy* (from the Greek *peirates*, venture),[7] *piraterie*, *pirataria*,

5 In the Mediterranean, the accumulation of capital in Italy or the Crown of Aragon was based on this type of plunder. These activities, though they disturbed commerce, made cities the places where pirates and privateers could find the necessary funding for their activities or sell their looted goods. Even smaller ports benefitted from piracy and privateering as 'artisanal support industries'. Simbula (1993); Simbula (2000) 369. We find a similar situation described in English sources, relating how wine from La Rochelle seized by pirates was sold in London markets. Tranchant *et al.* (2004) 27–50; Bochaca (2015).

6 Bernard (1968) 772–779. Gilliodts-Van Severen (1904–1906).

7 Piracy: any robbery or other violent action taken for private ends and without authorization by public authority, committed on the seas or in the air outside the normal jurisdiction of any

robeurs, seeräuber, raiders, terms associated with robbery or larceny and the illegal misappropriation of goods by merchants, outside all legal strictures; these words implied the disregarding of life, property, and the provisions of orders and treaties. In contrast, we find *corso* (from the Latin *cursus*, run), *course, corse,* and *privateering*[8] to identify what is, according to M. Mollat,[9] virtually a public service, a form of capitalist activity requiring sanction from the king and subject to regulation. Privateering activities had an official character, providing support in turbulent times and having no other purpose than to attack a declared enemy.

Thus the distinction: whereas the pirate destroys all documents on board a captured vessel, the privateer keeps them as a testimony of his actions. The pirate does not hesitate to murder the crew or to leave them stranded in foreign lands to avert legal action. In contrast, the privateer takes possession of a vessel, its cargo, and its crew and presents its documents upon his return as proof of service. The pirate acts outside the law; the privateer behaves in accord with the political strategies of the polity he serves. These differences may seem well defined, but documentary evidence complicates matters.[10] B. Caunedo del Potro recognizes the figures of transporter-merchant-pirate or mariner-merchant-privateer. The former's actions were criminal, the latter acts of service. Meanwhile, other authors state that Biscayans were not only shippers and merchants but actively engaged in piracy and combined trade, transport, and privateering activities, although the pirate was more a shipper than a merchant. We can, however, glean a third profile, that of the privateer who occasionally adopts the role of pirate.

It is certainly due to this ambiguity that, from the fourteenth century onwards, authorities set out to determine in writing what they could not resolve in practice, attempting to identify the scope of action of the two categories based on Mediterranean legislation. Hence we find licences, safe-conducts,

state. Because piracy has been regarded as an offense against the law of nations, the public vessels of any state have been permitted to seize a pirate ship, to bring it into port, to try the crew (regardless of their nationality or domicile), and, if they are found guilty, to punish them and to confiscate the ship. Encyclopædia Britannica. See also Heebøll-Holm (2013) 13.

8 'Privateering was carried on by all nations from the earliest times until the nineteenth century. Crews were not paid by the commissioning government but were entitled to cruise for their own profit, with crew members receiving portions of the value of any cargo or shipping that they could wrest from the original owners. Frequently, it was impossible to restrain the activities of privateers within the legitimate bounds laid down in their commissions. Thus, it often became difficult to distinguish between privateers, pirates, corsairs'. *Encyclopædia Britannica.*

9 Mollat (1975) 25; Mollat (1980) 743–749.

10 Ferrer Mallol (2006) 255–322; Aznar Vallejo (1997) 407–418; Bello León (1996), 63–97.

letters of marque and reprisal. Officially, piracy became an informal activity (marauding, crime, unlawful profiteering), whilst privateering was portrayed as a formal activity (service, loyalty, lawful profiteering).

The truth is that in towns, villages, and rural settlements, as well as at sea, larceny and petty theft have been and are inherent to the social order. 'The significant change that takes place as regards preceding periods is the creation of cities engaged solely in the practice of perfectly typified privateering',[11] which logically spills over into piracy. The *Partidas* covered theft at sea and, more specifically, on board ships, and transferred responsibility for theft or robbery onto the shipmaster, whether the crime was committed by the members of his crew or himself or was due to negligence or unforeseeable circumstances. They also cautioned against devious shippers who intended to secretly take possession of cargo under the excuse of false wreckage, another modality of piracy.[12]

Hence the Code of Maritime Custom of Barcelona (*Código de las Costumbres Marítimas de Barcelona*) devotes several chapters to theft by a shipmaster and his crew and outlines how to administer justice to anyone guilty of the 'malicious' jettisoning of goods.[13] The code also mentions the threat of pirates in several chapters, describing their actions as a 'hindrance by evil folks'. Included is a description of what can be considered attacks at sea: 'the meeting or chase with privateer or pirate vessels, chasing the merchant ship or detaining it, or forcing it to port, or preventing it from leaving the port by hindering its navigation'.[14]

The Ordinance of Segovia of 1347 devoted a section to legislation on attacks at sea. A year later, the *Cortes* of Alcalá described an increase in commercial traffic with Flanders and France, as well as the growing significance of the Castilian fleet in the Atlantic. The growth in traffic and commerce caused considerable friction with Gascons and the English and resulted in subsequent illegal actions. The *Cortes* deemed it necessary to attempt to curb these attacks. A similar reaction occured in the *Cortes* of León in 1349. At each gathering of the *Cortes* a new aspect of the phenomenon was addressed in legislation. Thus a legal corpus evolved to confront one of the worst scourges of the state and the Castilian economy. In 1351, the *Cortes* of Valladolid, in measures complementary to those of the Ordinances of Alcalá, reckoned that since peace had been reached between Biscayans and the English, forceful measures were

11 Mollat (1980) 743–749.
12 *Partida v, Tit. IX, ley 11; Partida v*, Tít., IX, ley 10.
13 Capmany y de Monpalau (1791) Chap. 66 and 67.
14 Capmany y de Monpalau (1791) 349.

necessary to protect commerce with Flanders.[15] So the *Cortes* of Palencia in 1388 decreed the creation of a body of judges along the coast who would have the mandate to repress piracy in the littoral.[16]

In the fifteenth century, the situation had not significantly changed. Atlantic traffic was still infested with threats, and the Castilian Crown remained committed to establishing even a modicum of stability for its Baltic commerce, the main pillar of its economy. The *Cortes* of Toledo decreed the organization of a commercial fleet with a proper security system. Later, the *Cortes* of Madrigal resolved to reorganize the kingdom's naval structure. These sorts of regulations became more numerous and intense during times of war. Hence, in 1475, on account of the war between Spain and Portugal, a royal decree signed by Fernando the Catholic ordained the seizure of French, Breton, German, and English vessels that were threatening the coasts and supporting the Portuguese, requesting pursuit on the 'sea of my reign and beyond'. Obviously, this order directly involved Biscayan vessels; mariners on those coasts were doubtless prepared and well equipped for the task.[17]

The Basque confraternities were also aware of the need to control the seas. In 1460, the confraternity of Guipúzcoa began regulating the matter. Later, in 1479, the confraternity of the towns and city (Orduña) of the Lordship of Vizcaya joined the fight against piracy.[18] This effort involved their specific statutes – its particular procedural and penal system being based on capital punishment – in the prosecution of a type of crime that in the Late Middle Ages had become an epidemic.

Moreover, in these cases, the heads of confraternities would act *ex officio*; that is, no formal indictment was necessary to initiate the legal proceedings, as expressed in the statutes of the confraternity of the towns and city of the Lordship of Vizcaya of 1479:

> Thus we decree that said magistrates and mayors of the Confraternity have (privative) judicial powers in all places and jurisdictions of said city and towns and that having knowledge of such cases from the said

---

15 Suárez Fernández (1997) 15, 281, 348.

16 Rivera Medina (2006) 117.

17 Ibidem, 118.

18 Hidalgo de Cisneros *et al.* (1986) 85. 'Prymeramente hordenamos que los jueses de la dicha Hermandad ayan juridiçion tan solamente en los casos seguientes […] sobre delitos cometydos en la mar dondequier e en qualquier manera que sea, asy çibilmente commo criminalmente' (Firstly we decree that judges of said *Hermandad* are to have jurisdiction solely in the following cases […] over crimes committed at sea, wherever and and in whatever form, both civil and criminal).

> Confraternity as mentioned above, by means of petitions and appeals from the claimant, and not in any other manner, save on [...] crimes of the sea or committed at sea, which they might gather knowledge of from their occupations.[19]

In 1489, a royal decree against privateering, signed in Valladolid by King Fernando, declares:

> To suppress and punish privateers, (who) infest and rob vessels and persons sailing the seas for trade, with great harm to the service to God, and to the service to our vassals and the state, and to the increase it offers with the practice of trade being diverted by the acts of said pirates, against whom we require be taken criminal action for the crimes they have committed and will commit, condemning them according to their guilt and misconduct, to pay and compensate for robberies, damage and losses of the claimants, and it is ordered that no vessel suspected of piracy be towed into port, even should they claim to bring victuals[20] for the towns; should they enter the port, they are to be arrested promptly and the merchandise and vessel confiscated, the crew detained, and subject to criminal punishment and penalty, and civil liabilities to compensate for robbery, damage, expenses and interests of the victims.[21]

19 'Yten hordenamos que los dichos corregidores e alcaldes de la dicha Hermandad ayan jured:ición en todos los lugares e juridiçiones de la dicha çibdad e villas e que conoscan de los dichos casos de la dicha Hermandad de suso espaçificados (sic), seyendoles pedido e querellado por la parte e non en otra manera, saluo sobre [...] delitos de la mar o cometydos sobre mar, que en esto puedan conosçer de su ofiçio'. Bazán (2006) 82.

20 On occasion pirate vessels entered ports under the pretext of requiring repairs. In this regard, the Lordship of Vizcaya promulgated the *Cuadernos de Hermandad y Fuero Viejo*, 'allowing only those ships requiring repairs carrying letters of marque, counter marque or reprisal to enter the port'. Hidalgo de Cisneros Amestoy *et al.* (1986).

21 'Por reprimir y castigar los corsarios, (que) infestan y roban los navios y personas que navegan por los mares mercantivolmente en grand deservicio de Dios, y nuestro daño, y deservicio de nuestros vasallos y de la cosa pública, la quales augmentada con el exercicio de la mercadería, y se desvía á causa de los dichos piratas, contra los quales queremos que sea procehido assi criminalmente por los delitos que han cometido y cometiesen, castigando aquellos segund sus culpas e deméritos, como civilmente a pagar y satisfacer los robos, males, daños y menoscabos de los dapnificados', y se ordena que ningún a ningún embarcación sospechosa de pirata se le permita atoaje en los puertos, aunque atraquen con el pretexto de traer vituallas para las villas, que en caso de entrar en el puerto se les tomas presto y se requisan las mercancías y el navío, que se aprese a su tripulación a el navío, y que contra ellos se 'criminalmente a debido castigo y punición, y civilmente a

Between the fourteenth and fifteenth centuries we can discern a growing awareness of the need to establish control mechanisms on maritime transport and commerce by various means: definition of the crimes, implementation of privative jurisdiction to deal with these harmful behaviours and protect the good of the 'republic', and the promulgation of ordinances and regulations furthered by local and regional powers and by the Crown. Furthermore, merchant confraternities enacted mutualist measures to contain the losses entailed by risks at sea.

3 Conflicts in the Commercial Sphere

In the power struggle between adjoining continental and insular territories during the fourteenth and fifteenth centuries, the English Channel and the sea lanes connecting Mediterranean and southern European markets with those of the Atlantic north played a leading role as a testing ground. Precisely during this period was there an attempt to stabilize the triangular relationship of England, France, and Castile, the latter being the articulating element between England and France.[22] The backdrop is the last great feudal conflict of the Middle Ages, the Hundred Years' War.

Within this context of war, private initiative retained a leading role as a complement to or substitute for naval fleets in maritime warfare during the Middle Ages. As such, a permanent pool of men and vessels[23] found, for lack of proper charters, a means of income in privateering or piracy. However, this fragile equilibrium was also affected by the Hanseatic League, which fought, legitimately, for the establishment of protectionist measures in an attempt to

---

satisfacción de los robos, daños, gastos e intereses en los dapnificados'. Fernández Duro (1900) Appendix 19.

22 Suárez Fernández (1959). The author analyses the incidence of war and politics in alliances, treaties, and truces directly affecting commercial traffic.

23 This concept of reserves for the defence of the maritime border was carried out in the South Atlantic when Juan de la Cosa was appointed to guard the Channel coast against the infestation of pirates and privateers as a contingency plan regarding the imminent arrival of the Fleet of the Americas. 'Relación de los maravedís que se han dado para gastos de las dos carabelas de que Juan de la Cosa va por Capitán para guarda e amparo de las naos que vienen de las Indias, e fué nueva que había ciertos amados [sic] que diz que hay una que se llama Juan de Granada Vizcaino'. Juan de la Cosa was a navigator, a pilot knowledgeable about the sae, a cartographer and to a certain extent a man of science, in addition to being a shipowner, daring explorer, and at times a captain, pirate hunter, or admiral. Ballesteros (1954) 345–346.

monopolize commercial traffic. Its efforts, eliciting reactions among the powers involved, generated diplomatic conflicts and defensive actions, embroiling mainly the English and the Castilians.

On this geographic, political, economic, and commercial 'canvas', criminals found a breeding ground for their misdeeds, attacking the property of others (limited at sea to ships and their cargo) and causing serious disputes as well as financial and human losses. Pirates were of all nationalities: English, French, Flemish, Genoese, Florentine, Catalan, Castilian. The focus of this chapter concerns the English and the *vizcaínos*, Biscayan or Basque pirates. The latter was also a frontier group to the extent that the country's political boundaries flowed into the town of Bayonne.[24]

The Biscayans were already known as shippers and pirates in the Mediterranean; Pero Paya, Pedro de Larraondo, Juan Garay, and other pirates-privateers were feared in the *Mare Nostrum* for their swift and precise actions. E. Ferreira Priegue attributed the success of their ships in the Mediterranean to two factors: their medium tonnage, which allowed them to be loaded rapidly and admit modest consignments; and the way their runs to the itineraries and ports of call accommodated the requests of the charterer, in contrast to the rigid calendars of Mediterranean merchant shipping.

One should add that in the Mediterranean, communication between ports of call was carried out by cabotage fleets; polities also restricted the number of ports where certain goods, like weapons, could be exported in order to simplify the control of taxes, banned goods, guarantees imposed on naval armaments, etc. Merchants in the Mediterranean were thus subject to a greater amount of political and military control than in the Atlantic.

In considering the Basques' success, one important element to highlight is the economic utility of not having to hire a specialized pilot for voyages to Flanders and England, their principal routes at the time when they began asserting their presence in the Mediterranean. They did sail that sea, however, and in doing so were likely forced to hire pilots possessing knowledge of the routes: negotiating the littoral, seabeds, winds, and currents was not to be left to improvisation.[25]

Likewise, and from the fourteenth century onwards, Biscayans were known in the Atlantic as 'sea vagrants', negotiating charters at various ports and undertaking more or less risky runs, sometimes under the guise of being serious

24 Lamaignère (1865) provides a detailed description of the relationship between pirates from both sides of the border.

25 Ferrer i Mallol (2006) 95–110. Ferrer i Mallol (2001); Ferrer i Mallol (1998) 509–524; Ferreira Priegue (1988) 490.

shippers and sometimes as pirates. They operated from the southern Atlantic to the North Sea,[26] merging Mediterranean port traffic with the 'North routes'. As noted by T. Guiard y Larrauri, the fleet of the Lordship of Vizcaya was

> for a long time as much military as it was mercantile and the belligerent and piratical nature of the locals was encouraged by the harshness of maritime relations during the fifteenth century and the immediate and sustained sequence of war endeavours, to which the mariners contributed, as is well known.[27]

Taken together, the disturbances and incidents caused by Biscayan pirates and robbers were a matter of great concern for the authorities and merchant and mariner associations of England,[28] Portugal,[29] Brittany,[30] France,[31] and Flanders,[32] in addition to institutions involved in the Genoa-Flanders route. Even the renowned 'keepers' of the Channel and the Atlantic, the Hanseatic League,[33] worried about Biscayan pirates. Biscayans could just as easily participate in the siege of Ceuta, serve in the Navy of Vizcaya, enrol as crew members in the voyages of Archduchess Juana,[34] or refashion themselves as sea robbers.

4 Theoretical Foundations and Case Studies

Conflicts that break out at sea are always framed by a real or desired border, allowing us to establish a vertical hierarchy of conflict, which can be supported by a transversal framework defined by its manifestations and the actors involved. Starting with the more intensive conflict, the Hundred Years' War, a second level follows. At this level we find disputes between territories. Finally, there are the conflicts generated within the communities themselves. The public and private sectors, if we may use these terms, are involved in their inception

26 Tranchant (2013) 19–32; Bochaca (2015) 87–99.
27 Guiard y Larrauri (1972) 37.
28 Childs (2003) 55–64; Childs (1995) 351–420; Caunedo del Potro (1984); Caunedo del Potro (1982) 9–54.
29 Barros (2005) 335–369. See also Miranda (2011) 155–175. Viúla de Faria (2010) 109–127.
30 Casado Alonso (1992) 81; Casado Alonso (2000) 29–50; Priotti (1993) 265–283.
31 Tranchant *et al.* (2008) 33–47.
32 Casado Alonso (1994) 177–247.
33 Wubs-Mrozewicz and Jenks (2013); Goris (1925); Czaja (2012) 235–248.
34 Guiard y Larrauri (1906) 452. Labayru y Goicochea (1967) Appendix no. 39; Fernández Duro (1893) 180.

and development, sharing the defence of a strategic cause and an interest in the maintaining of dominion over maritime commerce and commercial routes. This hierarchy of conflict, in turn, inevitably materializes on the borderline during times of war and uncertainty. The English Channel and the Bay of Biscay, in interaction with each other and both being obligatory points of passage along the 'North routes', are geographic elements of integration, fragmentation, and confinement, and in each case is a potent and dynamic no-man's-land.

Participation of the actors involved in the conflict, in the widest sense, derives from the needs and aims of the seats of power. First there are the rulers who, given particular family alliances or treaties, could change the course and purpose of their actions, escalating or attenuating their intensity. Second are the commercial power groups who aired their disagreements over the control of an area or market or the shipping of products. Third, there are the mariners, whose actions, whether formal or informal, generated conflicts that were isolated but exerted an impact on the stability of the commercial system as a whole. Here, precisely, one finds thieves, sea plunderers, and pirates.

In this sense, and referring specifically to informal maritime conflicts, F. Braudel seems to note the existence of a phenomenon derived from urban piracy and having a lower level of intensity that verges on that of petty theft.[35] Thus Braudel provides a vertical hierarchy determined by degrees of operative capacity. Piracy is here regarded as a business endeavour, carried out by men possessing some seafaring skills who are willing to venture out in a poorly fitted boat, hence proving their condition of necessity and poverty; when the opportunity presents itself, they attack similarly humble vessels. This sort of activity represents a sort of low-level piracy, in the sense that it does not impact the economic system but rather proves that violence at sea displayed a pyramidal distribution, deriving from an organized business endeavour and overstepping, certainly, the limits of legality.

Having established a hierarchy of conflict in terms of context and actors, I can expand on this theory and identify another characteristic related explicitly to piracy, treated in this study and defined by three ranks or levels. (1) Conflicts derived from activities of individuals who experience or consider piracy to be their main activity in the context of submerged economies. (2) Those conflicts solely occurring at times of disruption (as with shippers who use legal runs to make opaque profits) and sometimes including the participation of 'entrepreneurs' and other outside individuals. (3) Those occurrences responding to petty opportunism (of a low intensity), pointing up the widespread poverty in port environments. Within this configuration, the representation ranges

35 Braudel (1976) 292.

from associations created *ad hoc* (generally a family set-up) to professional pirates to the astute shipper and, finally, to the individual or individuals who, using poor means, will occasionally attack vessels. The differences among the diverse modalities reside basically in two aspects. On one hand, the continuity of piratical practice over time and, on the other, the armed capacity of the vessel used are key when establishing the capitalistic dimension of these endeavours.

This study's foundational premises follow a retrospective methodology, with analysis of the facts and cases conducted via documents in ports of origin and their complements held in repositories in ports of destination. The data for each has been collated. My main intention in this chapter is to offer a comprehensive vision of the phenomenon based on the analysis of individual cases.

*Case Studie*s

> The Spanish ports in the Bay of Biscay were inhabited by a race of hardy and adventurous seamen, famed for nautical skill and commercial enterprise, and at all times eager to display their hostility to the English mariners, their principal competitors on the ocean. The ships from these ports had formed a large fleet for their common protection, and had sailed up the Channel [...]. Their chief object was to trade with the mercantile cities of Flanders; but on their passage committed many acts of piracy; and when they were threatened with reprisals, boldly claimed the dominion of the seas, and defied the vengeance of those whom they had injured [...]. Edward determined to chastise the insolence of the Spaniards; and unwilling to yield the glory to his captains, took upon himself the command of the fleet. [...] Fourteen of the Spanish ships had been captured [...]. Edward landed in triumph at Winchelsea [...]. The men of Biscay were not dismayed by their loss; but it was soon discovered that the quarrel was equally detrimental to the interests of each party; and a truce for twenty years was concluded at London between the king of England and the maritime cities of the lordship of the king of Castile.[36]

This account reflects the predominant reality throughout the period in the relationship between the Lordship of Vizcaya and England. One finds evidence

36 This peace agreement was signed at 1 August 1351 at the port of Swyne between the Hermandad de las Marismas and Edward III of England after the battle of Winchelsea. Lingard (1819) 77–78.

here of the dispute for dominion over the European Atlantic; the need to sign peace treaties, given the symbiosis of the regional economies involved; the role of the Cinque Ports confederation in the defence of the Atlantic littoral and of English interests; the ongoing activity of Biscayan shippers in the English Channel; and the prevalence of informal activities and piracy that impeded traffic, disrupted trade, and marred relationships between the regions. In fact, the will to pacify the common seas led the English monarch to sign a peace treaty granting the federation of *Hermandad de la Marisma* or *Hermandad de la Marina de Castilla*[37] the freedom to trade in English waters. The English Crown demonstrated, via its individual actions, that peace was a priority for the economies of the region.

Previously, in 1317, Edward II had promulgated an arrest exemption for the shippers of Plencia, Bermeo, Bilbao, Lequeitio, and other Biscayan towns for debts and other offences.[38] In 1324, following a request by a merchant of Bermeo, Edward II granted all mariners, shipmasters of *naos*, and other men of the towns of Bilbao, Bermeo, Lequeitio, Plencia, and Portugalete protection of their transports for one year.[39] This license is but one of many bestowed upon the Biscayans in order to maintain the lines of commerce, which included trade in primary goods such as Basque iron, Castilian wool, and La Rochelle wine transported by Biscayan vessels. The protection of shipping structures under control of Biscayans and Cantabrian shipmasters continued during the reign of Edward III, who, from London or the English continental territories, endeavoured to safeguard the continuity of this traffic.[40]

Evidently, this relationship was sustained despite the pressures of disagreements and wars. However, on occasion the piratical actions of the Biscayans caused clashes with English authorities. In 1337, Castilian ships returning from Flanders attacked English vessels; the seized goods were claimed under English law through the person of the sheriff of Sandwich and the shipmasters and their crew were incarcerated, prompting a formal request for reparation.[41]

From the mid-fourteenth century onwards, English pirates assaulted and plundered Biscayan vessels en route to English and French ports. The incidents described in English sources provide a wealth of interesting information. For example, robbers, described as pirates, assaulted *naos* from the port of Bermeo,

37 Rivera Medina (2006) 117–133; Solórzano Telechea (2009–2010) 47.

38 *Calendar of Patent Rolls* (CPR), Edward II, vol. III, 20 November 1317.

39 Ibidem, Edward II, vol. V. Rochester, 30 September 1324.

40 Ibidem, Edward III, XVI. 1345. Letter of marque for protection of more than 40 vessels on the Cantabrian coast, of which 20% were Biscayan, with predominance by the ports of Bilbao and Portugalete, with 6 vessels.

41 CCR, Edward III, vol. II, 1337.

which had been loaded with wine at the port of La Rochelle. Such incidents took place during the second half of the fourteenth century. In these cases, claims for reparation were made, although sources do not clarify whether the victims actually received compensation.[42]

The increase in piracy occurred in parallel with the growth of merchant navigation. Incidents were more prevalent at specific times of year, corresponding to the chartering of fleets or convoys between May and September. Such timing indicates that the attacks were not random but rather demonstrated a certain degree of planning and intelligence. In this sense, information was vital, and the means of gaining it were varied. It was obtained via messages conveyed by sea or on land, by signals on land, through the use of lights or flags; news was gathered from the crews of other ships or from men on the boats that provided maintenance, going from one ship to the next.[43] At times, tavern chats became a means of intelligence gathering, if a tipsy mariner discussed a ship's route, destination, merchandise, or other information.

In the fifteenth century, there was a marked increase in robberies and assaults. In just the five-year stretch between 1400 and 1405, English pirates ransacked more than ten *naos* from Bilbao, Plencia, and Lequeitio. There was ample occasion for acts of robbery, assault, and the seizure of ships loaded with iron for the English market. It is worth remarking that the places where these incidents took place, preferably at the entry to ports such as Somerset or Portugalete, demonstrate how raiders sought to minimize their risk of losses and secure a worthy booty.[44] During the fifteenth century, in reaction to the pirates' strategies, merchants and authorities gradually imposed commercial instruments and regulations to counteract the increase in criminal maritime activities, or at least to preserve the investments of shipowners and merchants. Thus there emerged maritime insurance, surveillance fleets, and a legal framework articulated around the general average and funding mechanisms for the protection of fleets. Furthermore, licenses, safeguards, and maritime insurance were granted as a means to provide the necessary peace of mind for maritime navigation.

B. Caunedo del Potro has analysed the issuance of individual insurance to foreign merchants, granted by the Catholic Monarchs in the last quarter of the fifteenth century and coinciding with a rampant increase in piracy under cover

42 CPR, Edward III, vol. VII. This is a request for restitution for robbery and assault. The shipmasters – Pedro Martín (Bermeo), Pedro de Rete, and Juan de Mondragón (Bermeo) – are mentioned on three occasions.

43 Barros (2000) 16; Farelo (2013) 193–211.

44 CPR, Henry IV, vol. II.

of the intermittent wars being fought at the time.[45] W. Child has noted that the majority of English safe conducts issued to foreign vessels during the 1450s and 1460s were for Basque ships. This underlines the region's role as a principal provider of maritime transport services for England in general.[46]

In the Mediterranean scenario, the latter years of the fourteenth century and the early years of the fifteenth century, coinciding with a truce (1377–1414) in the Hundred Years' War, facilitated the expansion of privateers into the Mediterranean, where active or latent wars provided favourable conditions for them to act, including convenient bases of refuge and markets in which sell their spoils. Some years were particularly tricky due to the sustained activity of robber-pirates such as Pero Paya (a resident of Lequeitio), Sancho de Butrón (probably a resident of Plencia), or Pedro de Larraondo. Even while acting as shippers, these men all engaged in piracy, privateering, and even the occasional robbery.

Having analysed the English sources relating to Basque pirates, it is therefore possible to establish a hierarchy of larceny in the twofold scenario of mercantile synergies developed during the Late Middle Ages. On a primary level, there is larceny as a form of family business. In the last quarter of the fifteenth century, the more powerful lords of Bilbao, plentifully endowed with titles and fame, joined forces with mayors or the consuls and communal officers of the trading houses, later known as consulates, and struck deals and sealed commercial contracts.[47] Among these actors, the Arbolancha family stands out.[48] One of the town's most influential families, the owners of a stately tower house whose representatives could be found in the town government and in merchant and seamen confraternities, the Arbolanchas were renowned merchants, operating a transport and commercial concern. Juan and Sancho participated in this business, each assuming a very different role.[49] Juan, who appears as owner of the *nao* Santiago, was a legal merchant, engaging in the shipping and trade of local products and the importing of manufactured goods purchased at ports of call. Sancho was a pirate, who in 1484 attacked an English vessel and was accused, with other Biscayans, of robbery and assault. During the legal proceedings, the pirate and his companions were acquitted on the condition that they reinstate the stolen ship and goods to their rightful owner.

45 Caunedo del Potro (1984) 229–235.
46 Childs (1978) 149.
47 Guiard (1906) 482.
48 Guiard (1972) Introduction.
49 Enríquez Fernández *et al.* (1995) 55; Enríquez Fernández *et al.* (1995) 56. Enríquez Fernández *et al.* (1995) 70; García Fernández (1997) 11–40; García Fernández (2005) 282–284. García Fernández (2004); García Fernández (1997) 258.

On a secondary level, there was the practice of larceny as a way of life. In the Atlantic sphere, for example, the *nao* Santa Catalina, returning from England with cloth, tin, leather and other products and carrying a letter of safe conduct, was attacked in 1488 when entering the port of Huelva by La Robada, a *nao* belonging to Martín de Zarauz and Ochoa de Azúa from Bilbao. The attackers, all from the same town, assaulted the vessel:

> they went against them and fired many lombards until they captured the nao and all the merchandise it carried, and they took it to where they chose, and they are going about selling and wasting it in some of those cities and towns and places, and ports, causing great harm and damage; and the perpetrators are deserving of great punishment to their body and their property as transgressors of the safeconduct granted by their natural king, queen and lords. [...] They demand the restitution of the *nao*, the merchandise and the compensation of losses.[50]

In the Mediterranean, Pero Paya illustrates the profile of the shipper-pirate-robber who made this sort of activity central to his way of life. In 1397, a ship loaded with wool sailed from Mallorca to Barcelona. Nearing the island of Dragonera, the vessel was attacked by Pero Paya and endured such violence that part of the planking broke and the ship itself came close to sinking. The pirate seized what he considered most valuable, disregarding the protestations of one victim who, wielding the ship's cartulary, affirmed the cargo belonged to the Catalans and that they were at peace with Castile.[51] Although an isolated incident, this episode reveals, in the light of other sources, that this man faithfully paid the 'Centenario', or one percent of his earnings, to the church of Lequeitio.[52]

At the third level in the hierarchy is larceny as a community activity. This category refers to those vessels who would band together to attack a ship that they believed held valuable cargo. In 1476, Juan Matosin, from Dundee in

---

50 'recudieron contra ellos e les tiraron muchas lonbardas hasta que por fuerça los ouieron de tomar la dicha nao con todas las dichas mercaderias que en ella trayan, e lo lleuaron todo a donde quisieron, e lo andan vendiendo e malvaratando por algunas desas dichas çibdades e villas e lugares e por los puertos dellas, en lo qual ellos han resçibido grand agrauio e daño; e los que lo fisieron diz que mereçen padesçer gran des penas en sus presonas y bienes como quebrantadores de seguro e saluoconduto dado por su rey e reyna e señores naturales'. Piden a restitución de la nao, bienes y daños con su recrecimiento'. Enríquez Fernández (2002) 169.

51 Ferrer Mallol (1998) 509–524.

52 Rivera Medina (2008).

Scotland, accused a group of neighbours from Ondarroa, Lequeitio, Busturia, and Deva of stealing his *nao* and its cargo.[53] This case is particularly striking, as it reveals how under certain circumstances, several *naos* united in order to capitalize on an opportunity to make easy profits. First, it is worth highlighting that the protagonists were inhabitants of maritime towns known for their shipping activities; second, significantly, the actors are here identified by name, surname, filiation, and profession. In addition, among the names we find merchants, shippers, 'honourable men': that is, representatives of the municipal and local powers and oligarchy related to the 'ancients'. This evidence indicates that inhabitants of different towns and territories – who, whether because of need or greed, had transformed their locales temporarily into pirate towns – forged an alliance against a common target. Additionally, the presence of some of these individuals reveals that on occasion the assaults were carried out by skilled seamen, men of commerce who would venture out to sea for the profits to be had from the transporting of goods and who did not hesitate, when they saw fit, to assault other vessels. In sum, one finds here a veritable criminal maritime organization.

The claimant, Juan Matosin, declared that in June 1476, he sailed along the English coast on board his ship *Margarita de Dundi*, 'loaded with irons and cloth from Holland, glassware, pastel, spices, haberdashery, a copper candelabrum, and other goods for a value of 4425 crowns, without engaging in any provocation or harm'.[54] Trusting in the state of alliances between kingdoms, the ship sailed on, unconcerned, but it was attacked by a caravel and its company, shot at 'with gunpowder', assaulted, and boarded by force. Its cargo was robbed. In his claim before the Chancellery of Valladolid, the victim demanded restitution for damages and the court instructed the defendant to comply, under threat of a fine of 10,000 maravedis.

53 Enríquez Fernández (2002) 91. Toledo, 12 de mayo de 1480: 'Martín de Arancibia, San Juan Juan (*sic*) de Vnda, García de Arriola, Ochoa Migueles e Juan de Gorozica, Pedro de Galarza, Juan de Cerala, Domingo, su hermano, Martin Ruiz de Arancibia y Perico de Ytola, todos vecinos de la villa de Ondarroa; Domingo de Zarauz, Martin de Yarza, Juan Ochoa de Ormaegui (barbero), Ferrando, hijo de Iohan Iñiguez de Olea, Iohan Martinez de Licona, hijo de Iohan Martinez de Licona (carpintero), Rodrigo/ de Arteaga, Rodrigo del Puerto, Ferrando de Çereila, Ferrando, hijo de Martin García de Yarza, Machin de Muguertegui, hijo del tonelero, Ochoa de Mutio, vecinos de la villa de Lequeitio; y Juan Migueles de Aguirre, Perucho de Arrasate, (carpintero) morador en anteiglesia de San Pedro de Uscola, Martín Caleza de Deba, calafetero, e (blank), fijo de Martin Ruiz de Aranza, morador en anteyglesia de Ayspe, y Furtuno de Elorrio, vecinos e moradores del Condado de Vizcaya; y Pedro Vizcaya, vecino de Motrico, Juan Bon, vecino de la villa de Deba, San Juan Ferrandez de Zubelzu, vecinos y moradores de la Provincia de Guipúzcoa'.

54 Ibidem.

As proof of his testimony, the claimant explained how he had chased the pirates to the town of Ondarroa, where, to his surprise, he found the plundered candelabrum displayed in the town's church. This is not a minor detail. That the candelabrum was offered to the church confirms that the criminals needed to present the church authorities[55] with a part of the profits from their maritime activities. Also, this act proves how larceny was considered a lesser evil by the inhabitants of the towns – indeed a common enterprise carried out for the good of the town and its inhabitants. In other words, coastal dwellers did not frown upon piracy, engaged in as it was by representatives of various social ranks, impelled by a feeling of impunity and the idea of the common good.[56]

Finally, a fourth level comprises acts of occasional, low-intensity larceny. Estuaries, bays, coves, small ports, and islands provided convenient havens and favourable escape routes for pirates, especially those lacking experience and in possession of relatively few weapons. In 1484, Juan Escribano, an English merchant and Bristol resident, complained of the robbery of wine, sugar, and other goods before the *Corregidor* of Vizcaya:

> loaded in the port of Lisbonne, on a nao freighted in said city, eighty-one tuns of wine and three boxes of sugar, which could weigh ten bushels, more or less, all of which he says he was sending on the said nao with an agent of his to travel with it to the said town of Bristol; and at the port of the town of Muros [...][57]

His agent was kidnapped, and the shipowner was forced to pay 20 doblas in ransom. He claimed to know that the criminal was selling the stolen goods.

5 Conclusion

The increase in commercial traffic in the Late Middle Ages boosted the frequency of actions contrary to established rules in a still nascent maritime legal regime. Larceny emerged as an independent phenomenon. Nonetheless, as

55 Bernard (1968) 470.

56 See also the chapter by Heebøll-Holm in this volume.

57 'quel ovo cargado en la çibdad de Lisbona, en vna nao que en la dicha çibdat fleyto, ochenta e vn toneles de vino e tres caxas de açucar, que podia aver en ellas quinze arrouas, poco mas o menos, e onze sacas de hurzilla, que podian pesar diez quintales, poco mas o menos, todo lo qual el dis que enbiaua en la dicha nao con vn criado suyo que lo leuase y fuese con ello a la dicha villa de Bristol; e questando en el puerto de la villa de Muros'. Enríquez Fernández (2002) 184.

with other activities disruptive to maritime traffic, it is possible to determine a hierarchy dependant on the actors involved. So, based on case studies, one finds the organization of *ad hoc* family businesses, where each member seems to constitute a piece of a puzzle; associations with the sole purpose of participating in larceny as a way of life; and finally, the formation of community associations, where several vessels band together with the purpose of attacking a single ship.

In all cases, different degrees of solidarity were expressed towards the doers of the misdeeds by the representatives of all social levels in maritime communities: the lord, the officer, the merchant, the shipowner, the shipmaster, the artisan, and the priest. This is common in Atlantic and Mediterranean scenarios, and such support helped to partially undermine formal economic channels.

Acknowledgements

Research for this essay was conducted thanks to funding from the project *Solidaridad y/o exclusión en las fronteras marítimas. Castilla en la Baja Edad Media* (*HAR 2013-48433-C2-2-P*) and *The sea as a frontier. Legal transgressions in the Atlantic during the Late Middle Ages* (Ref. PGC2018-095719-B-I00), funded by the Ministry of Economics and Competitivity of Spain. I thank Prisca Toftegaard Habchi for her translation and revision of the text.

Bibliography

Arias Bonet, J.A., 'El derecho marítimo en las Partidas', *Revista de Derecho Mercantil* XLI (1968) 671–676.

Aznar Vallejo, E., 'Corso y piratería en las relaciones entre Castilla y Marruecos en la Baja Edad Media', *En La España Medieval* 20 (1997) 407–418.

Ballesteros, A., *La Marina Cántabra y Juan de la Cosa* (Santander 1954).

Barros, A., 'O Porto contra os corsários (a expedição de 1469)', *Revista da Faculdade de Letras. História*, 3rd series, vol. 1 (2000) 11–27.

Barros, A., 'O grande comércio dos "pequenos actores". Portuenses e Bascos na construção do sistema atlántico', *Revista Internacional de Estudios Vascos* 50 no. 2 (2005) 335–369.

Bazán, I., '"Degollaron a todos los dichos treynta e tres yngleses e asy degollados dis que los lançaron en la mar": Las hermandades vascas y la lucha contra la piratería en la Baja Edad Media', *Itsas Memoria. Revista de Estudios Marítimos del País Vasco* 5 (2006) 69–93.

Bello León, J.M., 'Apuntes para el estudio de la influencia del corso y la piratería exterior de los Reyes Católicos', *Historia. Instituciones. Documentos* 23 (1996) 63–97.

Bernard, J., *Navires et gens de mer à Bordeaux (vers 1400–vers 1550)* (Paris 1968).

Bochaca, M., 'La diplomatie du roi d'Angleterre au secours des intérêts commerciaux bayonnais: la gestion des relations avec les Castillans et les Portugais à la fin du XIIIe siècle' in J.A. Solórzano Telechea, B. Arízaga and L. Sicking eds., *Diplomacia y comercio en la Europa atlántica medieval* (Logroño 2015) 33–44.

Bochaca, M. et al., 'Le contrôle administratif, fiscal et juridique des ports du fond du golfe de Gascogne et de leurs accès fluviomaritimes à la fin du Moyen Âge' in A. Polónia and A.M. Rivera Medina eds., *La gobernanza de los puertos atlánticos, siglos XIV–XXI* (Madrid 2016) 87–99.

Braudel, F., El *Mediterráneo y el mundo mediterráneo en la época de Felipe II*. (Madrid 1976).

Capmany y de Monpalau, A., *Código de las Costumbres Marítimas de Barcelona* (Madrid 1791).

Casado Alonso, H., 'El comercio internacional burgalés en los siglos XV y XVI' in Ballesteros Caballero, F. et al. eds., *Actas del V Centenario del Consulado de Burgos* (Burgos 1994) 177–247.

Casado Alonso, H., 'El papel de las colonias mercantiles castellanas de los Países Bajos en el eje comercial Flandes-Portugal e islas atlánticas, siglos XV–XVI' in J.J. Ruiz Ibáñez, *Las vecindades de las monarquías ibéricas* (Madrid 2013) 355–374.

Caunedo del Potro, B., La *actividad de los mercaderes ingleses en Castilla (1475–1492)* (Madrid 1984).

Caunedo del Potro, B., 'Contribución al estudio del transporte marítimo en el mar Cantábrico', *Anuario Instituto Juan de la Cosa* 4 (1981–1982) 9–54.

Childs, W., *Anglo-Castilian trade in the later middle Ages* (Manchester 1978).

Childs, W., 'Commercial relations between the Basque Provinces and England in the Later Middle Age, c. 1200–c. 1500', *Itsas memoria: Revista de Estudios Marítimos del País Vasco* 4 (2003) 55–64.

Czaja, R., 'The changes of the navigation and the maritime trade in the Baltic Sea in the late medieval period' in J.A. Solórzano Telechea, M. Bochaca and A. Aguiar Andrade eds., *Gentes de mar en la ciudad atlántica medieval* (Logroño 2012) 235–248.

Enríquez Fernández, J. et al., *Archivo General de Simancas. Registro General del Sello. Vizcaya (1480–1482)* (San Sebastián 2002).

Enríquez Fernández, J. et al., *Libro de Autos Judiciales de la Alcaldía (1419–1499)* (San Sebastián 1995).

Enríquez Fernández, J. et al., *Libro de Acuerdos y Decretos Municipales (1463) de la Villa de Bilbao* (San Sebastián 1995).

Enríquez Fernández, J. et al., *Libro de Acuerdos y Decretos Municipales de la Villa de Bilbao (1509–1515)* (San Sebastián 1995).

Enríquez Fernández, J., et al., *Ordenanzas Municipales de la Villa de Bilbao (1477–1520)* (San Sebastián 1995).

Farelo, M., 'La mutualisation des risques et ses effets sur le fonctionnement des gouvernements des villes côtières portugaises au Moyen Âge', *Annales de Bretagne et des Pays de l'Ouest* 120 no. 2 (2013) 193–211.

Ferrer Mallol, M.T., 'Corso y piratería entre mediterráneo y atlántico en la baja edad media' in M. González Jiménez eds., *La península ibérica entre el mediterráneo y el atlántico, siglos XIII–XV* (Cádiz 2006) 255–322.

Ferrer I Mallol, M.T., 'Corsarios vascos en el mediterráneo medieval (siglos XIV–XV)', *Itsas Memoria. Revista de Estudios Marítimos del País Vasco* 5 (2006) 95–110.

Ferrer I Mallol, M.T., *Corsarios castellanos y vascos en el mediterráneo medieval* (Barcelona 2001).

Ferrer I Mallol, M.T., 'Transportistas y corsarios vascos en el mediterráneo medieval: Las aventuras orientales de Pedro de Larraondo (1406–1409)', *Itsas Memoria: Revista De Estudios Marítimos Del País Vasco* 2 (1998) 509–524.

Fernández Duro, C., *La Marina de Castilla desde su origen y pugna con la de Inglaterra hasta la refundición en la Armada Española* (Madrid 1893).

Ferreira Priegue, E., *Galicia en el comercio marítimo medieval* (La Coruña 1988).

Flores Díaz, M., 'Hombres, barcos e intercambios' in *Hombres, barcos e intercambios: El derecho marítimo-mercantil del s. XIII en Castilla y Aragón* (Madrid 1998).

Gacto, E., 'Historia *de la jurisdicción mercantil en España', Anales de la Universidad Hispalense* 11 (1971).

García Fernández, E., 'La cofradía de oficios en el País Vasco durante la Edad Media', *Stvdia Histórica. Historia Medieval* 15 (1997) 11–40.

García Fernández, E., 'Las cofradías de mercaderes, mareantes y pescadores vascas en la Edad Media' in B. Arízaga Bulumburu and J.A. Solórzano Telechea eds., *Ciudades y villas portuarias del Atlántico en la Edad Media, Actas del Seminario de estudios medievales de Nájera* (Logroño 2005) 257–294.

García Sanz, A., 'Cronología de las formas castellanas de los "Roles d'Oleron"' in M.R. Ayerbe Iríbar ed., *Estudios dedicados a la memoria del profesor L.M. Diez de Salazar Fernández* (Bilbao 1992) 289–302.

Goris, J.A., *Étude sur les colonies marchandes méridionales-portugais, espagnols, italiens-à Anvers de 1488 à 1567. Contribution à l'histoire des débrets du capitalisme moderne* (Louvain 1925).

Guiard y Larrauri, T., *Historia de la muy noble y muy leal de la Villa de Bilbao* (Bilbao 1906).

Guiard y Larrauri, T., *Historia del Consulado de Bilbao* (Bilbao 1972).

Gilliodts-Van Severen, L., *Cartulaire de l'ancienne estaple de Bruges. Recueil de documents concernant le commerce intérieur et maritime, les relations internationales et l'histoire économique de cette ville* (Bruges 1904–1906).

Hidalgo de Cisneros Amestoy, C., *Fuentes Jurídicas Medievales del Señorío de Vizcaya. Cuadernos Legales, Capítulos de la Hermandad y Fuero Viejo* (1342–1506) (San Sebastián 1986).

Hidalgo de Cisneros, C., *et al.*, *Colección documental del Archivo General del Señorío de Vizcaya* (San Sebastián 1986).

Heebøll-Holm, T., *Ports, Piracy and Maritime War. Piracy in the English Channel and the Atlantic, c. 1280–c. 1330* (Leiden and Boston 2013).

Iglesia Ferreirós, A. et. al., 'Estudios sobre los orígenes del Derecho Marítimo hispano-mediterráneo', *Anuario de Historia del Derecho Español* XXXIX (1969) 213–316.

Iglesia Ferreirós, A., 'Libro do Consulado da Mar', *Anuario de Historia del Derecho Español (AHDE)* LVI (1986) 219–439.

Iglesia Ferreirós, A., 'El Libro del Consulado de Mar', in Petit, C. de, *Ius Mercatorum al Derecho Mercantil* (Madrid 1997) 109–142.

Labayru y Goicochea, E., *Historia del Señorío de Bizcaya* (Bilbao 1967).

Lamaignère, E., *Los corsarios bayoneses: colección de episodios históricos marítimos* (San Sebastián 1865).

Lingard, J., A *History of England from the first invasion by the romans to the acension of Henry VIII* (London 1819).

Martínez Gijón, J., 'La jurisdicción marítima en Castilla durante la Baja Edad Media', *Les Grandes Escales. Recueil de la Societé Jean Bodin pour l'histoire comparative des institutions*, XXXII (1974) 347–363.

Miranda, F., 'Portugal y las redes mercantiles en la Europa Atlántica a finales de la Edad Media' en Carvajal de la Vega, D. et al. eds., *Redes sociales y económicas en el mundo bajomedieval* (Valladolid 2011) 155–175.

Mollat, M., 'Problèmes maritimes de l'histoire des croisades', *Cahiers de civilisation médiévale* 39–40 (1967) 345–359.

Mollat, M., 'De la piraterie sauvage à la course réglementée (XIVe–XVe siècle)', *Mélanges de l'Ecole française de Rome. Moyen-Age, Temps modernes* 87 no. 1 (1975) 7–25.

Mollat, M., 'Orientaciones para el estudio del corso y la piratería (siglos XIII)', *Anuario de Estudios Medievales* 10 (1980) 743–749.

Mollat, M., 'Essai d'orientation pour l'étude de la guerre de course et la piraterie (XIIIe–XVe siècles)', *Anuario de Estudios Medievales* 10 (1980) 743–749.

Pohlmann, H., 'Die Quellen des Handelsrechts' in H. Coing, *Handbuch der Quellen und Literatur der Generen Europaischen Privatrechtsgeschichte. Mittelalter (1100–1500), Die Gelehrten Rechte und die Gesetzgebung* (München 1973) 801–834.

Porras Arboleda, P.A., 'La práctica mercantil marítima en el Cantábrico Oriental (siglos XV–XIX). Primera parte', *Cuadernos de Historia del Derecho* VII (2000) 13–127.

Porras Arboleda, P.A., 'La práctica mercantil marítima en el Cantábrico Oriental (siglos XV–XIX). Segunda parte', *Cuadernos de Historia del Derecho* VIII (2001) 141–254.

Porras Arboleda, P.A., 'El Derecho Marítimo en el Cantábrico durante la Baja Edad Media: Partidas y Rôles d'Oléron' in B. Arízaga Bulumburu and J.A. Solórzano Telechea, eds., *Ciudades portuarias del Atlántico en la Edad Media* (Nájera 2005) 231–255.

Rivera Medina, A., 'Estado, negocio y corsarismo: Vizcaya desde el Medievo a la Modernidad', *Itsas Memoria. Revista de Estudios Marítimos del País Vasco* 5 (2006) 117–134.

Rivera Medina, A., *Estudio Histórico del Puerto de Lekeitio* (Vitoria-Gasteiz 2008).

Serna Vallejo, M., 'La autonomía jurídica de los ares: derecho propio, jurisdicciones privilegiadas y autogobierno', *Yvs Fugit* 16 (2009–2010) 197–218.

Serna Vallejo, M., 'La historiografía sobre los Róles d'Oléron (siglos XV a XX)', *AHDE* LXX (2000) 471–498.

Serna Vallejo, M., *Los 'Rôles d'Oléron': el 'coutumier' marítimo del Atlántico y del Báltico de época medieval y moderna* (Santander 2004).

Simbula, P., *Corsari e pirati nei mare di Sardegna* (Caglari 1993).

Simbula, P., 'I pericoli del mare: Corsari e pirati nel Mediterráneo basso medievale', in S. Gensini ed., *Viaggiare nel Medioevo* (Pisa 2000).

Suárez Fernández, L., *Navegación y comercio en el Golfo de Vizcaya. Un estudio sobre la política marinera de la Casa de Trastamara* (Madrid 1959).

Solórzano Telechea, J.Á., '"Las Nereidas del Norte": puertos de identidad urbana en la fachada cantábrica entre los siglos XII–XV', *Anales de la Universidad de Alicante. Historia medieval* 16 (2009–2010) 39–61.

Tranchant, M., et al., 'Aspects du commerce franco-castillan à la fin du Moyen Âge : la progression castillane dans le golfe de Gascogne' in J. Ph. Proitti et al., *Le commerce atlantique franco-espagnol. Acteurs, négoces et ports (XVe–XVIIIe siècle)* (Rennes 2008) 33–47.

Tranchant, M., et al., 'Géographie portuarie de la Galice à la Bretagna méridionale à l'aube des Temps Modernes', in A. Fernández et al., *Les ports du golfe de Gascogne de Concarneau à la Corogne (XVe–XXIe siècle)* (Paris 2013) 19–32.

Tranchant, M., et al., 'La violence en mer et dans les ports du golfe de Gascogne à la fin du Moyen Age: bilan et perspectives de recherche' in M. Augeron et al., *La violence et la mer dans l'espace atlantique (XIIe–XIXe siècle)* (Rennes 2004) 27–50.

Viúla de Faria, T. et al., 'Pur bonne alliance et amiste faire: Diplomacia e comércio entre Portugal e Inglaterra n final da Idade Média', *CEM. Cultura, Espaço & Memoria.* Revista do CITCEM 2 (2010) 109–127.

Wubs-Mrozewicz, J. and S. Jenks eds., *The Hanse in Medieval and Early Modern Europe* (Leiden 2013).

CHAPITRE 7

Lutte contre la piraterie et construction de normes partagées entre chrétiens et musulmans en Méditerranée médiévale

Dominique Valérian

1 Introduction

La piraterie est un phénomène ancien et endémique en Méditerranée, mais elle prend une dimension nouvelle avec l'arrivée de l'Islam. La fin de l'empire romain puis byzantin, et plus encore la conquête par les musulmans d'une grande partie des régions côtières de la Méditerranée (notamment au sud et à l'est), font désormais de cette région un espace partagé entre des pouvoirs chrétiens et musulmans multiples. Il n'y a donc plus une domination impériale unique, ni un droit unifié, mais une pluralité d'États qui développent leurs propres normes en matière de droit maritime[1]. Contrairement à la thèse émise par Henri Pirenne, et maintenant largement remise en cause[2], l'unité de la Méditerranée n'est pas brisée et l'arrivée de l'Islam n'empêche pas la navigation et le commerce de se développer à nouveau, après une période de crise aux VIIe et VIIIe siècles[3]: sous l'impulsion principalement des marins et marchands musulmans à partir surtout du IXe siècle, puis des Latins à partir du XIe siècle, la Méditerranée redevient un espace d'échanges intenses[4]. Shelomo D. Goitein a pu ainsi parler, à partir des documents de la Geniza du Caire, de « free-trade community », soulignant les nombreux facteurs d'unité de ce monde méditerranéen, parmi lesquels une certaine communauté de normes en partie héritées de l'époque antique[5]. Il est incontestable en effet que les marchands circulent librement sur une mer où aucune souveraineté exclusive ne s'affirme. A partir du XIe siècle en particulier, le commerce maritime se développe sous l'impulsion des cités Italiennes puis des ports de Provence et de la couronne

---

1 Valérian (2014a) 77–90.

2 Pirenne (2005) et Picard (2005) V–XLV, qui dresse un bilan historiographique du « débat » pirennien.

3 Celle-ci précède l'arrivée de l'Islam en Méditerranée, comme l'ont montré notamment les travaux des archéologues. Hodges, Whitehouse (1983).

4 Picard (2015), Lopez (1974).

5 Goitein (1978) 61; Goitein (1960) 29–42.

 | DOI:10.1163/9789004407992_009

d'Aragon, et on voit de plus en plus de négociants chrétiens latins venir et parfois s'installer pour des périodes plus ou moins longues dans les ports musulmans ou byzantins[6]. Les frontières politiques, mais aussi religieuses, ne sont donc pas un obstacle insurmontable pour ces marchands que les perspectives de profit poussent à voyager parfois très loin de leur patrie. Il n'en demeure pas moins – et c'est une différence fondamentale avec la période de domination romano-byzantine en Méditerranée – que cet espace est aussi le théâtre de conflits violents, non seulement entre chrétiens et musulmans, mais aussi, et sans doute plus encore, entre puissances chrétiennes. Certains visent à la conquête de territoires, mais aussi au contrôle de portions de la mer Méditerranée ou de routes maritimes, notamment par la domination sur les îles et des passages stratégiques.

La guerre n'a jamais empêché le commerce de se déployer, et elle n'est jamais permanente. Elle n'en reste pas moins le cadre général des relations en Méditerranée au Moyen Age. Plus généralement, le recours à la force et à la violence est récurrent, de la part des États mais aussi de pirates qui agissent à titre privé dans un espace maritime où aucune souveraineté ne s'exerce. La Méditerranée est en effet une mer libre, ce qui signifie que chacun est libre de naviguer et de commercer, mais aussi d'attaquer d'autres navires dès lors qu'ils sont considérés comme ennemis, et donc comme des cibles légales. L'élaboration progressive de normes communes, partagées par les différents États, a donc eu d'abord pour but d'encadrer et de réglementer cette violence, à défaut de pouvoir la faire disparaître totalement, de tracer des limites juridiques reconnues entre la violence légale, encadrée par les États et les normes, et celle qui est rejetée dans l'illégalité et à ce titre condamnable et susceptible de poursuites. Dans ce cadre, la question de la piraterie a longtemps été centrale dans les négociations diplomatiques comme dans la réflexion des juristes, menant à la rédaction et à la conclusion de traités de paix, mais aussi des codes de règlementation maritime. Progressivement, dans les derniers siècles du Moyen Âge, se construit donc la notion de piraterie légale, que l'on désigne de plus en plus, et de manière systématique à l'époque moderne, sous le terme de course.

Les historiens se sont interrogés sur la pertinence, pour le Moyen Âge, de cette distinction entre course et piraterie, notamment dans le sillage du XVe Colloque international d'histoire maritime de 1975 consacré à cette question[7]. Michel Mollat en particulier a contesté la possibilité d'une telle distinction juridique : 'Dans la zone atlantique… la distinction entre la course et la piraterie ne paraît guère plus aisée qu'en Méditerranée, du moins jusqu'à la fin du Moyen Age. […] Course et piraterie ne s'insèrent donc pas, de soi, dans les cadres définis d'un

6 Constable (2003).
7 *Course et piraterie* (1975).

type déterminé de l'économie ou d'un mode de relations publiques'[8]. L'absence d'émission de lettres de course officialisant une mission à caractère public interdirait selon lui de parler de course pour cette époque. Les mots de *cursus* ou *cursarius* apparaissent pourtant dès le XIIe siècle dans les sources, mais leur usage est encore indifférencié[9]. Pour autant, au-delà de la question de la terminologie, encore indécise jusqu'à la fin du Moyen Âge, un encadrement étatique de cette pratique, notamment par le prélèvement fiscal, se met bien en place et permet de distinguer course et piraterie. C'est le cas par exemple dans le contexte de la couronne d'Aragon, dès le XIIe siècle et plus encore à partir du XIVe siècle, où l'on voit la délivrance de licences de courses très formalisées, délimitant notamment les zones et les cibles autorisées[10]. Il est donc incontestable que les contemporains avaient une claire conscience de la frontière qui séparait la rapine de la prise légale, de bonne guerre. C'est ce qui apparaît sans ambiguïté dans les procès consécutifs à des actes de piraterie, qui visent à établir la culpabilité des accusés, ou dans les enquêtes destinées à déterminer si des captifs sont des prises de bonne guerre et peuvent être à ce titre vendus, ou s'ils doivent être libérés car leur prise est contraire au droit. Les arguments apportés par les parties concernées, comme les questions posées par les magistrats, montrent bien des limites juridiques reconnues permettant d'appuyer une décision judiciaire. Que l'activité légale soit encadrée ou non par des documents tels que des licences de course, on relève un effort des États pour réglementer la violence sur mer, au moins pour ce qui concerne leurs propres ressortissants. Pour autant, peut-on déceler une production de normes communes, partagées par les différentes puissances de Méditerranée, et en particulier entre les mondes chrétiens et musulmans, dont les traditions juridiques sont a priori totalement différentes ?

2 Une « loi internationale » de la mer ?

La régulation de la violence sur mer suppose en effet que les États puissent s'entendre sur des principes juridiques communs, voire sur des normes partagées et applicables dans un espace maritime sur lequel ne s'exerce aucune souveraineté internationalement reconnue. Le problème est dès lors de faire émerger un certain consensus sur la définition de ce qui est autorisé, légal, et de ce qui ne l'est pas, et donc de parvenir à une convergence des normes, au-delà des différences dans les codes de lois dans les différents pays. La question de l'existence d'un droit international de la mer a été posée, notamment par

8 Mollat (1975) 7.
9 Ibidem.
10 López Pérez (1995) 579–644.

Hassan S. Khalilieh qui parle de « loi maritime internationale », mais sans véritablement démontrer qu'elle existe à cette époque en Méditerranée[11]. Il est possible de comparer les corpus juridiques traitant des affaires maritimes, qui existent aussi bien à Byzance que dans les mondes musulmans ou latins, et montrent en effet des similitudes dans le traitement de certaines questions liées à la navigation ou au droit commercial[12]. Les plus importants sont le *Nomos Rhodion Nautikos*, collection de lois maritimes byzantines codifiées entre 600 et 800[13], le *Kitāb Akriyat al-Sufun*, traité de droit musulman attribué au juriste malikite Muḥammad b. ʿUmar (m. 310/923)[14], ou la monumentale compilation du *Consulat de mer*, rédigée entre le XIIe et le XIVe siècle en contexte catalan mais largement diffusée dans le monde latin[15]. Il faudrait y ajouter des codes propres à certaines cités, notamment italiennes, comme le *Breve Curiae Maris* et le *Breve dell'Ordine del Mare* de Pise (fin XIIIe–XIVe siècle) ou encore les *Statuts* de Marseille (XIIIe siècle)[16].

Pour autant, il est difficile de parler pour cette époque d'un droit international, avec un code unique qui serait reconnu par tous les États riverains de la Méditerranée. Les codes de lois maritimes promulgués le sont à l'usage des sujets du souverain ou des citoyens de la cité. Seul le *Livre du consulat de mer* peut éventuellement faire exception, en raison de sa très large diffusion, mais ses règles ne sauraient de toute manière s'appliquer aux musulmans ou aux sujets byzantins. On relève certes des similitudes entre ces différents codes, dues à la fois à un certain nombre de problèmes partagés liés à la navigation (naufrages, locations de navires, responsabilité des marins et des capitaines de navires, etc.) et à un héritage commun des corpus de droits anciens. Pour Byzance ou le monde latin cet héritage est assumé par les juristes, mais il est manifeste également dans le droit musulman, qui s'inspire notamment de la législation byzantine préexistante[17]. Pour les pays musulmans, la présence de populations côtières habituées au droit byzantin, en Orient mais aussi dans une certaine mesure au Maghreb où le *Digeste* de Justinien avait été diffusé, contribue à influencer les juristes musulmans lorsqu'ils doivent élaborer une législation pour régler les problèmes liés à la navigation. On retrouve alors des

11 Khalilieh (1998), chapter 5, 'Territorial waters, the freedom of the seas and maritime international law'.

12 La date de rédaction de ces codes montre que leur mise par écrit correspond toujours à des périodes de fort développement de l'activité maritime et de puissance navale.

13 Ashburner (1909).

14 *Kitāb akriyat al-sufun* (1983 et 2006).

15 Jados (1975).

16 Bonaini (1857) ; Pernoud (1935).

17 Voir, en particulier, Khalilieh (2006).

éléments existant dans le droit byzantin, en partie adaptés aux exigences de la *Sharīʿa*, mais aussi développés sur certains points. Les affaires maritimes étant absentes des sources du droit musulman (Coran et *Ḥadīth*), c'est principalement à travers un raisonnement par analogie (*qiyās*) avec les problèmes liés au transport terrestre que les juristes élaborèrent une législation propre à la navigation[18]. De même, la comparaison entre le droit byzantin et les codes élaborés dans le monde latin, notamment le *Consulat de Mer*, montre que nombre de principes du *Digeste* et de la *Loi rhodienne* se retrouvent à partir du XIe siècle en Occident, où l'on sait que ces deux textes étaient lus. Le cas du délestage des navires en cas de tempête, étudié par Olivia R. Constable et Hassan S. Khalilieh[19], montre ces points de convergence entre droits maritimes byzantins, musulmans et latins : seule une menace imminente justifie de jeter par-dessus bord une partie de la cargaison, il doit y avoir une juste répartition des pertes entre les marchands et la décision doit se faire d'un commun accord. Mais on relève également de nombreuses divergences de détail, par exemple sur l'inclusion ou l'exclusion, dans l'évaluation des pertes des effets personnels, du bateau et des salaires de l'équipage, sur l'estimation de la valeur des biens perdus ou sur les marchandises humaines. Dès lors peut-on vraiment parler, comme le fait Hassan S. Khalilieh, d'une « internationalisation de la loi de la mer » ? Les ressemblances que l'on peut constater sont d'abord liées à la similitude des situations sur lesquelles les juristes doivent se pencher et à des principes généraux communs, comme le droit de propriété. Il est vraisemblable qu'elles sont dues aussi à un héritage de traditions juridiques, notamment romaines et byzantines, ainsi qu'à des phénomènes d'emprunts facilités par la grande circulation des hommes et des idées. Pour autant les différences observées sont nombreuses, non seulement entre droits byzantins, musulmans et latins, mais aussi entre les écoles juridiques (*madhhab*) de l'islam ou entre les différentes nations marchandes de l'Europe latine, montrant des spécificités régionales qui, si elles portent souvent sur des points de détail, n'en sont pas moins réelles. Olivia R. Constable reconnaît finalement que

> the differences of opinion in medieval maritime law codes concerning jettison and general average, despite their underlying similarities, make it difficult to trace a clear line of connection between them[20].

---

18 Ibidem, 252.

19 Constable (1994) 207–220 (comparaison entre les droits byzantins et latins principalement, mais aussi avec la législation musulmane et juive); Khalilieh (2006) 150–194 (comparaison entre la *Loi rhodienne* et le *Kitāb akriyat al-sufun*).

20 Constable (1994) 220.

Surtout, aucune de ces lois ne fait autorité pour l'ensemble de la Méditerranée et on ne décèle pas de volonté d'uniformiser ces législations ni d'en imposer une particulière au détriment des autres. Elles n'abordent pas, en particulier, les problèmes qui pourraient surgir mettant en jeu des acteurs relevant de législations différentes. Qu'en était-il par exemple des biens d'un marchand musulman se trouvant à bord d'un navire catalan en cas de tempête ? On peut supposer que ce sont les dispositions du *Consulat de mer* qui s'appliquent pour tous à bord du navire, à moins que n'ait prévalu le principe de personnalité des lois. Mais les traités de droit, comme la jurisprudence, n'abordent pas la question – ce qui peut laisser supposer qu'elle ne posait pas vraiment de problème. L'application d'une loi particulière a pu se produire dans certains cas d'espace maritimes plus étroitement contrôlés par un pouvoir – ce qu'on appellerait aujourd'hui des « eaux territoriales ». Si aucune domination impériale ne s'exerce sur la Méditerranée, il a pu exister en effet des formes de revendication de souveraineté sur des portions limitées de mer. Il est plus ou moins admis que jusqu'à une distance donnée du rivage, une certaine souveraineté s'exerce, notamment pour des raisons de protection des côtes[21]. Ainsi, les traités de paix contiennent parfois une clause faisant obligation au souverain musulman d'assurer la sécurité des marchands sur terre *et* sur mer, ce qui suppose une forme de contrôle, au moins théorique, mais sans que soit précisée l'étendue spatiale de cette protection en mer[22]. De même certains États ont tenté d'imposer une souveraineté sur des portions de mers qu'ils pouvaient contrôler militairement – mais sans que cette domination ne soit reconnue par les autres États. C'est le cas par exemple de Venise dans l'Adriatique, mais aussi de la *taifa* de Denia, entre la côte orientale d'al-Andalus et la Sardaigne au XIe siècle[23]. D'une manière plus générale, ce droit maritime ne s'applique donc qu'aux navires et marchands d'un État donné et n'aborde pas les aspects internationaux, c'est-à-dire les relations entre acteurs de nations différentes, et on ne peut donc pas parler encore pour cette époque de droit international de la mer[24].

21 Khalilieh (1998) 138–141.

22 Voir, par exemple, le traité entre Venise et les Hafsides de Tunis en 1231 : …*ut genus Veneticorum sit salvum quando pervenerit in regnum Barbarie, hoc est Barbarem, et securitatem <habeat> tam in terra quam in mare, in rebus et personis, secundum quod consuetum est consuetudinis pacis.* Girardi (2006) 15.

23 Doumerc (2013) ; Travis Bruce (2010).

24 C'est la conclusion à laquelle arrive également Jean-Marie Moeglin dans le cadres des relations internationales dans l'Europe chrétienne médiévale. Moeglin et Péquignot (2017) 749 : 'Le droit international comme ensemble de règles et normes reconnues par tous et régissant les relations entre peuples et États est très largement resté au Moyen Âge une chimère que les références occasionnelles au *jus gentium* ne faisait que conjurer'.

3 Un discours sur la guerre reposant sur une opposition religieuse irréductible

Cette absence de cadre juridique internationalement reconnu n'a cependant pas empêché le développement des relations commerciales et le déplacement des marchands à l'étranger, et notamment en terre d'Islam. Les transactions économiques entre marchands étaient réglées de manière souple, grâce à la relative proximité des droits commerciaux et la reconnaissance réciproque des actes écrits, sans que l'on en perçoive toujours les modalités précises car les pratiques et coutumes n'ont guère été formalisées juridiquement[25]. De même les litiges et conflits mettant en cause des étrangers sont peu à peu encadrés, notamment par les traités de paix[26]. La régulation de la violence pirate pose cependant des problèmes plus complexes, car elle croise des considérations stratégiques, idéologiques, religieuses, autant qu'elle frappe les esprits et provoque des réactions collectives mettant en jeu l'opposition entre deux religions à prétention universelle qui entendent étendre leur hégémonie sur la Méditerranée. Elle est étroitement liée aux normes sur la guerre et la paix, et donc dans le cadre des relations entre chrétiens et musulmans à un discours de différenciation religieuse. Les textes, et notamment les chroniques, établissent ainsi une distinction claire entre fidèles et infidèles, et la piraterie est présentée comme une des manifestations de la guerre sainte, d'un côté comme de l'autre[27]. Dans les textes musulmans par exemple elle est, dès les premiers siècles de l'Islam, une des modalités de l'expédition annuelle que le calife ou son représentant a le devoir de mener au-delà des frontières pour accomplir le devoir de djihad de la communauté musulmane[28]. Au XIVe siècle encore, alors que la piraterie connaît une recrudescence importante sur les côtes du Maghreb, le chroniqueur Ibn Khaldūn décrit cette activité dans le port de Bougie, qualifiant les pirates de *ghuzāt al-baḥr*, et il désigne les chrétiens comme infidèles ou mécréants (*kufarā'*), ce qui renvoie dans les deux cas au lexique du djihad[29].

Le droit musulman concernant la paix repose également sur une distinction religieuse fondamentale, considérant que la guerre n'est légale que contre les pays non-musulmans, désignés de manière significative comme *Dār al-ḥarb* (territoire de la guerre, par opposition au *Dār al-Islām*). Les juristes construisent

25 Valérian (2009).
26 Valérian (2003).
27 Valérian (2014b).
28 Picard (2015) 93–98.
29 Ibn Khaldūn (2000) VI, 578, trad. III, 116.

alors une législation qui repose sur l'idée que l'islam, religion universelle, a vocation à s'étendre à l'ensemble du monde et qui considère que la paix est donc impossible. Seules des trêves de durée limitée sont admises, avec une typologie s'inspirant de l'exemple du prophète Muhammad et dépendant du rapport de forces entre les musulmans et leurs ennemis. En cas d'impossibilité de poursuivre les combats, il est ainsi admis de signer une trêve, pour une durée n'excédant pas en général dix ans (conformément à l'accord passé par Muhammad avec les Mekkois)[30]. Hors de ces périodes de trêve les États sont donc *de facto* en guerre, et la piraterie est légale.

4 La primauté des traités bilatéraux

Cette définition juridique de la guerre et de la paix, reposant sur des logiques religieuses, ne peut cependant pas servir à l'évidence de base à une norme commune entre chrétiens et musulmans. Si elle reste un cadre général dont il faut tenir compte pour ne pas heurter trop frontalement les élites religieuses, elle s'accommode dans la pratique d'une interprétation souple permettant des relations diplomatiques entre États, et la signature de traités bilatéraux qui obéissent à une logique purement politique et non pas confessionnelle. Dans le contexte multiculturel qui caractérise les ports méditerranéens au Moyen Age, c'est en effet souvent la nécessité de faciliter les affaires et les échanges qui a primé, permettant de s'accommoder, voire de contourner une norme générale parfois trop contraignante. En l'absence d'un droit international de la mer ce sont donc ces accords bilatéraux qui régissent les relations entre États en Méditerranée. De manière significative, lorsque dans la correspondance diplomatique apparaît une plainte, c'est à ces accords qu'il est fait référence, et non pas aux textes généraux de droit ou aux règlements maritimes des cités ou des royaumes. C'est donc à travers ces traités, de plus en plus détaillés au fur et à mesure que l'on avance dans le Moyen Age, que l'on peut voir émerger progressivement un certain nombre de règles régissant les relations en Méditerranée, qui pour certaines débordent du cadre des relations bilatérales pour apparaître comme des normes communes à l'ensemble de la région.

La chronologie de la construction de ces normes est cependant difficile à établir, car si certains problèmes ont trouvé une réponse formalisée dans le cadre des traités bilatéraux signés entre puissances, d'autres semblent s'être réglés de manière plus informelle, par une coutume restée non-écrite, au

---

30 Sur la législation musulmane sur la guerre et la paix, voir principalement Khadduri (1955).

moins dans un premier temps[31]. La correspondance diplomatique, qui montre non seulement les entorses à ces règles, mais aussi d'autres coutumes, non écrites, permet parfois de compléter les textes normatifs par l'analyse des pratiques visant à réguler les échanges et la violence sur mer, lesquelles ont dû connaître des phases d'expérimentation et de tâtonnements avant d'aboutir à des accords diplomatiques. Ce que l'historien peut bien suivre en revanche, est la mise par écrit et la diffusion de ces normes à l'ensemble de la Méditerranée. Ces traités montrent en tout cas le développement progressif de règles régissant les relations internationales, et plus précisément la sécurité des mers et le statut des étrangers. Ils permettent de comprendre sur quels principes juridiques partagés ils s'appuient et notamment la distinction, reconnue internationalement, entre course et piraterie.

À partir de la fin du XIe siècle, c'est-à-dire au moment où commence l'expansion maritime de l'Occident latin, on voit se multiplier les accords diplomatiques entre puissances chrétiennes européennes, mais aussi entre ces dernières et les pouvoirs musulmans ou Byzance. Les premiers ne sont connus que par des mentions qui en sont faites dans les chroniques, ou dans la correspondance diplomatique, et il est difficile d'en connaître avec précision le contenu et la forme. Peu à peu cependant ils sont mieux conservés, et leur longueur croissante montre la codification progressive et de plus en plus précise des règles régissant les relations entre puissances afin de répondre aux problèmes et conflits qui pouvaient survenir, sur mer comme dans les ports ou sur les côtes. Au début relativement sommaires, ils deviennent donc avec le temps de plus en plus précis, multipliant les clauses qui, pour certaines, sont liées à un problème ponctuel et conjoncturel, mais qui pour d'autres apparaissent comme des normes plus durables, que l'on retrouve répétées de traité en traité.

En apparence, ces accords maintiennent dans leur forme la fiction d'empires hégémoniques qui imposent leur domination en Méditerranée: dans le cas de Byzance ce sont des chrysobulles, présentés comme des privilèges concédés par l'empereur[32], et les traités signés avec les souverains musulmans se font dans le cadre d'une législation élaborée et fixée en grande partie au IXe siècle, dans un contexte de puissance de l'Islam, qui n'accepte des trêves que dans la mesure où celles-ci permettent d'espérer une reprise rapide de la guerre

31 Certaines règles ne furent cependant jamais formalisées dans des textes, comme par exemple pour les modalités d'associations commerciales entre chrétiens et musulmans. Les documents de la pratique, et la rareté des différents portés devant la justice, nous montrent qu'elles fonctionnaient bien, mais sans que l'on sache avec précision quelles normes étaient en vigueur.

32 Voir par exemple, pour les traités vénitiens, Pozza, Ravegnani (1993).

et de l'expansion[33]. Dans les faits cependant, il s'agit bien d'accords bilatéraux entre puissances, qui résultent des équilibres de puissances dans une Méditerranée désormais partagée et qui poussent à une adaptation du droit. Pour autant, si ces accords sont bilatéraux et dépendent d'un rapport de force variable entre les États contractants[34], on constate aussi que certaines normes se retrouvent dans d'autres contextes diplomatiques, signe de l'émergence de règles générales applicables à l'ensemble des relations internationales en Méditerranée, du moins en temps de paix. Celles-ci s'affranchissent alors en partie des normes appliquées dans tel ou tel État, en laissant en particulier de côté les distinctions confessionnelles qui en sont parfois le fondement, que ce soit dans le droit canonique chrétien ou dans le *fiqh* musulman. Ces textes deviennent alors la base des relations politiques en Méditerranée, définissant et codifiant la limite entre un état de paix (ou de trêve), régi par des règles communes, et un état de guerre, où tout est permis.

Ces règles ont donc d'abord et avant tout pour but de réprimer ou au moins d'encadrer la violence. Le principe de base, posé dès les premiers accords, est la sécurité garantie aux navires et aux marchands, dans les pays qui les accueillent mais aussi sur mer. Concrètement, ces clauses visent à interdire en temps de paix la violence privée, principalement la piraterie en mer mais aussi le droit de naufrage et plus globalement tout acte contraire à la sécurité des biens et des personnes dans les ports.

5 Lutte contre la piraterie et définition de la violence légale

C'est donc dans le cadre de ces accords de paix seulement que l'on peut parler de liberté de commerce et de navigation en Méditerranée – pour les relations entre chrétiens et musulmans au moins[35], hors des périodes couvertes par les traités, la piraterie est légale et rien, sauf la force, ne peut s'y opposer. Tout bateau ennemi peut alors légalement être attaqué et pillé, de même que les côtes d'un pays en guerre, et les personnes prises peuvent être emmenées en captivité

33 Khadduri (1955) 202–222.

34 C'est le cas notamment dans le domaine fiscal, les taxes portuaires et les exemptions pouvant varier selon les rapports de forces.

35 Entre puissances chrétiennes l'état naturel des relations est la paix, rompue par les activités de guerre, alors qu'à l'inverse entre chrétiens et musulmans la guerre est l'état normal des relations, interrompue par des trêves. Les licences de course délivrées dans les pays de la couronne d'Aragon autorisent ainsi la course contre les seuls bateaux chrétiens des pays en guerre avec la couronne, et contre tous les bateaux musulmans à l'exception de ceux des sultans en paix avec le roi d'Aragon. López Pérez (1995) 587.

et vendues. Le *Livre du Consulat de Mer* reconnaît cette pratique comme légale et prévoit ainsi:

> Si un bateau marchand est sur le point d'être intercepté par un navire ennemi, et qu'il y a à bord un ou plusieurs marchands, le patron doit leur demander s'ils souhaitent qu'il attaque et capture le navire ennemi. Si un marchand ou tous les marchands ou la majorité d'entre eux exprime son approbation à cette proposition, le patron peut procéder à l'attaque[36].

Cette distinction entre navires amis et ennemis est fondamentale, et permet notamment de définir la notion de « prise de bonne guerre » par les pirates[37]. C'est sur ce point que reposent de nombreuses plaintes visibles dans la correspondance diplomatique, avec deux points litigieux particulièrement discutés. Le premier porte sur la date de l'attaque par rapport à l'entrée en vigueur de la paix, mais il est en général facile à régler. En 1314, après la paix signée entre les Hafsides et la couronne d'Aragon, une correspondance est échangée entre les deux souverains à propos de la libération de captifs et la question qui est posée à chaque fois porte sur la date des faits, avant ou après la signature de la trêve[38]. Le deuxième concerne la question plus délicate de la nationalité des victimes et des pirates. À une époque où l'identité des personnes n'est pas toujours facile à déterminer, et avec des populations souvent mobiles dont les allégeances politiques peuvent être mouvantes, ce problème donne lieu à de nombreuses contestations, mais aussi à des manipulations de la part des pirates, non sans une certaine mauvaise fois parfois. En 1324 un certain Ibn Jundî, qui avait vendu des sujets du roi d'Aragon Jacques II, est soupçonné par ce dernier d'être originaire de Grenade, sultanat avec lequel un traité était en vigueur, mais le sultan répond que le pirate n'est pas son sujet et n'est donc pas concerné par le traité[39]. À l'inverse en 1304 le corsaire valencien Pere Ribalta, ayant capturé des sujets du sultan hafside malgré une trêve entre Tunis et le royaume d'Aragon, força les captifs à se déclarer originaires de Bougie, car il n'existait pas alors de trêve avec cette ville, en leur proposant une difficile alternative : s'ils acceptaient cette proposition, il s'engageait à les vendre comme esclaves à Pantelleria, île proche de Tunis où ils pourraient facilement se faire racheter ; s'ils refusaient en

36 Jados (1975) § 288.

37 À Valence au début du XVe siècle les captifs musulmans doivent être présentés devant le Bailli général qui les interroge pour vérifier la légalité de leur prise, et à l'issue de la procédure ils sont déclarés « de bona guerra ». Hinojosa Montalvo (1971).

38 Alarcón y Santón, García de Linares (1940), 288–290 (18 *jumadā* II 714 / 29 septembre 1314). Voir aussi Ibidem, 290–294 (26 *dhū l-qaʿda* 715 / 21 février 1316).

39 Ibidem, 47–49 (29 *dhū l-ḥijja* 724 / 17 décembre 1324).

revanche, il les vendrait en Romanie, d'où ils ne pourraient jamais revenir chez eux. Les captifs acceptèrent et furent donc vendus à Pantelleria. Mais Barthomeu de Malta, marchand de Messine monté à bord pour les acheter reconnut l'un d'entre eux, le patron du bateau capturé, qu'il avait vu lors d'un précédent voyage à Tunis, et il fallut libérer les prisonniers[40].

Ces discussions autour d'actes de piraterie, qui alimentent largement la correspondance diplomatique, montrent l'habileté des pirates à tirer profit des limites parfois floues de souveraineté. Mais les efforts des coupables pour prouver leur bon droit montrent surtout que, dans l'esprit des souverains comme de leurs sujets, il existait bien une frontière claire entre une violence légale contre des ennemis et des actions répréhensibles dans le cadre des accords de paix. Dès lors, la principale difficulté à laquelle ont dû faire face les souverains a été de définir des modalités de résolution des conflits et de condamnation des contrevenants afin d'éviter qu'une action isolée de piraterie n'entraîne une rupture de la paix. L'enjeu en effet n'est pas d'ordre moral, reposant sur une condamnation de principe de la piraterie qui n'existe pas à cette époque, mais bien pratique : tous les efforts, aussi bien par la diplomatie que par la construction progressive de normes, visent à éviter avant tout le cycle incontrôlable des représailles, sur mer et surtout dans les ports contre les ressortissants de la nation à laquelle est supposé appartenir le pirate, facteur de rupture de la paix et de perturbation des échanges. Il s'agit donc avant tout de trouver des solutions pour punir les seuls coupables en renonçant autant que possible au principe de responsabilité collective.

C'est sur ce point, plus que dans la définition de la paix ou de la guerre, que l'on assiste, au cours des derniers siècles du Moyen Âge, à une codification progressive, et de plus en plus précise, des pratiques et des procédures. Celles-ci apparaissent à la fois dans les traités de paix négociés par les ambassadeurs, mais aussi dans la législation des États et des cités maritimes. Elles semblent s'appuyer moins sur une réflexion juridique théorique ou des principes religieux – la question de la confession des coupables n'est jamais prise en considération – que sur une résolution pragmatique des situations de conflits. Dans les ports, la question de la résolution des conflits est assez vite réglée dans les traités de paix, car il existe des autorités, à la fois sultaniennes et consulaires, entre lesquelles les domaines de compétence judiciaire sont progressivement fixés[41]. Le principe général est que l'affaire est jugée par l'autorité dont relève l'accusé – souvent le consul pour les chrétiens, et le cadi pour les musulmans.

---

40 Archivo de la corona de Aragón, *Cartas Reales Diplomaticas, Jaime* II, *caja* 21, no. 4160 (26 juillet 1304).

41 Valérian (2003).

Ce choix, qui vise sans doute à écarter tout soupçon de partialité qui pourrait déboucher sur un cycle de représailles dommageable au maintien de relations de paix, se retrouve également pour les affaires de piraterie. Pour celles-ci cependant, la résolution du conflit est plus complexe, dans la mesure où en mer ne s'exerce aucune souveraineté, ce qui pose la question de l'autorité qui doit intervenir, juger et punir. En outre, le coupable est plus difficile à arrêter s'il trouve refuge dans son pays ou surtout ailleurs, hors de l'espace de souveraineté dans lequel peut s'exercer la justice. La règle qui s'impose très tôt dans les traités est que le pirate doit être arrêté et condamné par la juridiction dont il relève. Ainsi l'accord de 1234 entre Pise et les Hafsides de Tunis prévoit que 'si un Pisan ou quelqu'un des terres de Pise part en course contre les terres d'Africa ou de Bougie, les podestats et consuls des Pisans doivent faire justice aussi bien sur sa personne que sur ses biens'[42]. Au XIVe siècle, à Gênes, est même institué à cet effet un tribunal spécial, l'*Officium Robarie*, qui avait compétence pour recevoir des plaintes de victimes de pirates génois, même lorsque le plaignant était musulman[43].

Au-delà de la condamnation du fautif, ce qui compte est donc la réparation matérielle, par la restitution des biens quand elle est encore possible, ou par une compensation financière, ce qui suppose que l'on mette la main sur le coupable et qu'on puisse le faire payer, ce qui devait être souvent difficile dans la pratique[44]. Une première solution a été d'autoriser la victime à se rembourser en exerçant des représailles, mais encadrées et limitées aux pertes subies. Ce droit de marque est défini ainsi par René de Mas Latrie :

> droit concédé à un particulier par l'autorité souveraine dont il est le sujet, de reprendre, même par la force, son bien ou l'équivalent de son bien, sur un étranger ou les concitoyens de cet étranger, lorsqu'il n'a pu obtenir justice par les voies judiciaires du pays de son adversaire[45].

À la différence de la licence de course, accordée dans le cadre d'un état de guerre, le droit de marque s'inscrit dans un contexte de paix et vise à en assurer la pérennité en l'encadrant doublement : d'une part en le subordonnant à l'épuisement des recours légaux, et d'autre part en limitant les prises au préjudice subi. Il n'est donc accordé qu'après des procédures judiciaires et des

42 Mas Latrie, L. de (1866) 34.

43 Kedar (1985).

44 Les licences de course délivrées par les rois d'Aragon prévoient ainsi une caution et des garants. López Pérez (1995) 694.

45 Mas Latrie, R. de (1866) 530.

échanges diplomatiques, parfois longs, et s'il s'apparente à une justice privée[46], celle-ci se fait au nom de l'État. En 1263 par exemple, le roi d'Aragon Jacques le Conquérant autorise le Barcelonais Pere Ferrer à saisir jusqu'à mille besants de biens appartenant à des sujets hafsides, suite à une attaque menée contre lui par des pirates bougiotes dans le port de Stora[47], Cette solution, outre qu'elle reposait sur le principe de responsabilité collective et pouvaient entraîner à son tour des mesures de rétorsion, avait cependant l'inconvénient de dépendre d'une procédure longue et incertaine. Pour pallier le problème et permettre une indemnisation rapide des victimes et éviter d'entrer dans un cycle de violence, on institua en Europe, surtout à partir du milieu du XIVe siècle, des taxes spéciales, les *lous*, qui pesaient sur les transactions commerciales avec le port concerné par l'acte de piraterie[48]. En renonçant à faire payer le coupable, on remplaçait donc la violence incontrôlable des représailles par une taxe contrôlée par l'État et supportée collectivement par les marchands compatriotes de la victime, lesquels avaient tout à gagner au maintien de bonnes relations diplomatiques et de la paix.

Mais la question qui a le plus préoccupé les pouvoirs a été celle des captifs, qui posaient un problème à la fois économique, humain et religieux. Sans entrer dans le détail, une série de normes et de pratiques se met en place permettant le retour le plus rapide possible du captif dans son pays d'origine[49]. Ces normes reposent encore sur la distinction entre état de paix et de guerre : si le captif a été pris en temps de paix et donc illégalement, il doit être rendu aux siens gratuitement – ce qui peut poser le problème de l'indemnisation de celui qui l'a acheté au pirate. Dans le cas contraire, des procédures de rachat sont mises en place, codifiées avec parfois beaucoup de détails dans les traités de paix, en prenant en considération le droit de propriété du maître – on fixe par exemple l'obligation de le libérer contre une rançon dont le montant n'excède pas son prix d'achat[50]. Les négociations diplomatiques, accompagnées dans certains cas de l'envois d'ambassades, s'appuient sur ces règles pour permettre le retour des captifs, parfois avec des échanges collectifs, mais celles-ci servent

46 Il s'inspire sans doute du « droit de *faide* » connu dans l'Europe féodale. Moeglin et Péquignot (2017) 733–737.

47 Archivo de la corona de Aragón, Cancillería, Reg. 12, f. 14r (février-mars 1262). Depuis 1250, sans qu'une paix ait été formellement signée entre le roi d'Aragon et les Hafsides, un modus vivendi s'est installé, Jacques le Conquérant interdisant notamment les actes de piraterie. Dufourcq (1966), 90–91.

48 Aguiló (1904), López Pérez (1995) 785–806.

49 Valérian (2007).

50 Par exemple dans le traité entre la couronne d'Aragon et les Hafsides de 1403 (art. 7). Aguiló (1902) 351. Dans ce traité 12 articles sur 52 concernent le rachat des captifs.

aussi de base légale à des intermédiaires privés ou à des ordres religieux spécialisés dans la rédemption des captifs, comme les trinitaires ou les mercédaires, pour procéder aux rachats.

6 Conclusion

Dans cette Méditerranée désormais partagée entre puissances latines, grecques et musulmanes aucune autorité unique ne s'exerce plus, et on voit coexister plusieurs systèmes juridiques et religieux différents. La nécessité d'assurer la paix et les échanges pousse cependant à la reconnaissance de certaines règles et principes communs, à défaut d'avoir déjà un droit international reconnu par tous. L'existence de racines juridiques en partie identiques à ces législations, mais aussi de problèmes partagés qui n'ont rien de spécifiquement religieux, facilite ce processus. Un problème se pose cependant avec la régulation de la piraterie et plus largement de la violence entre chrétiens et musulmans, car elles touchent au droit de la guerre et de la paix, qui repose alors sur une distinction confessionnelle a priori irréductible, dans un contexte de rivalité à la fois politique et spirituelle. Les autorités religieuses continuent de produire un discours qui met en avant la séparation et l'inégalité fondamentale entre fidèles et infidèles, mais ce sont désormais les traités bilatéraux entre États qui deviennent le véritable fondement juridique des relations internationales.

Ces derniers visent alors à endiguer et encadrer la violence endémique en Méditerranée, d'une part en fixant une limite entre la violence légitime, en contexte de guerre, et celle qui est interdite en temps de paix, et d'autre part en luttant contre la justice privée et le cycle sans fin des représailles par la fixation de règles de résolution des conflits et l'affirmation du monopole étatique de la violence, sur terre comme sur mer. Ces règles se construisent de manière pragmatique, par une expérimentation dont on ne voit souvent que le résultat et qui vise à améliorer les conditions des échanges et de la navigation. Mais elles reposent aussi sur une réflexion partagée sur les bases légales de la guerre et de la paix, qui s'écarte de la norme religieuse opposant bloc à bloc chrétiens et musulmans, fondant les principes juridiques de relations entre États. Cela pose bien sûr la question de l'efficacité de l'action du pouvoir politique, qui reste souvent limitée, notamment sur mer, en raison de la faiblesse des moyens mais aussi du caractère encore souvent mouvant des appartenances nationales. Il n'en demeure pas moins que ces règles, répétées et précisées de traité en traité, sont de plus en plus communément admises comme source de loi, ainsi que le montre la correspondance diplomatique qui y fait régulièrement référence. Les derniers siècles du Moyen Âge, dans un contexte à la fois de rivalités de puissances, de conflits religieux et d'essor des échanges, sont à cet égard un moment décisif dans la construction de normes régulant la violence en Méditerranée, qui seront ensuite développées à l'époque moderne, servant de base à une distinction plus nette et admise entre course et piraterie, et à l'ébauche d'un droit « international » régissant les relations entre les États en paix.

Bibliographie

Aguiló, E. de K., 'Pau feta entre els reys de Aragó y de Sicilia de una part y el rey de Tunis de l'altre (1403)', *Boletín de la Sociedad Arqueológica Luliana* 9 (1902) 350–355.

Aguiló, E. de K., 'Mostres de lous passats per la redencio de catius cristians', *Boletín de la Sociedad Arqueológica Luliana* 10 (1904) 337–340.

Alarcón y Santón, M. et R. García de Linares, *Los documentos árabes diplomáticos del Archivo de la Corona de Aragón* (Madrid et Grenade 1940).

Ashburner, W. (ed. et trad.), *Nómos Rodiōn naytikós. The Rhodian sea-law* (Oxford 1909).

Bonaini, F. (ed.), *Statuti inediti della città di Pisa dal XII al XIV secolo*, 3 vol. (Florence 1857).

Bruce, T., 'Réseaux et territorialité dans la Méditerranée occidentale au XIe siècle: l'exemple de la taifa de Denia', *Mélanges de la Casa de Velázquez* 40 no. 2 (2010) 157–177.

Course et piraterie. Études présentées à la commission internationale d'histoire maritime à l'occasion de son XVe colloque international pendant le XIVe Congrès international des sciences historiques, San Francisco, août 1975, 3 vol. (Paris 1975).

Constable, O.R., 'The problem of jettison in medieval Mediterranean maritime law', *Journal of Medieval History* 20 (1994) 207–220.

Constable, O.R., *Housing the stranger in the Mediterranean world: lodging, trade, and travel in late antiquity and the Middle Ages* (Cambridge 2003).

Doumerc, B., 'L'Adriatique, une proie dans les griffes du lion vénitien (XIe–XVIe siècle)' in A. Nef ed., *Les territoires de la Méditerranée, XIe–XVIe siècle* (Rennes 2013) 15–34.

Dufourcq, Ch.-E., *L'Espagne catalane et le Maghrib aux XIIIe et XIVe siècles, de la bataille de Las Navas de Tolosa (1212) à l'avènement du sultan mérinide Abou l'Hassan (1331)* (Paris 1966).

Girardi, F., ed., *Venezia e il regno di Tunisi. Gli accordi diplomatici conclusi fra il 1231 e il 1456* (Rome 2006).

Goitein, Sh. D., *A Mediterranean society*, 1 (Berkeley, Los-Angeles et Londres 1978).

Goitein, Sh. D., 'The Unity of the Mediterranean World in the "Middle" Middle Ages', *Studia Islamica* 12 (1960) 29–42.

Hinojosa Montalvo, J.M., 'Confesiones y ventas de cautivos en la Valencia de 1409', *Ligarzas* 3 (1971) 113–127.

Hodges, R. et D. Whitehouse, *Mohammed, Charlemagne & the Origins of Europe* (Londres 1983).

Ibn Khaldūn, 'A. al-R., *Kitāb al-'Ibar*, ed. Shiḥāda, Kh. and Zakkār, S., *Ta'rīḫ Ibn Ḫaldūn*, (Beyrouth 2000), trad. Mac Guckin De Slane, W. et P. Casanova, *Histoire des Berbères* (Paris 1956).

Jados, S.S. (trad.), *The Consulate of the Sea and Related Documents* (Tuscaloosa, 1975).

Kedar B.Z., 'L'*Officium Robarie* di Genova: un tentativo di coesistere con la violenza', *Archivio storico italiano* 143 (1985) 331–372.

Khadduri, M., *War and Peace in the Law of Islam* (Baltimore 1955).

Khalilieh, H.S., *Islamic Maritime Law. An Introduction* (Leiden, 1998).

Khalilieh H.S., *Admiralty and Maritime Laws in the Mediterranean Sea (ca. 800–1050). The* Kitāb Akriyat al-Sufun *vis-à-vis the* Nomos Rhodion Nautikos (Leiden 2006).

Kitāb akriyat al-sufun, ed. Muṣṭafā A. Tāhir, 'Kitāb akriyat al-sufun wa l-nizā' bayna ahli-hā', *Les Cahiers de Tunisie*, 123–124 (1983), 5–52; trad. Khalilieh (2006) 273–330.

Lopez, R.S., *La Révolution commerciale dans l'Europe médiévale* (Paris, 1974).

López Pérez, M.D., *La Corona de Aragón y el Magreb en el siglo XIV (1331–1410)* (Barcelone 1995).

Mas Latrie, L. de, ed., *Traités de paix et de commerce et documents divers concernant les relations des Chrétiens avec les Arabes de l'Afrique septentrionale au Moyen-Âge* (Paris 1866).

Mas Latrie, R. de, 'Du droit de marque ou droit de représailles au Moyen Âge', *Bibliothèque de l'École des chartes* 27 (1866) 529–577.

Moeglin, J.-M., Péquignot, S., *Diplomatie et « relations internationales » au Moyen Âge (IXe–XVe siècle)* (Paris, 2017).

Mollat, M., 'De la piraterie sauvage à la course réglementée (XIVe–XVe siècle)', *Mélanges de l'École française de Rome. Moyen Âge-Temps modernes* 87 (1975) 7–25.

Pernoud, R. (ed.), *Le IVe Livre des Statuts de Marseille* (Paris, 1935).

Pirenne, H., *Mahomet et Charlemagne* (Paris 2005).

Picard, Ch., 'Préface' à Henri Pirenne, *Mahomet et Charlemagne* (Paris 2005) V–XLV.

Picard, Ch., *La mer des califes. Une histoire de la Méditerranée musulmane (VIIe–XIIe siècle)* (Paris 2015).

Pozza, M., Ravegnani, G., ed., *I trattati con Bisanzio: 992–1198* (Rome 1993).

Valérian, D., 'La résolution des conflits dans les communautés européennes dans les ports du Maghreb médiéval, entre métropoles et pouvoir local', in A. Nef et D. Valérian eds., *Communautés et pouvoirs en Italie et au Maghreb au Moyen Âge et à l'époque moderne. Actes du séminaire de Rome, 26–27 octobre 2001, Mélanges de l'École française de Rome, Moyen Âge* 115 no. 1 (2003) 543–564.

Valérian, D., 'Le rachat des captifs dans les traités de paix de la fin du Moyen Âge : entre diplomatie et enjeux économiques', *Hypothèses 2006* (Paris 2007) 343–358.

Valérian, D., 'Le recours à l'écrit dans les pratiques marchandes en contexte interculturel : les contrats de commerce entre chrétiens et musulmans en Méditerranée' in *L'autorité de l'écrit au Moyen Âge (Orient-Occident), XXXIX*e *Congrès de la SHMESP, Le Caire, 30 avril–5 mai 2008* (Paris 2009) 59–72.

Valérian, D., 'The making of the medieval Mediterranean', in P. Horden, Sh. Kinoshita, eds., *A Companion to Mediterranean History* (Chichester, Oxford, Malden 2014a) 77–90.

Valérian, D., 'La piraterie maghrébine à la fin du Moyen Âge : une forme maritime du djihad ?', in B. Heyberger and A. Fuess eds., *La frontière méditerranéenne du XV*e *au XVII*e *siècle. Échanges, circulations et affrontements* (Turnhout 2014b) 115–126.

CHAPTER 8

Towards a Criminalisation of Piracy in Late Medieval England

Thomas K. Heebøll-Holm

1 Introduction

According to Alfred Rubin, the first English monarch to criminalise explicitly piracy was King Henry VIII.[1] In a Statute from 1536, we read the following:

> Where traytors, pirates, thieves, robbers, murderers and confederates upon the sea, many times escaped unpunished, because the trial of their offences hath heretofore been ordered, judged and determined before the admiral, or his lieutenant or commissary, after the course of the civil laws, (2) the nature whereof is, that before any judgment of death can be given against the offenders, either they must plainly confess their offences (which they will never do without torture or pains) or else their offences be so plainly and directly proved by witness indifferent, such as saw their offences committed, which cannot be gotten but by chance at few times, because such offenders commit their offences upon the sea, and at many times murder and kill such persons being in the ship or boat where they commit their offences, which should witness against them in that behalf; and also such as should bear witness be commonly mariners and shipmen, which, because of their often voyages and passages in the seas, depart without long tarrying and protraction of time, to the great costs and charges as well of the King's highness, as such as would pursue such offenders : (3) for reformation whereof, be it enacted by the authority of this present parliament, that all treasons, felonies, robberies, murders and confederacies hereafter to be committed in or upon the sea, or in any other haven, river, creek or place where the admiral or admirals have or pretend to have power, authority or jurisdiction, shall be enquired, tried, heard, determined and judged [...] suffer such pains of death, losses of lands, goods and chattels, as if they had been attainted

1 Rubin (1988), 36 ff.

 | DOI:10.1163/9789004407992_010

> and convicted of any treasons, felonies, robberies, or other the said offences done upon the lands.[2]

This Statute contains several relevant statements concerning the subject of this chapter, the criminalisation of piracy in the late Middle Ages. Firstly, it grouped pirates, thieves, murderers and their co-conspirators with traitors. This was a new way of legally perceiving of pirates. By categorising them among the vilest of malefactors, it made their criminalisation possible. Secondly, it conceded that the English legal system was flawed with regard to the conviction of crimes committed at sea. The statute sought to remedy this. Thirdly, in terms of territory it clearly defined which water-territory was concerned, who had legal authority in those areas and what punishment pirates should suffer. Finally, it explicitly removed the legal demarcation between land and sea. However, the contents of the statute were not new at all. Rather the core tenets of it had been formulated 122 years previously by King Henry V in the Statute of Truces of 1414. That Statute is significant not only because it served as model for future English statutes on piracy, but also because at the same time it both incorporated and broke with past English legal presumptions and procedures about the sea.

It is the purpose of this chapter to investigate the medieval origins of the Statute of 1414, its historical context and its influence on English perceptions of the sea and pirates in the following decades. This entails an exploration of the perception and treatment of pirates in late medieval English legal institutions, and an investigation of the development of English royal notions of sovereignty and treason. It is the argument of this chapter that the criminalisation of piracy worked in tandem with these developments, but that the late medieval influence on this criminalisation and on the formation of maritime law has been overlooked by scholars of history and law alike.[3]

2 English Maritime Law and Policy before 1414

King Richard the Lionheart and King John I are traditionally credited with creating the first English navy and in general devoting attention to the sea. Nevertheless, this proved fleeting and a more coherent royal attention to maritime

2 4 Pickering (1762–1806), IV: 441–443.

3 See for instance Pitcaithly (2012), Rubin (1988).

matters had to await the years around 1300.[4] Around that time several events caused English maritime law and institutions to grow in importance. First of all, seaborne trade – especially in wine – was growing in volume and the existing legal institutions proved increasingly inadequate at dealing with maritime issues of conflict and trade. For instance, the *Rôles d'Oléron* – an international maritime law of a *ius gentium* character – was only concerned with regulating the relationship between crew, the shipmaster and the merchant. It did not deal with violent conflicts at sea.[5] Rather, such conflicts were to be adjudicated by the kings' courts or by bilateral and high-level diplomatic negotiations between the rulers whose subjects were involved. Such solutions gradually proved unsatisfactory for the rulers and to a certain extent also for mariners and mariners.

Probably directly connected to the development of an increasing international trade there was a rise of maritime predation. Some were legitimate reprisals and pseudo-legal feuds between maritime communities such as the Cinque Ports, Great Yarmouth, Bayonne, the ports of Normandy and those of northern Spain. Others were related to the wars and conflicts between England, France, Scotland and Flanders, and finally some seem to have been piracy, i.e. indiscriminate plunder with the purpose of immediate personal enrichment. Irrespective of the legality of these acts, they often spiralled out of control rendering even official naval operations quasi- or even overtly piratical. Especially England under King Edward II proved incapable of handling this situation. Meanwhile in the realm of political theory and institutions, both the kings of England and the kings of France began to implement Romanist notions of royal sovereignty over the territories of their kingdoms including what in an embryonic form was defined as territorial waters.[6] As a result of the Hundred Years War, the English ambitions of regulating traffic and security in the waters of the kingdom became more urgent. Thus, in the 1350s in the wake of the victory at Sluys in 1346 and the conquest of Calais in 1347, King Edward III introduced a number of reforms of the legal institutions dealing with maritime issues. Firstly, in 1353 Edward passed the Statute of the Staples which placed the staple courts under the protection of the king thereby effectively bringing them under the Crown. Further in the aftermath of the victory at the Battle of Poitiers, 1356, an institutionalisation and clarification of the legal competences of the admiralty was given greater priority. After the Peace of Brétigny (1360)

4 Gillingham (1997), Brooks (1929), Brooks (1925), Dick (2010) 57–58, 64–71, 185–186, Marsden (1894) I, xii–xxvii.

5 James (1971), 78, Renouard (1959), Ward (2009) 20–26.

6 For a survey of maritime predation in this period, see Heebøll-Holm (2013).

which *de facto* came close to give the English king's ambition to sovereignty over the English waters including the Channel and the French Atlantic coast not just in name but also in practice, Edward III officially founded the Court of Admiralty, which had extensive and supreme legal powers. A central purpose of the Court of Admiralty was to deal with cases of piracy, both in international and domestic relations, and to obtain international recognition as a court of maritime law.[7] This period of supremacy proved brief however because the French under Charles V rebuilt a powerful fleet that could challenge the English supremacy and because other English courts of law came to challenge the jurisdiction of an increasingly corrupt or mismanaged English Admiralty. Thus between 1375 and 1403 the Inquisition of Queenborough sat over three sessions and reformed the maritime laws of England. These entailed a precision, but also a curtailing of the jurisdiction of the admirals.[8] Further, in 1391 (reconfirmed in 1402) a Statute was passed that severely limited the powers of the Court of Admiralty.[9]

3 The Status of Piracy in the Middle Ages

A perennial problem for the English kings – and by extension for the jurisdiction of the admirals – was the status of maritime aggression. The English kings disposed of few ships themselves and if they wanted to exercise their power at sea they had to turn to the maritime and mercantile communities. These however had proven to be fickle allies. While it was seemingly not hard to mobilise them for royally authorised, but privately organised, operations of maritime war and predation against the enemies of the kingdom, the English mariners often took a somewhat liberal view of who was the enemy and who were neutrals. This was not necessarily a problem for the kings. Indeed, the English maritime community proved instrumental in guarding the waters of the kingdom during the first years of Henry IV's reign when the new regime was beset with uprisings in England and Wales, a covert war with the French and an open one with Scotland. However, these mariners were quite difficult to control, and a fair number of their operations could be termed piratical rather than privateering. The English kings until Henry IV most often had had to tolerate such behaviour, and indeed exploited it to their advantage. Nevertheless, the relationship remained ambivalent.

7 Heebøll-Holm (2018) 163–169.

8 Heebøll-Holm (2016) 47–53, Twiss (2012) I:133–177, Ward (2009) 23, 37–44, 206–218.

9 *PROME* Richard II: 1391, Item 30, *PROME* Henry IV: 1402, Item 47.

Further the English faced the problem that unlicensed maritime predation was not per se a criminal activity. Though English kings in the fourteenth century claimed to have enjoyed a modicum of sovereignty over the territorial waters of their realms, in practice the sea was legally more akin to a marcher area as between England and Scotland or France and Gascony. This meant that a feudlike custom, rather than sovereign law, was used for settling conflicts at sea. Despite the creation of the Court of Admiralty, the kings did not have any special jurisdiction in these matters, partly because maritime communities guarded their privileges fiercely, partly because the Court of Admiralty ruled by maritime law and not the laws of the realm, and finally because such maritime conflicts often involved people from different kingdoms who – since the seas were unterritorialised – could not be judged according the law of any kingdom. Further a central tenet in the custom of maritime conflict was the right to reprisal and self-defense, both derived from the laws of just war. Essentially, reprisal meant that one was allowed to recuperate through one's own means losses suffered unjustly against the perpetrator or one's fellow countrymen. Thus, reprisals entailed collective liability.[10] In principle, reprisals did not entail any authorisation of the use of force in the restitution. As such it was related to debt collection. However, given that governments usually lacked sufficient force and will to enforce the restitution for the plaintiff and moreover the accused would most often contest and resist the claim, the use of force was *de facto* tolerated. However, this often led the reprisals to change from an act of restitution to retaliation. Though the English kings had prohibited feuds or private wars in their kingdom, they were legally powerless in conflicts beyond the English territory including those at sea. This had caused problems for the Crown in the late Middle Ages, and in it 1293 even sparked a war between England and France, the Gascon War of 1294–97.[11] However, in the main, the reprisals and maritime feuds did not cause significant problems for the English government in the fourteenth century.

While the royal government got more control over the institutions of the kingdom, the maritime communities themselves had grown increasingly sophisticated in their organisation of the maritime predation by creating privateering syndicates of merchants, ship-owners and shipmasters. This practice saw early development around 1300 with for instance the Alard family of Winchelsea, but these syndicates seem fairly loose and localised. By the 1380s however they grew in scope and formed powerful syndicates coordinating on a national level. By 1400 they seem to have been present in most English ports of

10 Neff (2005) 76–82.

11 For a discussion of these problems, see Heebøll-Holm (2013) and Heebøll-Holm (2018).

a certain size and importance, but the most famous was one in Dartmouth. This organisation also made it hard for the English kings to stop them from self-serving actions. Especially the actions of the syndicates in the period 1405–1414 proved to be problematic for the Lancastrian regime. Probably around 1406 it spun out of control and became directly detrimental to royal foreign policies. Simply put, what began as an early version of privateering soon turned into outright piracy. As Henry IV's health deteriorated, his son, the future Henry V, began to reorganise the realm. In maritime issues, he in 1408 appointed his uncle Thomas Beaufort admiral for life thereby strengthening the authority of the admiral. The core of the problem was that though England had been able to make peace or truce with all nations sailing the Channel, the syndicates continued to harass Flemish and Breton trade. In addition to hurting trade, this caused massive diplomatic problems for the King Henry V who wished to reopen the war with France. To that end he needed the Bretons and the Flemish (under the rule of the Duke of Burgundy) to remain neutral. Accordingly, Henry had a clear incentive to stop their piracies.[12] But how? Existing laws and customs had left him and his predecessors in a deadlock, and he had to tread carefully to avoid alienating the maritime communities. After all he was still dependent on them if he wanted to wage war on France. The led to the passing of the Statute of Truces which provided Henry with a new legal tool to neutralise unrest and disobedience in England.

4 The Statute of Truces, 1414

In April 1414 the English Parliament convened to pass a number of statutes. The context for this Parliament was that trouble had been brewing in various parts of the kingdom, primary amongst these the 'Lollard Rising', whose alleged aims were capture of the king, overthrow of government and reform of the church. The purpose of the April Parliament was therefore the restoration of order and justice on land and sea, and it passed a new Statute on the Lollards, a reinforcement of the 1411 Statute of Riots and the Statute of Truces, the most novel of the three.[13] The immediate context for the passing of the Statute of Truces was a Crown initiative to crack down on privateers-turned-pirate. In Devonshire, centre of this activity and notoriously prone to resistance to royal control, a general *oyer and terminer* commission had opened in Exeter in

12 Kingsford (1925), Gardiner (1966), Pistono (1975), Pistono (1976a), Pistono (1976b), Pistono (1977), Pistono (1979), Ford (1979), Heebøll-Holm (2019a).

13 PROME Introduction 1414 Parliament, Matusiak (2013) 87–102.

February 1414. Several indictments targeted shipmasters whose actions had brought the peace with Brittany into jeopardy. However, as Devonshire had had to build local defences against Breton, French and Spanish raids and the West Country shipping and mariners contributed significantly to the local economy and naval defense,[14] the local juries refused to testify against their fellows. To them, the mariners' actions were just reprisals for the losses English shipping had suffered. Thus, their non-cooperation with the royal commissioner may well, argues Edward Powell, have caused Parliament to pass the Statute of Truces. On unlicensed plunder at sea, the Statute said:

> if any such murder, robbery, plunder, breaking of the king's truces and safe-conducts, and deliberate sheltering, abetting, supporting, advising, hiring, sustaining and maintaining of such persons is carried out in future by any of the king's lieges and subjects within the kingdoms of England, Ireland and Wales, or on the high seas [...] it shall be adjudged and determined as high treason committed contrary to the crown and dignity of the king. And that in every sea port there shall be made and appointed and assigned henceforth by the king, through his letters patent, one loyal man called a conservator of the king's truces and safe-conducts, who shall have at least forty pounds of land a year. And that the said conservator shall have the power and authority by the said letters patent, and also by commission of the admiral of England, to enquire into any such treasons and offences which are committed against the king's truces and safe-conducts on the high seas [...] as the admirals of the kings of England reasonably had and exercised before this time, in accordance with ancient maritime custom and law.[15]

14 Kowaleski (2014).

15 'qe tieux tuerie, robberie, espoillerie, rumperie des trieves et saufconduitz de roi, et voluntaries receit, abbettement, procurement, conseille, louere, sustenance, et maintenance de tieux persones affairez en temps avenir par ascuns des lieges et subgitz de roi, deinz les roialmes d'Engleterre, d'Irland et Gales, ou sur le haut meer, [...] soient adjuggez et determinez pur haut tresoun fait encontre la corone et dignite de roi. Et qe en chescun port de meer soit fait et assignee desorenavaunt par le roi par ses lettres patentz un loial homme, appelle conservatour des trieves et saufconduitz de roi, qe eit .xl. liverees de terre par an a meyns. Et qe le dit conservatour eit poair et auctorite par les dites lettres patentz, et auxi par commissioun del admiralle d'Engleterre, d'enquerer de toutz tieux tresons et offenses affairez encountre les trieves et saufconduitz de roi, sur le haut meer [...] come les admiralles des rois d'Engleterre devaunt ces heures resonablement, solonc l'aunciene custume et leie sur le meer usez, ount faitz, ou usez'. *PROME* Henry V: 1414, Item 23.

The Statute as a matter of fact grouped murder, robbery, plunder and the breaking of truces and safe-conducts together as high treason. While the first three categories pertain to criminal law and had always been the prerogative of the king's jurisdiction, the last two belonged to the *jus gentium* laws of war. However, they were essential to include if one wanted to curb piracy. While the king had no jurisdiction over sea as such, the breaking of his truces and safe conducts pertained not to maritime matters, but to matters of the king's person and dignity. In other words, it was a personal insult and a crime of *lèse majesté*. However, to bolster the king's legal authority in maritime matters, the Statute also mentioned that according to the ancient laws and customs of the sea there was a precedent of English royal jurisdiction over the sea, and the traditional obstacle of the legal difference between land and sea was overcome by stressing that the Statute was equally applicable in the kingdoms of the realm as well as on the high seas. Thereby a legal equality of the land and sea was achieved. Thus by combining murder etc. with the breaking of truces and safe-conducts, by effacing the difference between land and sea with reference both to the kingdoms of England, Wales and Ireland and by referring to ancient law and custom, thereby causing a territorialisation of the sea founded both on past and present and finally by involving the royal dignity, Henry V was able to construct a legal 'package' that circumvented past problems of handling piracy.

Moreover, by making the Statute applicable solely to his subjects on the British Isles he avoided the issue that in the past had caused such legal initiatives to flounder, namely the attempt to claim universal jurisdiction over pirates. This had resulted in doomed international negotiations as no foreign ruler would willingly allow their subjects to be judged by (partial) English courts of law. Further, earlier efforts had tried to establish criminalisation through bilateral agreements, but such efforts proved fleeting, not least because the navies of medieval rulers ultimately were merchants, mariners and shipowners who were licensed, hired or impressed to fight the enemies of the realm at sea.[16]

The Statute went to considerable lengths to describe the legal powers of the conservators.[17] The concept of conservators of the peace at sea was not a new invention though. In the first decades of the fourteenth century the English and French kings had at several points agreed to appoint such conservators to

16 For examples of such negotiations, see Heebøll-Holm (2013) 174–183, 200–223.

17 I have only reproduced a small section of these in the quotation above. It should be noted that the research has never been able to establish whether conservators were actually appointed though.

adjudicate conflicts between their subjects at sea. However, neither the French nor the English were actually committed to such a policy, and in any event, these attempts always wrecked on the power struggles of these kings. The main problem with this approach – in addition to the rivalry between the kings of England and France – was that they were bilateral and based on marcher law. Any infraction by either party was likely to jeopardize the construct as a whole.[18] Thus, in contrast to the past initiatives these conservators were exclusively to deal with English subjects and regulate their behaviour. The adjudication of such acts was left to these well-paid royal officers in the ports, appointed exclusively by the king and acting on the authority of the admiral. In this way, the stranglehold of syndicates led by local magnates and strongmen on the ports and their legal workings was formally broken and the high salary could ensure a minimum of corruption.[19]

Even though it is unknown if such conservators were ever appointed, the Statute still seems to have made a profound impression on the legal system and the syndicates alike. Two months after the passing of the Statute of Truces, a new commission was appointed to inquire into the Devonshire affair, but this time no locals were appointed. Rather, it was headed by the king's appointee, John Arundel, steward of the Duchy of Cornwall and a Lancastrian loyalist, and its findings were not to be judged locally, but at the King's Bench at Westminster. Now the Devonshire juries became cooperative and the commission secured 150 indictments, including a significant minority concerned piracy. Twenty shipmasters including three leading ship-owners were indicted.[20] Even though punishments never seem to have been actively imposed, the unrestrained piracy appears to have been curbed, and the king succeeded in enforcing truces and providing restitution.[21] From 1415–21 Henry V maintained patrols in the Channel to police the sea. These were very expensive, though, and even then, piracy, mutiny and self-serving actions by the contracted or impressed English sailors occurred, though more rarely than before.[22]

Thus, acts of unlicensed robbery at sea were made akin to high treason, the gravest crime in medieval England,[23] and this can effectively be interpreted as a *de facto* criminalisation of piracy. In the following we shall investigate

18 Chaplais (1951) 278, Chaplais (1982) I: 389–392. The first of such initatives may even date back to the reign of King John. See Brooks (1925).

19 Heebøll-Holm (forthcoming a).

20 Powell (1989) 201–207.

21 Sumption (2015) 402.

22 Friel (2015), 103, 128, Powell (1989) 208.

23 See for instance Bellamy (1970), 128–130, Cuttler (1981) 40–44, Gillingham (2008) 201–205.

two of the central tenets necessary for the rebranding of piracy as treason, namely sovereignty and treason.

5 Sovereignty, Treason and Piracy

The legal manoeuvre of making piracy akin to treason required the application and adaptation of Romanist ideas of sovereignty and treason to the situation in early fifteenth century England. The medieval reception of Roman sovereignty entailed the combination of the secular and religious power in order to achieve a theocratic station where the king essentially became God's viceregent. This was the aspiration of most late medieval kings, and it necessitated the combination of the often-synonymous notions of *iurisdictio*, *dominium*, *imperium* and *potestas*. This notion became more widespread during the late Middle Ages and meant a transformation of the distribution of power in society. In the early middle ages, the subject was bound to the ruler through fealty rather than obedience. Further, the fealty was reciprocal and indeed contractual. Both were bound by the laws of the kingdom in horizontal relationship of power. If either subject or ruler broke faith the fealty was dissolved. The subject would have the legal right to disobey the ruler. However, in the High Middle ages, the kings increasingly sought to be *lege soluti*.[24] For most rulers, sovereignty over the territorial waters of their realms was not the primary concern. However, England's geography and the political status of the English kings naturally led these kings to try out notions of sovereignty based on Romanist ideas.

The earliest known English claim to something akin to sovereignty over the territorial waters of England was voiced by the Benedictine monk, William of Malmesbury, who claimed that the Anglo-Saxon King Edgar I had enjoyed this right.[25] However, actual English or rather Plantagenet maritime power began in the twelfth century with the rule of Henry II. The maritime power of the early Plantagenets in effect rested not so much on public declarations as on the fact that in addition to ruling England and Ireland they controlled almost all of the French Atlantic coastline. However, for most of the thirteenth century, English kings were too preoccupied with domestic trouble to formulate a specific maritime policy. A century later English interest in sovereignty over the sea resurfaced as the *Rôles d'Oléron* were backdated to the rule of these first Plantagenets. Indeed, justification of English royal jurisdiction over the seas

24 Bellamy (1970) 10, Maiolo (2007), 143.

25 Sobecki (2008) 147.

was grounded on a claim that Richard the Lionheart gave the *Rôles d'Oléron*.[26] This renewed interest was in part stirred by the piratical feuds of the 1290s. In 1297 at the earliest, Edward I's negotiators with Flanders and Castile – and in 1306 with France – began to argue that the English kings since time immemorial – perhaps dating back to Edgar and most certainly to the reign of the early Plantagenets – had been in peaceful possession of the sea including the exclusive right and obligation to judge all trangressors there. In the settlement negotiations over piracy between France and England in 1306 at Montreuil, the English negotiators formulated it thus:

> since the kings of England by their right to the said realm have been in peaceful possession of the sovereign lordship of the sea of England and the islands there for as long as anyone can remember, they have by decree and the passing of laws, statutes and common and private rights been guardians of peace and justice between all manner of people from other lordships as well as their own subjects passing through these waters. By sovereign right with all manner of jurisdiction over high and low justice by the said laws, statutes, decrees and rights and by all other deeds, the right to sovereign lordship in the before mentioned places belong to them.[27] (my translation)

With regard to sovereignty – or perhaps rather sole jurisdiction over maritime trespasses – several phrases in this declaration are of importance to the development of sovereignty and the Statute of Truces. The notion 'peaceful' signaled unchallenged possession of sovereignty, and the term 'as long as anyone can remember' probably referred to the Romanist notion of *per longam consuetudinem* where rights could be conferred by the fact that it had been used for a long time. Finally, and based on the previous, the English king demanded sole jurisdiction in an international body of water that had never been governed by any lord.

These ideas were founded on the Roman empire's relationship with the sea (essentially the Mediterranean) where the jurisdiction over sea territory was

26 Heebøll-Holm (2013), 130–134.

27 'come les roys Dengleterre par raison du dit roialme, du temps qil ny ad memoire du contraire, averoient este en paisible possession de la sovereigne seigneurie de la meer Dengleterre et des isles esteans en ycele par ordinance et establisement de loiz, estatuz et deffenses communes et privees a garder pees et droiture entre tote manere des gentz tant dautri seigneurie come de leur propre par illeqes passantz et par sovereigne garde ove tote manere de conisance et justice haute et basse sur les dits loys, estatuz, ordinances et deffenses et par tous autres faitz, queux a la garde de sovereigne seigneurie appartenir purront en leux avantditz'. Chaplais (1982), I: 367.

the prerogative of the emperor because the coasts of the Mediterreanean were part of the territory of the emperor, even though Roman law officially declared the sea *res nullius*.[28] However by the twelfth-century the glossator Azo argued that jurisdiction over the sea could be claimed in two eays, either by grant of privilege or by long-established custom. Nevertheless, no legislation could be found to challenge the public nature of the sea and Azo's assertion was countered by the fact that fishermen and sailors by *ius gentium* had older claims to jurisdiction than the kings. Royal feudal practice of territorialisation over the coast through grants of use and rights from Crown to vassals, though confirming both the rights of local lords and Crown, could not initially overrule this *ius gentium*. In the thirteenth century, however, this notion was given more power with the introduction of the concept of *regalium*. This entailed an *a priori* legal and political privilege bestowed on a ruler, and it provided a basis for vindicating claims to territorial waters. By the fourteenth century a concept of defining territorial waters as the seas under a ruler's jurisdiction was founded on an active policing of the sea by the king's admirals. Thus, were admirals fundamental for the territorialisation of the sea as the Montreuil declaration stated elsewhere.[29] At this point though, the concept was only in its inception, and it had to await the post-glossator Bartolus of Saxoferrato later in the fourteenth century to find a clearer formulation. According to Bartolus, the admirals' primary task was to guard the sea (i.e. fight pirates), and he included islands and the waters between them and land as *regalia*. These were termed by Bartolus as districts, but it is important to note that the application of such concepts predate Bartolus. In 1311 Philip IV le Bel termed an assault on Rochelais merchants as happening *in mari infra districtus nostris* i.e. in French territorial waters and neither in fourteenth century England or France are there any explicit reference to Bartolus. Finally, no rulers in northern Europe had the actual means to conduct a coherent enforcement of their claims over the sea. As Sebastian Sobecki notes, a right that is not enforced or enforceable is reduced to a claim.[30]

King Edward I knew this, and it is unlikely that this argument was meant to state an inalienable right of the kings of England. Rather it was intended to counter the French kings' status as liege lords of the English kings. At this point it was but a bargaining chip to make the kings of England and France equals in

28 Sobecki (2008) 141; Heebøll-Holm (2013) 127.

29 Chaplais (1982) I, 367–368.

30 Sobecki (2008) 142–145, 148–149, Heebøll-Holm (2013) 14–15, *Foedera* 1307–1327, 146, Gauvard (2005) 49.

status.[31] Nevertheless, Edward III certainly knew how to exploit this claim. In 1338 or 39 all documents that could support a claim to English sovereignty at sea were collected into the so-called *Fasciculus de Superioritate Maris*, and Edward III was soon able to back-up his claims with actual naval power and success. In the 1350s Edward expanded and strengthened the judicial side of the English admiralty, and in 1361 he institutionalised the Court of Admiralty. With these successes Edward – supported by the Treaty of Brétigny – could confidently claim English royal sovereignty over the sea not only in theory but also in practice. He had largely recreated the twelfth century Plantagenet empire and contrary to his predecessors he ruled these territories as an – at the time – uncontested sovereign.[32] However in the later years of Edward III's and during Richard II's reign English maritime power crumbled. Henry V's pretensions were more modest than Edward III's though he still promoted the Romanist notions, especially *regalium*. Thus, the Statute of Truces did not claim universal jurisdiction over the sea, only royal jurisdiction over English mariners.

Central to all claims of sovereignty was the status of treason and rebellion. While the early medieval world allowed for the subject to disobey his ruler, the Romanist concept of sovereignty did not. As God's viceregent disobedience to the sovereign became treason liable to the most draconic punishments of the realm including the gruesome execution of the traitor, total forfeiture of one's goods and possessions and possibly also similar punishment of the traitor's children. Some factors made it easier to pass such a Romanist inspired concept of law and treason in England – contrary to most other European kingdoms – since William the Conqueror had declared noble private war and insurrections against the king illegal and punishable. Nevertheless, there was considerable resistance to the introduction of Romanist concepts, but kings like Edward III and Henry V persisted in using them.[33]

The charge of treason was old in English law, but it was not clarified and limited until Edward III's Statute of Treason of 1352. Here treason was defined as acting against the king's interests, including attempting as well as merely imagining the death of the king, his queen or his eldest son, sexual violation of female members of the royal family, waging war against the king or adherence to the king's enemies. Furthermore, treason was not confined to actions. Intent was the crucial point and that was what was required for a person to be established as a traitor.[34] However, the process of trial in cases of treason differed

31 Heebøll-Holm (2013) 188–189.
32 Heebøll-Holm (2016) 49–51.
33 Bellamy (1970) 10–14.
34 Leitch (2015) 22–23.

little in form from that used when the charge was felony or trespass. Though treason had been marked off from felony by the statute then apart from allowing for the declaration of certain crimes in Parliament no special procedures had been laid down.[35]

Further measures were needed in order for piracy (and indeed robbery and murder) to be viewed legally as treason. Megan Leitch argues that the Statute of Truces expanded the definition by claiming these acts was an infraction on the king's peace and by extension his word and honour. An injury to those equipped with royal safe-conducts or shielded by truce could thus constitute treason 'since harming someone under the king's protection constituted a denial of the king's authority. Thus, in English law, treason meant the breach or intended breach of a strictly hierarchical loyalty, with intent to effect critical harm'.[36] Further, Roman law principles reshaped by medieval legal customs had produced a law of arms that in the late Middle Ages was applicable to combattants in any war. This law of arms 'focused on breaches of the expected code of conduct between individual soldiers rather than on the polities on whose behalf the soldiers might be fighting'.[37] The act of making piracy treason was thus linked to breach of the king's word rather than against the polity.

The use of the charge of treason against pirates had been tried out at least twice prior to the passing of the Statute of Truces. In 1383, a number of Cornwall men led by John Treverthean the Elder were arrested and brought before the Chancery to answer charges of treason which may have been of piracy.[38] Perhaps more importantly, in 1411 John Prendergast and William Longe of Rye, notorious privateers turned pirates, were charged with treason for their actions against foreign merchants.[39] This was successful in the sense that though they did not suffer any punishment, in the future they did refrain from attacking neutrals. This case may well have been a testing ground for a nation-wide application of the charge. Furthermore, the use of the treason charge was not restricted to pirates, robbers or murderers. In 1418 Henry V used it against deserters in the wars in France.[40] Moreover, the charge of treason was also applied by the April 1414 Parliament for crimes committed on the Scottish March. These were to be judged as treason and aid to the enemy, Scotland, but here collusion with the enemy was clear and not circumstantial as it was in maritime case.

35 Bellamy (1970) 138.
36 Leitch (2015) 23–24, See also Keen (1965) 211.
37 Leitch (2015) 23–24, See also Keen (1965) 211.
38 *CPR* 1381–85, 257, Bellamy (1970) 156.
39 Given-Wilson (2016) 456–457, 486–488, Heebøll-Holm (forthcoming a).
40 Sumption (2015) 611.

Further, it was to be judged by Common Law by the sheriffs in the County courts. Finally, in 1414 the Lollard Sir John Oldcastle was judged for treason and outlawed, thus Lollardry was combined with rebellion and conspiracy and made coterminous.[41] In sum it was a legal measure that was tried out in a wide variety of different cases of disobedience to the king, and hence served as a general measure to strengthen royal control.

The inclusion of piracy as treason may also have hinged implicitly on the Roman notion of *perduellio* (treason).[42] In Roman public law the crime of *perduellio* encompassed a wide variety of misdeeds including military acts hostile to the state such as desertion and aiding the enemy, actions against the constitution of the state, maladministration by magistrates, violation of civic duties, personal injury done to magistrates, and crimes of *lèse majesté* agains the emperor, his dignity and his family.[43] However, *perduellio* as a term is especially interesting as it also pertained to piracy. While Roman Law did not hold any criminalization of piracy, Roman political discourse did. In *De Officiis,* Cicero wrote famously: 'a pirate is not included in the number of lawful enemies (*perduellium*), but is the common foe of all the world; and with him there ought not to be any pledged word nor any oath mutually binding'.[44] Cicero's condemnation of pirates has usually been taken by scholars of piracy (including myself) as a distinction between pirates and foreign, but legitimate, enemies. On a general level, this does not change the meaning of Cicero's dictum, it just accentuated the crime of piracy, namely that pirates were even more repulsive than the most heinous enemies of the state, who even then maintained a minimum of rights. However, this also meant that pirates were beyond the jurisdiction of the state. This really wasn't a problem for the Romans as a long as pirates were foreigners whose war at sea one wanted to delegitimize by labelling them as pirates.[45] However if the pirates were one's own subjects, such a discourse of exclusion would hardly do. Thus, the English king had to reshape this discourse of exclusion, if he wanted to criminalise English piracy. Therefore, he had to extend his sovereignty to the territorial waters of England and thereby grouping pirates with murderers, robbers and traitors. In regard to the sea, the Statute of Truces in effect implemented a Romanist concept of the sea which permitted Henry V to criminalise domestic pirates.

41 Bellamy (1970) 172.

42 For Ulpian's take on *perduellio*, see *The Digest of Justinian* (1998) IV, 318, Dig. 48.4.11.

43 Bellamy (1970) 2.

44 'nam pirata non est ex perduellium numero definitus, sed communis hostis omnium: cum hoc nec fides nec ius iurandum esse commune', Cicero (1968) III.29.

45 See for instance De Souza (1999), Gabrielsen (2013), Heebøll-Holm, Höhn and Rohmann (2019b).

It is worth noting though that English sovereignty at sea was never a purpose of the Statute. It was merely a foundation, but due to Henry's victories it became the effect. Indeed, as Bellamy notes:

> king [Henry V] was prompted to introduce Roman notions into the treason laws not so much to increase his own powers per se as to maintain a reasonable level of public order. The extension of the penalties for treason to lesser crimes both at this time and in the fifteenth century was intended to remedy complaints about lack of governance, which was a perennial grievance in the England of the later middle ages.[46]

Thus, by introducing a more modest notion of jurisdiction over the seas than his predecessors, but endowning this Statute with clearer and more powerful executive force, the Statute of Truces indirectly became the model on which future English jurisdiction over the sea was inspired.

6 Conclusion: The Statute beyond Henry V

After the death of Henry V in 1422 the English government began selling off the ships of the navy that he had built. In the long run, this would prove disastrous, but in the 1420s there really was no need for a large and expensive royal navy. The Statute of Truces seems largely to have been followed, and due to Henry's conquest of northern France, the Channel had become an English sea. Indeed, in 1420, Parliament proposed to Henry that he claim the Channel as English dominion (de facto sovereignty), justifying the proposal by reference to England's possession of both shores. However, Henry refused the invitation with the formula *soit avise par le Roy.*[47]

However, the political crisis precipitated by the Treaty of Arras (1435) which united Burgundy and France against England, the French reconquest of the traditional French privateering ports Harfleur and Dieppe and the siege of Calais in 1436 caused a feverish English attempt to mobilise the private naval ressources of the realm.[48] This entailed the Commons managing in 1435 to pass a seven-years suspension of the Statute of Truces in Parliament.[49] This *de facto* became a repeal as the Statute of Truces had been a source

46 Bellamy (1970) 14.

47 *PROME* Henry V: 1420, Item 17, Sobecki (2008) 149–150.

48 Meale (1996) 206–207.

49 PROME Henry VI: 1435, Items 24, 26, 28.

of concern and irritation for English shipmasters. As Ian Friel notes: 'the Statute seems to have had a deterrent effect of some kind. English merchants and sailors later claimed that the spirit of the legislation inhibited them from striking back at foreign pirates, undermining English common law rights and the tradition of reprisal'.[50] In 1436, in a general atmosphere of fear of an invasion, the Crown proceeded to issuing a mass of privateering licenses, and in 1442 the Crown tried to reorganise the naval resources of the kingdom around a royal fleet. The effort floundered however, and England reverted to the classic model of leaving the defense of the coasts to privateering syndicates thereby accepting a high degree of self-serving plunder of neutral shipping, especially Hanseatic. This acceptance only grew with reversals in France and growing fears of French invasion.[51] This seems to have spelled the doom for any thought of English royal control of the sea and by extension, criminalisation of piracy. However, the achievements of Henry V and more indirectly the Statute of Truces had been successful in a different area, that of public opinion. In the *Libelle of Englyshe Polycye* written between 1436 and 1438 as a response to the political crisis precipitated by the Treaty of Arras, the author prophetically argued that England's future lay at sea and maritime trade. The mercantilist focus is evident from the start of the poem, where it states that in order to protect trade, the admiralty (i.e. mastery of the Narrow Sea and other English waters), must be kept. Furthermore, the poem has a popular tinge to it as can be seen from its use of the term 'oure England'. So, the argument of the poem was that the king and council should give naval power equal attention to the military one, and that protection of English trade and merchants was much more important and valuable to England than waging costly dynastic wars in France.[52] Indeed 'oure England' indicated a change of perception from seeing the sea as the territory of the king of England to being the territory of the commonality of the English. Guarding it against pirates – in this case especially Bretons – was a special concern for the *Libelle*, and in any case the the book is a vindication for intregrating the sea with England's territory, thereby underlining the equality between land and sea.[53] Indeed Sebastian Sobecki summarises its importance thus:

50 Friel (2015) 101. See also, Rodger (1997) 147, Warner (1926) xviii–xix.

51 *CPR* 1429–36, 509–512, *PROME* Henry VI: 1435, Items 24, 26, 28, Richmond (1964), Griffiths (1981) 223–232.

52 Warner (1926) 1.

53 Sobecki (2008) 152–154.

> on a political, legal and, perhaps most importantly, cognitive level, the *Libelle* articulates the concept of territorial waters a century and a half before Albericus Gentilis is credited with having done so. The *Libelle*'s notion of the sea's territoriality rests on employing imperial *regalia* and authority as well as using precedent in the form of listing the 'cases' of three Kings of England. This claim is further strengthened by the need to curb piracy (corresponding to Bartolus's argument) and the constant reiteration of the political and territorial equality of land and sea.[54]

The *Libelle* was not alone in asserting this. The English historian John Capgrave (1393–1464) in 1453 repeated some of the Libelle's arguments,[55] and even the French herald in the *Débat des hérauts d'armes*, written between 1453–1461, begrudgingly admitted that the English for the time being had mastery of the sea, but that this sea power was founded purely on criminal pirates preying on peaceful trade.[56] It is beyond the scope of this chapter to treat the development of English maritime law and courts until Henry VIII's statute.[57] Suffice to say that the notion of English sovereignty over the sea and by consequence a right to criminalise pirates was not dead. Rather it continued to build on the Statute of Truces.

The Statute had not achieved a universal condemnation of pirates, and as it was eventually repealed it was confined to a footnote in the maritime policy of English medieval monarchs. However, this position ignores the intention and significance of this Statute in regard to medieval maritime law. In effect, this Statute did not come out of the blue nor was it as such destined to fail. It had a long history dating back (at the latest) to the beginning of the fourteenth century, and moreover, permitting me to speculate a bit in counterfactual history, it was not on the outset destined to fail. Rather, had Henry V not died in 1422 or the war effort in France not taken a turn for the worse – especially after 1429 – then it might have become a permanent feature of English maritime policy. Indeed, as Henry VIII's statute of 1536 demonstrate, the essence of the Statute was found sound enough to form the core of an English stance on piracy, albeit domestic. That was genius of the Statute: contrary to the past centuries, it only attempted to criminalise the subjects of the king of England. While this may initially seem counterintuitive, a strong and effective government like Henry V's turned it into a success. Moreover, strictly speaking the Statute was

54 Sobecki (2008) 158.
55 Griffiths (1981) 225, Sobecki (2008) 158.
56 *Le débat des hérauts d'armes de France et d'Angleterre* (1887) 25ff.
57 For this development, see for instance Sutton (2018).

not at first thought of as to bolster a bold claim to sovereignty over the territorial waters of England. Rather it was an initative to harness and control the unruly forces of England.[58] Ultimately, Henry did not want to control the sea. He wanted to control England and its institutions. To that end, the Statute worked in a circumstantial way to usher in a royal monopoly over the legitimate use of violence in society. Nevertheless, it came to form the embryo of what ultimately in the seventeenth century became a universal English criminalisation of piracy.[59]

Acknowledgements

The research for this article has generously been funded by the Danish National Research Foundation, DNRF102ID.

Bibliography

Primary Sources

Chaplais, P., ed., *English Medieval Diplomatic Practice*, Part 1, Documents and Interpretations, 2 vols. (London 1982).

Cicero, *On Duties*, William Miller, ed. (London 1968).

CPR – Calendar of the Patent Rolls (London 1891–1916).

Le débat des hérauts d'armes de France et d'Angleterre, L. Pannier and P. Meyer eds. (Paris 1877).

Foedera, Th. Rymer ed., vol. 1 part 2, 1272–1307 (London 1816).

Marsden, Reginald G., ed., *Select Pleas in the Court of Admiralty*, 2 vols. (London 1894).

Pickering, D., *The Statutes at Large, from the Magna Charta, to the End of the Eleventh Parliament of Great Britain, Anno 1761*, 46 vols. (Cambridge 1762–1807).

PROME – Parliament Rolls of Medieval England, Given-Wilson et al. eds. (Woodbridge 2005).

The Digest of Justinian, A. Watson ed. et trans, 4 vols. (Philadelphia 1998).

Twiss, Travers, ed., *The Black Book of the Admiralty*, 4 vols. (Cambridge 2012 [1871]).

Warner, George, ed., *The Libelle of Englyshe Polycye. A Poem on the use of Sea-Power, 1436* (Oxford 1926).

58 Matusiak (2013) 90–92.

59 Pitcaithly (2012) 125.

Secondary Literature

Bellamy, J.G., *The Law of Treason in the Later Middle Ages* (Cambridge 1970).

Brooks, F.W., 'Naval Administration and the Raising of Fleets under John and Henry III', *The Mariner's Mirror* 15 (1929) 351–390.

Brooks, F.W., 'William de Wrotham and the Office of Keeper of the King's Ports and Galleys', *English Historical Review* 40 (1925) 570–579.

Chaplais, Pierre, 'Règlement des conflits internationaux franco-anglais au XIVe siècle', *Le Moyen Âge*, 57 (1951) 269–302.

Cuttler, S.H., *The Law of Treason and Treason Trials in Later Medieval France* (Cambridge 1981).

De Souza, Ph., *Piracy in the Graeco-Roman World* (Cambridge 1999).

Dick, B., *Framing Piracy: Restitution at Sea in the Later Middle Ages* (unpublished PhD thesis, University of Glasgow 2010).

Ford, C.J., 'Piracy or Policy: The Crisis in the Channel, 1400–1403', *Transactions of the Royal Historical Society*, Fifth series, vol. 29 (1979) 63–78.

Friel, Ian, *Henry V's Navy* (Stroud 2015).

Gabrielsen, V., 'Warfare, Statehood and Piracy in the Greek World' in N. Jaspert and S. Kolditz eds., *Seeraub im Mittelmeerraum* (Paderborn 2013) 133–154.

Gardiner, D., 'John Hawley of Dartmouth', *Reports and transactions of the Devonshire Society* 98 (1966) 173–205.

Gauvard, C., 'Punir le crime' in C. Gauvard, *Violence et ordre public au Moyen Age* (Paris 2005) 48–65.

Gillingham, J., 'Enforcing old law in new ways: professional lawyers and treason in early fourteenth century England and France', in P. Andersen, M. Münster-Swendsen and H. Vogt eds., *Law and Power in the Middle Ages: Proceedings of the Fourth Carlsberg Academy Conference of Legal History 2007* (Copenhagen 2008) 199–220.

Gillingham, J., 'Richard I, Galley-Warfare and Portsmouth: The Beginnings of a Royal Navy', in *Thirteenth Century England*, VI (1997) 1–15.

Given-Wilson, Ch., *Henry IV* (Yale 2016).

Griffiths, R.A., *The Reign of King Henry VI* (Stroud 1981).

Heebøll-Holm Th.K., 'Law, order and plunder at sea: a comparison of England and France in the fourteenth century', *Continuity and Change* 32 (2017) 37–58.

Heebøll-Holm Th.K., 'Piracy, Patriotism and Profit in England around 1400', in Th.K. Heebøll-Holm, Ph. Philipp and G. Rohmann eds., *Merchants, Pirates, and Smugglers. Criminalization, Economics and the Transformation of the Maritime World* (Frankfurt 2019a) 33–55.

Heebøll-Holm Th.K., 'The Origins and Jurisdictions of the English Court of Admiralty in the Fourteenth Century', in A. Mussun and N. Ramsay eds., *Courts of Chivalry and Admiralty in Late Medieval Europe* (Woodbridge 2018) 149–170.

Heebøll-Holm, Th.K., *Ports, Piracy and Maritime War. Piracy in the English Channel and the Atlantic, c. 1280–c. 1330* (Leiden 2013).

Heebøll-Holm, Th.K., Ph. Höhn, and G. Rohmann, 'Introduction' in Th.K. Heebøll-Holm, Ph. Höhn and G. Rohmann eds., *Merchants, Pirates, and Smugglers. Criminalization, Economics and the Transformation of the Maritime World* (Frankfurt 2019b) 9–30.

James, M.K., *Studies in Medieval Wine Trade* (Oxford 1971).

Keen, M., *The Laws of War in the Middle Ages* (Abingdon 1965).

Kingsford, C.L. 'West Country Piracy: The School of English Seamen', in C.L. Kingsford, *Prejudice and Promise in Fifteenth Century England* (Liverpool 1925 [1962]) 78–106.

Kowaleski, M., 'Warfare, Shipping, and Crown Patronage: The Impact of the Hundred Years War on the Port Towns of Medieval England', in M.M. Elbl ed., *Money, Markets and Trade in Late Medieval Europe: Essays in Honour of John H.A. Munro* (Leiden 2014) 233–254.

Leitch, M., *Romancing Treason. The Literature of the Wars of the Roses* (Oxford 2015).

Maiolo, F., *Medieval Sovereignty. Marsilius of Padua and Bartolus of Saxoferrato* (Delft 2007).

Matusiak, John, *Henry V* (London and New York 2013).

Meale, C.M., '*The Libelle of Englyshe Polycye* and Mercantile Literary Culture in Late-Medieval London' in L. Boffey and P. King eds., *London and Europe in the Later Middle Ages* (Turnhout 1996) 181–228.

Murray, K.M.E., *The Constitutional History of the Cinque Ports* (Manchester 1935).

Neff, S.C., *War and the Law of Nations* (Cambridge 2009).

Pistono, S.P., 'Henry IV and Charles VI: the confirmation of the Twenty-Eight-Year Truce', *Journal of Medieval History*, 3 (1977) 353–366.

Pistono, S.P., 'Henry IV and John Hawley Privateer 1399–1408', *Reports and Transactions of the Devonshire Association* 111 (1979) 145–163.

Pistono, S.P., 'Flanders and the Hundred Years War: the Quest for the *Trêve marchande*', *Bulletin of the Institute of Historical Research*, vol. 49, no. 120 (1976a) 185–197.

Pistono, S.P., 'Henry IV and the *Vier Leden*: Conflict in Anglo-Flemish Relations 1402–1403', *Revue belge de philologie et d'histoire* (1976b) 458–473.

Pistono, S.P., 'Henry IV and the English Privateers', *The English Historical Review* 90 (1975) 322–330.

Pitcaithly, M., 'Piracy and Anglo-Hanseativ Relations, 1385–1420' in R. Gorski, *Roles of the Sea in Medieval England* (Woodbridge 2012) 125–146.

Powell, E., *Kingship, Law, and Society. Criminal Justice in the Reign of Henry V* (Oxford 1989).

Renouard, Y., 'Le grand commerce des vins de Gascogne au Moyen Âge', *Revue historique* 221 (1959) 261–304.

Richmond, C.F., 'The Keeping of the Seas during the Hundred Years War, 1422–1440', *History* 49 (1964) 283–298.

Rodger, N.A.M., *The Safeguard of the Sea: A Naval History of Britain, 660–1649* (London 1997).

Rubin, A.P., *The Law of Piracy* (Honolulu 1988).
Sobecki, S.I., *The Sea and Medieval English Literature* (Woodbridge 2008).
Sumption, J., *Cursed Kings. The Hundred Years War IV* (London 2015).
Sutton, Anne F., 'The Admiralty and Constableship of England in the Later Fifteenth Century: The Operation and Development of these Offices, 1462–85, under Richard, Duke of Gloucester and king of England', in A. Musson and N. Ramsay eds., *Courts of Chivalry and Admiralty in Late Medieval England* (Woodbridge 2018) 187–214.
Ward, R., *The World of the Medieval Shipmaster* (Woodbridge 2009).

CHAPITRE 9

L'émergence du pirate atlantique dans le royaume de France à la fin du Moyen Âge

Pierre Prétou

1 Introduction

L'histoire de la piraterie comme chef d'accusation, utilisé comme outil de régulation justicier par la royauté française, demeure largement méconnu dans sa chronologie médiévale. Les choses existent-elles lorsque l'on ne rencontre pas les mots dans les archives pour les dire ? Force est de constater que les chefs d'accusation ne sont pas hors du temps. Ils nécessitent l'observation historique attentive, au risque d'acclimater ou de transposer la modernité dans une approche régressive. En peu de mots, le problème d'histoire médiévale que soulève la piraterie est l'apparition du terme qui vient sublimer des crimes existants par ailleurs – vol, coups et blessures, captures des personnes – au prétexte que, commis en mer, ils en viendraient à offenser Dieu, la royauté qui existe par sa grâce et la chose publique que cette dernière incarnerait. Entre les agressions commises en mer et la piraterie, la victime se voit soudain ajoutée sa nation et ce changement bouleverse l'histoire du droit des représailles qui quitte alors le monde des compensations financières issu de l'expérience méditerranéenne du *corso* pour aller à la rencontre des crimes énormes que l'on ne saurait réparer sans exécution et pénalité extraordinaire. Or, le Moyen Âge français méconnait largement tant l'existence de la fameuse distinction qui sépare la course et la piraterie, que la différence qui existerait entre armement privé et public. Ces élaborations apparaissent néanmoins tardivement dans un contexte d'essor des circulations sur les mers bordières atlantiques, de conflit franco-anglais sur la Manche et de maturation des états souverains modernes. Si l'expérience maritime méditerranéenne fondait un socle juridique, nous soutiendrons ici que c'est sur les mers bordières de l'Atlantique que devait naître une nouvelle mécanique de règlement des conflits qui embarquait à son bord un stéréotype criminel supposé hérité de l'histoire romaine. Le pirate français émergea au terme de cette évolution médiévale tardive, imbriquant ici un contexte de rivalités souveraines chrétiennes, une genèse de l'Etat justicier moderne et une mise en sujétion des hommes. Il nous faut néanmoins partir d'un vide lexical, une absence quasi complète du terme 'pirate', que l'expérience

 | DOI:10.1163/9789004407992_011

atlantique devait remplir avant qu'elle ne soit soulevée par l'essor de la souveraineté tardive.

2 Les mots de la violence en mer

Dans les sources françaises, les mots qui caractérisent la violence en mer se rencontrent dans trois gisements classiques – littérature, réglementations et actes judiciaires – avant de différer selon l'espace maritime qui en furent le cadre, selon qu'il s'agisse de la Méditerranée ou de l'Océan Atlantique. Or, dans tous les cas, des hésitations lexicales se constatent qui confirment une genèse tardive des mots, bien qu'inspirée des rédactions romaines issues de l'Antiquité[1]. Le terme pirate, bien connu du corpus cicéronien et, partant, de tous les lettrés du Moyen Age frottés de latin, ne se lit que rarement dans les écritures médiévales[2]. Le mot a lentement disparu des rédactions au haut Moyen Âge, si bien qu'il ne se rencontre qu'à la manière d'un hapax. Il refait surface à partir du XIIIe siècle dans un contexte de réappropriation de la littérature latine, en particulier à l'occasion de la traduction des grands textes historiques de l'Antiquité, tel le *Ab Urbe Condita* de Tite-Live. C'est dans la seconde moitié du XIIIe siècle, que les rédacteurs des *Faits des Romains* engagent pour la première fois le mot français 'pyrate' ou 'pirathe'[3]. Dès lors, cette traduction change le sens que l'historien peut affecter à ces termes car, une fois entré dans le français médiéval, le 'pirate' n'est plus une évocation de lettré, mais bien une appropriation contemporaine du terme. Toutefois, malgré cette évolution, le moyen Français n'y fit pas large accueil et l'usage demeure isolé, tant les mots du 'larronage de mer' s'imposent par leur fréquence. Celui qui méfait en mer est donc avant tout un 'escumeur de mer', ou un 'larron de mer', qui a 'pillé et robbé' plus qu'il n'a 'piraté'[4]. De même, le fait de 'monter sur mer', ou de 'courir sus' se maintient-il en usage tardivement, rappelant ici les traditions du *corso* méditerranéen : une violence certes, mais le lexique n'emporte pas immédiatement une culpabilité criminelle. Que l'on soit en paix, ou en guerre, n'importe finalement que peu pour ces termes. En revanche, le 'larron de mer' vient qualifier

1 Un exemple dans Cheyette (2004) 45–68.

2 Nous avons indiqué des pistes dans Prétou (2014) 37–48.

3 Voir ici 'Li fes des Romains', seconde moitié du XIIIe siècle : Paris, Bibliothèque nationale de France (désormais BnF), Français 726. Voir également le lexique de Pierre Bersuire dans : Paris, Bibliothèque Sainte-Geneviève, ms. 0777, f. 385.

4 Les occurences sont très nombreuses, pieces d'archives comme chroniques. Pour un exemple, voir Jean Froissart, Chroniques, Livre I, § 91. Voir également les commentaires de Thomas Heebøll-Holm (2013).

plus nettement celui qui agit en dehors de ces cadres, mais il n'est que rarement l'objet des rédactions.

La condamnation pour faits de 'piraterie' se révèle également quasi absente de toutes les sources judiciaires françaises. Si le terme n'est pas méconnu des gens de droit qui l'emploient à l'occasion dans leurs plaidoiries en latin, sa version française se révèle moins assurée[5]. Le mot ne vient pas s'associer aisément aux contextes militaires lors desquels des gens de guerre auraient méfait. Car le Moyen Âge français n'a pas inventé le crime de guerre, mais 'l'excès de guerre', hérité de la notion romano-canonique '*excessus*'. Ainsi 'Le fait de faire guerre à nos sujets comme s'ils feussent nos ennemis' est-il répréhensible, de même qu'avoir saisi des hommes en temps de paix 'comme s'ils feussent prins de bonne guerre'[6]. Ces malfaiteurs donc, 'n'ont pas bien obey' et les décisions de justices visent *in fine* leur obéissance et le crime qui y est lié. L'exemple des frères Plusqualec dans la décennie 1430 l'illustre. Pour avoir saisi, volé et attaqué dans les pertuis charentais, ils se rendent coupables de 'destrousses et mises à rançons' illégitimes[7]. Et le procès de prendre, au lendemain de la Praguerie, un tour nettement politique qui fait l'économie des termes de la piraterie : l'objectif était de condamner l'obéissance due au roi et non de sublimer une protection souveraine des mers. Ces procès condamnent donc, mais préparent également la grâce des coupables visés que l'on fait revenir dans le service du roi. Aussi la piraterie se révèle-t-elle absente du lexique employé par les actes car les mots qui aggraveraient perturberaient aussi leur rentrée en grâce finale. Par conséquent, les violences commises en mer n'entrent guère dans la liste des crimes réputés irrémissibles depuis Charles V[8]. L'incendie, le viol de pucelles, le sacrilège, ou encore le guet-apens qui concourent au *crimen maiestatis* ne visent pas les faits commis en mer, bien que s'embusquer ou incendier s'y rencontre aisément. Dans tous les cas, ces élaborations ne s'appliquent guère aux Sarrasins rencontrés en Méditerranée, car il est toujours honorable de les combattre et de paraître s'être croisé.

Sans surprise, conséquence ou raison des propos évoqués *supra*, c'est le crime de piraterie lui-même qui échappe aux réglementations royales. Le modèle de l'ordonnance d'Henri III en 1584, qui dispose l'emploi des supplices justiciers à l'encontre des pirates dans son article 64, est en réalité une création parfaitement moderne. Les ordonnances maritimes médiévales françaises ne

---

5 Voir le terme 'piratarum' ensuite translate en 'prinsez et robées' dans une affaire dieppoise de 1370 : France, Paris, Archives nationales de France (désormais ANF), $X^{1A}22$, fol. 13 et s.

6 Nous avons developpé cette question dans Prétou (2010) 63–72.

7 Voir *Archives historiques du Poitou*, t. II, (Poitiers 1873), 217–251.

8 Voir l'ordonnance de 1364 : *Ordonnances des Roys de France de la troisième race … vol. 3*, 1364 (Paris 1732), 124.

déploient rien de tel et éludent tout emploi du lexique pirate. Si des monuments juridiques classiques réglementent les activités marinières médiévales, elles n'emploient pas plus le terme. En Méditerranée, le *Consolat de la mer* blâme certes la '*male gent*'[9] qui méfait en mer mais il s'arrête à ces mots. En revanche, dans l'Atlantique, les *Jugements de la mer* ou 'Rôles d'Oléron' s'en distinguent en ce qu'ils enregistrent le terme 'pirate' pour qualifier les crimes commis sur mer[10]. Toutefois, cette rédaction, si elle marque une plus grande sensibilité de cet espace maritime à un tel lexique, il n'en reste pas moins que les articles qui en font état sont des rédactions postérieures de la première moitié du XVIe siècle : elles ne sont pas médiévales[11]. Reste alors le droit de la marque, qui aurait pu faire naître une distinction entre course et piraterie. Lettres de représailles, licences de 'soy défendre' et 'pignorations' ne sont pas méconnues des archives françaises[12]. Toutefois, ces documents constituent avant tout une pratique, et non un droit, que les affaires génoises traitées au Parlement de Paris démontrent[13]. L'expérience de la marque est avant tout une relecture comptable, engageant la solidarité des pertes. Cette tradition médiévale ne se relie que difficilement au retour du droit romain à partir du XIIIe siècle, car l'accusation en piraterie qui en découlerait viendrait analyser des coupables et des mauvais sujets du roi, plus que des patrimoines endommagés en mer qu'il conviendrait de restaurer.

3 L'Atlantique comme laboratoire lexical

Plusieurs exemples de violences commises en mer permettent de distinguer l'évolution culturelle française qui fait émerger les termes de la piraterie, avant tout dans les récits atlantiques. Un premier cas emblématique surgit avec les agissements d'Eustache Le moine dans l'Europe du Nord-Ouest au début du XIIIe siècle. Il s'agit d'un premier cas de forban qui nait dans le contexte du conflit franco-anglais après 1204, lorsque la commise de la Normandie fait de la Manche une frontière politique. Eustache, petit noble du Boulonnais qui

9 Nous signalons la mise en ligne d'une édition numérique du *Llibre del Consolat de mar* : [http://www.lluisvives.com/servlet/SirveObras/jlv/09255007699869439647857/index.htm].

10 Article 44. Voir l'édition Pardessus (1828).

11 L'article 44 est un ajout, également present dans l'édition du Grand routier de la mer de Pierre Garcie, que J.-M. Pardessus a cru bon d'ajouter aux redactions anciennes des coutumes de la mer.

12 Timbal (1958) 109–138.

13 Chavarot (1991) 51–89.

monte sur mer par vindicte envers le comte de Boulogne, navigue alors entre deux couronnes en conflit auxquelles il vend alternativement ses services. Ce contexte déclenche une forme de soustraction de sujétion que sa décapitation finale à l'issue de la bataille de Sandwich en aout 1217 rattache ostensiblement à la punition pour crime de désobéissance. Les sources normandes et anglaises accablent fortement le personnage et Mathieu Paris risque les termes '*pirata nequissimus*'[14]. Néanmoins, l'écriture vernaculaire ne translate guère et y voit avant tout une figure du traître au sens féodal du terme[15]. Déloyal, tyrannique, sans aveu, il suscite donc la juste colère du roi à son encontre. 'Maltyran', le récit d'Eustache est l'occasion de blâmer la tyrannie d'exercice comme d'usurpation qui se distingue du pouvoir juste des rois. Malgré l'emploi du lexique pirate latin, il s'agit donc d'une affaire d'obéissance féodale secouée par l'apparition d'une frontière maritime. En somme, un premier traître des mers. Ce récit gagne donc à être comparé avec son inverse, celui de Don Pero Niño, un hidalgo qui, au début du XIVe siècle, opéra tant en Méditerranée que dans l'Atlantique. A la différence d'Eustache, le récit du castillan – le *Victorial*[16] – encense ses actes qui, fait très rare dans le corpus médiéval, anoblissent le personnage pour ce qu'il fit en mer. Or, la logique du récit distingue nettement ce qu'il fit contre les Sarrasins, de ses campagnes auprès de Charles Savoisy pour le compte du roi de France et contre les Anglais dans l'Atlantique. Chef de guerre en Méditerranée occidentale, il s'honore de faire la Croisade, non sans attaquer les Marseillais qui menacent les routes commerciales de la Castille, ce qui engendre des conflits diplomatiques insolubles[17]. De même, il se livre aux razzias, incendies et captures sur les rivages de la Manche dans une lecture militaire classique. Et le lexique pirate de ne pas parvenir à se fixer sur le personnage, merveilleux croisé défendant l'honneur de son roi sur toutes les mers. En Méditerranée, la lutte contre les Sarrasins abolit donc tout lexique pirate, au point d'éluder d'autres agissements plus contestables qui seront finalement reprochés aux Normands qui l'accompagnaient sur la Manche[18]. En cela, Don Pero Niño se rapproche des Boucicaut que l'on retrouve sur la Manche comme en Méditerranée orientale. Cumulant les charges de Maréchal et d'Amiral, ils y défendent l'honneur de leur roi tant par la guerre que par la croisade. A Famagouste

14 Mathieu Paris, *Chronica Majora*. Néanmoins, le point de vue de l'auteur, favorable à la cause anglaise, accable particulièrement Eustache.

15 Ce que démontre un poème octosyllabique du XIIIe siècle, ultérieur aux événements. Voir l'édition : Holden et Monfrin (2005).

16 Voir l'édition Llavador (1997).

17 Voir ici Ferrer Mallol (2000).

18 En particulier pour les attaques menées sur les îles anglo-normandes auxquel Don Pero Niño ne participa pas.

en 1401, aux Italiens clamant avoir été spoliés, Jean Le Maingre, pour contrer toute accusation en piraterie, de déclarer : 'tout ce qui se trouvait sur les terres sarrasines, il lui était licite de s'en emparer'[19]. La croisade fait donc rhétoriquement échec à l'élaboration du lexique pirate quand bien même les frères Boucicaut auraient-ils dépassé les cadres, comme ils le firent en incendiant les rivages de la Tamise en 1380.

A la fin du Moyen Âge, les affaires atlantiques deviennent un laboratoire d'un contentieux maritime nouveau lié à l'essor des amirautés et des traités internationaux que la sauvegarde des rois conforte. Une ordonnance française de 1373 fondait le tribunal des prises et fonctionnement de l'Amirauté[20]. Pour autant, le texte ne contenait aucun pirate, mais des 'mauvaises prinses'. Le principe de la décimation faite au nom du roi y était disposé. Cette réglementation devenait décisive sur l'atlantique, c'est à dire dans les rapports diplomatiques entre états royaux modernes. Au Parlement de Paris, elle infléchissait la pratique qui, bien qu'amorcée avec les affaires génoises, s'appliquait désormais sur les affaires du Ponant[21]. D'un point de vue quantitatif, ce sont donc les affaires atlantiques qui enflent et qui concernent principalement les rapports avec l'Angleterre ou la Castille. Les accords internationaux et autres tentatives de régulation a posteriori des conflits maritimes jouent ensuite un rôle décisif dans la maturation de ces régulations. Par exemple, entre 1411 et 1414, le duc Jean V de Bretagne et le roi Henri V d'Angleterre avaient ainsi tenté d'équilibrer les comptes des dommages que Bretons et Anglais s'étaient infligés par le passé[22]. En 1445 à Châlons-sur-Saône, Charles VII et le duc de Bourgogne procédaient de même afin de liquider les tensions opposant les Flamands aux Normands[23]. En venant ainsi dégonfler une masse d'affaires que la procédure criminelle n'aurait jamais pu résoudre, le procédé ouvrait une voie pour la criminalisation d'un petit nombre irréductible. C'est donc en creux que le pirate devait faire son apparition.

Si aller contre les Sarrasins sur mer s'accompagnait d'une réception tardive de la Croisade, dans l'Atlantique, un raisonnement différent se devait de voir le jour. Sur le fondement de la pratique ancienne du *corso* méditerranéen, il fallait bâtir un stéréotype du bon combattant en mer, renouvelé par l'honneur du service de son roi. Un premier prototype élaboré surgit des dernières décennies de la Guerre de Cent Ans. Pierre de Brézé, sénéchal de Normandie l'illustre

19 *Chronique* d'Antonio Morosini, an 1403 ; *Société de l'Histoire de France*, 1898, tome I, p. 6.

20 Ordonnance de Charles V sur l'Amirauté du 6 décembre 1373. Voir BnF, NAF 10251. Cf. Ordonnances, VIII, 640.

21 Voir Chavarot (1991) 51–89.

22 Mollat (1975) 7–25.

23 Mollat (1975) 7–25.

magnifiquement. L'exceptionnelle conservation de la comptabilité de ses armements démontre une intention de se conformer à la décimation des prises en mer qui anticipe le fonctionnement de l'Amirauté introduit par l'ordonnance de 1373[24]. Cette pièce d'archive confirme ce que l'imagerie des manuscrits français royaux démontre par ailleurs, car Pierre de Brézé est célébré pour son action en mer dans les miniatures des *Vigiles de Charles VII* selon Martial d'Auvergne[25]. L'imagerie le montre déployant toute son emblématique sur mer, avant cri de guerre et assaut vaillant sur un adversaire prévenu. Les codes justes de la guerre sont donc ici employés et le sénéchal y ajoute la commission royale à l'Amiral, la restitution du mal pris et la conservation des preuves étayée par l'enregistrement comptable. Au final, cela explique l'insertion du prototype de ce bon officier en mer dans les *Vigiles*, c'est-à-dire à mettre au crédit de l'œuvre du roi Charles VII. En creux, il démontre ce qu'il ne faut pas faire : s'embusquer, ne pas montrer pavillon, ne pas compter, ne pas payer la décimation. Il ne restait qu'à le nommer 'corsaire', ce que le Moyen Âge français ne fit pas, mais ce motif amorçait tout de même le retour de celui qui ne se conforme pas aux bons usages ainsi promus : le pirate.

4 Le retour de l'ennemi de la chose publique

Le terme français 'pirate' fait un retour splendide dans la littérature tardive. Il vient toutefois se greffer sur des élaborations classiques qu'il faut ici rappeler. Le navire, artefact culturel, évoque fondamentalement une matière religieuse depuis l'Antiquité. De même, la réception médiévale de la navigation peine à s'extraire d'une représentation du pèlerinage des âmes sur les eaux, tant les motifs maritimes se multiplient dans le corpus biblique. Or, les ouvrages de dévotion moderne de la fin du Moyen Âge en accentuent encore les contours[26]. Ainsi que le proclame le *Calendrier des Bergers* : 'L'homme mortel au monde bien est comparable au navire'[27]. Le malfaiteur en mer est donc régulièrement celui qui fait échec au pèlerinage maritime, tel le démon envoyé pour empêcher l'âme de s'élever lors de son périple nautique. Ce motif s'associe à d'autres, plus volontiers profanes, qui font des larrons en mer des obstacles aux amoureux tentant

24 Voir Chantilly, Musée Condé, 1 AA 39. Édition Contamine (2003) 319.

25 Voir la miniature sous la rubrication 'Comment Breze et autres Françoys furent courir en Angleterre' BnF, Ms français 5054, f. 241.

26 Voir Guillaume de Digulleville, *Le pèlerinage de vie humaine*. BnF, Français 376.

27 Voir ici : *Calendrier des bergers*, 1493. Bibliothèque municipale Angers, France. SA 3390, fol. 42.

de se réunir d'amour lointain[28]. Et le roman tardif d'exploiter alors le stéréotype du pirate qui attaque les voyageurs, mais que des Croisés de passage délivreront opportunément. Cette inspiration hybride plusieurs imaginaires que le succès des histoires des Romains vient renouveler à partir du règne de Jean II le Bon. Translaté en français dans les *Faits de Romains* et dans les *Décades* de Tite Live, le mot 'pirate' s'infiltre dans l'essor des traductions françaises d'une littérature très prisée par la Cour de France. Les exemplaires royaux peints de Valère Maxime, ou encore de la *Cité de Dieu*, parce qu'ils insèrent des histoires de pirates ayant défié de prestigieux chefs antiques, assurent un retour en force du motif. L'imaginaire de la croisade s'efface donc au bénéfice du bon chef auquel se comparent les rois de France de la fin du Moyen Âge. César et Pompée y émergent particulièrement en raison de la lutte qu'ils menèrent contre les pirates en Méditerranée. La miniature célèbre donc ces chefs par autant d'épiphanies peintes qui émaillent les exemplaires commandités par l'entourage des Valois[29]. S'y ajoutent les suppliques des communautés littorales qui dénoncent les nids de pirates venus de la mer que le souverain doit s'honorer de purger[30]. Retour du motif de la caverne de voleur autrefois déployé par l'abbé Suger? Les textes évoquent volontiers les 'roches de mer' qui accueillent les larrons de mer et le Prince, tel Pompée, de devoir les en déloger[31]. Désormais, une littérature fait la promotion évidente d'une main forte accompagnant les actions souveraines sur les flots.

Dans ce contexte culturel et politique, une capture de la licéité des actions réalisées en mer voit le jour. Une première étape se constate en 1313 à Poissy, lorsque Philippe le Bel, par ordonnance, dispose une confiscation royale de la justice des prises. Philippe VI la renouvelle en 1335 et c'est sur ce fondement que le Parlement de Paris intervient et s'impose à toute autre cour de justice. En 1443, Charles VII dispose une ultime avancée en réservant explicitement

---

28 Charles d'Orléans, *Ballades*, XXVIII : 'Dieu vueille celle nef garder / Des robeurs escumeurs de mer, / Qui ont à Dangier alliance ; / Car, s'ilz povoient, par rudesse / M'osteroient ma desirance, / Et le tresor de ma liesse'.

29 Voir par exemple : 'César capturé par les larrons de mer', BnF, Ms français 251, folio 216 v°. *Faits des Romains*. Atelier de Richard de Montbaston, fin XIVe siècle ; 'Pompée combattant les pirates', BnF, Ms français 105, folio 46. *Histoire du saint Graal*. Atelier du maître de Fauvel, 1ère moitié du XIVe siècle.

30 Voir l'exemple de la Saintonge : 'Mémoires présentés au roi Charles VII par les délégués de la ville de Poitiers pour le détourner d'établir la gabelle en Poitou et en Saintonge', ed. *Archives historiques du Poitou*, t. II, 1973, 258–259.

31 Voir ce motif dans *Histoire du Saint Graal, Joseph d'Arimathie*, 2e quart du XIVe siècle. BnF, Français 105, fol. 46 : 'Comment Pompees assailli pluiseurs larrons en une roche de mer et comment il fist faire un grant feu devant l'uis d'une cave qui en la roche estoit pour les larrons estaindre dedens'.

ces affaires à la seule cause souveraine. Les traités internationaux s'infléchissent alors. Vers 1450, une tentative franco-castillane de sécuriser la voie commerciale unissant la Biscaye aux Flandres le démontre[32]. Au règlement global des compensations versées de part et d'autre, le souverain français ajouta une taxation sur toutes les importations castillanes, forme de fiscalisation de la marque, pour assurer la paix des navires, anticiper le dommage, confisquer la vengeance sur mer, et donc tenter de réguler *a priori* les prises, et non plus *a posteriori*. Ce pas se révèle décisif et il s'ajoute à un renforcement du droit de la naturalité puisque la marque ne frappait pas les naturels du royaume où elle était édictée. Les marchands l'avaient bien compris puisqu'ils s'évertuaient à obtenir des lettres de naturalité leur permettant d'extraire leurs biens des représailles licites. En toute matière, la sauvegarde royale s'était infiltrée dans les textes qui sécurisaient ces évolutions, faisant des contrevenants de possibles agresseurs de la majesté des rois qui porte avec elle le bien de la 'chose publicque'. Si le Sarrasin méditerranéen était ennemi de Dieu, le pirate émergeant allait être celui des rois par la grâce de Dieu, ces souverains qui prononcent désormais la marque et qui, en conséquence, s'étaient appropriés en creux la définition du pirate.

Un traité signé entre Aragon et France en 1485 parvenait pour la première fois à un préambule définissant par approche commune une paix de navires soutenue par le bien public[33]. Dès lors, une stigmatisation de 'l'ennemi de tous' était permise. Les premiers stéréotypes de criminels aggravés viennent alors se séparer de ceux que l'on appellera plus tard les corsaires. Les pirates n'obéissaient à personne et tuaient leurs captifs. Cette cruauté en faisait des ennemis du genre humain qui offensaient Dieu et, par conséquent, les majestés que la divinité avait institué sur terre. La capture de la marque permet donc *in fine* aux souverains de définir la licéité des agressions en mer, faute de pouvoir les interdire. En creux, c'est donc bien la piraterie qui émergeait de la marque. Réservée par le roi et contrôlée par l'Amiral, l'absence de lettres impliquait nécessairement que l'illicéité rencontrât l'offense faite à la majesté puisque cette dernière produisait la seule licéité valide sur mer. Face à cette mécanique culturelle, juridique et politique, habitée en creux d'ennemis imaginaires et de bon comportements promus par les états souverains, il convient de retenir une très insistante observation de la fidélité des hommes une fois engagés en mer. Plus qu'une appropriation des eaux qui aurait conduit à une première définition des eaux territoriales, il s'agit d'une mise en sujétion des mariniers : un crime d'obéissance donc, parfaitement politique, même si le crime de mutinerie

32 Mollat (1975) 7–25.

33 Mollat (1975) 7–25.

n'émerge pas encore de ces élaborations, puisque qu'une Marine royale n'avait pas encore véritablement vu le jour. En cela, l'élaboration tardive de la piraterie rejoint la trajectoire des accusations en brigandage et en fausse monnaie, dans une identique chronologie qui voit se dresser des ennemis imaginaires de la genèse de l'Etat justicier moderne. Le pirate, comme le faux monnayeur ou le brigand, ne sont pas de simples voleurs à punir. Leur crime a été aggravé ou sublimé par une réception tardive, car leurs agissements n'offensent désormais plus que les seules victimes, mais également la communauté toute entière, la *res publica*, portée par les rois.

5 Conclusion

Au final, d'intenses productions de discours voient naître l'accusation française en crime de piraterie. Le pirate français nous semblera toutefois avoir émergé avec plus d'évidence des expériences atlantiques que des traditions méditerranéennes. La raison paraitra assez simple : affronter des Sarrasins ne présentait pas le même sens juridique qu'affronter des Chrétiens, si bien que la géopolitique religieuse explique cette maturation tardive[34]. La fragmentation souveraine rencontrée sur les rivages des mers du Ponant, surexcitée par le conflit franco-anglais, joua ici un rôle décisif. Ce que le Moyen Âge français y créa en premier lieu fut une singularisation des crime commis, les 'robbeurs escumeurs de mer' du XIIIe siècle. Ces mêmes ennemis furent ensuite transformés en 'pirates' au XVe siècle au terme d'une évolution qui avait été escortée par les formules classiques de la souveraineté moderne : 'voulans la chose publicque prospérer en notre royaume'. Cette évolution remarquable du champ pénal laisse toutefois un perdant : les marchands. Le crime, parce qu'il sort du champ comptable – puisque l'aggravation du crime n'est pas évaluable et mène à la mort pénale – sort des traditions du *corso* et des compensations financières de tradition méditerranéenne. Il laisse aux Etats le pouvoir d'autoriser et d'interdire, en deux outils d'apparence distincte qui n'en sont en réalité qu'un : la course et la piraterie, saisis ici dans leur genèse française atlantique et médiévale.

Bibliographie

Chavarot, M.-C. 'La pratique des lettres de marque d'après les arrêts du parlement (XIIIe-début XVe siècle)', *Bibliothèque de l'École des Chartes*, t. 149 (1991) 51–89.

34 Voir le chapitre de Dominique Valérian dans ce volume.

Cheyette, F., 'The Sovereign and Pirates, 1332', *Speculum* 45, no. 1 (1970) 45–68.

Contamine, C. 'A l'abordage ! Pierre de Brézé, grand sénéchal de Normandie, et la guerre de course (1452–1458)', in P. Bouet et V. Gazeau, *La Normandie et l'Angleterre au Moyen Âge* (Caen 2003) 307–358.

Ferrer Mallol, M.T., *Corsarios castellanos y vascos en el Mediterráneo medieval* (Barcelona 2000).

Heebøll-Holm, Th., *Ports, Piracy and Maritime War. Piracy in the English Channel and the Atlantic, c. 1280–c. 1330* (Leiden et Boston 2013).

Holden, A.J. and J. Monfrin, *Le Roman d'Eustache le Moine* (Louvain 2005).

Llavador, R.B., *El Victorial* (Salamanca 1997).

Mollat, M., 'De la piraterie sauvage à la course réglementée (XIVe–XVe siècle)', *Mélanges de l'École française de Rome, Moyen Âge, Temps modernes* t. 87 no. 1 (1975) 7–25.

Pardessus, J.-M., *Collection de lois maritimes antérieures au XVIIIe siècle* (Paris 1828).

Prétou, P., 'Abolir l'excès de guerre : le pardon royal face à la guerre de Guyenne', 1444–1463' in M. Houllemare et Ph. Nivet éds., *Justice et guerre de l'Antiquité à la Première Guerre mondiale* (Amiens 2010) 63–72.

Prétou, P., 'Du larron écumeur de mer aux pirathes : les genèses de l'accusation en piraterie à la fin du Moyen Âge français' in M. Battesti éd., *La piraterie au fil de l'Histoire, un défi pour l'État* (Paris 2014) 37–48.

Timbal P.-C., 'Les lettres de marque dans le droit de la France médiévale' *Recueil de la société Jean Bodin* t. X (Bruxelles 1958) 109–138.

CHAPTER 10

Maritime Conflict among Hundred Years' War Allies

Tiago Viúla de Faria

1 Introduction

Around 1420, four ships freighted by Portuguese and Flemish merchants that had been laden in Lisbon were stopped off Winchelsea by a small armed flotilla consisting of two balingers and a larger ship. Sir John Arundel, the flotilla's commander, ordered the taking of the merchant ships in the name of the English Crown, thus preventing their crossing to their final destination of Sluys. Held at their own expense and peril, the Portuguese shipmaster Piers Gonsalves (Pêro Gonçalves) and his three partners protested the action to the English parliament.[1] They claimed that the goods on board belonged solely to persons in Flanders and Portugal, and thus they had nothing to do with the enemy. The mariners' second claim was significant. They expected to be released, 'sicome les lieges du Portyngale sount et ount estes *toutditz amys et bienvoillantz al Roialme d'Engleterre*' (my italics), which suggests that seafarers operating in the Anglo-Portuguese context were aware, if only in broad strokes, of the existence of certain rights that could assist them. In expectation of royal favour, they invoked the bonds of friendship and favourable disposition (or so they argued) which had traditionally brought together the subjects of Portugal and those of England. Yet though the Portuguese might be considered friends, this did not suffice to keep their ships from being captured on an English royal mandate, nor even to prevent the valuables they carried from being held.

Regardless of the identity of the participants, such incidents in the medieval Atlantic were not uncommon. To be clear, conflict was a given even in civilian interactions, and conflict management was part and parcel of societal relations.[2] But if this particular event is to be taken at face value, then a problem involving the inadequacy of practice versus form becomes obvious, as geopolitical and economic dimensions were interlocked. European markets and the networks of trade were sustained by burgeoning trans-'national' ties, whereas polities (under the sway of their ruling elites) communicated with each other in a slowly morphing 'system' of allegiances and counter-allegiances. Of course,

1 TNA SC 8/85/4210.
2 Lantschner (2015), Wijffels (2017).

 | DOI:10.1163/9789004407992_012

the strength and depth of links varied and depended on a number of factors. Most pointedly, the Anglo-French dynastic and territorial quarrels, which eventually developed into the Hundred Years' War, put time-honoured political and economic practices to the test. In some way, and to a greater or lesser extent, the Anglo-French dilemmas spanned all of Europe's Atlantic seaboard from Cádiz to Lübeck.[3] Strains among English, Portuguese – however 'friendly and well-wishing' as they may have been – and other nautical colleagues should not be surprising.

What follows concerns the ongoing linkage of two traditional allies to sea-bound conflict and its management and resolution, as modified by 'international' politics and policymaking, with vagaries arising due to the Hundred Years' War. The discussion first seeks to characterize the terms of a 'special relationship' against the backdrop of economic, political, and military ties. It then identifies frequent causes of conflict among the English and the Portuguese and the role played by domestic resources in tandem with external relations as conflict-management channels. In the concluding section, I question whether there existed forms of conflict specific to inter-polity alliances, and the extent to which formal bonds of friendship were helpful to 'allied' seafarers when all was said and done. Central to this subject is evidence from the UK central archives on matters including criminal investigations, letters of protection and safe conduct, military service, legal cases, royal correspondence with local officials, diplomatic documentation, and private petitions for the redress of injury.[4] Sources from the Portuguese side, which almost completely lack legal, fiscal, and criminal accounts, are comparatively thin.

2 Underpinnings

Before the Hundred Years' War the English and the Portuguese had longstanding and relatively well-established commercial relations, characterized by steady if comparatively modest trade. The Portuguese had been featured among England's customary trading partners in Edward I's *carta mercatoria* of 1303, and it is probable that English factors could be found in Lisbon before 1350.[5]

3 Blockmans and Wubs-Mrozewicz (2017), Jeggle (2014) especially 56–58, Curry (2001) 149 ff., Minois (2010) 725–730 ('De la chrétienté à l'Europe des nations'), and still helpfully Perroy (1933).

4 An overview of the most relevant records is given at <http://www.nationalarchives.gov.uk/help-with-your-research/research-guides/medieval-maritime-personnel-and-ships/> (accessed 12 November 2018).

5 *Munimenta*, 205–211, CCR Edward III, vol. 9, 491. On the trade see Childs (2013).

There is, however, reason to believe that claims of a workable, unwavering Anglo-Portuguese friendship, made by merchants like Pêro Gonçalves, perhaps had less to do with time-honoured connectedness and generic pleas for *amicitia* than with official stipulations.[6] More specifically, a set of treaties – which arose from the Iberian ramifications of the Anglo-French conflict – provided norms of interaction. Although merchants had earlier become directly involved in Anglo-Portuguese agreements – Portugal's marine communities had signed a treaty with Edward III in 1353 – none had the sway of the treaty of perpetual friendship and alliance that conjoined Richard II of England (and France) and João I of Portugal on 9 May 1386.[7]

Known as the Treaty of Windsor, the pact was a reaction to the existing coalition between the Valois monarchy in France and the Trastámara rulers of Castile. The Trastámaras posed an additional threat to English territorial interests in France and, through Lancastrian dynastic claims, in Castile, too. Not least thanks to support from Valois troops, the Trastámara kings posed a genuine menace to the self-rule of Portugal under its traditional elites.[8] In establishing 'ligae, amicitiae, confoederationes, et uniones firmae, perpetuae, et reales', the primary goal of the 1386 treaty was to set out measures of mutual protection in the face of the Castilians and the French. The treaty was a step ahead of conventional inter-regnal tactics in that it comprised 'omnes et singuli vassali vel subditi regnorum'. In other words, it expressly took in society at large – including the 'mercatores', who, along with other groups, were singled out.[9] The implications here should be stressed. In particular, articles two and nine of the treaty were instrumental because they set new grounds for socioeconomic procedure. In allowing individuals the freedom of travel and the right to become residents in the other country, the treaty made them answerable to local laws and customs. In the event of a breach of treaty, the sovereign was to answer for the actions of his subjects. Thus the Crown was made accountable for the redress of claims, the payment of injuries, and the punishment of infractors. In addition, the treaty could be renewed at the accession of every new monarch. And it typically was, which helped to confirm it as a day-to-day instrument of the law.

Indeed, for many people the ramifications of something that encroached considerably on the economic sphere and its agents would have been clear,

6 Lesaffer (2004) 34–37.

7 Along with a military compact dating from 1373, the two treaties are summarized in Faria and Miranda (2010) 110–114.

8 On these developments see especially Russell (1955).

9 *Foedera*, vol. 7, 515–521.

since knowledge of the treaty – from hearsay, the written record, or official proclamation – likely seeped into everyday mercantile interactions. Sometime before 28 August 1379, Richard II directed enquiries on whether certain English subjects had been treated as friends in Lisbon up to that point. Simultaneously he ordered the release of a Portuguese crew who had been kept under arrest in Plymouth on the proviso that they declare their friendship towards the English king and realm.[10] It seems likely that suspicions had arisen after Portuguese royal ships had joined the Castilian fleet in attacks against the English earlier in the decade. For all intents and purposes, it was not clear where 'the Portuguese' stood and whether they should be trusted. The extent to which such perceptions were shaped by fluctuations in the international political arena is evident from claims made, around the same time, by French merchants at the *parlement de Paris* that a group of Portuguese merchants who had accused them of wrongdoing were allies with the English in the war.[11]

There is evidence to suggest a change of perception in 1386. Let us consider some fifteenth-century examples across a range of some twenty years, all of which are taken from documents dealing with marine-related injury and resolution. In 1404 a royal proclamation directed to the main coastal towns of the South stated that the merchants of Portugal should not be subjected to robbery and mischief, as such harassment would be contrary to Henry IV's alliance with the king of Portugal.[12] In question was the treaty of 1386, which Henry had renewed without modification only months before.[13] In another example, dating from some time between 1419 and 1423, Gil de Tavira of Algarve brought a case before the English chancery. He stated that the constable of Bordeaux, John Radcliffe, with others 'del flotte dengleterre' had seized cargo – French wine transported on a Castilian ship – belonging to him. After the wine was sold in Cornwall, Gil de Tavira sought redress as a subject of Portugal and therefore an ally of England.[14] In a third example, from 1444, a Portuguese crew, driven ashore at Cornwall, sought food and assistance and in their dealings with the locals emphasized Anglo-Portuguese friendship. Their ship was nonetheless plundered. The unfortunate crew complained directly to the English Crown.[15] This last episode, it is worth remembering, took place nearly a century after the signing of the 1353 Anglo-Portuguese commercial treaty and a good three generations after the 1386 Windsor treaty. Despite the rapidly

10 *CCR* Richard II, vol. 1, 268.
11 Miranda (2017) 21.
12 *CCR* Henry IV, vol. 2, 317.
13 Faria (2012) 70–71.
14 TNA C 1/73/76.
15 *CPR* Henry VI, vol. 4, 289–290.

changing circumstances of the Hundred Years' War, the friendship claim had spanned this entire period with only minor differences in phrasing.

A rhetoric of unwavering goodwill and friendship thus seems to have developed in connection with the alliance, informing Anglo-Portuguese mercantile interactions some time between the late fourteenth and the early fifteenth centuries. Seamen did not necessarily take such amicable bonds (even as they expressed them) too seriously or much to heart, nor did this rhetoric by itself forestall incidents of conflict. This is not to say that Portuguese and English merchants showed no interest in cooperating, let alone that they were outright rivals. Quite the contrary: ties of solidarity may well have bound commercial peers together, their claims emerging out of documentary assurances of protection that supposedly, from a legal standpoint, were reliable. Indeed, it would seem that the 'binding friendship' argument had originated from the top down as part of a rhetorical toolkit. A joint ruling, framed in terms of an alliance, had been formulated at the political centre, and its substance drew largely from the experiences shared by the subjects of both realms. From a certain point onwards there was the expectation that, because of its basis in law, such rhetoric could be harnessed to repair losses and damages resulting from conflict.

By definition, Anglo-Portuguese exchanges were framed by the Atlantic. Conflict was no exception. Communications by land were territorially cut off by France and Castile, thus making it difficult for people, merchandise, equipment, and supplies to reach their destinations even during periods of truce. Irrespective of shape, scope, or complexity, almost every Anglo-Portuguese interaction – be it economic or military – used the ocean. Besides the influence of geography itself, the interplay among actors was further conditioned once the marine space had developed into a full-fledged war zone. Not only were naval resources indispensable for trade and the exchange of agents and news, they also enabled the transportation of armed forces and provisions, diplomatic missions, and of course the patrolling of the seas – to such an extent that resources directly under the royal wing were often found lacking. As a result, civilian means were routinely used and thus joint Anglo-Portuguese enterprises (military and political) materialized. This was probably the alliance's greatest drawback for those whose livelihood depended on crossing the Atlantic undisturbed, calling at the ports of both countries. What is more, treaty dispositions specifically identified enemies in common and set in place obligations of mutual defence, which increased the likelihood that civilian vessels would be regarded as potential prey. International warfare, and Anglo-Portuguese arrangements in particular, came to affect seafarers on two broad levels: in the remit of armed operations, and, more widely, because they bred maritime insecurity.

3 The Crown: Protective and Predatory

Of all human-induced sea hazards, piracy was probably the most widespread. But as merchant ship captains began engaging in piratical activity, governments found the stratagem worth incentivizing. Losses (mostly material) were inflicted on the enemy, but with disruption to trade and communications as an inevitable byproduct. Besides licensing their own privateers, governments might turn a blind eye towards – and even more or less overtly support – aggression by civilians, as long as it was targeted. What might seem like improvised lawlessness escalating into retaliation was in fact deliberate action, reliant partly on sentiments of partisanship and 'national' belonging. It is not surprising, for instance, that the depredations suffered by the English almost continuously during the 1370s and '80s at the hands of French and Castilian shipping were reprised following the deposition and murder of Richard II, as resentment took over the Paris court. Without ever declaring war on Richard's usurper, Henry IV, the Valois were likely largely responsible for the outpouring of violence in the Channel at that time.[16] Ships hoisting the flag of powers siding with either of the main belligerents were frequently involved – Castile's continuing support of the French became particularly noteworthy – and these politically tinted naval offensives undertaken by civilians lasted well into the fifteenth century.[17]

All this activity impinged on Anglo-Portuguese relations quite significantly. Naval clashes between Castilians and the English in the early 1400s caused the Portuguese considerable political embarrassment, upsetting their respective relations with England and Castile. When the two enemies preyed upon each other in Portuguese waters, sometimes just beyond harbour, as was the case in Lisbon and Cascais, they were in breach of Portuguese sovereignty. A petition registered the complaints of a Bristol merchant whose cargo, worth an astounding £4,000, had been lost to a Castilian ship near Lisbon, leading to the (allegedly unjust) arrest of *le Marie* of Bilbao by English officials.[18] In another episode, a ship belonging to merchants of Biscay and Galicia was attacked by Englishmen 'in portu ville de Lagos' in Algarve. That the incident came under Portuguese jurisdiction was too evident to be ignored, and João I of Portugal, seizing the diplomatic opportunity on offer, quickly stepped in to mediate between the Castilian merchants, who were making claims for reparation, and the English Crown (his intervention generated a batch of royal correspondence

---

16 Some of the points made in this paragraph are amply demonstrated in Ford (1979).

17 See for instance Childs (1978) 42.

18 TNA SC 8/216/10796. Additional cases in Carus-Wilson (1967) 45–46.

throughout 1407 and 1408). The matter was resolved when, at João's request, the plaintiffs obtained permission from Henry IV to bring their grievances before the latter's royal officials. Significantly, the letters of safe conduct issued in England for the Castilian merchants did not reach them directly; rather, they were sent through the Portuguese king.[19] It could be that the rule of law and the dispensation of justice in an alien jurisdiction provided a justification for the Portuguese king's intervention. Still, it should not be surprising that in such a case the management of otherwise petty marine conflicts were intertwined with the workings of international politics, as matters were taken to the highest level. The involvement of prominent figures likely explains why the procedures around the Lagos incident were copied down in the Portuguese chancery, in a cartulary of the key Anglo-Portuguese diplomatic instruments.[20]

The Lagos incident's political undertones can be fully revealed if one considers the diplomatic context. At exactly the same time that the Castilian merchants' saga was unfolding, Portuguese and Castilian envoys were engaged in difficult talks that aimed to put a definitive end to a longstanding dispute over the Portuguese throne. In 1402, during the latest conversations, the Castilians had unsuccessfully tried to persuade the Portuguese to lend them and the French armed support specifically against the English. The Castilian representatives singled out piracy and the English Crown itself as being responsible for anti-Castilian violence: the memorandum of negotiations claimed that (in the Castilians' view) the English government had secretly been behind piratical actions and was therefore guilty of breaching the terms of the truce.[21] Conflict at sea – whether involving merchant shipping, military shipping and personnel, or a mixture of both – mirrored the international status quo. As such, it was ripe to be exploited politically. In managing the Lagos dispute, Henry IV's choice of words in a letter to his ally João I is telling: he called the Castilians 'adversarii vestri' rather than 'nostri'.[22] This preference subtly voiced English diplomatic aspirations to win over the Castilian court. That a dispute among sailors should attract such levels of attention in the first place can be understood in light of the relationships of allegiance versus controversy that were held among these various intersecting polities. Both João I and Henry IV were keen to take advantage of the situation. Even such a small-scale event, because it involved members of polities at odds, had sufficed to feed policymaking at a complex, international level.

---

19 PT/TT/GAV 18, *mç*. 7, no. 28, ff. 36 r.–8 v.; transcribed in *Gavetas*, vol. 9, 135–137.

20 PT/TT/GAV 18, *mç*. 7, no. 28. The manuscript is now in the *Reservados* collection.

21 Suárez (1960) 28 ff.

22 *Gavetas*, vol. 9, 135.

The effects of naval depredation were also far-reaching due to Anglo-Portuguese trade being deeply embedded in mercantile relations. Commerce being constant, material resources were generally available at the most important ports. Friendly political relations made it easier for governments to utilize such means, relying both on the networks of professionals and on the assets themselves. This had significant implications. In the years leading up to the 1386 treaty, the Portuguese government had mandated that its envoys to Richard II obtain unlimited credit at their destination. The objective was to acquire the funds necessary to raise a mercenary army in England for immediate service in Portugal. Although the loans were taken out in the name of the Portuguese ruler, the property of Portuguese merchants was what was offered as surety.[23] The operation's yield is impossible to estimate, other than to note that between 1384 and 1385 several trips via the sea transported a relatively small armed force to Portugal, where it served under governmental orders.[24] The fundraising operation's impact on the Portuguese merchant community at large was doubtless damaging. Lenders, failing to be paid the debts they were owed by the Portuguese Crown, began to turn their attention to private Portuguese nationals, whose property was seized wherever it could be found, including the English ports where goods awaited to be sold or shipped in transport. Reimbursement was slow and arduous, causing an escalation in reprisals between merchants (with the royal debts consistently being stated as their underlying reason). This continued until the settlement of the arrears, some thirty years after the original loans had been contracted.[25]

Merchants, along with the exchanging of blows over the forceful seizure of property, also sought more sophisticated means of reparation. It was vital to the Portuguese government's financiers to be conversant with the full terms of business. Some time before 10 July 1397, a certain John Reynold of Bodmin, Cornwall, requested from the English exchequer a transcription of the powers originally awarded to the Portuguese ambassadors in 1385, probably to determine who exactly was to be held accountable for the loans. He was duly provided with a transcript.[26] This man was likely the same John Reynold who in 1403 was ordered to restore 50 ox hides, 47 tuns of wine, and one pipe of honey which he had seized in the port of Sandwich from a Lisbon merchant in lieu of sums owed to him by the king of Portugal.[27] The Portuguese merchant – who,

23 TNA E 30/307.
24 Faria (2011) 263–265.
25 Faria (2009) especially 221–222.
26 TNA C 47/30/8/1.
27 *CCR* Henry IV, vol. 2, 196.

stripped of his livelihood, had fallen into hardship – filed successive pleas with the royal chancery, which the local authorities took some time to acknowledge.[28] The views of the two merchants about accountability were plainly at odds, leaving it to the English administration to come to a solution. English officials were required to draw upon common procedure but also to interpret the ambassadorial papers at issue. Moreover, dealing positively with the harmful effects of Anglo-Portuguese war politics was also a concern for business partnerships, as in the case of a group of Southampton merchants who had hired the services of a London mercer, John Holbech, to recover a loan they had made to the Portuguese. This time around (c. 1391), the plaintiff (Holbech) chose to turn to the English parliament, claiming that he had found it impossible to recover the money he was owed, which in turn had made his employers refuse to cover his costs. The deal, Holbech declared, had thrown him into poverty. Luckily for him, the petition met with success and the Southampton businessmen were forced to pay up – even if they themselves still awaited compensation.[29]

Merchants and other seafaring folk in the Anglo-Portuguese environment might make representations directly to the crown. Most often, their intention was to forestall trouble in the first place. Letters of safe conduct and of protection were issued throughout this period, both collectively and on behalf of individuals. As expected, they multiplied during bouts of piracy or intense military activity and during periods of weak royal surveillance of the seas. In 1445, two English merchants sought assurances from Afonso V of Portugal, even though both were residents of Lisbon. Letters of protection, declaring the intention to guard the men from attempted reprisals and the seizure of goods by Portuguese citizens, were handed out in response.[30] In 1455, at Henry VI's request, Afonso issued general letters of protection to ensure that *the merchants, masters, sailors, and all people of England* could travel safely.[31] Franchises of this kind typically were valid for one year and might be extended, depending on the circumstances. Additional, *ad hoc* measures could be set in motion, probably to mitigate the effects of judicial processes that were moving too slowly. That same year, the merchants of Porto addressed themselves directly to Afonso V's officials with detailed written accounts of the losses they had suffered at the hands of the English. These reports, to be included in the royal

28 TNA SC 8 301/15034, /217/10810, /217/10816.

29 Faria (2009) 217.

30 PT/TT/CHR/I, *liv.* 25, fol. 27 v., documents 3 and 4.

31 PT/TT/CHR/I, *liv.* 15, fol. 66 v., documents 1 and 2, dated 15 and 28 January 1455.

business to be conducted in a diplomatic mission that was soon to depart for England, were to be taken straight to Henry VI.[32] As such, it seems possible that they were used as a bargaining chip in Anglo-Portuguese negotiations, especially when one considers that Afonso V had earlier granted a general protection.

On top of this, the allied governments responded to intimidation and violence between civilians by occasionally enacting joint policy. For instance, in the aftermath of the congress and treaty of Arras (1435), rocketing levels of seaborne aggression led the two governments to demand that mariners (whether English or Portuguese) produce written proof of nationality whenever they were approached at sea.[33] That these sorts of methods were called upon only serves to confirm the sheer inefficacy of the overarching bilateral agreements on the ground, even if plaintiffs kept citing them. Besides the presence of private actors showing little regard for treaty stipulations, opportunists were to be found even among civic and royal officialdom. In summer 1433 a sizeable armed mob led by five Exeter men took from a Portuguese ship (after customs had been paid) goods worth an estimated £400, plus the crew's coffers. The criminal leaders included John More, John Hull, and William Attwyll. These men were, respectively, a future mayor of Dartmouth, a soon-to-be MP for Exeter, and a royal searcher of ships at Exeter and Dartmouth. It took two years for chancery to finally issue orders for the perpetrators' arrests in June 1435. It remains unclear whether the Portuguese did achieve any satisfaction in the matter, since More and Hull came to enjoy parliamentary immunity and Attwyll continued to serve in royal office for a further twelve years.[34]

Problems of this kind were not exclusive to the power structures of middling English sea towns. Allegations made against public officers in Lisbon indicate there was opportunism there, too, and yet again one finds the interpenetration of civic and Crown spheres. In or shortly before 1454, English merchants – Lisbon-resident and others – insisted that the Portuguese king see to their many complaints. These grievances included the claims that royal officials helped themselves to ships' cargo at will; that officials picked out the best items of merchandise to be sold, for too little money, to select clients of their choice; that they colluded with the customs magistrate and the tax collector (*almoxarife*); that they unlawfully overcharged the merchants; that civil

32 On 9 January 1455: *Livro antigo*, 193.

33 Faria (2012) 82.

34 London, History of Parliament Trust, unpublished articles on Hull, John (of Larkbeare in St Leonard, Devon) and Attwyll, William (of Exeter, Devon) for 'Commons, 1422–1504', editor Linda Clark. I am grateful to the History of Parliament Trust for allowing me to see these articles in draft.

servants – judicial, administrative, and fiscal – in the customs house demanded gratuities which were then split among themselves; and even that the clerks asked for fees in exchange for tasks which everybody knew were free of charge.[35] The Lisbon customs facility, it seems, was rife with corruption – this being the only authorized point of entry into Portugal of cloth, by far the main English import – but it is possible that it was somewhat restrained after the protest.[36] In all, disruptions to Anglo-Portuguese economic life and the well-being of its traders were endemic. The status quo remained markedly at odds with the written assurances exchanged by the allies in matters encompassing the safety of ships, people, and goods; shelter taken during travel; the experience at ports; and the very dependability of institutions.

4 Negotiating the War

If seafarers and marine entrepreneurs routinely suffered the rippling ramifications of conflict, such effects were felt even more deeply when their involvement in the Hundred Years' War was direct. In addition to using them as surety, the Crown often relied on the means of private merchants for the military operations – seizing, for example, ships along with crews and gear for royal service. How exactly the impressment of civilian shipping worked at this level is difficult to say (for example, was formal permission to levy ships always necessary?), but the practice seems to have been common especially in England, where royal sea power was patchy at times and war needs were recurring. Because of the lack of means, it was therefore essential to look for non-state resources.[37] For example, in 1372 four Portuguese merchant ships docked at Falmouth and Plymouth were held (and eventually released) for Edward III's use, perhaps in connection with English operations for the relief of Thouars in Poitou, their masters taking out indentures for service with the king's officials.[38] The following year, a Portuguese emissary had at least half a dozen (Portuguese) ships detained at Bristol and Southampton for the transport of troops to Portugal. The ships were kept stationed for about six weeks, if not longer.[39] Very sizeable numbers of civilians and material resources could be

35 Barros (1950) vol. 10, 246–270. See also Chapman and Shillington (1907) chapter 5.

36 Another set of grievances put forward only a few years later, in 1458, was less adversarial in that regard: Barros (1950) vol. 10, 271–275.

37 Lambert (2017) 26–31; also Cushway (2011) especially chapter 3.

38 TNA C 47/2/46/1 to 5. The Poitou operations are mentioned in Russell (1995) 7; Shillington (1906) 120.

39 Russell (1955) 197, n. 2.

implicated when military needs became exceptionally strong. In 1380–81, around forty ships were used to transport a force of 3,000 soldiers and equipment to Portugal;[40] and in 1386, almost ninety ships, manned by an astounding 2,765 seamen in total, were required for an even larger army.[41]

Arrangements made for an Anglo-Portuguese campaign in 1381–82 shed some light on the practicalities of royal arrests. In terms of duration, naval service for that particular mission ranged from a couple of weeks, as with the 50-ton *Le Stephan* of Lisbon, with a crew of fourteen, to over half a year, as with the 1500-ton *St Luke* of Lisbon, with a crew of 28. The rates of payment depended on a ship's size and the duration of service. The *Stephan*, for example, elicited a total pay of £57 16s., and the *St Luke* £90 5s. Such terms were not to everyone's satisfaction, as masters and owners manifested their unwillingness to serve. On this occasion, the arrest met with the claim that the practice was actually in contravention of the terms of the Anglo-Portuguese alliance. A few of the vessels were discharged from duty as a result.[42] Apart from the availability and readiness of appropriate ships, drafting was determined according to need. The ships selected for service varied significantly in size. In 1417, among the transports seized in Bristol at Henry v's behest for the invasion of Normandy, besides Portuguese shipping (the 80-ton *Margarete* of Porto, belonging to João Afonso with a Portuguese master), were much larger boats, the biggest of which, weighing 300 tons, came from Denmark, another of Henry's allies.[43] Merchant vessels were most frequently employed to transport armies, as in this case, but they were also used to transport military equipment and were employed as well in diplomatic missions. On occasion, the two sorts of uses were combined: in 1421 two Portuguese ships waited at Southampton to embark on a voyage that would take a couple of emissaries back to Portugal, along with horses, armour, and weaponry.[44]

Besides having repercussions on the marine society on a broader scale, the allies' armed needs exerted an obvious impact on individual seafarers. A case described in court proceedings dating from 1441, involving one Vasco Rodrigues, originated in a ship's impressment for military service. While on its way back to Portugal laden with merchandise from Flanders, a storm drove Vasco Rodrigues's ship ashore at Dartmouth, where royal officials requisitioned it for the transportation of troops to Gascony. During this trip, felons of

40 TNA C 47/2/49/2.

41 Russell (1955) 412–413 and n. 2.

42 Biggs (2009).

43 *CCR* Henry v, vol. 1, 397. Both Portugal and Denmark were listed as England's allies in a declaration of an Anglo-French truce dated 13 October 1416 (vol 1, 369).

44 *CCR* Henry v, vol. 2, 168.

Breton origin seized the ship and its cargo, valued at 1,000 marks altogether, threw the whole crew into prison and held them for ransom. Rodrigues decided to stand as surety for the release of his companions, which resulted in three years of captivity. Upon release, he opted to return to England, taking lodgings in London on borrowed money, and to file for compensation. He had suffered all his losses, he claimed, because of his personal service to King Henry VI. Yet Rodrigues was again incarcerated, this time because of debts accumulated in England that allowed him to pay the costs of living there. He was imprisoned for a further three years until he finally received a pronouncement in his favour. He could expect restitution to be paid in several instalments over three years. At this point, Rodrigues was no longer able to support himself. Eventually he gave up on the reparations he was entitled to and abandoned England for good.[45] For him – and others for sure – reliance on the Anglo-Portuguese alliance and the countries' friendship had achieved very little, if anything.

By now it should be clear that the various upshots of conflict and the allied responses to the Hundred Years' War were widely felt and were at times disastrous. Doubtless the war was also costly for Anglo-Portuguese commerce. Trade between the two nations, W.R. Childs has argued, contracted during 1381 because English and Portuguese merchant ships had to suspend their business activities because they were involved in a major military operation that year.[46] Still, there was money to be made off the war. As is observable in Anglo-Portuguese maritime relations, conflict opened up opportunities for economic enrichment. Encompassing as well the lack of safety at sea, the wartime logic of alliances and counter-alliances went both ways: (private) resources, as they were summoned, became hampered, and because naval conflict produced marine violence and concomitant losses, trade was contaminated. However, plunder and the like offered obvious material rewards for successful pirates, privateers, and their employers. Regarding ship arrests, we have already seen that crews drafted on a military contract could expect paid compensation. Moreover, shipmen might still be able to make the travel they engaged in during hostilities into a kind of commercially oriented activity by obtaining marketable goods at stops along the way. Finally, as war politics and mutual ill will made access to English ports more difficult for Castilian merchants, Anglo-Portuguese trade had an opportunity to flourish.[47]

45 *CPR* Henry VI, vol. 3, 515, 543, and vol. 4, 29–30.

46 Childs (1997) 35–36.

47 Childs (1997) 34.

Eventually private investors played a significant role in easing the costs of conflict. The Crown frequently relied on them for funding, but most of what can be gleaned about financial risk-taking in the Anglo-Portuguese war business comes from the complaints of investors. This is not to say that every deal would end up a failure. On the contrary: that investment spanned several points in time suggests investors' responsiveness as well as the ongoing prospect of revenue. For one thing, not every merchant objected to being involved in military activity, probably because the potential earnings made risk more manageable and ultimately worth taking. The 27,000 *libras* obtained by Fernando I of Portugal in 1383 to defray war costs came from two wealthy Lisbon citizens. They had agreed to organize a sale of wine worth 21,000 *libras* so as to generate a profit of 6,000 that would then be channelled into the royal coffers. In return, the two merchants were awarded the prize of collecting the *sisas* tax in full, levied on all sales of wine and meat in Lisbon, for four months. In 1395 they filed suit against the Crown, claiming that they had been prevented from collecting the proceeds. In their estimation, the interest surpassed 200,000 *libras* in the new currency.[48] English entrepreneurs were just as willing to take chances, as is shown by a bond taken by two Portuguese military recruiters with a group of Londoners around 1384–86. Among the creditors were Henry Green and Thomas Morieux, both knights and officials in Richard II's court. Nicholas Brembre, the mayor of London and a wealthy merchant close to the king, was another lender. These men had agreed to finance the two envoys, even though these envoys were already in arrears with other London creditors.[49] The transaction, which involved well-placed individuals, was surely but one of many sealed at the time. In fact, the Portuguese fundraising operation in England appears to have triggered a gigantic investment in war – which seems to have been paid back only around 1412 or possibly later and may have led to a temporary mistrust from potential creditors.[50] Nonetheless, the incredible loans drafted between 1384 and 1386 in both Portugal and England stand as testament to the readiness of merchants and other economic players to gamble in the business of war.

Civic authorities and institutions proved equally resourceful in their own responses to the war. To pick one example, the Portuguese ambassadors sent to England in 1384, in addition to having orders from the Crown, also received

48 'Todo aquello que da dicta renda das dictas sisas poderom aver no tempo que a nom teverom nem correrom o quall interesse estimavam a duzentas mill libras da moeda antiga'. AML-AH *Livro 1° de Sentenças*, document 19.

49 TNA E 30/1279; Russell (1955) 370 and n. 1; Jones (1968) 189.

50 Faria (2009) 223.

independent mandates from the cities of Lisbon and Porto to contract ships and to recruit militias for municipal use. The soldiers were to be paid out directly from the town coffers. Porto, on the authority of the municipal council, even sent a transport ship (a *barinel*) to England to carry troops explicitly intended for the city. A further 10,000 franks were invested in the recruitment of 'many' English archers and men-at-arms to serve around Portugal. About 700 of them pulled ashore in April 1385 to garrison Porto. In fact, Porto did not shy away from royal requests to finance later military operations, despite the Crown's reputation for being notoriously late in its payments.[51] Moreover, certain institutions and services developed out of the need to protect the welfare of seafaring communities. The flourishing of bonds (*bolsas*), for instance, in Portugal was due to the risks in travelling the regions most affected by the Anglo-French conflict, namely the Atlantic coastline from La Rochelle to Bruges, including meridional England.[52] As with private individuals, strains induced by warfare had increased the preparedness of sea-minded collectives, helping to make them more resilient.

5 Conclusion

As might be expected, sea-mediated relations were far from trouble-free, even as they took place among 'amys et bienvoillantz' – as the late medieval, 'allied' peoples of Portugal and England broadly called themselves. Although claims of friendship and goodwill, grounded in political assertions, were repeatedly stated, conflict (more or less violent, ranging from formal proceedings to robbery, assault, and even murder on occasion[53]) was part and parcel of the relationship, even as supervised – usually quite ineffectually – by the allied polities. The very notion of alliance was double-faceted. On a deeper level, it rested on a tradition of free enterprise and commercial partnership, and, from a certain point onwards, on constitutionalism via 'international' lawmaking. Both facets, however, came up quite short in preventing disruptions and disputes, and even in improving conflict management in the remit of the Anglo-Portuguese sphere. Whatever the benefits of the Anglo-Portuguese special relationship, they were somewhat lessened by the comparatively high levels of attrition between members of the two polities.[54] In the context of dispute management, the alliance

51 *Vereaçoens*, 390–393, Russell (1962) 419–433.
52 Barros (1950) vol. 9, 357–539.
53 *CPR* Henry VI, vol. 3, 176.
54 Miranda (2017) 17–18.

was not a dead letter since merchants kept recalling it even as the Hundred Years' War tapered off in the mid-fifteenth century. But its palpable failure to stop violence (sanctioned and non-sanctioned alike) shows that, in practice, the alliance was but one of several tools in the conflict-management kit.

One problem was that late medieval public mechanisms of 'international' joint procedure, in this case the Windsor treaty and its derivations, remained too vague. They failed to hollow out the jurisdictional voids which prevented the implied mercantile communities from managing and resolving litigation within what should have functioned like a common platform. It is not likely, therefore, that the formalization of alliance represented a vast – or even a clear – improvement on the means and access to conflict resolution, and surely not among the English and the Portuguese. Whatever the economic and judicial privileges of alliance, the official procedures at large were comparable to those already available to other Atlantic merchants and merchant collectives. They consisted of the ability to petition higher bodies (local and royal tribunals, parliament, chancery) through challenges and lawsuits, and to appeal directly to kings and peers within the oligarchy with requests for intervention (through letter-writing and diplomacy, for example). It was left to the skills and knowhow of individuals and collectives to determine the ways, and the extent to which, the norms set out in malleable instruments of governance such as the 1386 Windsor treaty were implemented. Merchants and other entrepreneurs still felt the need to come together and act as a group, such as when the English in Lisbon and the people of Porto lobbied separately before King Afonso V, or at times when efforts of commercial and royal diplomacy entwined.

Thus, popular perceptions and the royal outlook should not be confused. Many in England and in Portugal were dissatisfied with wartime royal policy. To think of conflict as a nationally unified compound ('the enmity existing between England and Castile', 'the Anglo-Portuguese military partnership', and so on) is especially problematic when non-military, commercially engaged agents are at issue. Yet the notion of 'national' collectives is not entirely anachronistic in this context and remains useful; the king can still be regarded as the personification of his subjects, and his subjects as enveloped in the extension of the royal political purpose. This much can be gleaned from the litigation management records, spanning the whole of the Hundred Years' War, that drew upon the alliance as a set of norms. 'The Portuguese', 'the English', or 'the Spanish' (meaning those of Castile) were indeed taken collectively as distinct entities, definable through provenance and natural allegiance to a certain sovereign.

Last of all, since the working relationship between allies was highly susceptible, as it were, to the whims of war, formal alliances created their own sets of problems. Paradoxically, alliances contributed to heightened conflict, generating further political decision-making in turn. Regardless of the guarantees given them, subjects still suffered wrongdoing by 'representatives' of the political opponents of either Portugal or England, or of both countries. In this regard, the sea proved especially fertile. Remarkably, Anglo-Portuguese relations were remodelled and re-placed within the functioning of a specifically marine setting. The ocean equally challenged the link existing between polities and conflict-management as removed from warfare, strictly speaking. Marine actors as ubiquitous as corsairs, pirates, bands of criminals, and indeed all manner of opportunists showed little concern for such prearranged political alignments. In stark contrast with what one finds in state-level proceedings, one of the outlaws in a 'pan-national' pirate flotilla led by a group of Castilians operating off Galician coasts at the turn of the fourteenth century was a man who went by the name 'Juan el Inglés'.[55] Across its many manifestations, sea-girt conflict in the Hundred Years' War cannot but call into question the implications of alliance and its real value during this period.

Bibliography

Unpublished Documents

Arquivo Municipal de Lisboa – Arquivo Histórico [Lisbon], Chancelaria Régia (AML-AH).

Arquivo Nacional – Torre do Tombo [Lisbon], CHR/I (Chancelaria de D. Afonso v) (PT/TT/CHR/I).

Arquivo Nacional – Torre do Tombo, GAV (Gavetas) (PT/TT/GAV).

The National Archives [Kew, London], C 1 (Court of Chancery) (TNA).

The National Archives, C 47 (Chancery Miscellanea) (TNA).

The National Archives, E 30 (Diplomatic Documents) (TNA).

The National Archives, SC 8 (Ancient Petitions) (TNA).

Published Documents

As Gavetas da Torre do Tombo, A.S. Rego ed., 12 vols (Lisbon 1960–1977) (*Gavetas*).

Calendar of the Close Rolls, preserved in the Public Record Office, H.C.M. Lyte et al. eds., 47 vol. (London 1900–1963) (*CCR*).

Calendar of the Patent Rolls, preserved in the Public Record Office, H.C.M. Lyte et al. eds., 53 vol. (London 1891–1916) (*CPR*).

55 Suárez (1960) 22.

Foedera, conventiones, litterae, et cujuscunque generis acta publica inter reges Angliæ et alios…, 20 vols, T. Rymer ed. (London, 1704–1735) (*Foedera*).

Livro antigo de cartas e provisões dos senhores reis D. Afonso V*, D. João* II *e D. Manuel I do Arquivo Municipal do Porto*, A.M. Basto ed. (Porto 1940) (*Livro antigo*).

Munimenta Gildhallae Londoniensis: Liber Albus, Liber Custumarum et Liber Horn, vol. 2, part 1, H.T. Riley ed. (Rolls Series, vol. 12) (London 1860) (*Munimenta*).

'Vereaçoens': anos de 1390–1395. O mais antigo dos livros de vereações do Município do Porto existentes no seu Arquivo, A.M. Basto ed. (Porto 1937) (*Vereaçoens*).

Secondary Literature

Barros, H.G., *História da administração publica em Portugal nos seculos* XII *a* XV, vols. 9 and 10 (Lisbon [1950]).

Biggs, D., '"A Voyage, or Rather an Expedition, to Portugal": Edmund of Langley's Journey to Iberia, June/July 1381', *Journal of Medieval Military History* 7 (2009) 57–74.

Blockmans, W., and J. Wubs-Mrozewicz, 'Maritime Integration from the Seaside: A Comparative Synthesis', in W. Blockmans, M. Krom and J. Wubs-Mrozewicz eds, *The Routledge Handbook of Maritime Trade around Europe, 1300–1600* (Abingdon and New York 2017) 446–481.

Carus-Wilson, E.M., *The Overseas Trade of Bristol in the Later Middle Ages* (New York, 2nd edition 1967).

Chapman, A.B., and V.M. Shillington, *The Commercial Relations of England and Portugal* (London 1907).

Childs, W.R., *Anglo-Castilian Trade in the Later Middle Ages* (Manchester 1978).

Childs, W.R., 'Anglo-Portuguese Relations in the Fourteenth Century', in J.L. Gillespie ed., *The Age of Richard* II (Stroud 1997) 27–49.

Childs, W.R., *Trade and Shipping in the Medieval West: Portugal, Castile and England. A Series of Lectures* in memoriam *for Professor Armindo de Sousa, given in the University of Porto, November 2009* (Porto and Turnhout 2013).

Curry, A., 'War, Peace and National Identity in the Hundred Years' War', in Hartmann, A.V., and B. Heuser eds, *War, Peace and World Orders in European History* (London and New York 2001) 141–153.

Cushway, G., *Edward* III *and the War at Sea: The English Navy, 1327–1377* (Woodbridge 2011).

Faria, T.V., 'The Politics of Anglo-Portuguese Relations and their Protagonists in the Later Middle Ages (*c.* 1369–*c.* 1449)' (DPhil thesis, University of Oxford 2012).

Faria, T.V., '"Por proll e serviço do reino"? O desempenho dos negociantes portugueses do Tratado de Windsor e suas consequências nas relações com Inglaterra (1384–1412)' in M.H.C. Coelho, S.A. Gomes and A.M.R. Rebelo eds, VI *Jornadas Luso-Espanholas de Estudos Medievais: A Guerra e a Sociedade na Idade Média (6, 7 e 8 de Novembro de 2008). Actas*, vol. 2 (Porto de Mós, Alcobaça and Batalha 2009) 209–227.

Faria, T.V., 'Tracing the "Chemyn de Portyngale": English Service and Servicemen in Fourteenth-Century Portugal', *Journal of Medieval History* 37 (2011) 257–268.

Faria, T.V., and F. Miranda, '"Pur bonne alliance et amiste faire": Diplomacia e comércio entre Portugal e Inglaterra no final da Idade Média', *Cultura, Espaço & Memória* 1 (2010) 109–127.

Ford, C.J., 'Piracy or Policy: Crisis in the Channel, 1400–1403', *Transactions of the Royal Historical Society* 29 (5th series) (1979) 63–78.

Jeggle, C., 'Interactions, Networks, Discourses and Markets', in Caracausi, A., and C. Jeggle, eds, *Commercial Networks and European Cities, 1400–1800* (London 2014) 45–63.

Jones, R.H., *The Royal Policy of Richard II: Absolutism in the Later Middle Ages* (Oxford 1968).

Lambert, C., 'Henry V and the Crossing to France: Reconstructing Naval Operations for the Agincourt Campaign, 1415', *Journal of Medieval History* 43 (special issue: 'Agincourt in Context: War on Land and Sea') (2017) 24–39.

Lantschner, P., *The Logic of Political Conflict in Medieval Cities: Italy and the Southern Low Countries, 1370–1440* (Oxford 2015).

Lesaffer, R., 'Peace Treaties from Lodi to Westphalia', in R. Lesaffer ed., *Peace Treaties and International Law in European History. From the Late Middle Ages to World War One* (Cambridge 2004) 9–44.

Minois, G., *La guerre de Cent Ans: naissance de deux nations* (Paris [2008] 2010).

Miranda, F., 'Conflict Management in Western Europe: The Case of the Portuguese Merchants in England, Flanders and Normandy, 1250–1500', *Continuity and Change* 32 (special issue: 'Merchants and Commercial Conflicts in Europe, 1250–1600') (2017) 11–36.

Perroy, É., *L'Angleterre et le grand Schisme de l'Occident. Étude sur la politique réligieuse de l'Angleterre sous Richard II (1378–1399)* (Paris 1933).

Russell, P.E., *The English Intervention in Spain and Portugal in the Time of Edward III and Richard II* (Oxford 1955).

Russell, P.E., 'Os Ingleses em Aljubarrota: um problema resolvido através de documentos do Public Record Office, Londres', *Revista Portuguesa de História* 10 (1962) 419–433.

Shillington, V.M., 'The Beginnings of the Anglo-Portuguese Alliance', *Transactions of the Royal Historical Society* 20 (new series) (1906) 109–132.

Suárez Fernández, L., *Relaciones entre Portugal y Castilla en la época del Infante Don Enrique, 1393–1460* (Madrid 1960).

Wijffels, A., 'Introduction: Commercial Quarrels – and How (Not) to Handle Them', *Continuity and Change*, 32 (special issue, 'Merchants and Commercial Conflicts in Europe, 1250–1600') (2017) 1–9.

CHAPTER 11

In the Shadow of Other Empires: Genoese Merchant Networks and Their Conflicts across the Atlantic Ocean, ca. 1450–1530

Carlo Taviani

This chapter deals with commercial conflicts which arose among certain traders in the Atlantic area – the southern Iberian Peninsula (Seville, Cadiz, Lisbon, Majorca, Malaga) and the Atlantic archipelagos close to the African continent (Madeira, the Canaries, Cape Verde) – between 1450 and 1530.[1] It focuses on a specific group of traders who moved from Genoa on the Italian Peninsula to Portugal and Spain. From there they traded in the islands of the African and the American Atlantic. Spanish, Portuguese, English, French, and Italian (Genoese and Florentine) merchants were attracted by the resources of the African continent. The present chapter focuses on commercial conflicts which involved European traders in the Atlantic. First, it shows the difficulties historians encounter in finding information on commercial conflicts which involved people and traders on the African continent. Second, it maintains that in order to understand commercial conflicts in the Atlantic it is useful to explore its entanglements with the Mediterranean. It establishes differences among the various commercial conflicts which arose between European traders and focuses on the Genoese. It posits that to study these traders it is useful to explore the institutions and networks involved with Genoa from abroad. Finally, it focuses on the Genoese system of conflict resolution and on the history of certain offices.

1 Conflicts and Silent Trade

Many commercial conflicts which arose along the shores of West Africa, in the West African hinterlands, and in the African archipelagos of the Atlantic during

1 This chapter has been conceived together with another essay which deals with the Genoese and the quest for gold. Taviani (forthcoming). The paragraphs on the Genoese diaspora and on the 'silent trade' in this chapter have similarities with two paragraphs in that essay. I have added here more results on the subject of the 'silent trade', on the notaries, and the Genoese network. Abulafia (2008).

 | DOI:10.1163/9789004407992_013

the fifteenth and early sixteenth centuries will probably remain unknown. The interactions between the people who came from Europe and the people of Africa or those of the Atlantic islands are not described in the written sources of pre-colonial Africa, and often the sources in European languages do not focus on these kinds of commercial contacts.

Among the European traders who reached the Atlantic during the fifteenth and early sixteenth centuries, the Italians and particularly the Genoese, together with famous Portuguese and Spanish traders, played an important role in the commerce conducted between West Africa and the Americas. Genoese traders in West Africa have not been studied separately from Spanish and Portuguese traders.

When the Genoese in the fourteenth century explored and traded in the Canaries they enslaved the Guanches people and brought them to North Africa to sell them. We do not know anything about prior commercial relationships or conflicts that may have existed between the Guanche and the Genoese. Very early in the sixteenth century, along with their Portuguese counterparts, Genoese traders acquired and enslaved people from Africa and sold them in the American Atlantic via the archipelagos of Cape Verde. We do not know much about the commercial relationships that the Portuguese *lançados* (mainly Jewish middlemen), the Portuguese, and the Italian traders established with these Africans in order to enslave members of their group. We can imagine that there were commercial conflicts amongst the complex and violent exchanges between Christian Europeans and the peoples of Africa, both the Muslim traders and the African people of sub-Saharan Africa – probably many more such conflicts than those which arose within the community of European merchants (Portuguese, Spaniards, Italians, etc.) on the one hand, or between traders within West Africa, on the other. However, there remains little in the historical record about these clashes, and often what exists is largely mythological.

A series of classical sources – among the most famous a passage in Herodotus – and subsequently certain medieval Arabic, European Renaissance and later European references report a commercial practice which has been named the 'silent trade'. According to various sources, people in sub-Saharan Africa (as well as in other parts of the globe) swapped goods and gold through a nonverbal form of exchange – that is, without ever meeting face to face. The two parties deposited goods in a specific space at two different moments. Upon seeing what the other had left in this place, one party to the trade would adjust the quantity of their own goods (to make for an equitable exchange) without ever meeting the other party. When one of the traders was satisfied, this trader (or group) took the other party's goods and went away; the other party claimed the remaining goods. This phenomenon has been extensively studied since at least the nineteenth century.[2] Since the initial studies conducted by early-nineteenth-century German scholars, this practice has been considered a means of transaction connected to conflicts, an idea that many others, such as Karl Polanyi and Paulo de Moraes Farias (who has contested the very reality of the silent trade), have expanded upon. Gustav Schmoller considered the silent trade to be a mixture of trust and mistrust because its traders were not involved in a deep exchange.[3] Max Förster, an anthropologist and a colleague of Aby Warburg, was interested in silent exchange as an early form of commerce, and Richard Henning compared the silent trade with the *Wieland Sage* of English mythology.[4] According to Förster and Henning, silent trade was practised amongst people who could not speak to each other, not only because they did not know each other's language but because they were sometimes at war.[5] The necessity of acquiring metals led to a sort of forced commercial exchange.[6] This powerful myth, enduring for hundreds of years from Herodotus to the European Renaissance, could be regarded as a phenomenon related to cross-cultural commerce and to conflicts and their resolutions. Even though the hostilities were not directly related to this sort of trade, but – according to this hypothesis – pre-existed it, we can imagine that they also affected trading transactions. What lies behind this myth will remain unexplored because of the lack of source material. The study of the African past is in fact very difficult, because sources are scarce as compared to European material.

The following chapter focuses on the relationships and conflicts of a group of Italian traders who, far from their home city, traded in the shadow of the Portuguese and Spanish powers in the Atlantic. The sources analysed for the moment mostly provide information about the Genoese and their European counterparts, but they are indirectly related to Africa.

---

2 Green (2013), Bonner (2010), Dolfsma and Spithoven (2008), Giardina (1986), North (1977), de Moraes Farias (1974), Price (1967), Polanyi (1963), Bovill (1929–1939), Henning (1917), Förster (1907), Schmoller (1900–1904).

3 Schmoller (1900–1904).

4 Förster (1907), Henning (1917). For the contact between Aby Warburg and Max Förster, see the database of the Warburg Institute Archive, *ad indicem*: http://wi-calm.sas.ac.uk/CalmView/advanced.aspx?src=CalmView.Catalog. One of the shelves of Warburg's library is denominated 'prehistoric trade'.

5 Ibidem.

6 Ibidem.

2 The Genoese Trade Diaspora in the Atlantic

From the fourteenth to the seventeenth centuries, Genoese traders were active from North Africa to the Atlantic, from Asia (in the Indian Ocean) to the Black Sea, and from the Iberian Peninsula to the Low Countries and England. From the beginning of the fourteenth century onwards, Genoese traders could be found in the southern Iberian Peninsula, having established their companies mainly in Seville, Cádiz, Jerez, Puerto Santa María, Malaga, and Lisbon.[7]

Over the decades, they expanded their businesses outwards towards the archipelago off the western coast of Africa: Madeira, the Canaries, Cape Verde, and São Tomé. Madeira – where many Genoese merchant families became residents – was crucial for the production of slave plantation sugar.[8] So too the Canaries, which were 'rediscovered' by the Genoese navigator, Lanzarotto Malocello, at the beginning of the fourteenth century.[9] As has been mentioned, during the same century Genoese traders enslaved the indigenous people of Tenerife (Canaries), the Guanches, and sold them into slavery in North Africa. In the following century and in the early sixteenth century, they established sugar plantations there. In 1461, Cape Verde was reached by the Genoese navigator Antonio Da Noli, who was then given the title of 'discoverer' by King Afonso v of Portugal and was later made governor of the island. Cape Verde also became an important center for the slave trade. Exploration and trade were typical activities engaged in by members of the Genoese diaspora, but while the latter has been extensively investigated, the former has been much less studied. Genoese in the Atlantic not only reached Africa from the west but also tried to penetrate it from the north. As regards the Maghreb, for example, Antonio Malfante travelled to Tlemcen (southern Algeria) in 1452 and wrote an account – the first made by a European Christian – of the legendary city of Timbuktu, known today for its old endangered libraries, but in earlier times for its being a trading post for gold and slaves.[10] In earlier centuries Tunis, Oran, and Bugia had already become important trading posts for Genoese and Italian merchants, who exchanged goods from Genoa and the rest of Europe with merchandise brought by caravan from Africa through the Sahara. The Iberian Peninsula and the crown of Atlantic islands formed a commercial hub between Africa and Europe.

7 Verlinden (1970), 100, 123 and de Sopranis (1939).
8 Vieira (2004), Camacho (1961), Galloway (1989), Rau (1964).
9 Verlinden (1958).
10 De La Ronciere (1918), di Tucci (1934).

Though the city of Genoa was geographically remote, it was relevant within this trading diaspora that extended to the Maghreb and the Atlantic. To resolve conflicts and to create partnerships, Genoese traders needed a complex social and institutional system whose core was located in Genoa. It was formed by two major components. On the one hand, there was the web of families among whom the traders could find investors and mediators for commercial conflicts arising abroad; on the other, there was notarial institutions. In the period from around 1450 to the early sixteenth century, the Genoese network which was projected towards the Atlantic used notaries and their authority to transmit sources to their relatives and business partners, to resolve commercial conflicts with other Genoese or with business partners who had business in Genoa (Florentines, along with Portuguese and Spanish traders), to build new businesses, and to transplant institutions. Genoese merchants in the Atlantic traded under the flags of Spain and Portugal. At the beginning of the sixteenth century, this Atlantic trade was flowing towards the New World; Genoa, at this point, was far away from this diaspora. When the Americas opened up new markets and provided new goods, the Genoese moved westwards, becoming the bankers and merchants of the Spanish Empire.

Although the traders came from Genoa, this does not necessarily imply that they brought goods to Genoa or to the Italian Peninsula. As has been studied by Jacques Heers, the trade balance remained in favour of the Spanish Peninsula. The commercial hub was the Spanish peninsula and Northern Europe. Furthermore, the Genoese traders were located in the Spanish peninsula; their trade was located there and projected itself outwards towards the Atlantic and Africa.[11]

The role of the Genoese has been recognized and studied mostly for their so-called explorers and adventurers: Christopher Columbus; Antonio da Noli (1461), the discoverer of Cape Verde; Antonio Malfante, who went to Tlemcen and collected information on Timbuktu (1452); Antoniotto Usodimare, who accompanied the more famous Alvise Cadamosto in Guinea (1455); and Niccoloso da Recco, who rediscovered the Canaries (1341).[12] These so-called Genoese explorers need to be contextualized as part of the story of the Genoese trading networks. The vast Genoese trading networks represent what were essentially commercial contacts between Europeans and Africa. The 'explorers' were only the tips of the icebergs of wider trading networks. This perspective

11 On this, see Taviani (forthcoming).

12 The literature on Christopher Columbus is too extensive to be accounted for here; for Antonio da Noli, Antonio Malfante and Nicoloso da Recco, see Verlinden (1958), Peragallo (1904), Caddeo (1928).

may help us gain a more accurate view of relations between Africa and Europe, a vantage that would be less Eurocentric since it regards 'exploration' as a component of commercial exchange and exploitation.

The literature on the Genoese on the Spanish Peninsula and the Atlantic is extensive. Together with the seminal works of Enrique Otte and Ruth Pike, the efforts of many other scholars have been devoted to this subject and have involved the use of Spanish and Portuguese archives, but the documentation in Genoa has not been explored systematically.[13] Economic historians consult merchant ledgers extensively in order to track down the activities of traders, yielding particularly fruitful insights for places such as Florence, where account books have been well preserved. There are, however, far fewer Genoese ledgers from this period.[14] Nonetheless, notarial deeds are rich in information, even if this information is sometimes difficult to parse: although certain notarial deeds possess a title to explain the kind of deed it is, others have no such title. Table 11.1 illustrates the most frequent titles of notarial deeds for the period between the end of the fifteenth and the beginning of the sixteenth century.

Some of the categories are very common, such as will or power of attorney, but others – the *mahona* or the *alberghi*, and even the *commenda* contracts – much less so. The *commenda* and the *mahona* were business partnerships, but whereas the *commenda* is famous and was diffused along the entire Mediterranean, the *mahona* was specific to Genoa and a few other places.[15] The *alberghi* was a kind of kinship partnership and is typical of medieval Genoa.[16] The notarial deed denominated 'albergo' was usually a list of people of that *albergo*.

Although notarial deeds as a whole in the earlier centuries have been studied, there are no comprehensive studies of fifteenth-century Genoese notarial deeds. Not all commercial activities were recorded or appear in documents written in front of a notary during this period, while it seems probable that

---

13 For the Genoese in Spain, see Airaldi (1966), Álvarez (1992), Andújar Castillo (1999), Arienzo (1993) and (1998), Assini (1994), Balletto (1976), Bitossi (2004), Boscolo and Bibiano (1986), Boscolo (1974) (1981) and (1984), Coca Castañer (1973) (1980) (2000) (2007), Doria (1986), Esposito (1989), Fábregas (2001) (2004) (2005), Fossati Raitieri (2001a) (2001b), Gioffrè (1961), Igual Luis (1992) (1997), Martignone (1974), Pike (1966), Spinola (1868) (1868), Otte (1963) (1965) (1986) (1996), Verlinden (1970); for the contact with the Genoese in Portugal, see Musso (1976), Peragallo (1891) and (1904), Alessandrini (2006), D'Arienzo (1998), Rau (1954) (1966), Verlinden (1961). An exception on the use of Genoese sources is the work of Fabregas (2004).

14 Taviani (forthcoming).

15 Taviani (2018) 431–434.

16 Grendi (1975).

TABLE 11.1 Titles of deeds

Original name	Translation
Compositio	Composition
Procura	Power of attorney
Testamentum	Will
Naulitiatio	Itinerary of the ship
Commenda	Business partnership
Calculus Rerum	Inventory
Manumissio	Manumission
Datio in solutum	Giving in payment
Sententia arbitralis	Arbitral sentence
Fidecommisso	Trust
Venditio	Sale
Maona	Business partnership
Albergo	Kinship partnership

SOURCE: ARCHIVIO DI STATO DI GENOVA, NOTAI ANTICHI

private writings were extensive. It is possible to hypothesize that – among the commercial deeds – what has been recorded by notaries refers to conflicts or phenomena which could not be resolved in private.[17]

Because of their great variety, any systematic study of Genoese notarial documents would be quite a daunting task. The challenge involved is probably the reason – together with the lack of a complete index – why projects devoted to the extensive use of notarial archives in Genoa never came to fruition and remained a dead letter.[18] The present research refers to around 10,000 notarial deeds, with one-tenth referring to the Genoese diaspora on the Iberian Peninsula. The core of this research project is the notarial documentation preserved in Genoa, but an examination of Genoese documents – as will be shown with the case study of the Cattaneo family below – can be fruitfully integrated with a study of the documentation housed in Seville (notarial archives and *Casa da India* archives), Lisbon (*Archivo do Torre do Tombo*), and the notarial archives of the Canaries. As mentioned, the Genoese merchant network in place during the period considered here (ca. 1450–1530) was mainly projected into the

17 I want to thank Valentina Ruzzin for sharing her thoughts on this subject.

18 For example the very promising project of Fernand Braudel, Carlo Cipolla, and Roberto Lopez: see Taviani (forthcoming).

Atlantic islands and the Iberian Peninsula, and its commercial ties with Genoa were weak (even black enslaved people are mentioned only very rarely in the Genoese documentation). The notarial connection was, however, stronger and more important. The sources do not contain information about the goods the Genoese traded in. That kind of data is more likely to be found in Seville or Lisbon.

What follows relates to two kinds of conflicts: (1) those involving the rivalry between the Spanish and the Portuguese in the Atlantic and West Africa which involved the Genoese; and (2) the internal conflicts which arose among two or more groups of Genoese traders. A third variety of conflicts – those which arose between Genoese and non-Spanish or non-Portuguese European traders, such as the English traders – is not considered here.

3 Genoese Trade with the Spaniards and Portuguese

The decades preceding the Treaty of Tordesillas in 1494 saw many conflicts between the Portuguese and the Spanish empires. Some had been regulated by the papal bulls, such as the *Romanus Pontifex* (1459) and *Inter Caetera* (1456). However, those efforts did not resolve the situation. The Castilian-Portuguese war that arose in the period 1475–1480 led to the Canaries being declared Spanish in 1479. These events were relevant moments with regard to the control of the Atlantic. The islands of Madeira, the Canaries, Cape Verde, and São Tomé were vital trade centers which allowed Europeans to exploit West Africa and, later, the New World.

A few examples show that the involvement of Genoese traders in the activities of the Spanish or the Portuguese led to violent commercial conflicts. In 1453, a Genoese merchant aboard a Catalan ship had his hands cut off when the vessel was approached by a Portuguese ship off Guinea.[19] In 1481 there were rumors at the court of Portugal that Florentine and Genoese merchants were stealing secrets about Mina in Guinea; and in 1471 a Genoese was reported to be the first to purchase pepper on the Malgueta coast.[20]

We can look at some of these examples as a form of Genoese participation in Portuguese and Spanish exploration, but we can also consider these various clues to represent a symptom of administrative and economic stress. The Portuguese court was greatly invested in the defence of its geographic and commercial secrets. Conflicts were created by the Genoese trading in the shadow

19 Blake (1942) 17.
20 Ibidem.

of the Portuguese and the Spanish empires. Jewish or Armenian merchants – which have been studied to a much greater extent – were highly competitive and this situation also caused conflicts. In the early sixteenth century the Genoese not only traded but also occupied various offices. During the period examined here, for example, the *Almoxarife* (taxation office) of the island of Fuego in Cape Verde was occupied in 1512 by Antonio Spinola, a Genoese.[21] Even more importantly, the *Feitor de Casa da India* in Portugal, in the same period, was also a Genoese, Antonio Salvago.[22]

Around 1515 the king of Portugal forbade English merchants to trade in slaves with Africa. The order was issued by the Genoese *feitor*, Antonio Salvago.[23] We know that some English merchants, such as Roger Marlom, Sebastian Cabot, and others, traded with the Genoese during this period.[24] We can hypothesize that the Genoese used their administrative and commercial networks to conduct business with other merchants (English merchants, for example) and that the administrative offices were used to trade with other Genoese merchants and, at the same time, could be useful when conflicts arose. Genoese traders perhaps used the administration of the Portuguese empire itself to resolve commercial conflicts or difficult administrative situations.

4 Internal Genoese Conflicts

In Genoa several offices dealt with commercial conflicts, but merchants, often relying instead on an informal network of agents and intermediaries, did not always use them. Considering the role of offices or of intermediaries, it is possible to distinguish schematically at least three major levels of conflict resolution. A first level of conflict resolution involved the role of the offices. Among the most relevant is the office called *Officium Mercantiae* (Office of the Goods). It had been reassembled and rules were issued on its role in 1404 during the French dominion over Genoa. It lasted until 1530.[25] Initially a political office, it was ruled by officials who were appointed via elections. Half of the representatives were drawn from the *populares* (merchants and artisans), the other half from the nobles. In 1530 the Genoese transformed it into the *Rota Civile*.[26] Appointed experts in law were appointed to rule this office. By the end of the

21 *Historia Geral de Cabo de Verde* (1990) 192.
22 Torre do Tombo, Nucleo Antigo, 881, 372
23 Ibidem.
24 Dalton (2012) and (2016).
25 Savelli (2017).
26 Ibidem.

sixteenth century it had become a model for other cities and countries, such as the Low Countries.

Some commercial conflicts were resolved by the *Ufficium Robarie* (office of the pirates), though its activities have mostly been documented from a political perspective.[27] The oldest sources pertaining to this office are from 1301.[28] They stated that the office had the power to punish all thefts committed by the Genoese against people who were not enemies of the Commune of Genoa.[29] At the end of the fourteenth century the role of the office was more strongly oriented towards the control of political unrest.[30] Between the end of the same century and the beginning of the fifteenth century the office's activities were reduced until eventually it became defunct.[31]

Another important office was the *Ufficio dei Rupti* (office of the bankruptcies), which was created in 1423. It reserved the right to check the account books of Genoese merchants and citizens. Its magistrates could regulate controversies among quarreling parties or among debtors and creditors. A few years later, in 1429, the office was abolished and its activities were taken up by the *Ufficio di Moneta* and the *Ufficio dei Banchi*, whose activities are recorded particularly for the period 1465–1467.[32] The office of the *Rupti* resumed its activities in 1474.[33] Its rules stated that the magistrates of the office were in charge for six months. Debtors who went bankrupt were to end up in debtors' prisons (*carcere male paghe*).[34] According to the regulations, there would be a fine levied against people from every place in the Genoese lands who hid a fugitive debtor.[35] Debtors could not participate in councils or dress in silk or use any silver or gold object.[36] Certain commercial conflicts which arose in the Crimea were regulated by the *Officium Gazarie*, whose main duties were to superintend the administration of Caffa and the other trade posts and cities in Crimea and the regulation of navigation in the same area.[37] It was created around 1313.

27 Roccatagliata (1990).
28 Ibidem.
29 Ibidem, 17.
30 Ibidem, 50–68.
31 Ibidem, 81.
32 Archivio di Stato di Genova (ASG), Ms. 266, cc. 114r-v. For the activities of the office, see ASG, *Notai Antichi*, 669 (for the years 1423–1459), *Notai Antichi* 769 (for the activities of the 1460s), *Notai Antichi* 841 (for the activities of the 1450s), *Notai Antichi* 841 bis (for the years 1465–67). The documents have been located by Rodolfo Savelli. See Savelli (2017).
33 Archivio Storico del Comune di Genova, 110 bis, E22, c. 25r.
34 Ibidem, c. 26r.
35 Ibidem, c. 27r.
36 Ibidem, c. 27v.
37 See Forcheri (1974). See also Khvalkov (2018).

The second level of conflict resolution was that of the *probi viri de tabula*, a group of intermediaries appointed monthly or yearly. This group's activities have not been recorded often in the sources and have not yet been well investigated.

The third level of conflict resolution was informal. The parties nominated an arbiter who was an expert in law or one or more merchants who were experts in goods. The notary acted in two phases:

1) The parties nominated the arbiters and asked for a deadline.
2) The composition was concluded in front of him.

As will be shown in subsequent case studies, sometimes these different levels interacted and a resolution was reached via a system which mixed the role of one or even two offices and that of an informal agreement. Disentangling this matter is complicated by the typology and the conservation of the sources. One of the difficulties encountered by scholars in describing the process of commercial conflict resolution in Genoa is that the activities of several offices were recorded by a notary and his documents have been preserved together with other kind of sources. For example, a folder for Battista Parisola contains deeds from the period 1462–1465. Among this material we find deeds related to the activities of intermediaries who resolved commercial conflicts and to the activities of the *Ufficium Mercantiae*, which acted alone.[38]

5 Case Studies

The following case studies show how conflicts arose among the Genoese abroad in the Atlantic and how they were resolved with the theoretical models shown above.

The first case involves Christopher Columbus. The very famous source related to this case took the name 'the Assereto document'.[39] It has been considered proof that Christopher Columbus was Genoese, since it mentions him as 'Genoese'. On 25 August 1479 Christopher Columbus spoke in front of the *Officium Mercantiae* because he was involved in a case between Lodisio Centurione and the brothers Paolo and Cassano Di Negro. Lodisio Centurione had sought to acquire a certain amount of sugar. Columbus had been sent to Madeira by Paolo di Negro, who wanted to acquire the sugar and bring it to Lodisio Centurione.[40] Columbus went to Madeira, but Paolo di Negro had been

38 ASG, *Notai Antichi* 769, 40, 118 (for the first case); 48, 120 (for the activities of the *Ufficium Mercantiae*).

39 Assereto (1904).

40 Ibidem 12.

unable to send the money, which came to 1290 ducats. The provider of sugar was disappointed, since Columbus did not have the money to pay him (he only had 103 ducats). At the same time, the ship which had to be used to bring the sugar arrived; its owner Ferdinando Palensi – was also upset, since he wanted to be paid for the use of his ship, even if the sugar was much less. At that point, in fact, Columbus had sold other goods to pay for at least a part of the sugar. The situation was complex since Columbus had to pay two parties at the same time without having much money to do so. In this case the *Officium Mercantiae* dealt with the conflict and resolved it – forcing one of the parties, Paolo di Negro, to pay Lodisio Centurione.[41]

Another case shows the overlapping role of different offices. On 15 September 1469 the *Officium Mercantiae* took a decision on a conflict pitting Thomas Coche of London, who was represented by his procurator Lorenzo Testa, against the Genoese Christophorus Cattaneo.[42] In this case, the *Officium Mercantiae* acted together with the *Officium Banchorum*, which in that period had been substituted for the *Officium Rupti*. In another conflict, between Simone Cattaneo, a merchant in London, and Gaspar Cattaneo, the *Officium Banchorum* forced Gaspar to pay Simone. In this case the office acted alone.[43]

The third case involves the *Probi Viri de Tabula* and the Cattaneo, an important Genoese family whose activities are important since they are connected with the very beginning of the transatlantic slave trade. Until now, experts on the history of the transatlantic slavery have usually considered that the first organized transatlantic voyages and cargos were organized during the 1530s.[44] At the same time they also admit that it is possible to find a few commercial voyages in earlier years of sixteenth century, but state that it was usually the king of Portugal who gave the *Casa da Guiné* permission to do this.[45] However, as has been documented, some private merchants, such as the Genoese Cattaneo family, had already acquired enslaved people from West Africa in Cape Verde and had sold them to other Genoese merchants in the New World in 1513.[46] Here new evidence is presented that documents the activities of this family, and in particular of Alessandro Cattaneo, who was also involved in

41 Ibidem 13.

42 ASG, *Notai Antichi*, 841, n. 10, September 19, 1469. The conflict is also recorded at the date of April 10, ASG, *Notai Antichi*, 841, n. 2.

43 ASG, *Notai Antichi*, 841 bis, 2, 6 February 1466.

44 Green (2012).

45 Green (2012).

46 Dalton (2016) 99.

another shipment in 1516. The information related to Alessandro's activities can be obtained from a constellation of documents preserved in Seville, Lisbon, and Genoa.[47] This case study is useful in illustrating how different archival perspectives can shed light on the Genoese commercial diaspora which spread outwards from Genoa as far as Santo Domingo. Furthermore, these two glimpses of the Cattaneo family's business practices in 1513 and 1516 require scholars to focus on this family and others to verify the hypothesis that certain investors had already been systematically involved in the slave trade at the beginning of the sixteenth century.

The Genoese sources also contain information about the use of the second degree of intermediation, the *Probi Viri de Tabula*. In 1519 Caesar Cattaneo, a citizen of Genoa and a son of Leonardus, made his will in Genoa and mentioned that his son Antonio had died in Cape Verde, where his son Alessandro was also a resident.[48] Caesar had previously given 500 ducats to Antonio. When Antonio died Caesar took the 500 ducats back for himself and for a group of Genoese, who probably invested in Antonio's trade: 200 ducats went to Lorenzo Cattaneo, the Genoese consul in Portugal, 200 went to himself and 100 were given to Francesco Lomellini and, since the latter was deceased, to Battista Spinola, son of Tomaso. Caesar also declared that Alessandro owned him 300 ducats plus 400 which the latter had received for his emancipation, while Giovanni, another son, owed him only 400 ducats for his emancipation. He decided that Giovanni had to receive the same amount of money as Alessandro. Should they not find a solution, he stated that two *probi viri* should be named. The person who had initiated the conflict should be fined 500 ducats.

6 Informal Agreement

From the middle of fifteenth to the beginning of the sixteenth century, various members of the Centurione family were trading in gold. They were among the richest merchants and bankers in Genoa.

47 The Spanish sources in Seville are in Archivo Protocolos de Sevilla (APS), Record of Bernal Gonzalez Vallesiilo, file 15, book I (13 December 1513), file 15 (21 October 1516). Quoted in Pike (1966), 101 and 194 n. 10 and 15 and studied by Dalton (2016) 99. The Portuguese sources are in Torre do Tombo and were published in *Historia Geral de Cabo de Verde* (1990) 167, 245. The Genoese sources are in ASG, *Notai Antichi*, 1286, Giovanni Costa, doc. 619 (15 luglio 1519) and have been identified by Andrea Lercari, see Cattaneo della Volta and Lercari (2017) 187.

48 ASG, *Notai Antichi*, 1286, Giovanni Costa, doc. 619 (15 luglio 1519).

TABLE 11.2 The quest for gold of the Centuriones

Name	Partnership	Location	Date	Gold	Purpose
Federico Centurione	Unknown	Mina de Oro (El Mina Castle in West Africa)	1486	attempt	
Federico Centurione	Stefano Centurione and Giuliano Calvo	New World	1507	attempt	
Federico Centurione	Unknown	Portugal	1513		Received gold 'de la Tyba' (gold powder)

SOURCE: TAVIANI (FORTHCOMING)

Table 11.2 shows a small dataset reflecting the Centuriones' involvement in the quest for gold covering the years 1465 to 1513.

In 1465 Nicholas and Jacobo Marihoni were engaged in a dispute with Francesco Centurione and Thomas Piccamiglio.[49] The disagreement revolved around a quantity of wheat and Valencian drapes which were exchanged in the Kingdom of Tlemcen for sub-Saharan gold (*aurum tiberi*).[50] The Marihoni gave Centurione and Piccamiglio 628 *doublas* and 2 tominas of gold (*aurum tiberi*). A group of mediators (people known to both the parties) resolved the conflict. The mediators were Tadeo Spinola, Luca Pinelli, Johannis and Franciscus Spinola.[51] This notarial deed involved both the Centurione and the Marihoni families. The further away from Genoa the Genoese traded, the smaller was their Genoese network. When Genoese families traded with sub-Saharan Africa via North Africa, only a small group of merchants from Genoa were able to reach these remote places.

---

49 ASG, *Notai Antichi*, 869, 31 March 1466, c. 150.
50 Ibidem.
51 Ibidem.

7 Conclusion

As this chapter has shown, the Genoese were involved in the Atlantic trade and interacted with Portuguese and Spanish merchants and officials. To resolve conflicts they used their network and the institutions in Genoa. The first part dealt with the various kinds of conflicts; the second with conflicts among the Genoese traders.

Often the investment for trading came from Genoa, from members of the older generations of a family: these people had accumulated money from businesses in other places such as the Levant (the Black Sea, which was a Genoese territorial domain before the Ottoman conquest, or in the Eastern Mediterranean Sea, such as Chios, and Cyprus, as in the case of the Centurione family). In such cases the conflicts occurred within the same family.

More often, however, notarial deeds contain information about commercial conflicts between two families or groups of merchants which were then resolved in front of a Genoese notary and – even more importantly – using Genoese witnesses and mediators (like the case studies presented here). Genoese mediators played an important role in resolving these kinds of disputes, since they were often socially or economically linked to the parties involved in the conflict. This may be the reason why the merchants of the Genoese diaspora employed Genoese notaries even when they themselves lived far away. Genoese notarial deeds and the social, economic, and kinship ties within Genoese society performed a regulatory function whenever conflicts arose. Thus not only is the role of the notary relevant, but also that of the social network. Spanish and Portuguese archives lack richness in their fifteenth-century material, especially when compared to Italian and to Genoese archives in particular; if we want to study the Genoese network, the archives in Genoa offer a variety of possibilities. The rich Genoese network behind the so-called explorers and adventures is very well represented in Genoese notarial deeds.

Bibliography

Abulafia, D., *The Discovery of Mankind: Atlantic Encounters in the Age of Columbus* (New Haven 2008).

Airaldi, G., ed. *Genova e Spagna nel secolo 15: il 'Liber damnificatorum in regno Granate' (1452)* (Genova 1966).

Albuquerque, L., and Madeira Santos, M. E., *Historia Geral de Cabo Verde. Corpo Documental II* (Lisboa 1995).

Alessandrini, N., 'La presenza italiana a Lisbona nella prima metà del Cinquecento', *Archivio storico italiano* 164 no. 1 (2006) 37–54.

Álvarez, J., 'El Libro de los privilegios de los genoveses del Archivo de Simancas. Descripción', in de Silos Manso, D., Triguero, M.T. and Abejón, M., ed., *El libro de los privilegios concedidos a los mercaderes genoveses establecidos en Sevilla* (Madrid 1992) 18–32.

Andújar Castillo, F., 'Los genoveses en el reino de Granada: comercio y estrategias mercantiles' in E. Belenguer Cebrià, *Felipe II y el Mediterráneo, vol. 1: los recursos humanos y materiales* (Madrid 1999) 357–376.

Assini, A., 'L'archivio del collegio notarile genovese e la conservazione degli atti tra Quattro e Cinquecento' in V. Piergiovanni ed., *Tra Siviglia e Genova. Notaio, documento e commercio nell'età colombiana* (Milano 1994) 213–228.

Balletto, L., 'Mercanti genovesi a Siviglia alla metà del Quattrocento', *Medioevo. Saggi e rassegne* 2 (1976) 109–115.

Balletto, L., 'Famiglie genovesi nel Nord-Africa' in Geo Pistarino ed., *Dibattito su Grandi Famiglie del Mondo Genovese fra Mediterraneo ed Atlantico. Atti del Convegno, Montoggio, 28 ottobre 1995*, Accademia Ligure di Scienze e Lettere. Collana di monografie 13 (1997) 49–71.

Bitossi, C., 'Genova, Napoli e Spagna tra Quattro e Cinquecento: l'avvicinamento silenzioso' in G. Galasso and C.J. Hernando Sánchez eds, *El reino de Nápoles y la monarquía de España: entre agregación y conquista (1485–1535)* (Roma 2004) 495–514.

Blake, J.W., *Europeans in West Africa, 1450–1560: Documents to Illustrate the Nature and Scope of Portuguese Enterprise in West Africa, the Abortive Attempt of Castilians to Create an Empire There, and the Early English Voyages to Barbary and Guinea* (London 1942).

Bologna, M., ed., 'L'Archivio della famiglia Sauli, di Genova', *Atti della Società Ligure di Storia Patria*, Nuova Serie vol. XL (CXIV) Fasc. II. (2000).

Bonner, M., 'The Arabian Silent Trade: Profit and Nobility in the "Markets of the Arabs"' in P.M. Sijpesteijn, R.E. Margariti and A. Sabra eds., *Histories of the Middle East: Studies in Middle Eastern Society, Economy and Law in Honor of A.L. Udovitch* (Leiden 2010).

Boscolo, A., 'Gli insediamenti genovesi nel sud della Spagna all'epoca di Cristoforo Colombo' in A. Boscolo ed., *Saggi di storia mediterranea tra il XIV e il XVI secolo* (Rome 1981).

Boscolo, A., 'Il genovese Francesco Pinelli amico a Siviglia di Cristoforo Colombo' *Nuova rivista storica* 68 (1984) 355–366.

Boscolo, A., 'La prima politica mediterranea di Ferdinando I d'Aragona' in *Atti del 1° Congresso Storico Liguria-Catalogna, Ventimiglia-Bordighera-Albenga-Finale-Genova, 14–19 ottobre 1969* (Bordighera 1974) 349–360.

Bovill, E.W., 'The Silent Trade of Wangara', *Journal of the African Society* 29 (1929–1930) 27–38.

Brilli, C., *Genoese Trade and Migration in the Spanish Atlantic, 1700–1830* (Cambridge 2016).

Caddeo, R., *Le navigazioni atlantiche di Alvise da Ca' da Mosto, Antoniotto Usodimare e Niccoloso da Recco* (Milano 1928).

Camacho, Guillermo, and Perez Galdos, 'El cultivo de la cana de azucar y la industria azucarero en Gran Canaria, 1510–1535', *Anuario de estudios atlánticos* 7 (1961) 11–60.

Camacho, Guillermo, and Perez Galdos, 'Málaga, colonia genovesa (siglos XIV y XV)', *Cuadernos de estudios medievales* 1 (1973) 135–144.

Camacho, Guillermo, and Perez Galdos, 'Los Genoveses en Málaga durante el reinado de los Reyes Católicos', *Anuario de estudios medievales* 10 (1980) 619–650.

Camacho, Guillermo, and Perez Galdos, 'Genoveses en la corte de los Reyes Católicos: los hermanos Italian', *Moneda y monedas en la Europa medieval, siglos XII–XV, XXVI Semana de Estudios Medievales Estella* (Pamplona 2000) 457–483.

Chiavari Cattaneo Della Volta, E. and A. Lercari, *I Cattaneo Della Volta: vicende e protagonisti di una millenaria famiglia genovese* (Genoa 2017).

Coca Castañer, L. de, 'Genova y el Reino de Granada (siglos XIII–XV)' in S. Cavaciocchi ed., *Relazioni economiche tra Europa e mondo islamico, secc. XIII–XVIII*, 2 (Grassina 2007) 267–294.

Dalton, H., 'Into Speyne to Selle for Slavys: English, Spanish, and Genoese Merchant Networks and Their Involvement with the "Cost of Gwynea" Trade before 1550' in T. Green ed., *Brokers of Change: Atlantic Commerce and Cultures in Precolonial Western Africa* (Oxford 2012) 91–124.

Dalton, H., *Merchants and Explorers: Roger Barlow, Sebastian Cabot, and Networks of Atlantic Exchange 1500–1560* (Oxford 2016).

D'Arienzo, Luisa, 'Le colonie genovesi di Siviglia, Cadice, Jerez e Puerto de Santa Maria alla vigilia del viaggio di scoperta colombiano attraverso una fonte fiscale sulla guerra di Granada (l'assedio di Baza del 1489)' in L. Arienzo, *Sardegna, Mediterraneo e Atlantico tra medioevo ed età moderna: studi storici in memoria di Alberto Boscolo*. Vol. 3: *Cristoforo Colombo e la sua epoca* (Rome 1993) 133–183.

D'Arienzo, Luisa, 'Mercanti genovesi tra Siviglia e Lisbona nel Quattrocento' in A. Boscolo and B. Torres Ramírez eds., *La presenza italiana in Andalusia nel basso Medioevo* (Bologna 1986).

D'Arienzo, L., 'Banchieri e mercanti genovesi in contatto con Cristoforo Colombo in Portogallo', in *Case commerciali, banchieri e mercanti italiani in Portogallo: convegno* (Lisbon: Istituto italiano di cultura in Portogallo, 1998) 51–66.

D'Esposito, F., 'Presenza italiana tra i Conquistadores ed i primi colonizzatori del Nuovo Mondo (1492–1560)' in *Presencia italiana en Andalucía, siglos XIV–XVII, Actas del III Coloquio Hispano-Italiano* (Sevilla 1989) 493–518.

De Moraes Farias, P.F., 'Silent Trade: Myth and Historical Evidence', *History in Africa*, 1 (1974) 9–24.

Dolfsma, W. and A. Spithoven, '"Silent Trade" and the Supposed Continuum between OIE and NIE', *Journal of Economic Issues* 42 no. 2 (2008) 517–526.

Doria, G., 'Conoscenza del mercato e sistema informativo: il know-how dei mercanti-finanzieri genovesi nei secoli XVI e XVII' in A de Maddalena and H. Kellenbenz eds., *La Repubblica internazionale del denaro tra XV e XVII secolo* (Bologna 1986).

Fábregas García, Á., 'Aprovisionamiento de la seda en el reino Nazarí de Granada. Vías de intervención directa practicadas por la comunidad mercantil genovesa', *La España medieval*, 27 (2004) 53–75.

Fábregas García, Á., *La familia Spinola en el reino nazarí de Granada. Contabilidad privada de Francesco Spinola (1451–1457)* (Granada 2004).

Fábregas García, Á., 'Estrategias de los mercaderes toscanos y genovesos an el reino nazari de Granada. Una primera aproximacion a través de la correspondencia Datini', *Serta antiqua et mediaevalia*, 5 (2001) 259–304.

Fábregas García, Á., and A. Malpica Cuello, 'Los genoveses en el reino de Granada y su papel en la estructura económica nazarí' in L. Gallinari ed., *Genova. Una 'porta' del Mediterraneo* 1 (Genoa 2005) 227–258.

Forcheri, G., *Navi e navigazione a Genova nel Trecento* (Genova 1974).

Förster, M., 'Stummer Handel und Wielandsage', *Archiv fur das Studium der neueren Sprachen* (1907) 303–308.

Fossati Raiteri, S., 'I mercanti-banchieri genovesi nella Spagna del secolo XV', *Serta antiqua et mediaevalia* 5 (2001) 237–258.

Fossati Raiteri, S., 'La nazione genovese tra Cordova e Siviglia nel secondo '400', G. Petti Balbi ed., *Comunità forestiere e 'nationes' nell'Europa dei secoli XIII–XVI* (Naples 2001) 283–298.

Galloway, J.H., 'The Atlantic Sugar Industry: ca. 1450–1680' in *The Sugar Cane Industry: An Historical Geography from Its Origins to 1914* (New York 1989) 48–83.

Giardina, A., 'Le merci, il tempo, il silenzio. Ricerche su miti e valori sociali nel mondo greco e romano', *Studi storici* 27 (1986) 277–302.

Gioffrè, D., 'Documenti sulle relazioni fra Genova ed il Portogallo dal 1493 al 1539', *Bulletin de l'Institut historique Belge de Rome* 33 (1961) 179–316.

Goldthwaite, R., E. Settesoldi and M. Spallanzani, *Due libri mastri degli Alberti. Una grande compagnia di Calimala (1348–1358)* (Florence 1995).

Goldthwaite, R., E. Settesoldi and M. Spallanzani, 'The Practice and Culture of Accounting in Renaissance Florence', *Enterprise & Society* 16 (2015) 611–647.

Green, T., 'Silent Trade', *History in Africa*, Special 40th Anniversary Issue (2013) 3–6.

Green, T., *The Rise of the Trans-Atlantic Slave Trade in Western Africa, 1300–1589* (Cambridge 2012).

Grendi, E., 'Profilo storico degli alberghi genovesi', *Mélanges de l'Ecole française de Rome. Moyen Âge*, temps modernes 87 no. 1 (1975) 241–302.

Heers, J., *Le livre de comptes de Giovanni Piccamiglio, homme d'affaires génois; 1456–1459* (Paris 1959).

Heers, J., *Gênes au XVe siècle. Activité économique et problèmes sociaux* (Paris 1961).

Hennig, R., 'Der stumme Handel als Urform des Außenhandels', *Weltwirtschaftliches Archiv* 11 (1917) 265–278.

Igual Luis, D. and G. Navarro Espinach, 'Los genoveses en España en el tránsito del siglo XV al XVI', *Historia. Instituciones. Documentos* 24 (1997) 261–332.

Igual Luis, D. and G. Navarro Espinach, 'Valencia y Sevilla en el sistema económico genovés de finales del siglo XV', *Revista d'historia medieval* 3 (1992) 79–116.

Khvalkov, I., *The Colonies of Genoa in the Black Sea Region: Evolution and Transformation* (New York, NY, 2018).

Martignone, F., 'Rapporti tra genovesi e catalani nel XV secolo', *Atti del 1° Congresso Storico Liguria-Catalogna, Ventimiglia-Bordighera-Albenga-Finale-Genova* (Bordighera 1974) 513–522.

Musso, G., *Genovesi e Portogallo nell'età delle scoperte. Nuove richerche d'archivio* (Genova 1976).

North, D., 'Markets and Other Allocation Systems in History: The Challenge of Karl Polanyi', *Journal of European Economic History* 6 (1977), 703–716.

Otte, E., 'Empresarios españoles y genoveses en los comienzos del comercio transatlántico: la avería de 1507', *Revista de Indias* 93–94 (1963) 519–530.

Otte, E., 'Das genuesische Unternehmertum und Amerika unter den Katholischen Königen', *Jahrbuch für Geschichte von Staat,* Wirtschaft und Gesellschaft Lateinamerikas 2 (1965) 30–74.

Otte, E., 'Il ruolo dei Genovesi nella Spagna del XV e XVI secolo', *La repubblica internazionale del denaro tra XV e XVII secolo* (Bologna 1986) 17–36.

Otte, E., *Sevilla y sus mercaderes a fines de la Edad Media* (Sevilla 1996).

Otte, E., ed., 'Due documenti riguardanti le relazioni di Genova col Portogallo', *Atti della società ligure di storia patria* 1ª serie, 23, no. 2 (1891) 715–732.

Peragallo, P., *Cenni intorno alla Colonia Italiana in Portogallo nei Secoli XIV, XV e XVI* (Torino 1904).

Pike, R., *Enterprise and Adventure. The Genoese in Seville and the Opening of the New World* (Ithaca, New York 1966).

Polanyi, K., 'Ports of Trade in Early Societies', *The Journal of Economic History* 23 no. 1 (1963) 30–45.

Price, J.A., 'Conditions in the Development of Silent Trade', *Kroeber Anthropological Society Papers* (1967) 67–79.

Rau, V., 'Uma familia de mercadores italianos em Portugal no seculo XV: os Lomellini', *Revista da Faculdade de Letras* XXII (1956) 5–32.

Rau, V., 'The Settlement of Madeira and the Sugar Cane Plantations', *Afdeling Agrarische Geschiedenis. Bijdragen* 11 (1964) 3–12.

Roccatagliata, A., ed., *L'Officium robarie del comune di Genova: da ufficio della pirateria a ufficio dei ribelli (1394–1397)* (Genova 1989).

Roncière, C. de la, 'Découverte d'une relation de voyage datée du Touat et décrivant en 1447 le bassin du Niger', *Extrait du Bulletin de Géographie historique et descriptive* (Paris 1918).

Savelli, R., *Politiche del diritto e istituzioni a Genova tra medioevo ed età moderna* (Genoa, 2017) http://www.academia.edu/34681992.

Schmoller, G., *Grundriß der allgemeinen Volkswirtschaftslehre* (Munich 1900–1904).

Silva de Jesus, J., 'A Casa de Viseu, o comércio da Guiné e os genoveses', in T. de Matos and J.P. Oliveira Costa eds, *A herança do Infante* (Lisbon and Lagos 2011) 305–322.

Sopranis, H.S. de, *Los Genoveses en Cádiz antes del año 1600* (Jerez 1939).

Spinola, M., ed. 'Relazione sui documenti ispano-genovesi dell'archivio di Simancas', *Atti della società ligure di storia patria* 1ª serie, 8 (1868) 365–402.

Spinola, M., L.T. Belgrano and F. Podestà eds. 'Documenti ispano-genovesi dell'archivio di Simancas', *Atti della società ligure di storia patria* 1ª serie, 8 (1868) 1–291.

Taviani, C., 'Companies, Commerce, and Credit', C. Benes, *A Companion to Medieval Genoa* (Leiden and Boston 2018) 427–447.

Taviani, C., 'The Genoese Merchant Network and Gold (ca. 1450–1530)', forthcoming.

Tucci, R. di, *Nuovi documenti e notizie sul genovese Antonio Malfante, il primo viaggiatore europeo nell'Africa occidentale (1477)* (Rome 1934).

Urbani, R., *'Genova e il Maghrib tra il '400 e '500'*, Genova, la Liguria e l'oltremare tra Medioevo e età moderna, 2 (Genoa 1976) 185–206.

Verlinden, C., 'Lanzarotto Malocello et la découverte portugaise des Canaries', *Revue Belge de Philologie et d'Histoire* 36 (1958) 1173–1209.

Verlinden, C., 'Navigateurs, marchands et colons italiens au service de la découverte et de la colonisation portugaise sous Henri le Navigateur', *Le Moyen Age* (1958) 467–497.

Verlinden, C., *The Beginning of Modern Colonization* (Ithaca and London 1970).

Verlinden, C., 'Relations commerciales entre Gênes et le Portugal à l'époque des grandes découvertes', *Bulletin de l'Institut historique Belge de Rome* 33 (1961) 163–178.

Vieira, A., 'Sugar Islands: The Sugar Economy of Madeira and the Canaries, 1450–1650' in Schwartz, S.B., *Tropical Babylons: Sugar and the Making of the Atlantic World, 1450–1680* (Chapel Hill 2004) 42–84.

CHAPTER 12

Handling Conflicts in Long-Distance Trade: A View of the Mediterranean through the Experience of Merchants Operating in the Kingdom of Valencia in the Late Sixteenth-Century

Ana Belem Fernández Castro

1 The Institutional Framework of the Kingdom of Valencia

The Kingdom of Valencia occupied a privileged position on the map of Mediterranean ports. Lying in the middle western area of the *Mare Internum*, its ports, from the Middle Ages onwards, were points of connection and exchange through which goods and people circulated, as well as being obligatory staging posts on the most active trade routes in the region.[1] The sixteenth century, to which this study is confined, was a period complicated by the economy of the kingdom, whose maritime orientation rendered it subject to the tensions of the Mediterranean.[2] The wars that pitted the Hispanic Monarchy against the Turk, France, England and the United Provinces were the backdrop which set the context for Valencian sea trade, an activity historically framed by conflict.[3]

War was, in effect, an aggravated form of violence which severely disrupted long-distance maritime commerce, because it had a direct impact on the most important and serious problem affecting trade: non-fulfilment of commercial agreements. This was the essence of what Avner Greif calls the 'fundamental problem of exchange' (FPE). Overcoming it was an indispensable prerequisite of commerce, which required that merchants should be confident *ex-ante* that both their personal safety and their goods would be protected, and certain of the profitability of the business transaction and the economic capacity of their

---

1 Igual (2017) 210–228; Iradiel (2017); Iradiel (2006) 111–129.

2 As indicated by the fiscal sources through which Valencian economic history has been reconstructed. Salvador (1972); Castillo (1967); Blanes (2003); Ling (1974); Casey (1979); Franch (1986).

3 Hattendorf (2004) 130–138; Cancila (2007). Following Mckenzie's definition, we consider conflict as the violence inflicted by multiple actors (not only national states) on different spheres like economics, politics, or even individual psychology. McKenzie (2013) 1–3.

 | DOI:10.1163/9789004407992_014

partners to comply with their obligations *ex-post*.[4] To put it another way, the rationale of the FPE lay in maximising profits and minimising – or at least containing – losses, a task in which the strategies used by merchants to handle conflicts played a key role: the profitability of business transactions depended on them, even that of transactions disrupted by violence, because of the expectation of being compensated for losses suffered.

The main aim of this study is to identify the strategies employed by the mercantile actors involved in Valencian maritime trade in the last quarter of the sixteenth century to manage the disputes that arose in contractual transactions. These resulted both from violence at sea (at the hands of privateers or the forces of nature) and from the inability of trading partners to meet their contractual obligations, giving rise to financial losses for which affected parties demanded redress. But how did those who suffered a maritime/mercantile conflict claim compensation in the Kingdom of Valencia? How did the strategies they used to manage disputes operate in practice and how effective were they?

Institutions were the instruments through which merchants handled conflicts, providing a crucial underpinning for the development of trade. Douglass North was the first to highlight this support[5] and to emphasise the multiple (formal and informal) institutional alternatives available to merchants to optimise the profitability of their business. North's contributions – and more recently those of Greif – have profoundly influenced the recent development of social sciences, specifically their understanding of institutions as systems of social rules and factors regulating behaviour.[6]

In the legal context, the ability of institutions to influence the behaviour of individuals is known as jurisdiction. In the culture of the *ius commune* jurisdiction was understood as the authority to create law,[7] and it carried with it the power to administer sanctions over the actions of persons subject to the control of the jurisdictional body.[8] Societies in the *Ancien Régime* accommodated multiple jurisdictional spheres in family, corporate, societarian and also, of course, judicial contexts. Legal historians have characterised this with the term legal pluralism.[9]

4 Greif (2000) 251–284.

5 North (1991) 22–40; Milgrom, North, Weingast (1990) 1–23.

6 North (1990); Greif (2006) 30; Greif (1997) 57–94.

7 Costa (1969); Meccarelli (1998); Clavero (1996) 15–38; González (2003) 223–241.

8 Benton, Ross (2013) 1–17.

9 Vallejo (2009) 1–13; Garriga (2006) 59–106; Benton (2002); Grossi (1995); Merry (1988) 869–896.

The Kingdom of Valencia displayed a remarkable degree of legal pluralism, expressed in its variety of both legislation and institutions. Confining ourselves to institutions expressly dedicated to the administration of justice, as well as mechanisms such as conciliation or arbitration, the composite nature of the Hispanic Monarchy[10] fostered a confluence of jurisdictional bodies at various levels pertaining to the municipality, the kingdom and the monarchy as a whole, forming a highly complex institutional apparatus which contributed to the range of institutional options available in Valencia for handling mercantile disputes. On the one hand, the Civil and Criminal Justices (*Justicia Civil* and *Justicia Criminal*) were the judges who heard cases at local level. The mercantile court of the Consulate of the Sea (*Consulado del Mar*), whose competence extended over the whole kingdom, also operated in this sphere. On the other hand, the *Bailía General*, a royal institution competent in matters related to crown property, such as taxation and administration of justice in maritime and foreign trade matters,[11] was another institutional alternative available to Valencian merchants. The monarch, as the supreme source of justice in Hispanic political culture,[12] also played a part in the judicial life of the Kingdom of Valencia through the Viceroy, the representative of sovereign power, with the political and judicial support of the Royal Audience (*Real Audiencia*), the highest court in the kingdom, second only to the Council of Aragon (*Consejo de Aragón*), which acted as the supreme court of appeal.[13]

This list is not exhaustive and is intended merely to illustrate the enormous range of the Valencian institutional repertoire, which offered merchants numerous alternative institutions through which to confront the problems of contractual transactions. But which institutions did they use? How and why did merchants choose jurisdictions?

In the following pages we seek to shed some light on these questions on the basis of Valencian judicial and notarial sources[14] which provide details of the jurisdictional activity of some of the institutions available in the Kingdom of Valencia. First we shall address the structural role of contracts and mercantile networks in the strategy implemented by traders to manage conflicts in maritime trade, emphasising the part they played in articulating other institutions

10 Elliot (2009) 1–24; Elliot (1997) 48–71.

11 Ghazali (2013) 355–356; Lalinde (1963) 371–419.

12 Prodi (2008) 155–161; Hespanha (1992); Nieto (1988).

13 Belchí (2006) 38–40; Canet (1986); Pardo (2011) 337–348; Arrieta (1994).

14 Mainly the court records of the Royal Audience located at the *Archivo del Reino de Valencia* (ARV) and the notarial deeds preserved at the *Archivo del Colegio del Patriarca* (ACP), particularly the documentation elaborated by the notaries Antoni Joan Zamora and Joan Nofre Masquefa.

merchants used to tackle the problems of long-distance trade. We shall then explore the jurisdictional operation of some of the institutions available in the Kingdom of Valencia, such as the foreign consul (*consul de nación extranjera*), out-of-court conciliation, arbitration, the Consulate of the Sea and the civil courts, specifying the institutional advantages and limitations of each and how those features had a decisive impact on the way merchants used and combined institutions as part of their strategy for handling conflicts.

2 The Basis of Long Distance Trade: Contracts and Mercantile Networks

Contracts were the essential institutional basis of Hispanic trade in general and Valencian trade in particular. They constituted the prime coordination tool available to any merchant, as well as providing proof – predominantly in writing[15] – of the rules of the game established by the contracting parties themselves, which in turn gave shape to the trust underpinning credit relations,[16] through a series of clauses specifying both the objectives of the transaction and the ways in which possible disputes would be handled. Thus contracts were the foundation of conflict management, and the institutional strategy adopted by merchants to claim damages for breach of agreements was articulated around them.

Valencian laws (*fueros*) provided for certain contractually-based legal instruments which were highly effective for handling international conflicts: the executory clause (*cláusula ejecutiva*) and the waiver of own forum and change of jurisdiction clause (*cláusula de renunciación del propio fuero y variación de juicio*).[17] Merchants trading in Valencia, especially those involved in maritime trade, systematically included both these clauses in their contracts, because of the procedural advantages they provided and the fact that they facilitated conflict management, even in cases that extended beyond the borders of the kingdom.

The executory clause was a guarantee of compliance with obligations, as it had immediate legal and financial consequences for the party that breached the contract. Including it in the agreement empowered the parties to ask any

15 The complexity that mercantile transactions acquired in the Modern Era was one of the main reasons of the turn to written culture in the commercial culture of the Hispanic world, where notaries became crucial for the development of trade. Extremera (2003–2004) 188; Herzog (1996) 15–16; Burns (2010); Hook (2013) 61–74.

16 Klein, Hillebrand, Nooteboom (2005) 832.

17 Obarrio (2002) 36–37.

court in the kingdom to enforce the contract against the breaching party; in other words, to force that party to comply with its outstanding obligations by applying material pressure through seizure of its property in order to guarantee that the creditor would be reimbursed.[18] The executory clause was an effective mechanism for applying pressure which acted not only on the debtor's property but also on their person, since the creditor could request imprisonment of the debtor if the latter did not have sufficient goods to guarantee payment of the debt.[19]

Valencian law stipulated that proceedings for enforcement had to be initiated in the courts of the respondent's place of residence,[20] which was inconvenient for creditors operating in distant enclaves and lacking a support network to enable them to act through intermediaries. Adding the waiver of *own forum* and change of jurisdiction clause solved the problem, as it meant that the right to choose and alter the jurisdiction used to compel the breaching party was reserved for the creditor, limiting debtors' chances of evading legal actions taken against them by invoking special jurisdictional privileges.[21]

Normally merchants specified the competent jurisdictions for settling their differences in advance, by mutual agreement, sometimes indicating a specific institution, sometimes leaving the choice of jurisdiction to the discretion of the creditor, and even authorising any of the jurisdictions lying within the maritime ambit in which the partners' business was conducted. This jurisdictional openness was essential for recovering credit in long-distance trade, as it reduced transaction costs by expanding the range of institutions available for handling the dispute.[22] A significant case is the arbitration to which the Genoese merchants Simbaldo Lavachi and Francisco Lomelín Veneroso submitted; the former lived in Alicante while the latter operated in Granada. Both represented the economic interests of other Genoese active at various points in the Mediterranean, and therefore, to ensure compliance with the arbitration award, the parties agreed to waive their own forums and recognise the competence of any of the jurisdictions available in Granada, Cartagena, Alicante, Valencia and Genoa.[23]

---

18 Lumbreras (1960); Fairén (2004).

19 Tomás y Valiente (1960); Alejandre (1970) 3–24.

20 Obarrio (2002) 37.

21 Canet (1984) 58–60.

22 About the importance of the institutional availability in the geographic framework of business transactions, see Olcina (2017); Cordes (2013) 290–291.

23 ARV, Royal Audience, Lawsuits, Part II, Letter J, Appendix, no. 806. Arbitration agreement signed by the parties on 16 July 1576.

Recognising the jurisdiction of authorities scattered over such an extensive geographical area implied that the parties had the material and human resources to enable them to implement a strategy that included using institutions located outside their place of residence. However, merchants' access to institutions was asymmetric and determined by the economic and social context of each merchant.[24] Long-distance trade was therefore a risky and expensive enterprise usually engaged in by merchants who were economically and socially capable of overcoming the setbacks inherent in international transactions (not only the losses caused by a shipwreck or an attack by privateers, but also – and primarily – those occasioned by non-fulfilment of contracts). These were the merchants who could use and combine jurisdictions on an international scale, as they were protected by a financial position that gave them access to foreign institutions and by a social network that represented their interests in those institutions.

Juan del Lago was such a merchant. Born in Burgos, he was a businessman active in banking and in Mediterranean and Atlantic trade, especially in the wool sector. He also owned ships such as the Santa María de Montenegro, which was the subject of a serious dispute against the Ragusan ship-master Juan Simón Merissa in 1591. Merissa seems to have appropriated the ship for more than six years, sparking off intense judicial proceedings involving the Judge of the Royal Household (*Alcalde de Casa y Corte*) in Madrid, the Council of Castile, the Viceroy of Valencia and the Royal Audience, as well as the assistance of several Genoese notaries and of the Mayor of Seville (*Asistente*) in compiling evidence which enabled Lago to recover the ship and obtain compensation of 12,000 ducats for use of the vessel.[25]

The basis of international conflict management was the availability of a mercantile support network. Being included in the international economic circuits enabled merchants to activate jurisdictions in various geographical locations through the good offices of other merchants, who were part of their social capital.[26] Juan del Lago did not need to go to Madrid or Valencia in person in order to pursue Merissa in the courts, as he had a network of agents who set the Hispanic judicial machinery in motion on his behalf, enabling him to remain in Florence while the proceedings were being conducted.[27]

---

24 The analysis of this context is an essential methodological question to understand merchants' strategies of conflict resolution. Kuehn (1994) 11–74; Tate (2013) 235–244.

25 ARV, Royal Audience, Lawsuits, Part I, Letter J, no. 1208 and 1211. Joan del Lago against Blas de Marcos for the ownership of the ship Santa María de Montenegro. Year 1591.

26 Crespo (2015) 47–68; Miranda (2017) 21–23.

27 According to the power of attorney made on 18 April 1591 before the notary Gaspar de Velas, Juan del Lago's agents in Madrid were Martín de Aguiza and Francisco de Castillo. ARV, Royal Audience, Lawsuits, Part I, letter J, no. 1211.

For mercantile networks to function in practice as institutional instruments of conflict management, legal devices were needed to legitimise the intervention of third parties in disputes in which the property of others was at stake. A key legal tool for this purpose was the power of attorney or letter of procuration (*poder* or *procura*), through which grantors or principals authorised the attorney or agent, by means of a contract, to represent their financial interests in a lawsuit.[28] Power of attorney to handle a dispute empowered the representative to choose the institutional mechanisms to resolve it, a decision-making capacity that directly compromised the grantor's assets, since obtaining redress of damages depended on the effectiveness of the strategy implemented by the attorney. In this sense attorneys were always people of trust, and in Valencian mercantile experience that trust conformed to the criteria formulated by Francesca Trivellato,[29] concerning the cognitive and professional competences of merchants, their knowledge of the market and of institutions, and also their professional prestige, measured in terms of their financial capacity and the abundance of social capital they could call upon.

These criteria by no means excluded other factors traditionally associated with mercantile trust, such as kinship, religion or ethnicity as marks of cultural identity. Indeed, all these elements interacted, underlying the strategies employed by merchants to handle conflicts. We can see this interaction in the choice of the Genoese Anfrán Sauli as an agent for certain Valencian merchants[30] involved in two maritime incidents being heard in the Genoese courts. They included his partner and relative Joan Batista Sauli, whose familiarity with Anfrán was doubtless the decisive factor in his appointment, together with his good reputation as a merchant and banker in the markets of Genoa and Lyon[31] and his extensive knowledge of Genoese institutional processes. The first power of attorney was granted in 1581 to recover the goods carried on the settee Santa María which had been taken by Muslim privateers on its voyage from Valencia to Genoa and was later recaptured in Provence.[32] Two years later, in 1583, Sauli appears again in the notarial registers as the legal

28 Canet (1984) 15. The representation of the economic interests of a person in litigation was already regulated in Roman law through the figure of the *procurator ad litem*. Guzmán (2004) 208–212.

29 Trivellato (2009).

30 Among them some powerful merchants who controlled the Consulate : Luis Camarena; Dionisio Gamir; Gaspar Salvador; Gaspar Ocaña; Pedro Romero; Martín de Arays; Joaquín Arnau; Miguel Ángel Urnader; José Albert; Antonio Jaime Vila; Jaime Carmona.

31 Lapeyre (1982) 246.

32 ACP, Protocols, 1606. Power of attorney registered on 29 July 1581.

representative in Genoa of the insurers of the Santa María, the San Pedro and the San Juan, which had been wrecked on the Ligurian coast.[33]

Mercantile networks were the backbone of conflict management in long-distance maritime trade, underpinning the operation of institutions established abroad, through the intermediary role of trusted agents who decided the institutional strategy to be adopted to solve a conflict and obtain redress for the losses it had caused. Foreigners were vitally important for forming networks, especially the Genoese, who constituted one of the largest foreign merchant communities in Early Modern Spain. In the Kingdom of Valencia, most of those present in the last quarter of the sixteenth century were Genoese, Milanese and French.[34] Many of these foreigners settled permanently in Valencia, contributing enormously to the economic development of the kingdom in general, and in particular that of the local merchants, who established credit relationships with them. On the one hand, the Kingdom of Valencia, with its geographical advantages, its trade and its banking tradition, offered foreign merchants an opportunity for economic growth. On the other, the foreigners represented an asset for Valencian merchants, who took advantage of the resources of those foreigners and their access to international circuits to expand their own business.

3 Foreign Consuls: The Institutional Defence of Mercantile Diasporas

The Foreign Consul is the figure that best represents the firmly established position mercantile diasporas acquired in foreign countries. The term consul is of Roman origin; in that context, it denoted a magistracy whose competence was limited to the municipal sphere. Mercantile diasporas adopted the term to refer similarly to a magistracy within the community they founded abroad.[35] The prerogatives of the consul depended on the state of relations between the foreign nation and that of the host territory, although they generally held jurisdictional and administrative competences within the merchant community. In any case, the purpose of the consul was to represent and defend his compatriots against the political authorities of the territory in which the community settled.[36]

33 ACP, Protocols, 1608. Power of attorney registered on 8 February 1583.

34 Salvador (1996).

35 Ferreira (1995) 193–194.

36 Steensgaard (1996) 180–181; Aglietti (2013) 105; Coulon (2004) 179–188; Bartolomei (2013) 247–258; Girard (1934) 124–129; Miranda (2010) 198–200.

We have some references to foreign consuls in the Kingdom of Valencia in the Modern Era,[37] and I propose to supplement these with the information I have found in the archives on the activity of the French consul active in Valencian territory at least from 1575 to 1585, Glaudo Martí.[38] On more than one occasion Martí had to present himself before Valencian jurisdictions to represent and defend the interests of the members of his nation. In January 1581, for example, he appeared before the city's councillors (*jurados*) to request permission for the goods being transported on certain French ships which had arrived at the Grao to be unloaded. News of the plague which had been ravaging France since 1579 had led the municipal authorities to prohibit all contact with any person or merchandise originating from the affected areas,[39] and for this reason the ships in question had been prevented from putting into port.

Glaudo Martí presented the councillors with numerous statements issued by the authorities of the ports at which the ships had previously called, certifying the good health status both of the crew and of the goods they were carrying.[40] At first the councillors authorised the unloading of the ships in port, but the operation was interrupted at the behest of the then current Viceroy, the Duke of Nájera, who ordered that the French ships should leave at once. They remained at anchor off the Valencian coast until a storm drove one of them aground. The Viceroy interpreted this as a malicious manoeuvre by the French sailors and therefore ordered the affected vessel and its cargo to be destroyed.

With the help of consul Martí, the master of the ship that had been destroyed brought a case in the Council of Aragon demanding reimbursement of the value of the vessel and of the goods it was carrying. The situation was serious and required the intervention of a French embassy, which presented its complaints to Philip II over the treatment received by its compatriots in Valencia. Indeed, the pressure from the ambassador led the king to summon the Duke of Nájera to explain his actions, which, in Emilia Salvador's view, caused the Viceroy to be removed from office.[41]

The institutional strategy that mercantile actors used to handle conflicts depended on the material and social resources at their disposal. The diplomatic

37 In the ports of Valencia and Alicante there were many consuls of nation during the modern era representing the interests of merchant communities coming, for example, from Genoa, Florence, Naples, Malta, Venice, the Low Countries or England. Montojo (2005) 353. Castillo (1967) 63.

38 Villalba (2014) 231.

39 Lorite (2001–2002) 255–256.

40 *Archivo Municipal de Valencia* (AMV), judicial records of the *Racional*, pp. 51. Request submitted by Glaudo Martí, consul of the French nation, on 24 January 1581.

41 Salvador (1972) 137–139.

channel is presented as an institutional resource used by mercantile diasporas to manage disputes that affected their collective economic interests, particularly when those interests were threatened by the authorities of the host region, as is clear from the conduct of the Duke of Nájera. But diplomacy was also the institutional mechanism par excellence used by political and economic powers when they found themselves embroiled in maritime disputes that harmed their economic interests.[42] Those powers included Spain and Portugal, empires with a solid naval and commercial tradition which exposed them to the damaging effects of conflict at sea.

The diplomatic channel involved sending agents to the scene of the conflict to take charge of handling it through the local institutions. In March 1575 Antón Ruiz, a servant of the king of Portugal, presented himself to the Marquis of Mondéjar, the Viceroy at that time, to bring a criminal action against a group of French sailors who had stolen some Portuguese ships on the high seas when they were returning from Guinea to Portugal loaded with slaves and goods. According to Ruiz's reports, the French bandits had made off in the settee Santa Catalina to the port of Denia, where they disembarked and sold the stolen goods.

Ruiz asked for an exemplary punishment to be imposed on the miscreants, but it was not a simple matter because of factors such as the flight of the accused, threatening of witnesses and concealment of evidence, which prevented the judges of the Royal Audience from convicting the culprits. Perhaps the delay in providing a solution to the dispute was the reason why a Portuguese embassy was sent to Madrid. Don Duardo de Casteloblanco pressed Philip II to intervene to solve the conflict, and on 6 July 1575 Philip wrote to the judges of the Royal Audience ordering them to dispense justice promptly.[43] In this letter the king emphasised the obligation of the Valencian authorities to assist the French consul and his wife, who were holding some witnesses essential to establishing the truth of the case in safe keeping and were receiving threats from the French sailors who had fled from justice.

The foreign consul features as an intermediary between the group of merchants he represented and the political authorities, both those of his country of origin and those of his nation's host community. I presume it was consul Martí who informed the king of France of what had happened and asked him to intervene and send an embassy to Madrid. But the conflict over the Portuguese ships is especially useful for the light it sheds on the consul's representative function. Glaudo Martí intervened in the criminal proceedings not to

42 Miranda (2017) 25–27.

43 ARV, Royal Audience, Lawsuits, Part III, Appendix, no. 6659. Joan Batista Noguera, Ausiás Palmir and Felip Mallol for their salaries as guards of the ship Santa Catalina.

protect the French sailors who stole the Portuguese ships but to protect the witnesses who would help to clarify what had occurred and were being threatened by the French fugitives. The foreign consul was an individual post, intended to exercise a dual role, representing both the political authorities of the consul's country of origin and the mercantile elite established abroad.[44] Although the consul was a representative and a defender of his nation, that defence had clear limits: those of the consul's own professional prestige and those imposed by the political power he represented. Protecting alleged criminals would have compromised Martí, making him an accomplice in the crime, which would have had adverse consequences for his business and for French-Spanish political relations.

Another distinctive institutional feature of foreign consuls in the Kingdom of Valencia should be noted: they had no jurisdiction to resolve lawsuits. According to Ulbert, until the sixteenth century the foreign consul acted essentially as a judge for the members of his colony and with the passage of time he turned into a political representative completely dissociated from the mercantile elite.[45] The case of Valencia is the exception to the rule and constitutes an early precedent for the rules imposed by the Consular Regulations of 1765, by which foreign consuls lost all jurisdictional capacity in Hispanic territory.[46]

In the Kingdom of Valencia the monopoly of mercantile jurisdiction was exercised by the Consulate of the Sea. That exclusive jurisdiction was asserted by an order from the Baile dated 9 April 1554, warning the Ragusan consul, Joan Batista Barzi, to desist from judging mercantile cases between Ragusans or other merchants of any nation, as the jurisdiction competent to judge their lawsuits was the Consulate.[47] However, foreign consuls did not in fact refrain from settling mercantile disputes, since in practice the jurisdictional ban did not prevent them from resolving other merchants' litigation in their capacity as traders, rather than consuls, through mechanisms such as arbitration or conciliation. What is true is that the monopoly of mercantile jurisdiction claimed by the Consulate of the Sea, in the sense of competence over disputes between merchants and questions concerning trade by land and sea in the Kingdom of Valencia, had an impact on the development of Valencian institutions and consequently on the range of institutional options available to merchants to handle conflicts.

---

44 Steensgaard (1996) 202–221; Ferreira (1995) 194–198.

45 Ulbert (2006) 9–20.

46 Aglietti (2013) 114.

47 A copy of the order can be found in ARV, Royal Audience, Lawsuits, Part II, Letter G, no. 219. Geroni de Vecchi and Joan Pablo Dada about the accounting of their partnership. Year 1565.

The exclusive jurisdictional purview of the Consulate of the Sea applied throughout the kingdom, which was inconvenient for merchants residing outside Valencia, especially those in Alicante, who had to travel to the capital to gain access to the specialised jurisdiction of the Consulate. From the second half of the sixteenth century the port of Alicante underwent an unprecedented economic boom, encouraged by a fiscal reform in 1550 which halved the customs duties levied on Castilian goods exported through it.[48] Alicante became the leading centre for exports of wool to the Mediterranean, primarily to northern Italy, where there was a well-developed textile industry. The revolt of the United Provinces reinforced this situation, and around 1570 merchants engaged in the Castilian trade that was channelled towards northern Europe from the Bay of Biscay redirected wool exports to Italy through Alicante.[49]

Despite the economic development Alicante achieved in this period, the port was without a consulate until the eighteenth century as a result of opposition from the mercantile elite which controlled the Consulate in Valencia.[50] Although the *Bailía* of Orihuela (later transferred to Alicante in 1647) had been available to the merchants of Alicante since medieval times, it was evidently unequal to the task, judging by the constant protests from merchants in Alicante who pointed out how damaging the lack of a consulate was to their business. The Crown responded to the complaints of the merchant community with an institutional reform. Following a visit and an appraisal (*juicio de residencia*) of the justices and officials of Alicante in 1636, Dr Martín de Funes drew up a set of ordinances which recognised the *Baile* as a maritime or consulate judge, competent to deliver summary judgment on commercial cases arising there, both at first instance and on appeal if the litigants so wished.[51] Naturally, the Consulate of the Sea opposed the reform, but its leaders could do no more than retain jurisdiction as an appeal court for reviewing the decisions of the Bailía, provided that the litigants wished it to do so.[52]

4 Handling Conflicts Out of Court: The Role of Conciliation and Arbitration in Long Distance Trade

Jurisdictional clashes aside, the sources show that merchants, especially foreign merchants passing through the Kingdom of Valencia, preferred to use institutions that offered swift and inexpensive solutions to problems. These were

48 Casey (1979) 81; Montojo (2007) 87–90.
49 Franch (2008) 625; Alberola (1998) 15–24; Blanes (2008) 275–301.
50 Figueras (1957) 51–61; Montojo (1992) 61.
51 Figueras (1957) 66–71.
52 Franch (2009) 309.

normally found in procedural mechanisms that were readily accessible in the private sphere, such as bilateral negotiation, out-of-court conciliation and arbitration.

In the area of bilateral negotiation it was the merchants themselves who brought about the resolution of their conflicts without third-party intervention. Dealing with the dispute directly enabled merchants to avoid both the delays and costs and the formalities of a trial, a very useful method when one of the parties – or both – urgently needed to travel elsewhere, as was very often the case in the mercantile and maritime profession. However, the viability of this tool also depended on the complexity of the dispute; it proved highly effective for handling conflicts that involved modest sums of money.

This can be seen in the argument between Joan Batista Sauli, already mentioned above, and the Ragusan sailor Pedro de Sorgo, captain of the ship Santa María de la Gracia, in 1583. The two parties appeared before the notary Joan Nofre Masquefa to agree between themselves the terms on which they would settle their dispute over non-fulfilment of the shipment of 90 sacks of wool which were supposed to travel to Genoa from the port of Valencia.[53] The same procedure was followed in 1580 by the Corsican merchants Bastian de Antoni and Parsiq Paniale, resident in Marseille, to resolve an issue of freight shipments which pitted them against the master of the settee Nuestra Señora de la Gracia, Bartolomé Sernati. As in the previous case, the parties turned to a notary, Antoni Joan Zamora, to enshrine their agreement in a public deed, although in this case the mechanism chosen to settle the dispute was arbitration.[54]

Economic and legal historians[55] ascribe a prime position to arbitration in the list of institutions merchants used to resolve their conflicts, because of the advantages it brought to mercantile life. The most compelling of those advantages was its procedural economy, enabling the parties to cut the cost and time of settling the dispute[56] thanks to the informality and flexibility of the process, which was cost-free in some places.[57] These qualities made it much more expeditious than formal court hearings and a favourable alternative to ordinary proceedings.[58]

Speed, flexibility and economy were the very qualities merchants were looking for in the institutions they used to handle their conflicts, and in the two cases cited above the parties abandoned proceedings they were pursuing in the Consulate of Valencia to opt for settling out of court and arbitration as

53 ACP, Protocols, 1608. Agreement registered on 20 March 1583.
54 ACP, Protocols, 22019. Agreement made on 1 March 1580.
55 Ogilvie (2011) 297; Gelderblom (2013) 104–105; Jenks (2013) 265; Burset (2016) 621.
56 Merchán (1981) 45–46; Gelderblom (2013) 105; Ogilvie (2011) 300; Todd (2016) 9–10.
57 Like in London. Todd (2016) 9–10.
58 Ascheri (1989) 34.

alternatives less onerous to their interests. It is quite understandable that foreign merchants, unfamiliar with the institutional life of the city, should have gone directly to the Consulate of the Sea, merely for reasons of competence, to resolve their differences. However, hearings in the Consulate could also be lengthy and costly, and this would explain the discontinuance of actions. In consular proceedings the court costs were borne by the litigants, and they included the services of the bailiffs who carried out the formalities and the salary of the court clerk who recorded the proceedings. If the case went to appeal, the litigants also had to pay the judge of appeal's salary.[59]

Although arbitration was a process conducted outside the courts, arbiters acted as judges and their decisions were legally binding on the parties.[60] This concept was of Roman origin.[61] To describe arbitration as an infrajudicial or extrajudicial process, as some historians have done,[62] is therefore inappropriate in the Valencian context.[63] Although arbiters often had no judicial training, their activity was recognised in the Hispanic kingdoms as exactly equivalent to that of any other magistracy. Their status as judges distinguished them from arbitrators or amiable compositeurs, whose functions were limited, according to the doctrine of the *ius commune*, to mediating a rapprochement between the opposing parties and who were not empowered to administer justice.[64]

In Valencia arbitration clearly appears as a highly formalised practice in which the arbiters complied with the privileges (*fueros*) of the kingdom, using these to make their awards in accordance with the jurisdictional model of the *ius commune*, which based the administration of justice on observance of law and weighing of the evidence.[65] Thus the arbitral awards analysed highlight the legalist stamp of the *fueros* and the mercantile law regulated in the Book of the Consulate of the Sea (*Libro del Consulado del Mar*).[66]

In the dispute between Joan Batista Sauli and the French ship-master Francés Farant in 1597 over the shipment of a certain quantity of wheat, the influence of the provisions of the Book of the Consulate is clear. The case arose because Sauli failed to deliver the wheat to Farant at the time established in

59 *Libro del Consulado del Mar* (LCM), chapter 36 of the *Orde Judiciari*.
60 Martone (1984) 72–127; Merchán (1981) 70–77; Royo (2016) 168–169.
61 Godfrey (2004) 125; Valiño (2003) 483–539.
62 Garnot (1996); Garnot (2000) 103–120; Soman (1982) 369–375.
63 Criticism shared by Royo (2016) 143.
64 Royo (2016) 168–169; Godfrey (2004) 126–128; Fowler (1976) 133–147; Vallejo (1994) 211–270.
65 Ajello (1976) 339–341; Picó (2007) 1497–1518; Vallejo (1998) 19–46; Canet (1983) 22.
66 Barrero (1980) 471–478.

the contract of affreightment.[67] Consular legislation stipulated that the ship-master was obliged to make his ship available to the merchants at the time and place laid down in the contract. Similarly, the merchants were obliged to deliver the goods to the ship-master at the time and place stipulated. If one of the parties failed to comply with its obligations, it was obliged to compensate the other for its losses, unless the breach was due to force majeure.[68] The Book established that if the parties specified a fine to be charged in the event of a breach of the contract, the breaching party was under duty to pay it. Otherwise, if the parties did not stipulate a penalty, then in order to assess the penalty to be imposed on the breaching party they had to submit the case to the judgment of two good men versed in the maritime arts.[69] The case between Sauli and Farant conformed to these provisions, and for this reason they appointed the merchants Hieroni Delfino and Joan Porta as their arbiters.

Pursuant the Book regulations, the arbiters ruled that Sauli should fulfil the contract of affreightment as soon as the wheat was returned to him, as it had been confiscated at the behest of the Solicitor-General (*procurador fiscal*) of Valencia. That was the reason why Sauli did not deliver the wheat on time, and the arbiters judged it to be a just impediment[70] which exempted him from paying the total value of the shipment and the ship-master's costs as a penalty.

The evidence of compliance with the laws of the Kingdom and the regulations of the Book of the Consulate refutes the arguments of Oscar Gelderblom and Antonio Miguel Bernal that arbitration offered merchants the opportunity to settle their disputes on the basis of their own law, enabling foreign merchants to retain their jurisdictional autonomy even in foreign territories.[71] Besides, applying legal principles other than those of local law would only make sense in arbitrations between parties from the same country, where all those involved, including the arbiters, shared the same legal background. In sixteen cases out of thirty arbitrations analysed, one of the parties was foreign to the Kingdom of Valencia. In all cases the arbiters chosen by the parties were natives of Valencia or foreigners fully integrated into the community, many of them permanent residents, who were familiar with local law and institutions, even in the eight arbitrations in which both parties were foreign and shared the same national origin.

67 ACP, Protocols, 1621. Arbitration judgement registered on 2 February 1597.

68 LCM, chapters 234–235, 260.

69 LCM, chapter 235.

70 LCM, chapter 101.

71 Gelderblom (2013) 105; Bernal (2008) 518.

Maritime/mercantile conflicts required judicial solutions capable of ensuring that trade agreements were complied with expeditiously and at low cost, even at long distance. Arbitration was one of those solutions, though it was not an infallible method. The main problem with arbitration was that the arbiters lacked coercive resources to force the parties to comply with the award. Merchants who had not obtained a favourable result from the arbitral award often turned to other jurisdictions in search of a jurisdictional solution that would benefit their interests, arguing, for example, that the arbiters lacked jurisdictional powers and that their position in the process was merely to issue an opinion in the nature of a judgement of *arbitrium boni viri*.[72] This led those affected by non-compliance with the award to apply to the courts for them to oblige the breaching party to respect the arbitral decision and recognise the full jurisdictional authority of arbiters if they had so stipulated in the arbitration commitment. In the Kingdom of Valencia the royal and noble authorities had an obligation to uphold arbitration commitments and to enforce awards when asked to do so by those involved.[73] There was therefore a dynamic of constant interaction between arbitration and the courts of ordinary jurisdiction which demonstrates the limited autonomy of the practice of arbitration in Valencia.

5 The Role of the Consulate of the Sea and the Civil Courts in Mercantile Conflict Management

As already mentioned, the complexity of the conflict influenced the type of institution merchants used to manage it. In matters where substantial sums of capital were at stake, such as disputes arising from shipwreck, attacks by privateers or cases in which the financial liability of the contracting parties was uncertain, the effectiveness of bilateral negotiation, out-of-court conciliation and arbitration was limited. In such cases merchants preferred to turn to institutions that specialised in trade matters, such as the Consulate of the Sea, and even the civil courts, where the administration of justice was in the hands of jurists with the coercive resources necessary to oblige merchants to comply with their judgments and to face the financial liability resulting from them.

From its foundation in 1283 the Consulate of the Sea offered Valencian merchants a specialised form of justice, administered directly – in the sixteenth century – by a merchant and a seafarer, who took up the position of consuls

72 Merchán (1981) 70–77; Martone (1984) 3–21.

73 Royo (2016) 156.

every year[74] and judged cases related to maritime and terrestrial trade according to the usages and customs of the sea. That was the institution's area of expertise and its main attraction,[75] and it was always linked, both substantively and procedurally, to civil jurisdiction.

Indeed, the influence of Valencian *fueros* played a decisive part in formulating the *ius mercatorum* created in the Consulate of the Sea, calling into question the conclusions of historians who dissociate mercantile justice from the *ius commune*. The Judicial Order of the Valencian Court of the Consuls (*Orde Judiciari de la Cort dels Consols de Valencia*), one of the basic texts of the Book of the Consulate of the Sea which regulated the judicial process in the Valencian Consulate, stipulates that the consuls should resolve cases briefly and summarily, solely *facti veritate atenta* (looking to the truth of the facts), according to the usages and customs of the sea.[76] These principles embody the jurisdictional model to which all mercantile communities in medieval and early modern Europe aspired and provide the theoretical content of the *ius mercatorum*, an essentially procedural form of law resting on legal principles and local practices as sources for deciding cases.[77]

From a purely procedural point of view, the influence of the common law is present in the regulations of the *Orde Judiciari*, a source that proposes a rapid plenary hearing as a model of summary justice.[78] This hearing was characterised by an initial phase of pleadings between the litigants, followed by an evidentiary phase, leading to the judgment of the consuls. The hearing could be conducted orally or in writing, and the key to its brevity lay in eliminating the formal act of the *litis contestatio*, defining and limiting the procedural deadlines and eliminating interlocutory appeals.[79] In the rapid plenary hearing judgment was not obtained immediately, as a procedural order had to be observed, and this required an investment of time by the litigants, who received in return the assurance of a judgment based on the pleadings and the evidence they presented. This legal certainty which prolonged the proceedings was the purpose of ordinary jurisdiction[80] and it was also present in the procedural model of the *Orde Judiciari*.

74 By virtue of a privilege from 14 March 1493, King Ferdinand the Catholic officially integrated merchants into the Consulate of the Sea, originally reserved to sea men.

75 Calafat (2011) 141–154.

76 LCM, chapter 31 of the *Orde Judiciari*.

77 Cordes (2005); Donahue (2005); Basile, Bestor, Coquillette, Donahue (1998) 13–85.

78 Fairén (1984) 11–20.

79 Fairén (1984) 10; LCM, chapters 1–43 of the *Orde Judiciari*.

80 Alonso (2001) 23.

The lengthiness of civil proceedings was largely the result of the procedural resources available to litigants for having judgments reviewed. One of these resources was appeal, which was also available in Valencian consular jurisdiction. Indeed, the procedure for appealing the consuls' judgments was that established in the *fueros* for the civil courts,[81] and it was the Civil Justice of the city who heard appeals against the judgments passed by the Consulate's judge of appeal (a figure created in 1284[82]) when these reversed the decisions of the consuls. In this sense, merchants could have consular judgments reviewed twice: first before the judge of appeal, and then, if his judgment reversed the judgment at first instance, before the Civil Justice.

The Civil Justice's unfamiliarity with *mercatura* was offset by the involvement of two merchants who advised him on his decisions, and by the participation of the entire merchant community, who, according to the protocol laid down in the Book for pronouncing judgments, assembled in the public square to debate the appropriateness of the proposed solution.[83] This provision demonstrates the control exercised by the Valencian merchant community over the administration of justice – despite referral to ordinary jurisdiction – through which it was possible to supervise and certify the conduct of members of the community.

The complexity of mercantile conflicts also led to the presence in the Consulate of lawyers who advised the consuls on their decisions. In the case pursued by the merchants Francisco Sasso and Nicolás Inglar in 1599 over a debt, the consuls appointed the jurist Andreu Roig to advise them on the admissibility of seizing Inglar's assets in the context of his bankruptcy, as the matter was regulated by the *fueros* of the kingdom.[84] The presence of lawyers in European mercantile courts was a common phenomenon, as is shown by the experience of the *Mercanzia* court in Siena, the *Rota* in Genoa and the Consulate in Seville,[85] and is a clear sign of the influence of civil law on mercantile law, whose development was necessarily linked to the former.[86]

From the point of view of substantive law, Galgano and Gelderblom have pointed out that civil courts were not competent to settle mercantile disputes,

81 García (1984) 88–89.

82 García (1961) 21.

83 LCM, chapters 11–15 of the *Orde Judiciari*. These formalities can be observed in ARV, Royal Audience, Lawsuits, Part III, Appendix, no. 6497. Glaudo Guillermi and Pere Andreu about the insurance of some merchandises. Year 1569.

84 ARV, Royal Audience, Lawsuits, Part II, Letter F, no. 770. Judgement published on 12 June 1599.

85 Ascheri (1989) 29–34; Piergiovanni (2012) 903–914; Fernández (2017) 487–488.

86 Piergiovanni (1997) 71–90.

as their judges, almost always jurists specialising in *utrumque ius* (civil and canon law), were unfamiliar with the practices and customs governing the maritime-trading profession.[87] In the Kingdom of Valencia the magistracy was indeed a position reserved for trained lawyers,[88] but that does not necessarily mean that the judges were incompetent in mercantile matters. In the jurisdictional methodology of the *ius commune* judges were considered to have the ability to identify what was just in a specific case in the light of a plurality of sources of law[89]. Those sources could be commercial practices and customs, accessible to judges through the litigants themselves, who stated them explicitly during the proceedings, or consulted directly in customary compilations such as the above-mentioned Book of the Consulate of the Sea.[90]

The accessibility of maritime customs to civil judges can be seen in the case brought before the judges of the Royal Audience by the Frenchman Joan Augier in 1582 to establish ownership of a galleon that he was disputing with Jaume Carmona and other Valencian merchants. According to Augier, he was the legitimate owner of the galleon Santa María y San Juan and of the fish it was carrying, as his partners, Vicenzo Prados and Guillermo Burgal of Marseille, bought it in Algiers and sent it to Valencia, where it was impounded at the request of Carmona. As evidence, Augier presented the deed of sale made by the Christian notary Pedro de Ribera, certifying that he was the owner of the ship and of its cargo.[91] However, Jaume Carmona's side claimed that the galleon and the tuna were his property, as the barrels of fish were marked with the signs that identified the merchandise as his. Carmona stated that the tuna were loaded by his agents on the shore at Barbate (Cadiz) to be sent to Valencia under the command of the Catalan ship-master Arcis Segrera. But Segrera died on the voyage to Valencia, and the crew (consisting mainly of French sailors) took advantage of the situation to mutiny and divert the vessel to Algiers, where they sold the ship and its cargo.[92]

The judges of the Audience considered that both parties' claims were legitimate and were supported with sufficient evidence. However, they ruled that the sale of the ship and the tuna in Algiers was valid and that they therefore

87 Galgano (1993) 38; Gelderblom (2013) 126–133.

88 From 1645 onwards, persons without any legal training were accepted as judges in the Royal Audience. Canet (1993) 50.

89 Grossi (2007) 281; Bravo (1991) 111–163; Vallejo (1992); Vallejo (1998).

90 Wijffels (2005) 274.

91 ARV, Royal Audience, Lawsuits, Part I, Letter J, no. 845. Document submitted by Joan Augier on 8 November 1582.

92 ARV, Royal Audience, Lawsuits, Part I, Letter J, no. 845. Interrogation made by Jaume Carmona on 10 November 1582.

belonged to Joan Augier. In Valencian and Aragonese law judges were obliged to state the grounds and reasons for their judgments.[93] Thanks to this we know that the judges attributed the ship and the fish to Augier in compliance with the provisions of the Book of the Consulate of the Sea, which stipulated that the sale or gift of goods stolen by enemies at sea must be considered as valid as any other contract.[94]

Civil courts such as the Royal Audience regularly resolved mercantile disputes, and merchants even bypassed the specialised jurisdiction of the Consulate to fight their cases directly in those courts. This phenomenon coincided with the increase in litigation rates in the courts of kingdoms such as Castile and England,[95] and from a quantitative point of view it demonstrates repeated use of the courts as instruments for recovering credit and handling disputes. Unfortunately, the poor condition of much of the judicial documentation of the Civil Justice, together with the dispersal and fragmentation of the sources from the Royal Audience and the *Bailía General*, has prevented me from estimating the litigation rate in the main Valencian courts. However, I believe that in the Kingdom of Valencia there was also an upward trend in litigation that was particularly marked in commercial cases, due to the advantage of the courts' prerogative of taking firm measures to force compliance with contracts.

Merchants themselves recognised the coercive effectiveness of the courts in the powers of attorney they granted to their representatives abroad, authorising them to demand satisfaction of their claims in or out of court, referring expressly to seizure of debtors' property and their possible imprisonment as judicial mechanisms to force them to comply with their undertakings.[96] The fact is that legal action and ordinary jurisdiction were indispensable institutional instruments for recovering credit in long-distance trade, despite the reluctance to litigation characteristic of conventional legal attitudes among merchants in early modern Europe, whereby it was considered an affront to the good manners that ought to prevail in the mercantile profession.[97] Those good manners meant choosing amicable institutional mechanisms such as conciliation or arbitration to settle professional differences, mechanisms that also had

93 Garriga, Lorente (1997) 97–114.

94 ARV, Royal Audience, Lawsuits, Part I, Letter J, no. 845. Decision of 27 April 1583.

95 Kagan (1991); Muldrew (1993).

96 Joan Batista Sauli gave power of attorney to the Genoese merchant Leonardo Recio, to take legal actions before any judge or tribunal of the Hispanic kingdoms against Jerónimo Gropalle, Sauli's debtor. Recio was specifically commissioned to demand the seizure and sale of Gropalle's wealth, or even his imprisonment in order to grant the payment of the debt. ACP, Protocols, 1608. Power of attorney made on 24 January 1583.

97 Petit (1997) 63; Petit (2008) 25–26.

procedural advantages for those involved, such as the brevity and the low cost of the process.

But conciliation and arbitration were not infallible mechanisms for solving disputes, and in many cases their effectiveness depended on the option of intervention by the courts, forcing compliance with awards. As previously noted, conflicts in which large sums of money were at stake required sure jurisdictional remedies that guaranteed litigants' property rights, rather than rapid, low-cost solutions. For this reason, knowing how to take legal action and having a knowledge of law were essential skills for early modern merchants,[98] enabling them to overcome the fragmentation of the legislative framework typical of legal pluralism and providing them with an essential instrument for recovering credit, an indispensable requirement for continuity of long-distance trade: litigation.

6 Conclusions

Efficiency was a decisive factor in the institutional choices merchants made to handle conflicts, which were also conditioned by the economic and social capital merchants could call upon. Such efficiency, in the framework of the FPE, was not only measured according to the brevity and low cost of the institutional practices, but essentially with regard to the satisfaction of the needs that urged merchants to resort to institutions: maximising economic profits despite the risks of the maritime context and minimising losses when conflicts arose. In this manner, after the analysis of the jurisdictional performance of some of the institutions merchants used to handle conflicts in the Kingdom of Valencia, I arrive to the following conclusions:

a) The internationalization of commerce required legal mechanisms that made viable the management of conflicts that transcended jurisdictional boundaries. In the kingdom of Valencia contracts were key legal instruments that supported long distance trade, in which merchants established the ways of handling possible disputes taking advantage of the resources available in the *fueros*, such as the executory clause and the waiver of own forum and change of jurisdiction clause. These clauses allowed merchants to select the institutions that would have exclusive competence to enforce commercial agreements, which certainly simplified conflict management. However, to handle disputes that traversed different political frontiers also required the support of a network of

98 Jeannin (1995) 385–387.

agents that represented and defended merchants' financial interests abroad. Both institutions (contracts and mercantile networks) were the backbone of commercial conflict management since merchants articulated around them other institutional tools used to tackle the problems of commerce.

b) The foreign consul was an institutional alternative to handle conflicts in the kingdom of Valencia, albeit its competence was limited to the representation and defense of his compatriots against the Valencian political authorities. Foreign consuls had no competence to settle directly commercial disputes in Valencia since the Consulate of the Sea monopolized mercantile jurisdiction. However, consuls were not prevented from settling commercial disputes in their capacity as traders, rather than as consuls, through mechanisms such as arbitration or conciliation.

c) Out-of-court conciliation and arbitration were institutions that merchants frequently used to handle disputes because they offered swift and inexpensive solutions to some problems. Both institutions appear in the sources as highly efficient jurisdictional mechanisms to resolve simple conflicts involving modest sums of money, but ineffective to resolve complex legal conflicts in which large amounts of capital were at stake. Moreover, arbiters lacked coercive resources to force the parties to comply with the award, whose enforcement depended on the intervention of courts.

d) The aim of the jurisdiction of the Consulate of the Sea was also to offer rapid and low cost solutions to the problems of commerce. However, these jurisdictional aspirations coexisted in practice with a generalized need of legal certainty in the forms of conflict management among early modern merchants, which reshaped Consulate's jurisdiction. In this manner, the jurisdictional practice of the Consulate was highly influenced by *ius commune*, a legal tradition backed by the observance of law and weighing of the evidences as guarantees of a certain administration of justice. This jurisdictional model was typically found in civil courts and could be the reasons why merchants commonly resorted to institutions like the Royal Audience to handle their conflicts through litigation.

e) Maritime/commercial conflict management depended on a plurality of institutions that interacted and complemented each other. This complementarity is observed in different cases: On the one hand, commercial networks were core elements in the operation of institutions that merchants employed to handle disputes in long distance trade such as arbitration or litigation in public courts, which required the intervention of authorized third parties to make them work. On the other hand, the enforcement of arbitration awards relied on the coercive powers of public courts. Finally, albeit foreign consuls were useful diplomatic instruments, they have no jurisdictional powers to settle commercial disputes in the kingdom of Valencia, a limitation that forced foreign merchants to resort to local institutions to settle disputes. This evidence supports Regina Grafe's hypothesis about the success of long distance trade. Grafe argues that commerce was not the result of a single or better institution, but the result of institutional variety and complementarity.[99] Both characteristics are present in the strategies merchants used for conflict management in the Kingdom of Valencia, and they appear to be essential for an effective compensation for the damages produced by conflictive events and therefore for commerce development.

Bibliography

Aglietti, M., 'El debate sobre la jurisdicción consular en la monarquía hispánica (1759–1769)' in M. Aglietti, M. Herrero and F. Zamora, eds., *Los cónsules de extranjeros en la Edad Moderna y a principios de la Edad Contemporánea* (Madrid 2013) 105–118.

Ajello, R., *Arcana Juris. Diritto e politica nel settecento italiano* (Napoli 1976).

Alberola Romá, A., 'Relacions econòmiques entre el País Valencià i Europa durant l'edat moderna: aproximació al cas d'Alacant' in *Pedralbes: Revista d'historia moderna* 18 (1998) 15–24.

Alejandre García, J.A., *La quiebra en el derecho histórico español anterior a la codificación* (Sevilla 1970).

Alonso Romero, M.P., 'El solemne orden de los juicios. La lentitud como problema en la historia del proceso en Castilla' in *Anuario de la Facultad de Derecho de la Universidad Autónoma de Madrid* 5 (2001) 23–54.

Antunes, C., *Globalisation in the Early Modern Period. The Economic Relationship between Amsterdam and Lisbon, 1640–1705* (Amsterdam 2004).

Arrieta Alberdi, J, *El Consejo Supremo de la Corona de Aragón, 1494–1707* (Zaragoza 1994).

Ascheri, M., *Tribunali, giuristi e istituzioni dal Medievo all' Età Moderna* (Bologna 1989).

Barrero García, A.M., 'El Derecho Romano en los Furs de València de Jaime I' in *Primer Congreso de Historia del País Valenciano* (Valencia 1980) 471–478.

Bartolomei, A., 'De la utilidad comercial de los cónsules. Problemáticas y estado de la cuestión (Europa y el mundo mediterráneo, siglos XVII, XVIII y XIX)' in M. Aglietti, M. Herrero and F. Zamora eds., *Los cónsules de extranjeros en la Edad Moderna y a principios de la Edad Contemporánea* (Madrid 2013) 247–258.

99 Grafe (2015).

Basile, M.E., J.F. Bestor, D. Coquillette and C. Donahue eds., *Lex Mercatoria and Legal Pluralism: A Late Thirteenth-Century Treatise and its Afterlife* (Cambridge 1998).

Belchí Navarro, P., *Felipe II y el virreinato valenciano (1567–1578). La apuesta por la eficacia gubernativa* (Valencia 2006).

Benton, L., *Law and Colonial Cultures. Legal Regimes in World History, 1400–1900* (Cambridge 2002).

Benton, L. and R. Ross eds., *Legal Pluralism and Empires. 1500–1850* (New York 2013).

Bernal, A.M., 'La contabilidad como instrumento de conciliación y arbitraje en la Carrera de Indias (siglos XV–XVIII)' in *Anuario de Estudios Atlánticos* 54 (2008) 513–540.

Blanes, R., 'El comercio marítimo de Alicante hacia Valencia en el segundo cuarto del seiscientos (1626–1650)' in *Revista de Historia Moderna* 26 (2008) 275–301.

Blanes, R., *El puerto de Valencia: encrucijada de rutas, productos y mercaderes, 1626–1650* (Valencia 2003).

Bravo Lira, B., 'Iudex minister aequitatis. La integración del derecho antes y después de la codificación' in *Anuario de Historia del Derecho Español* 60 (1991) 111–163.

Burns, K., *Into the Archive. Writing and Power in Colonial Peru* (Durham and London 2010).

Burset, C.R., 'Merchant Courts, Arbitration, and the Politics of Commercial Litigation in the Eighteenth-Century British Empire' in *Law and History Review* 34 no. 3 (2016) 615–647.

Calafat, G., 'Expertises et Tribunaux de Commerce. Procédures et réputation à Livourne au XVII siècle', *Hypothèses* 14 (2011) 141–154.

Cancila, R., ed., 'Mediterraneo in armi (secc. XV–XVIII)', *Quaderni Mediterranea* 4 (2007).

Canet Aparisi, T. 'Derecho y administración de justicia en la formación del reino de Valencia', *Estudis: revista de historia moderna* 10 (1983) 7–32.

Canet Aparisi, T., 'La Audiencia valenciana: estructura de poder y grupo de servicio', *Pedralbes. Revista d' historia moderna* 13 (1993) 45–52.

Canet Aparisi, T., *La audiencia valenciana en la época foral moderna* (Valencia 1986).

Canet Aparisi, T., ed., *Práctica y Orde Judiciari de les Causes Civils de Contenciosa Jurisdicció* (Valencia 1984).

Caracausi, A.; Jeggle, C., eds., *Commercial Networks and European Cities. 1400–1800* (London 2014).

Casado Alonso, H., 'Las colonias de mercaderes castellanos en Europa (siglos XV y XVI)' in H. Casado Alonso ed., *Castilla y Europa. Comercio y mercaderes en los siglos XIV, XV y XVI* (Burgos 1995) 15–56.

Casey, J., *The Kingdom of Valencia in the Seventeenth Century* (Cambridge 1979).

Castillo Pintado, A., *Tráfico marítimo y comercio de importación en Valencia a comienzos del siglo XVII* (Madrid 1967).

Clavero, B., 'La Monarquía, el Derecho y la Justicia' in E. Martínez Ruiz, M. Pazzis eds., *Instituciones de la España Moderna. Las Jurisdicciones* (Madrid 1996) 15–38.

Cordes, A., 'Litigating Abroad. Merchants' Expectations Regarding Procedure before Foreign Courts According to the Hanseatic Privileges (12th-16th C.)' in P. Andersen, K. Salonen, H. Moller, H. Vogt eds., *Law and Disputing in the Middle Ages* (Copenhagen 2013) 281–299.

Cordes, A., 'The Search for a Medieval Lex Mercatoria' in V. Piergiovanni ed., *From Lex Mercatoria to Commercial Law* (Berlin 2005) 53–68.

Coronas González, S., 'La jurisdicción mercantil de los consulados del mar en el Antiguo Régimen (1494–1808)' in F. Ballesteros, H. Casado, A. Ibáñez, S. Escolar eds., *Actas del IV Centenario del Consulado de Burgos, 1494–1994* (Burgos 1994) 249–280.

Costa, P., *Iurisdictio. Semantica del potere político nella pubblicistica medievale, 1100–1433* (Milano 1969).

Coulon, D., 'Los consulados catalanes en Siria (1187–1400). Algunos datos de historia e historiografía' in R. Narbona Vizcaíno ed., *XVIII Congrés Internacional d'Història de la Corona de Aragó. La Mediterrània de la Corona d'Aragó, segles XIII–XVI* (Valencia 2004) 179–188.

Crespo Solana, A., 'El más amplio Atlántico: redes mercantiles y comunidades globales' in J. Iglesias Rodríguez, R. Pérez García, M. Fernández Chaves eds., *Comercio y cultura en la Edad Moderna. Actas de la XIII Reunión Científica de la Fundación Española de Historia Moderna* (Sevilla 2015) 47–68.

Crespo Solana, A., 'Nación extranjera y cofradía de mercaderes: el rostro piadoso de la integración social' in M.B. Vilar, P. Pezzi eds., *I Coloquio Internacional los Extranjeros en la España Moderna* (Málaga 2003) 175–188.

Crespo Solana, A., ed., *Comunidades transnacionales: colonias de mercaderes extranjeros en el mundo Atlántico*, 1500–1830 (Madrid 2010).

Donahue, C., 'Benvennuto Stracca's De Mercatura: Was There a Lex Mercatoria in Sixteenth-Century Italy?' in V. Piergiovanni ed., *From Lex Mercatoria to Commercial Law* (Berlin 2005) 69–120.

Elliot, J.H., 'A Europe of Composite Monarchies', *Past and Present* 137 (1992) 48–71.

Elliot, J.H., *Spain, Europe and the Wider World, 1500–1800* (New Haven and London 2009).

Engle Merry, S., 'Legal Pluralism', *Law & Society Review* 22 no. 5 (1988) 869–896.

Extremera Extremera, M.A., 'La pluma y la vida. Escribanos, cultura escrita y sociedad en la España moderna (siglos XVI–XVIII)' in *LITTERAE. Cuadernos sobre cultura escrita* 3–4 (2003–2004) 187–206.

Fairén Guillén, V., *Importancia de los tribunales consulares: el Consulado del Mar de Valencia* (Valencia 1984).

Fairén Guillén, V., *Sobre la historia del juicio ejecutivo sumario en Valencia. La Ordinació del rey Don Martín I de 1403. Con un apéndice sobre la Ley sevillana de 1360* (Valencia 2004).

Fernández Castro, A.B., 'Showing the Truth to the Judge: The Role of Proofs in the Consulate of Seville during the Late 16th Century' in *Anuario de Historia del Derecho Español* LXXXVII (2017) 477–493.

Ferreira Priegue, E., 'Cónsules de castellanos y cónsules de españoles en el Mediterráneo bajomedieval' in H. Casado Alonso ed., *Castilla y Europa. Comercio y mercaderes en los siglos XIV, XV y XVI* (Burgos 1995) 191–240.

Figueras Pacheco, F., *El Consulado Marítimo y Terrestre de Alicante y Pueblos del Obispado de Orihuela* (Alicante 1957).

Fowler, L., 'Forms of Arbitration' in S. Kuttner ed., *Proceedings of the Fourth International Congress of Medieval Canon Law* (Città del Vaticano 1976) 133–147.

Franch Benavent, R., 'El comercio marítimo y la manufactura de la seda en la Valencia del siglo XVI' in R. Franch Benavent and R. Benítez Sánchez-Blanco ed., *Estudios de historia moderna en homenaje a la profesora Emilia Salvador Esteban* (Valencia 2008) 619–636.

Franch Benavent, R., 'El Consulado y los Cuerpos de Comercio' in J. Hermosillo Plá ed., *La ciudad de Valencia: historia, geografía y arte de la ciudad de Valencia* (Valencia 2009) 307–310.

Franch Benavent, R., *Crecimiento comercial y enriquecimiento burgués en la Valencia del siglo XVIII* (Valencia 1986).

Gacto Fernández, E., *Historia de la jurisdicción mercantil en España* (Sevilla 1971).

Galgano, F., *Lex mercatoria: Storia del diritto commerciale* (Bologna 1993).

García Sanz, A., *Llibre del Consolat de Mar. Estudi Juridic* (Barcelona 1984).

García Sanz, A., 'La influencia de los consulados de mar de Barcelona y Valencia en la erección del consulado de Burgos (1494)', *Boletín de la Sociedad Castellonense de Cultura* 45 (1969) 227–228.

García Sanz, A., 'Las apelaciones en el Consulado' in *Boletín Castellonense de Cultura*, 37 (1961) 17–25.

Garnot, B., ed., *L'infrajudiciaire du Moyen Age à l'époque contemporaine* (Dijon 1996).

Garnot, B., 'Justice, Infrajustice, Parajustice et Extra Justice dans la France d'ancien régime', *Crime, Histoire & Sociétés* 4 (2000) 103–120.

Garriga, C., 'Justicia animada: dispositivos de la justicia en la monarquía católica' in *Cuadernos de Derecho Judicial* 6 (2006) 59–106.

Garriga, C. and M. Lorente, 'El juez y la ley: la motivación de las sentencias (Castilla, 1489, España, 1855)' in *Anuario de la Facultad de Derecho de la Universidad Autónoma de Madrid* 1 (1997) 97–114.

Gelderblom, O., *Cities of Commerce. The Institutional Foundations of International Trade in the Low Countries, 1250–1650* (Princeton and Oxford 2013).

Ghazali, M., 'Le tribunal du Baile General de Valence. Pour une connaissance de la captivité et de l'esclavage en Méditerranée, XVe–XVIIe siècle' in *Cahiers de la Méditerranée* 87 (2013) 355–381.

Girard, A., 'Note sur les consuls étrangers en Espagne avant le Traité des Pyrénées' in *Revue d'histoire moderne* 12 (1934) 124–129.

Godfrey, M., 'Arbitration in the Ius Commune and Scots Law' in *Roman Legal Tradition* 122 (2004) 122–135.

González Alonso, B., 'Jueces, justicia, arbitrio judicial. Algunas reflexiones sobre la posición de los jueces ante el Derecho en la Castilla moderna' in *Vivir el Siglo de Oro. Poder, cultura e historia en la Época Moderna* (Salamanca 2003) 223–241.

Grafe, R., 'Was There a Market for Institutions in Early Modern European Trade?' in *Union in Separation. Diasporic Groups and Identities in the Eastern Mediterranean, 1100–1800* (Roma 2015) 593–609.

Greif, A., 'Contracting, enforcement, and efficiency: economics beyond the law' in *Proceedings of the Annual World Bank Conference on Development Economics* (Washington 1997) 239–265.

Greif, A., 'The fundamental problem of exchange: A research agenda in Historical Institutional Analysis', *European Review of Economic History* 4 (2000) 251–284.

Grossi, P., *L'Europa del diritto* (Roma-Bari 2007).

Grossi, P., *L'ordine giuridico medievale* (Roma 1995).

Guzmán Brito, A., *Derecho Privado Romano* (Santiago de Chile 2004).

Hattendorf, J.B., 'The Sea as an Arena for Conflict' in D. Finamore ed., *Maritime History as World History* (Florida 2004) 130–138.

Herzog, T., *Mediación, archivos y ejercicio. Los escribanos de Quito, siglo XVII* (Frankfurt am Main 1996).

Hespanha, A.M., *Poder e Instituçoes no Antigo Regime* (Lisboa 1992).

Hoock, J., 'Règle et loi dans le discours commercial de la première modernité' in F. Pia and L. Braguier-Gouverneur ed., *Normes et Transgressions dans l'Europe de la Première Modernité* (Rennes 2013) 61–74.

Igual Luis, D., 'Valencia. Opportunities of a secondary node' in W. Blockmans, M. Krom and J. Wubs-Mrozewicz eds., *The Routledge Handbook of Maritime Trade around Europe. 1300–1600* (London and New York 2017) 210–228.

Iradiel, P., 'El siglo de oro del comercio valenciano' in Aguilar Civera, I., coord., *El comercio y el Mediterráneo. Valencia y la cultura del mar* (Valencia 2006) 111–129.

Iradiel, P., *El Mediterráneo medieval y Valencia: Economía, sociedad, historia* (Valencia 2017).

Jeannin, P., 'Distinction de compétences et niveaux de qualification : les savoirs négociants dans l'Europe moderne' in F. Angiolini and D. Roche eds., *Cultures et formations négociants dans l'Europe moderne* (Paris 1995) 363–397.

Jenks, S., 'Conclusion' in J. Wubs-Mrozewicz and S. Jenks eds., *The Hanse in Medieval and Early Modern Europe* (Leiden and Boston 2013) 255–281.

Kagan, R., *Pleitos y pleiteantes en Castilla, 1500–1700* (Salamanca 1991).

Klein Woolthuis, R., B. Hillebrand and B. Nooteboom, 'Trust, Contract and Relationship Development', in *Organization Studies* (2005) 813–840.

Kuehn, T., *Law, Family and Women: Toward a Legal Anthropology of Renaissance Italy* (Chicago 1994).

Lalinde Abadia, J., *La Gobernación General en la Corona de Aragón* (Zaragoza 1963).

Lapeyre, H., 'Les marchands étrangères dans le royaume de Valence aux XVe et XVIe siècles' in H. Kellenbenz ed., *Fremde Kaufleute auf der Iberischen Halbinsel* (Wien 1970) 100–117.

Lapeyre, H., *La Taula de Canvis en la vida económica de Valencia a mediados del reinado de Felipe II* (Valencia 1982).

Ling, R., *Long-Term Movements in the Trade of Valence, Alicante and the Western Mediterranean, 1450–1700* (California: Unpublished PhD-thesis 1974).

Lorite Martínez, M.I., 'Las autoridades valencianas ante la amenaza de la peste en el siglo XVI' in *Saitabi: revista de la Facultat de Geografia i Història* 51–52 (2001–2002) 245–258.

Lumbreras Valiente, P. 'Aportación a la historia del juicio ejecutivo en el derecho patrio' in *Revista de Derecho Procesal* 2 (1960) 243–252.

Martone, L., *Arbiter-Arbitrator. Forme i giustizia privata nell' età del diritto comune* (Naples 1984).

Mckenzie, F., 'Introduction: The Intersection of Trade and Conflict since 1500' in L. Coppolaro and F. Mckenzie eds., *A Global History of Trade and Conflict Since 1500* (London 2013) 1–3.

Meccarelli, M., *Arbitrium, Un aspetto sistematico degli ordinamenti giuridici in età di diritto comune* (Milan 1998).

Merchan Álvarez, A., El arbitraje. Estudio histórico jurídico (Seville 1981).

Milgrom, P., D. North and B. Weingast, 'The role of institutions in the revival of trade: the law merchant, private judges, and the Champagne fairs' in *Economics and Politics* 2 (1990) 1–23.

Miranda, F., 'Commerce, conflits et justice : les marchands portugais en Flandre à la fin du Moyen Âge' in *Annales de Bretagne et des Pays de l'Ouest* 117-1 (2010) 193–208.

Miranda, F., 'Conflict management in western Europe: the case of the Portuguese merchants in England, Flanders and Normandy, 1250–1500', *Continuity and Change* 32 (2017) 11–36.

Montojo Montojo, V., 'El comercio de Alicante en los reinados de Felipe II y Felipe III. Una construcción desde la cooperación' in *Cuadernos de Historia Moderna* 32 (2007) 87–111.

Montojo Montojo, V., 'Crecimiento mercantil y desarrollo corporativo en España: los consulados extraterritoriales extranjeros (ss. XVI–XVII)' in *Anuario de Historia del Derecho Español* 62 (1992) 47–66.

Montojo Montojo, V., 'Guerra y paz bajo Felipe III: el comercio del Levante español y sus relaciones clientelares, familiares y profesionales', *Chronica Nova* 31 (2005) 349–378.

Muldrew, C., 'Credit and the Courts: Debt Litigation in a Seventeenth-Century Urban Community', *The Economic History Review, New Series* 6 (1993) 23–38.

Nieto Soria, J.M., *Los fundamentos ideológicos del poder real en Castilla. Siglos XIII–XVI* (Madrid 1988).

North, D., 'Institutions, transaction costs and the rise of the merchant empires' in J.D. Tracy, ed., *The Political Economy of Merchant Empires. State Power and World Trade, 1350–1750* (Cambridge 1991) 22–40.

Obarrio Moreno, J.A., *Estudios de tradición romanística: el proceso en el ordenamiento foral valenciano* (Valencia 2002).

Ogilvie, S., *Institutions and European Trade. Merchant Guilds, 1000–1800* (Cambridge 2011).

Olcina Pita, V., 'Commercial Litigation across Religious Borders: Rendering Justice for Valencian Merchants in Fifteenth Century North Africa and Granada', *Comparative Legal History* 5 no. 1 (2017) 88–106.

Pardo Molero, J.F., 'Virreyes en la tierra. Sobre la delegación del poder regio en la monarquía católica (1480–1550)' in E. García Hernán, M.P. Ryan eds., *Francisco de Borja y su tiempo. Política, religión y cultura en la Edad Moderna* (Valencia-Roma 2011) 337–349.

Petit, C., 'Mercatura y Ius Mercatorum, Materiales para una antropología del comerciante premoderno' in C. Petit ed., *Del ius mercatorum al derecho mercantil* (Madrid 1997) 15–70.

Petit, C., 'Del usus mercatorum al uso de comercio. Notas y textos sobre la costumbre mercantil', *Revista da Facultade de Direito – UFPR* 48 (2008) 7–38.

Picó Junoy, J., 'Iudex iudicare debet secundum allegata et probata, non secundum conscientiam: storia della erronea citazione di un brocardo nella dottrina tedesca e italiana', *Rivista di Diritto Processuale* 62 (2007) 1497–1518.

Piergiovanni, V., 'Courts and Commercial Law at the Beginning of the Modern Age' in *Norme, scienza e pratica guiridica tra Genova e l'Occidente medievale e moderno* (Genova 2012) 903–914.

Piergiovanni, V., 'Derecho mercantil y tradición romanística entre Medioevo y Edad Moderna. Ejemplos y consideraciones' in C. Petit ed., *Del ius mercatorum al derecho mercantil* (Madrid 1997) 71–90.

Prodi, P., *Una historia de la justicia. De la pluralidad de los fueros al dualismo moderno entre conciencia y derecho* (Buenos Aires 2008).

Royo Pérez, V., 'El arbitraje en la documentación medieval valenciana. La caracterización de la institución arbitral en la práctica documental de las comarcas del Els Ports y El Maestrat entre 1232 y 1412', *Anuario de Historia del Derecho Español* 86 (2016) 141–195.

Salvador, E., 'Mercaderes extranjeros en la Valencia de los siglos XVI y XVII. Entre atracción y rechazo' in L.M. Enciso Recio ed., *La burguesía mercantil en la Edad Moderna* (Valladolid 1996) 1137–1155.

Salvador, E., *La economía valenciana en el siglo XVI. Comercio de importación* (Valencia 1972).

Smith, R.S., *Historia de los consulados de mar, 1250–1700* (Barcelona 1978).

Soman, A., 'L'infrajustice à Paris d'après les archives notariales', *Histoire, économie et société* 3 (1982) 369–375.

Steensgaard, N., 'Consuls and Nations in the Levant from 1570 to 1650' in S. Subrahmanyan, ed., *Merchant Networks in Early Modern World* (Aldershot 1996) 179–221.

Tate, J.C., 'Competing Institutions and Dispute Settlement in Medieval England' in P. Andersen, K. Salonen, H. Moller, H. Vogt eds., *Law and Disputing in the Middle Ages* (Copenhagen 2013) 235–244.

Todd, M., 'For Eschewing of Trouble and Exorbitant Expense: Arbitration in Early Modern British Isles', *Journal of Dispute Resolution* 1 (2016) 1–18.

Tomás y Valiente, F., 'La prisión por deudas en el derecho castellano y aragonés' in *Anuario de Historia del Derecho Español* 30 (1960) 249–490.

Trivellato, F., *The Familiarity of Strangers. The Sephardic Diaspora, Livorno, and Cross-Cultural Trade in the Early Modern Period* (New Haven and London 2009).

Ulbert, J., 'Introduction. La fonction consulaire à l'époque moderne: définition, état de conaissances et perspectives de recherche' in J. Ulbert, G. Bouëdec eds., *La fonction consulaire à l'époque moderne. L'Affirmation d'une institution économique et politique, 1500–1800* (Rennes 2006) 9–20.

Valiño Arcos, A., 'La recepción del arbitraje romano en Els Furs de València', *Excerptum es Studia et Documenta Historiae et Iuris* 69 (2003) 483–542.

Vallejo, J., 'Acerca del fruto del árbol de los jueces. Escenarios de la justicia en la cultura del ius commune' in *Anuario de la Facultad de Derecho de la Universidad Autónoma de Madrid* 2 (1998) 19–46.

Vallejo, J. 'Amor de árbitros. Episodio de la sucesión de Per Afán de Ribera el Viejo' in J.M. Scholz ed., *Fallstudien zur Spanischen und Portugiesischen Justiz 15. Bis 20.* Jahrhundert (Frankfurt am Main 1994) 211–270.

Vallejo, J., 'El cáliz de plata. Articulación de órdenes jurídicos en la jurisprudencia del ius commune', *Revista de Historia del Derecho* 38 (2009) 1–13.

Vallejo, J., *Ruda Equidad, Ley Consumada. Concepción de la Potestad Normativa, 1250–1350* (Madrid 1992).

Vaquero Piñeiro, M., 'Mercaderes catalanes y valencianos en el Consulado de Roma', *Revista d'Història Medieval* 9 (1998) 151–170.

Villalba, M.T., 'Los franceses en la documentación procesal valenciana del quinientos: los testimonios como fuente de información biográfica' in R. Franch Benavent, F. Andrés Robres and R. Benítez Sánchez-Blanco eds., *Cambios y resistencias sociales en la edad moderna. Un análisis comparativo entre el centro y la periferia mediterránea de la monarquía hispánica* (Madrid 2014) 223–232.

Wijffels, A., 'Business Relations between Merchants in Sixteenth-Century Belgian Practice-Orientated Civil Law Literature' in V. Piergiovanni ed., *From Lex Mercatoria to Commercial Law* (Berlin 2005) 255–290.

CHAPTER 13

Mediterranean and Atlantic Maritime Conflict Resolution: Critical Insights into Geographies of Conflict in the Early Modern Period

Cátia Antunes and Kate Ekama

1 Introduction

Traditionally, the history of the Mediterranean has been paramount to understand the history of Western Europe. For that reason, major historiographical works have been devoted to this liquid space. For Fernand Braudel, the Mediterranean was a means of connection between territorial worlds that seemed apparently separated. For him, the water separated as much as it connected, as encounters took place over the water and on its shores. The structural, conjunctural and eventmential history of the Mediterranean translated the lived cultural experiences of peoples and polities alike that shared a similar cultural tradition, regardless of religious and political divisions.[1] In the continuation of Braudel's work, David Abulafia stressed the connectivities engendered by the Mediterranean itself, as he argues for the power of maritime entanglements for the creation of specific spaces of social, economic, cultural and religious exchange that stretch beyond the borders of the sea into the territories around it and close-by liquid spaces like the Atlantic.[2] This cultural spill-over of the Mediterranean exchanges is particularly powerful when it comes to the resolution of maritime and commercial conflicts in the Renaissance and the Early Modern periods. For Maria Fusaro, maritime and commercial interactions in the Mediterranean resulted in the development of a Mediterranean legal culture that was applied more broadly (beyond trade and far away from the Mediterranean), thus pushing the Mediterranean experience beyond the Braudelian framework or Abulafia's connectivities.[3]

Even if later than the Mediterranean historiographical tradition, the Atlantic also has been attentively studied by different generations of historians. After World War II, the history of the Atlantic as a category was conceptualized

1 Braudel (1966).
2 Abulafia (2011).
3 Allaire and Fusaro (2017) 257–284; Fusaro (2015).

 | DOI:10.1163/9789004407992_015

and developed by specialists like Charles Boxer or Stuart Schwartz.[4] For these historians, European maritime expansion overseas and the exploitation of the Atlantic space had resulted in a clear division of spheres of influence and economic systems, where the nature and structure of the South Atlantic complex was separate from the North Atlantic complex and its Caribbean 'periphery'. This historical category of the South Atlantic lived on and was further explored within the nexus of the Portuguese colonial development as paramount to bridging economic and social systems West and East of the Cape of Good Hope.[5] This strand of literature however underlined the connections between the South Atlantic and the Indian Oceans rather than the links with the North Atlantic.

The early tradition of looking at the Atlantic as a historical category was reinvigorated in the beginning of the twenty-first century when Bernard Bailyn and David Armitage 'rediscovered' the concept and postulated a new methodological approach to this historical category.[6] The historical results of this development have been mixed. On the positive side, new histories of entanglements, rather than comparisons, have arisen, especially about areas and subjects traditionally considered peripheral.[7] On the negative side, the category 'Atlantic' history has been mostly adopted by Anglo-Saxon historians who tend to disguise studies of the British empire in the Americas under the premises allowed by Atlantic history.[8] The exception to this trend has been the efforts of historians of the Dutch Atlantic in portraying Dutch participation in the African and American trades and societies as separated from a 'national'/empire perspective.[9] Furthermore, new insights from Global History would suggest that thinking of the Atlantic as a contained space, as much as the Mediterranean, fails to emphasize the role this waterway played in the histories of the Pacific and the Indian Oceans.[10]

Following up on these traditions, we propose to enquire in this chapter whether it is historiographically productive to look at maritime and commercial conflict in the Mediterranean and the Atlantic as separate analytical categories. In this chapter, we de-construct the idea of Mediterranean and Atlantic as geographical units of analysis for the understanding of maritime conflict

4 Boxer (1952); Schwartz (1995) 48–59.

5 Russell-Wood (1992); Alencastro (2000); Benton (2000) 27–56.

6 Armitage and Braddick (2005) 11–27; Bailyn (2005).

7 'AHR Forum' (2007) 710–799; Cañizares-Esguerra (2018).

8 Armitage and Braddick (2005); Elliott (2006); Games (2008).

9 Postma and Enthoven (2003); Klooster and Oostindie (2014); Roitman and Oostindie (2014); Klooster (2016).

10 Gereffi and Korzeniewicz (1994); Knight (2014) 87–101; Antunes (2017).

resolution. Based on a broad range of primary sources that cross different chronologies and 'national' spheres of influence, we reflect upon three specific questions that seem paramount to understand the nature of maritime conflict resolution in general and specifically in the targeted areas covered by the current work: the nature of geographical concepts in historical analysis; the central role played by maritime connectivity in establishing spheres of legality and illegality; the implication of defining regimes of property rights, subjection and belonging of maritime agents.

2 Uncontained Nature of Geography in History: De-Constructing the Idea of Maritime Spaces

In May 1730 two Dutch East India Company (VOC) ships from the Chamber Amsterdam, the *Purmerlust* and *Ter Horst*, set sail for Batavia (Indonesia). Four months later both ships returned to Texel (island/port a few miles off Amsterdam).[11] What happened in those intervening months was certainly a story of drama and danger for the individuals involved. Not long after the ships began their voyage, they were captured by four Algerian privateers. The two ships were forcibly sailed to Algiers where they were held for some time.

Dutch ships sailing the Atlantic were often forced to face sailing Algerian privateers. During the late 1600s there were a number of skirmishes between Dutch and Algerian vessels. For instance, in 1690, near the Canary Islands, skipper Gilles Brouwer fought off three Algerian pirate ships for seven hours before he could continue his journey, for which action he was rewarded with a gold chain worth 100 silver ducats.[12] In 1696, Dirk Lovelt did not survive an encounter with two Algerian pirate ships but his widow received the amount of *f*1000 as a sign of the VOC's appreciation. In order to curb this violence at sea, a treaty was concluded with Algiers but repudiated in the mid-1710s. Thereafter, privateers threatened Dutch shipping as far north as the English Channel. The States General responded by providing convoys and small squadrons of warships to protect the vessels. Their first success came in 1724 – Captain Schrijver, of the Admiralty of Amsterdam, captured an Algerian privateer. Two years later, in 1726 the Dutch concluded peace with Algiers. Over the

11 For details of the *Purmerlust*'s voyages, dimensions and other specifics, see https://www.vocsite.nl/schepen/detail.html?id=10854 (accessed 2018-05-31). For similar details of the vessel *Ter Horst* see https://www.vocsite.nl/schepen/detail.html?id=10488 (accessed 2018-05-31). The case involving the two ships comes out of Kate Ekama's PhD dissertation research: Ekama (2018) 161–167.

12 At the time worth about 250 Dutch guilders.

following years, Captain Schrijver made a number of trips to Algiers where he was involved in ransoming the crews of Dutch ships captured and enslaved by the Algerians.[13]

Captain Schrijver was also instrumental in negotiating the release of the *Purmerlust* and *Ter Horst*.[14] The two company vessels were released on the condition that a number of sea chests were left behind in Algiers. Eleven chests containing specie bought the two vessels' release.[15] The ships were free to continue their voyage via the Cape of Good Hope to Batavia. However, the voyage was abandoned. The change in course came as a result of mutiny on board. Reportedly, 'the petty officers…and all the crew, both sailors and soldiers, mutinied and rebelled'.[16] A stand-off ensued between the officers and crew on one side, and the skippers on the other side. The mutinous crew refused to sail the vessels any further (exactly why was later disputed), they presented the skippers with a round robin, and demanded that they return to Holland. The skippers reportedly responded 'that they would rather die than go to Holland'.[17] The situation took days to resolve. Eventually, on 14 July 1730, the skippers conceded to the officers' and crew's demands. The two VOC ships set sail for Texel.[18]

The VOC's investigations of the causes of the mutiny revealed that the crew were concerned that they would be held financially responsible for the eleven chests which were left in Algiers. They refused to continue their voyage to Batavia, concerned that when they arrived there, their salaries would be docked. The skippers of the *Purmerlust* and *Ter Horst* were at pains to assure the crew that they would not be held responsible for the value of the chests, even offering a signed guarantee. The crew did not accept their assurances.[19] This finding

13 Bruijn (1974) 88; Bruijn (2008) 149; Bruijn (1973) 161–175.

14 NA, Hoge Raad Holland en Zeeland, 3.03.02, inv.nr. *833* (1741) Geëxtendeerde sententies, scans 5–6 ff. 4r–v, scan 14 f. 12v.

15 NA, Hoge Raad Holland en Zeeland, 3.03.02, inv.nr. *833* (1741) Geëxtendeerde sententies, scan 6 f. 4v, scan 7 f. 6r.

16 Original: '*Bootsman, schieman, constapel met hunne maats Quartiermeesters, zeilmakers, timmerlieden met hare maats, also ook alle het gemeene volk zo wel matrozen als soldaten hadden gemutineert en gerebelleert*'. NA, Hoge Raad Holland en Zeeland, 3.03.02, inv.nr. *833* (1741), Geëxtendeerde sententies, scan 6, f. 4v.

17 Original: '*dat zij liever sterven wilden als naar Holland gaan*'. NA, Hoge Raad Holland en Zeeland, 3.03.02, inv.nr. *833* (1741), Geëxtenteerde sententies, scan 6, f. 5r.

18 NA, Hoge Raad Holland en Zeeland, 3.03.02, inv.nr. *833* (1741) Geëxtenteerde sententies, scan 9, ff. 7v-8r; inv. nr. *673* (1741), Resolutie, scan 6. The *resolutie* indicates that the mutiny began on 9 July and according to the *geëxtenteerde sententie* the ships turned for Texel on 14 July.

19 NA, Hoge Raad Holland en Zeeland, 3.03.02, inv.nr. *833* (1741) Geëxtenteerde sententies, scan 10, f. 9r. It would not have been the only mutiny to be caused by worries over pay: in

was significant in the company's case because it absolved the company of any role in the cause of the mutiny.

The two vessels' unplanned return to the Dutch Republic was followed by a decade long legal dispute against the VOC Chamber Amsterdam over sailors' wages. It was not the sailors themselves who sued the company for their pay; investors in VOC sailors' wage accounts took the directors of the Amsterdam chamber to court to resolve their conflict over the payments. The case was pursued from city court to provincial court and finally to the High Court of Holland, Zeeland and West-Friesland.[20] The court records generated by the legal proceedings between Reijnier de Wolf, Anthonij Carstens and their fellow investors in sailors wages, on the one side, and the directors of the Amsterdam Chamber on the other side, bring to light events at sea and the ways in which they were handled. The resolution of one conflict sparked another, which in turn led to further disputes, culminating in the case against the company.

In opposition, De Wolff and Carstens claimed that the company was at fault for not providing the *Purmerlust* and *Ter Horst* with 'Turkish passes' and that fear of sailing without passes was the cause of the mutiny on board the two ships. In fact, De Wolff and Carstens asserted that the two vessels were captured because they had not carried the necessary passes, that is, the VOC had not issued the *Purmerlust* and *Ter Horst* the letters or passports they needed for protection. The VOC countered the former allegation: firstly, according to the company the Dutch consul in Algiers had secured 'complete Turkish passes' for the two vessels; and secondly, the mutiny occurred three weeks after leaving Algiers by which time neither vessel could have been in danger from privateers.[21] There was thus no hindrance to the *Purmerlust* and *Ter Horst* continuing on their voyage from the company's point of view.

The eventful voyage of the *Purmerlust* and *Ter Horst*, albeit curtailed, sparked the dispute between De Wolff and Carstens and the VOC Chamber Amsterdam directors over the payment of wages to the group of investors. Twelve men had invested in the wage accounts of the crew of the two vessels and they pooled their claims, totalling over 20,000 guilders, when they proceeded against the chamber directors in the city court in Amsterdam.[22] The

---

1608 crew onboard the *Oude Zon* mutinied, sparked by fears that they would not be paid for their work seeing as their contracts had already expired. Ketting (2002) 257.

20 The High Court documents: NA, Hoge Raad Holland en Zeeland, 3.03.02, inv.nr. 833 (1741), Geëxtenteerde sententies, scans 2–22, ff. 1r-20v; inv. nr. 673 (1741), Resoluties, scan 5–6.

21 NA, Hoge Raad Holland en Zeeland, 3.03.02, inv.nr. 833 (1741) Geëxtenteerde sententies, scan 17 ff. 15v-16r.

22 On the secondary market for employees' wage accounts see Van Bochove and van Velzen (2013).

Aldermen ruled against them in 1732. Nine of the twelve decided to appeal the verdict, which they did in the Provincial Court of Holland. That court confirmed the earlier sentence in the VOC's favour. Undeterred, the nine men, headed by De Wolff and Carstens, then proceeded on appeal to the High Court of Holland, Zeeland and West-Friesland where for the third time their claim to the sailors' wages was denied. It is the records of the legal proceedings which bring to light the eventful voyage of the two vessels and the linked disputes which began with the capture of VOC ships.

The capture and ransoming of the VOC ships *Purmerlust* and *Ter Horst* is an example of how the VOC was literally caught up in Mediterranean affairs. The VOC's sphere of operations – its charter area from the Cape of Good Hope eastwards – did not protect or exclude the company from Atlantic pursuits and forceful detainment in the Mediterranean. As this case underlines, the conceptual containment provided by the geographic notions of 'Mediterranean' and 'Atlantic' seem to be reductive when analysing the events surrounding these two ships. They sailed under the jurisdiction and exclusive privileges attributed by the States General via charter to the VOC (translated into exclusive rights to affairs in the Indian Ocean), failed to defend themselves by protection offered by the company's charter, or the existence of an Ottoman passport, resulting in the Atlantic apprehension of the ships, and the subsequent diplomatic conflict resolution regarding the Atlantic capture within the premises followed by the protocol and the rules as understood in the Mediterranean world at large and in Algiers in particular. Knowledge specialists like Captain Schrijver take centre stage as intermediaries not only between the United Provinces, the VOC and the Algerian privateers, but also as mediators in maritime conflicts arising in multiple maritime spaces.[23] We need then to conclude, that the actions of historical actors like the chartered companies, privateers and intermediaries in the resolution of maritime conflicts result in the necessity to de-construct the idea of oceanic segregation ('Mediterranean world' or 'Atlantic history') to understand the uncontained nature of liquid spaces. This is more so necessary when companies with charters to operate in the Indian Ocean are physically captured in the Atlantic and disputed in the Mediterranean, as if for maritime actors borders between oceanic spaces were virtual rather than real.

As we will argue below, the VOC pursuit of Atlantic operations was not only a contingency of having to cross the Atlantic Ocean into its oceanic charter located in the Indian Ocean. The company actively participated in multiple

23 Captain Schrijver was not alone in negotiating the fate of Dutch crews and ships with Barbary privateers. Van Gelder (2015) 175–198.

Atlantic adventures and claims that included the trade in enslaved Africans on the West Coast of Africa during the 1650s and the capture of Portuguese Indiamen for the whole of the first half of the seventeenth century, as we will see next.[24]

3 Maritime Connectivity: The Boundaries of (Il)legality

For about one hundred years after Vasco da Gama's arrival in Calicut in 1498, Europeans in service of the Portuguese Crown explored both shores of the Indian Ocean and reached further to the East, to China and Japan. Following this first spur of overseas maritime expansion, by the end of the sixteenth century, partnerships in Dutch cities started to pull up capital and invest in voyages to Asia, also known as *voorcompagnieën*.[25] These temporary partnerships shared the knowledge brought from Portuguese Asia by Jan Huygen van Linschoten (1563–1611), former secretary of the Portuguese Archbishop of Goa,[26] and the availability of capital in the largest cities as a result of the Dutch participation in the Baltic trade.[27] Although successful, the *voorcompagnieën* were short lived. The incursions in Asia led to major competition in the domestic markets for the Asian products they imported and the solution found for this problem was the creation of a single company that held the exclusive rights to trade into Asia. Those exclusive rights were translated into a charter in 1602 and the new company was appropriately named *Vereenigde Oostindische Compagnie* (United East India Company), commonly known as VOC.

Contrary to the *voorcompagnieën*, the VOC comprised large fleets that entered the Portuguese maritime and territorial domains in the South Atlantic and the Indian Ocean. These fleets were as interested in conducting trade as they were in privateering, an activity they perceived as necessary for the Portuguese to accept the Dutch presence in the Indian Ocean and to penetrate the Asian markets alongside – or instead of – the men serving the *Estado da Índia*. New research on the VOC violence against the Portuguese fleets of *Carreira da Índia* estimates that a total of 163 ships were captured between the entrance of the VOC in the Indian Ocean and 1625. These ships belonged to the *Carreira da Índia* and to Portuguese traders in Asia. During the period 1601 to 1609, the majority of the captures took place in the Indian Ocean, around Ceylon and

24 Van Welie (2008) 47–96.
25 Gaastra (2003) 17–23.
26 Van Linschoten (1910).
27 Van Tielhof (2002); van Bochove (2008).

Melaka, while in the period between 1610 and 1619 the captures moved from the Indian Ocean to the Indonesian archipelago, to return in the period between 1620 and 1625 to the Indian Ocean and the Bay of Bengal.[28] In this last period, however, an interesting phenomenon took place: two of the Portuguese ships captured by the VOC were taken in the South Atlantic after a pursuit around the Cape of Good Hope.

The VOC violence against the Portuguese ships of *Carreira da Índia* had two consequences. On the one hand, the Dutch violence of the Indian Ocean was not contained in that space, but spilled over into the Atlantic, a space where the VOC did not hold a presumption of jurisdiction or sovereignty, as its charter related solely to activities East of the Cape of Good Hope. On the other hand, the capture of the Portuguese Indiamen in the South Atlantic threatened the legal and exclusive rights of the Dutch West India Company (WIC), whose charter of 1621 stated clearly that the geographical limitations of its charter were contained in the Atlantic space,[29] leaving the VOC maritime captures in the South Atlantic in a situation of illegality.

However, the disputes between the VOC and the WIC in the South Atlantic were not exclusively related to capturing Portuguese Indiamen as prizes of war. In the years that followed the creation of the WIC in 1621, the precise location of the VOC refreshment station and settlement which grew into the city of Cape Town was a continuous fight between the VOC and the WIC. The WIC rightfully claimed that the VOC's settlement was situated within its Atlantic jurisdiction, seeing as the fort lay to the west of the line through the Cape of Good Hope (Kaap Goede Hoop, Cabo da Boa Esperança), which divided the two charter areas. The conflict between the two companies followed shortly after the question of financial rescue for the WIC via merging with the VOC had been answered by the VOC paying the WIC a large sum of money to avoid being burdened by the WIC's financial woes during the 1640s. It is likely that the WIC raised the conflict over Cape Town to elicit a similar sum in compensation and formal recognition of the VOC incursion into the WIC's charter area. The Cape remained in the WIC charter area, and the VOC continued to conduct activities, namely slave trading, on the West Coast of Africa during the 1650s.[30]

The boundaries of oceanic containment set out in the VOC and WIC charters defined, at least within the Dutch context, the frontier of legality and illegality to which both companies had to adhere. In practice, and when it came to maritime violence and territorial definitions of sovereignty, the interaction between the companies resulted in the need for maritime (and other forms of)

28 Murteira (2016) 202–203, 260, 297.

29 Article 1, Charter 1621, published in de Laet (1644) I 6–8.

30 Verstegen (2002) 39–48.

conflict resolution, as the VOC took prizes of war (the Portuguese Indiamen) in an Atlantic space where it did not hold jurisdiction, to the detriment of the rights adjudicated in exclusive privilege to the WIC. Furthermore, oceanic containment seems to have been impossible to uphold as the conflicts of the Indian Ocean were literally pursued into the Atlantic, in a less known form of maritime connectivity that blurred boundaries of legality and illegality supposedly established by oceanic containment as prescribed in the companies' charters. Regimes of legality and illegality were thus fluid, as is oceanic containment, a reality that resulted in the development of loopholes and grey areas that were prone to provoke and condition maritime conflicts and their consequent resolution.

4 Property Rights, Regimes of Subjection and Belonging of Maritime Agents

Similar to what happened with the VOC in the Indian and Atlantic oceans, the WIC was involved in privateering in various capacities. Company vessels cruised the Atlantic as privateers themselves, and company vessels were also potential victims of privateers operating under different imperial frameworks.[31] Furthermore, the WIC granted private merchants permission to conduct privateering in the company charter area. The federalised organisation of the company meant that this was arranged at chamber level, and the goods taken prize were sold off by the individual chambers.[32] It was this latter involvement which drew the WIC into a maritime conflict around property rights, subjection and belonging.

During the 1650s, the WIC Chamber Zeeland joined a dispute which was already at an advanced stage of litigation. The parties had proceeded in the city court in Vlissingen. Dissatisfied with the Aldermen's sentence, one party appealed to the High Court at which point the chamber joined the legal dispute.[33]

31 Francke (2000) 119–140.

32 The WIC consisted of five chambers, which operated under the board of directors, the Gentlemen Nineteen, and after 1674, the Gentlemen Ten. Equipping and sending out ships was organised by each chamber, and the goods brought back were sold off by the individual chambers. Selling recognition goods – that is, goods traded by private merchants who essentially leased the company monopolies – and prize was similarly decentralised. The extent of decentralisation comes through in the company's founding charter. Charter published in de Laet (1644) I 6–31.

33 NA, Hoge Raad Holland en Zeeland, 3.03.02, inv. nr. 754 (1662) Geëxtenteerde sententie, scan 58, ff. Lvi v-Lvii r. This case is discussed in Kate Ekama's PhD dissertation: Ekama (2018) 238–241.

The original dispute arose between two captains over goods which had been taken prize in the Atlantic in May 1650. The mid-seventeenth century was a period of hostility between the Dutch and Portuguese which manifest itself in, amongst other things, privateering. From 1645 onwards, the Portuguese in Brazil revolted against Dutch rule, which led to an increase in Dutch privateering against Portuguese vessels in the Atlantic. West India Company cruisers and to an even greater extent Zeeland privateers inflicted damage on the Portuguese fleets, capturing approximately 220 Portuguese Brazil traders between January 1647 and December 1648. As a result, 'substantial quantities' of sugar were shipped to the Republic, and the WIC profited by taking a percentage of the prize.[34] Privateering continued into the 1650s, the early years of which were a period of uncertainty regarding the legitimacy of prizes. Between 1649 and 1653 there was no truce between the Dutch and Portuguese, nor was there a final treaty. In 1654 the Dutch lost their colony in Brazil to the Portuguese. But it was only in 1661 that a final treaty was drawn up, and then ratified the following year.[35]

It was in this context of hostility, insurrection and privateering that Captain Jan Daniels departed Lisbon for Cape St Augustine (Cabo Santo Agostinho) in Portuguese Brazil, on board a vessel named *Eduard.* In Portuguese Brazil, he took on board 500 chests of sugar, and at least four rolls of tobacco, perhaps other goods too, for the account of Portuguese and English merchants resident in Lisbon. On the return journey, the *Eduard* encountered a hostile Dutch ship in the vicinity of the Azores. The vessel was Captain Lambert Bartelsz's (*Roode*) *Zeeuwsche Leeuw.* Bartelsz was a privateer: he had letters of reprisal (*brieven van repressallien*) against the Portuguese granted by the States General, and commission from the WIC, so it comes as no surprise that he readied his men for a battle against the *Eduard*. Jan Daniels also claimed that he was ready to fight, however, his officers and crew considered it prudent to agree to terms of surrender with Bartelsz instead. They reached an agreement on 22 May 1650. The *Eduard* and the *Zeeuwsche Leeuw* sailed for Vlissingen, and after arrival there the sugar and tobacco was unloaded from the vessel and the goods were (going to be) sold at company auction. Jan Daniels heard about the impending sale of both the Portuguese goods loaded on the ship, as well as those for the account of the 'English nation' in Lisbon, against which he protested by means of a warrant of seizure for the English goods. Bartelsz and the chamber did not

34 Boxer (1957), 201–203; Antunes and Roitman (2015).

35 On the loss of Dutch Brazil, see Boxer (1957) 240–241.

heed the arrest and sold the goods at auction anyway. In response, Jan Daniels instituted legal proceedings.

Interestingly, the foreign merchants chose to begin legal proceedings in the city court in Vlissingen. As foreign merchants, they would have been allowed to begin proceedings in the High Court.[36] However, they chose not to, perhaps preferring to be heard in a Zeeland court rather than in The Hague. In addition to Daniels, the other claimants in the case in the city court were men, and a woman, on whose accounts 42,5 of the chests of sugar on board the *Eduard* had been transported. The Vlissingen Court passed a verdict on 26 October 1655 which Daniels *et al* considered to be a misjudgment, and so they appealed the case. It appears that the foreign merchants bypassed the Court of Holland and appealed the Vlissingen verdict in the High Court.[37] Moreover, that they were foreign meant that they received lenience from the court insofar as the rules of beginning an appeal were concerned. They had in fact taken too long between the verdict of the lower court and lodging their appeal with the High Court, but the High Court overlooked this, attributing their tardiness to their 'foreignness' (*uijtlandicheijt*) and ignorance of the legal system, and allowed their appeal. The High Court granted them leave to appeal in September 1658. For three and a half years the High Court dealt with the matter: the parties swelled and their lawyers explored legal avenues, before the judges passed their verdict in February 1662. They overturned the Vlissingen court's sentence and instead ordered Bartelsz, his associates, and the Chamber Zeeland to return the 42,5 chests of sugar and four rolls of tobacco to Daniels *et al* or pay them their value plus interest dating from the time legal proceedings began in Vlissingen.[38]

The most interesting of the legal arguments revolved around subjection. The important question was whether the merchants on whose accounts the goods were shipped were Portuguese or English. If the members of the English Nation in Lisbon were considered subjects of the Portuguese Crown, then their goods could be claimed as prize under the letter of reprisal which Bartelsz carried. However, if the merchants were in fact considered English – which was the argument that they made to the court – then their goods could not be sold off as legitimate prize.[39] In the end, the court concluded that the English Nation in

36 Punt (2010) 7–8.

37 Theoretically, the case should have first been appealed in the Provincial Court. See LeBailly and Verhas on *omisso medio*: LeBailly and Verhas (2006) 14.

38 NA, Hoge Raad Holland en Zeeland, 3.03.02, inv. nr. 754 (1662) Geëxtenteerde sententie, scan 43, 48, ff. xLi v, xLvi v–xLvii r.

39 NA, Hoge Raad Holland en Zeeland, 3.03.02, inv. nr. 754 (1662) Geëxtenteerde sententie, scans 45–46, 54–55, xLiiii r-v, Liii v–Liiii r.

Lisbon were not in fact subjects of the Portuguese Crown. The court ordered the sugar and tobacco be returned to the merchants. The merchandise was specified as belonging to ten individuals, one of whom was an English noblewoman resident in Lisbon, Johanna Veere, to whom a half chest was due, and another of whom, on whose account there were eight chests, was Johan Busschel.[40] The latter was most likely the court's rendering of the name John Bushell, brother of Edward, who was in this period the Brazil Company's London agent.[41] Not only is it striking to see the detail of the judges' consideration of the subjection argument – who was born where and the implications thereof – but furthermore, in their judgment, the High Court bench protected the rights of foreigners against subjects of the States General and the WIC, following the rule that subjection determined property rights and thus rendered specific products in a ship rightful or wrongful prizes of war.

Surprisingly, at no point in the sentence or attendant resolution is the term 'prize' used in reference to the goods. Perhaps the framing of the case in terms other than prize was a means of avoiding the problem of jurisdiction. The jurisdiction of the Admiralty court over such a case should have been clear cut: prize cases were adjudicated by the Admiralty in the port in which the goods entered the Republic.[42] The involvement of foreigners, surely common in prize cases, should not have complicated the Admiralties' jurisdiction. A possible explanation is that the private nature of the contract between the Chamber Zeeland and the privateer shifted the case into the jurisdiction of the city court in Zeeland rather than the Admiralty court in that province. Be that as it may, the case between the captains was heard in first instance in the Vlissingen city court and sentenced by the burgomasters and aldermen of that city.

The case of the property rights of the English Nation in Lisbon being defined by the regime of subjection they fell under is not surprising, though. Since the end of the sixteenth century, Dutch courts had been plagued by matters relating to prizes of war being disputed by different merchant nations, not least the Portuguese Nation of Amsterdam, in a perennial fight to define property rights according to subjection. The Nation used two sets of arguments to claim its right to goods taken as prizes of war in the Atlantic and elsewhere in

40 NA, Hoge Raad Holland en Zeeland, 3.03.02, inv. nr. 754 (1662) Geëxtenteerde sententie, scan 47, f. xLvi r.

41 Shaw (1998) 116.

42 Prior to the creation of the Admiralties, prize cases were heard in multiple courts, including the Court of Holland and the Great Council of Malines. Prud'homme van Reine and van der Oest (1991) 24. Louis Sicking has addressed the jurisdictional tensions in maritime conflicts between the Court of Holland, that is the provincial court, and the Admiralty which was first established in Zeeland. Sicking (2004) 453–458.

the world. On the one hand, if the goods had been taken by Dutch privateers, the members of the Nation often claimed being subjects of the States General, as stated in the privileges provided to the Nation by the City of Amsterdam and later on the States General. At the same time, when goods were taken by Spanish privateers in Dutch ships, they would claim the goods to belong to members of the Nation as subjects of the king of Spain.[43] The claims continued even when the Portuguese Nation faced institutions like the Inquisition, against whom they would claim to be subjects of the States General and thus exempted from persecution or confiscation of assets.[44] As the disputes between the Portuguese Nation and Iberian institutions and privateers, on the one hand, and the Dutch privateers, on the other hand, ensued during most of the first half of the seventeenth century, the States General issued a resolution in 1651 declaring that all members of the Portuguese Nation would be considered, from then on, subjects of the States General of the United Provinces, in a move that possibly created the first 'national' citizens in Western Europe.[45]

Shifting notions of property rights provoked maritime and commercial conflict around the world and raised strong disputes regarding regimes of subjection and belonging of maritime agents (freighters, skippers, crews, etc), regardless of the maritime time spaces where conflicts arose. These two elements were thus paramount to determine the (il)legality of prizes of war in multiple maritime spaces, testing the limits of institutions in their ability to determine and design regimes of property rights concomitant to regimes of subjection.

5 Maritime Conflict in the Atlantic and the Mediterranean: Conclusions

The VOC and WIC transgressions in the Atlantic, the capture of their fleets by Mediterranean privateers, or the disputes of the English Nation in Lisbon or the Portuguese Nation in Amsterdam for captures in the Atlantic and the Mediterranean reflect the broad variety of commercial conflicts that arose with maritime interactions between different countries, diverse companies and varied firms. Although different, these cases were common in the Early Modern period and they showcase the necessity of looking at commercial conflict resolution resulting from maritime encounters within the particularities of the conflicts themselves, rather than the maritime spaces where they took place.

43 Antunes and Roitman (2015).

44 Antunes (2011) 221–238.

45 Roitman (2012) 55–90.

As we have argued, encounters in the Mediterranean and the Atlantic and the Indian Ocean created spillovers that opened up the conflicts taking place in one specific space to a space of resolution in a totally different maritime universe. In this sense, maritime encounters and commercial conflict contributed heavily to increase the connectivity of the maritime spaces, defying thus the idea that conflict resolution could be anchored in one specific space or within a specific tradition. Geographical containment seems thus an unfruitful avenue to pursue the study of international maritime conflicts.

Since geographical containment of maritime spaces seems to have been unimportant for the way commercial and maritime conflict took place and the way it was solved, we have looked at the possibility to, instead of thinking about maritime spaces, replace them by frameworks of (i)legality, mostly defined by institutions, through charters, laws, treaties or conventions. Also in this case, we demonstrate that the boundaries of (i)legality are fluid, as fluid are the means and mechanisms to resolve maritime and commercial conflicts, a conclusion supported by recent explorations on the meaning of (i)legality in the maritime world in general.[46] In maritime spaces where multiple jurisdictions were at play between different polities, but also between different institutions within the same polity, jurisdictional competition arose and with it the space for individuals and groups of interest to move to challenge the boundaries imposed by each one of the known jurisdictions.[47] This challenge often translated into conflict resolution by means of judicial procedures.

Creativity and ingenuity seem to have been the key factors when maritime agents pushed and crossed boundaries of legality. These attributes are more so interesting in the cases when groups of individuals endlessly (re)defined their status of subjection as a mechanism of defining for themselves different regimes of property rights. This fluid definition of identities and concomitantly of property rights showcases that maritime and commercial conflict were often less a matter of where the problem arose geographically, but rather a matter of using identity fluidity as an instrument in judicial procedures against states, institutions and fellow merchants.

Maritime connectivity as a driving force to define spheres of legality and illegality and the implication of defining regimes of property rights according to claims of subjection encapsulate an overarching narrative of conflict over jurisdictions, rather than conflicts that arise specifically because of particular maritime spaces and/or activities. We thus conclude that maritime conflicts

46 Antunes, Salvado and Post (2016) 23–52.

47 See also the chapter by Ana B. Fernández Castro in this volume.

led to conflicts over jurisdictions (defined by regimes of property rights and subjection regimes), which were not geographically exclusive of specific maritime spaces. This means that maritime conflicts were not geographically contained and can thus only be understood within a logic of maritime connectivity or entanglement.

Bibliography

Abulafia, D., *The Great Sea: A Human History of the Mediterranean* (London 2011).

'AHR Forum: Entangled Empires in the Atlantic World', *American Historical Review* 112 no. 3 (2007) 710–799.

Alencastro, L.F., *O Trato dos Viventes: formação do Brasil no Atlântico Sul, séculos XVI e XVII* (São Paulo 2000).

Allaire, B. and M. Fusaro, 'Litiges maritimes et disparités légales en Méditerranée 1610–1659: les gens de mer Nordiques face à la justice marseillaise', *Cahiers de la Méditerranée* 94 (2017) 257–284.

Antunes, C., *Cutting Corners: When Borders, Culture and Empire do not Matter* (Inaugural Lecture, Institute for History, Leiden University, 2017).

Antunes, C., 'Prosecuting the Persecutor: Contracts, Sugar, Jews and Inquisitors, 1580–1640', *Mediaevalia* 32 (2011) 221–238.

Antunes, C. and J.V. Roitman, 'A war of words: Sephardi merchants, (inter)national incidents, and litigation in the Dutch Republic, 1580–1640', *Jewish Culture and History* 16 no. 1 (2015) 24–44.

Antunes, C., J.P. Salvado and R. Post, 'Het omzeilen van monopolie handel: smokkel en belastingontduiking bij de handel in braziliehout, 1500–1674', *Tijdschrift voor Sociale en Economische Geschiedenis* 13 no. 1 (2016) 23–52.

Armitage, D. and M.J. Braddick, 'Three Concepts of Atlantic History', in Armitage, D. and M.J. Braddick, eds., *The British Atlantic World, 1500–1800* (Basingstoke 2005) 11–27.

Bailyn, B., *Atlantic History: Concepts and Contours* (Cambridge 2005).

Benton, L., 'Legal Regime and the South Atlantic World, 1400–1750: Jurisdictional Complexity as Institutional Order', *Journal of World History* 11 no. 1 (2000) 27–56.

Bochove, C. van, *The Economic Consequences of the Dutch. Economic Integration Around the North Sea, 1500–1800* (unpublished PhD dissertation, Utrecht University, 2008).

Bochove, C. van and T. van Velzen, 'Loans to salaried employees: the case of the Dutch East India Company, 1602–1794', *European Review of Economic History* 18 (2013) 19–38.

Boxer, C., *Salvador de Sá and the Struggle for Brazil and Angola, 1602–1682* (London 1952).

Boxer, C., *The Dutch in Brazil, 1624–1654* (Oxford 1957).

Braudel, F., *La Méditerranée et le monde méditerranéen* (Paris 1966).

Bruijn, J.R., 'Cornelis Schrijver' in Akveld, L.M. et al, eds, *Vier eeuwen varen. Kapiteins, kapers, kooplieden en geleerden* (Bussum 1973) 161–175.

Bruijn, J.R., 'Dutch men-of-war – Those onboard c. 1700–1750' in B.H. Slicher van Bath, ed, *Acta Historiae Neerlandicae: Studies on the History of the Netherlands* (The Hague 1974) 88–121.

Bruijn, J.R., *Schippers van de VOC in de achttiende eeuw aan de wal en op zee* (Amsterdam 2008).

Cañizares-Esguerra, J., ed., *Entangled Empires. The Anglo-Iberian Atlantic, 1500–1830* (Philadelphia 2018).

Ekama, K. *Courting Conflict: Managing Dutch East and West India Company disputes in the Dutch Republic* (unpublished PhD dissertation, Leiden University, 2018).

Elliott, J.H., *Empires of the Atlantic World: Britain and Spain in America, 1492–1830* (New Haven 2006).

Francke, J., '"Een sware equipage": de bemanningen van de admiraliteit Zeeland en de commissievaart tijdens de Negenjarige Oorlog (-1697)', *Tijdschrift voor Zeegeschiedenis* 19 no. 2 (2000) 119–140.

Fusaro, M., *Political Economies of Empire in the Early Modern Mediterranean. The Decline of Venice and the Rise of England, 1450–1700* (Cambridge 2015).

Gaastra, F.S., *The Dutch East India Company: Expansion and Decline* (Zutphen 2003).

Games, A., *The Web of Empire. English Cosmopolitans in an Age of Expansion, 1560–1660* (Oxford 2008).

Gelder, M. van, 'The Republic's Renegades: Dutch Converts to Islam in Seventeenth-Century Diplomatic Relations with North Africa', *Journal of Early Modern History* 19 (2015) 175–198.

Gereffi, G. and M. Korzeniewicz, eds., *Commodity Chains and Global Capitalism* (Westport 1994).

Ketting, H., *Leven, werk en rebellie aan boord van Oost-Indiëvaarders (1595-±1650)* (Amsterdam 2002).

Klooster, W., *The Dutch Moment. War, Trade, and Settlement in the Seventeenth-Century Atlantic World* (Ithaca 2016).

Klooster, W. and G. Oostindie, *Realm between Empires. The Second Dutch Atlantic, 1680–1815* (Ithaca 2014).

Knight, G.R., 'Commodity Chains, Mercantile Networks and the Early Years of the Batavia Firm of Maclaine Watson (1820–1840)', *South East Asia Research* 22 no. 1 (2014) 87–101.

Laet, J. de, *Historie ofte iaerlijck verhael van de verrichtinghen der geoctroyeerde West-Indische Compagnie, zedert haer begin, tot het eynde van 't jaer sesthien-hondert ses-en-dertich; begrepen in derthien boecken, ende met verscheyden koperen platen verciert.*, vol. 1 (Leyden 1644).

LeBailly, M-C. and C.M.O. Verhas, *Hoge Raad van Holland, Zeeland en West-Friesland (1582–1795). De hoofdlijnen van het procederen in civiele zaken voor de Hoge Raad zowel in eerste instantie als in hoger beroep* (Hilversum 2006).

Linschoten, J.H. van, *Itinerario. Voyage ofte schipvaert van Jan Huygen van Linschoten naer Oost ofte Portugaels Indiën, 1579–1592*, J.H.C. Kern, P.A. Tiele, P.J.B.C. Robidé van der Aa eds., 2 vols. (The Hague 1910).

Murteira, A., 'A navegação portuguesa na Ásia e na rota do Cabo e o corso neerlandês, 1595–1625' (unpublished PhD dissertation, New University of Lisbon, 2016).

Postma, J. and V. Enthoven, eds., *Riches from Atlantic Commerce: Dutch Transatlantic Trade and Shipping: 1585–1817* (Leiden 2003).

Prud'homme van Reine, R.B. and E.W. van der Oest, eds., *Kapers op de kust. Nederlandse kaapvaart en piraterij 1500–1800* (Vlissingen 1991).

Punt, H.M., *Het vennootschapsrecht van Holland. Het vennootschapsrecht van Holland, Zeeland en West-Friesland in de rechtspraak van de Hoge Raad van Holland, Zeeland en West-Friesland* (Deventer 2010).

Roitman, J.V., 'Creating Confusion in the Colonies: Jews, Citizenship, and the Dutch and British Atlantics', *Itinerario* 36 no. 2 (2012) 55–90.

Roitman, J.V. and G. Oostindie, eds., *Dutch Atlantic Connections, 1680–1800. Linking Empires, Bridging Borders* (Leiden 2014).

Russell-Wood, A.J.R., *A World on the Move: the Portuguese in Africa, Asia, and America, 1415–1808* (Manchester 1992).

Schwartz, S., 'Expansion, Diaspora, Encounter: Approaches to the Historiography of the South Atlantic', *Itinerario* 19 (1995) 48–59.

Shaw, L.M.E., *The Anglo-Portuguese Alliance and the English Merchants in Portugal, 1654–1810* (Aldershot 1998).

Sicking, L., *Neptune and the Netherlands: State, economy and war at sea in the Renaissance* (Leiden 2004).

Tielhof, M. van, *The 'Mother of all Trades'. The Baltic Grain Trade in Amsterdam from the Late 16th to the Early 19th Century* (Leiden 2002).

Verstegen, M., *Kaapstad. Een onwettig kind van de VOC: Een juridisch-politieke visie op de ontstaan van Kaapstad* (Zaltbommel 2002).

Welie, R. van, 'Slave Trading and Slavery in the Dutch Colonial Empire: A Global Comparison', *New West Indian Guide* 82 (2008) 47–96.

CHAPTER 14

The Commercial Practices of Portuguese Jewish Merchants in London and Their Dispute with Samuel Hayne, Riding-Surveyor for his Majesty's Customs, 1680

Catarina Cotic Belloube

1 Introduction

In the second half of the seventeenth century, a small community of Portuguese merchants, mostly of Jewish origin, was present in London. Living ostensibly at first as Catholics under the protection of the Spanish ambassador in London, these merchants found in England a certain degree of toleration for their religious practices. After lengthy negotiations with the different governments that ruled England at the time, a petition signed by several of the community's important merchants was given a favourable reply by the king, and in 1663 they received permission to settle officially in the kingdom, openly practice their religion, and be active members of the merchant community.[1] It remained a small community comprising about 1500 to 2000 members at its height in the beginning of the eighteenth century but it was in a favourable position to profit from English commercial development. Because its members' legal status remained uncertain and they could not swear Christian oaths due to their religious beliefs, limits were imposed on their economic activity (reduced admission to monopoly trading companies, restriction of the number of brokers allowed to take part in the commodities exchange in London). However, because they sustained a complex network of correspondents (who were sometimes close family members) in most of the important ports connected to the Atlantic trade, these merchants had an advantage when engaging in the English Plantation Trade. No matter that their foreign-born status could cause problems under the new restrictions to English colonial trade put in place

1 Roth (1964), Katz (1996), Hyamson (1951).

 | DOI:10.1163/9789004407992_016

during the middle of the century (unless granted a special dispensation, they could have no share in English vessels and had to pay steeper customs' duty): they quickly became non-negligible commercial actors in the region.

Such easy access to a restricted market could be considered problematic given the close ties of the London-based Portuguese merchants to Amsterdam and to the markets of England's main economic rival. Such connections, indeed, sufficed to render Jewish traders suspicious in the eyes of other merchants as well as royal officers, who accused them of engaging in unfair (and illegal) trading practices that violated English regulations. Among the several legal actions led by merchant competitors as well as royal officers at the time was the seizure in 1671 of a ship in Jamaica, an action justified by the colonial authorities via the claim that a Jew could never be an English subject. Another disputed seizure, this time in England, involved the *Experiment*, a ship whose cargo belonged, at least in part, to members of the Jewish community in London; it was stopped at Falmouth in 1680 en route to Amsterdam from Barbados. This latter affair highlights several concerns of particular interest relating to English colonial trade: the disparity between the strictures of commercial regulation and the actual practices of the actors involved in the Plantation and Dutch trade; the difficulty determining the legal status of Jewish merchants, whose identity and rights were constantly subjected to reinterpretation and abuse; and the tendency, due to these uncertainties, for direct conflict to arise with royal officers who interpreted the law strictly.

A well-documented case, the *Experiment* has been an example used to illustrate certain aspects of Atlantic trade in the seventeenth century, most notably by Holly Snyder, who cites it to discuss the restrictions faced by Jewish merchants because of their religious and social status while working in the colonial trade of the Atlantic region.[2] Christian Koot uses the same case in his description of the evolution of inter-imperial trade in the region during the late seventeenth century.[3] Much of the knowledge of the episode comes from the account of Samuel Hayne, Riding-Surveyor for his Majesty's Customs. One aspect of his text that has not yet been explored in a detailed way is its precise description of the Atlantic trade, in particular its illegal or quasi-legal aspects. His testimony offers a firsthand account of the strategies used by actors in long-distance trade to circumvent customs while maintaining a presence in trade routes under the sway of stringent regulations.

2 Snyder (2009) 53–56.

3 Koot (2011) 117–118.

2 The Immediate Context: The Acts of Navigation and the Creation of a National Monopoly on Long-distance Trade

The readmission of the Jews to England coincided with the implementation, in 1651 and 1662, of the Acts of Navigation, which closely regulated English imports and exports. The context of these acts was England's commercial rivalry with the United Provinces and the 'post-1647 English shipping slump',[4] as well as three seventeenth-century military conflicts (1652–1654, 1665–1667, 1672–1674) that pit the two nations against each other. These conflicts appear to have been a symptom of 'a deep, underlying conflict of interest between the English and the Dutch mercantile systems'[5] and the force behind the push for stricter regulation of its trade. Indeed, by the end of the seventeenth century (certainly after 1672), the English had displaced the Dutch as the dominant commercial force, particularly in Northern Europe. Their economy was 'based not on a buoyant growth of exports, but on a long phase of import-led growth and intense commercial rivalry'.[6] At about the same time England's political classes began to assert more strongly the idea that the benefits from trade as well as shipping and entrepot activity should be restricted to English subjects – including, at the time, Irish citizens and colonists. This constraint on colonial markets was perceived as both a right and a necessity: since the Dutch were so skilled in trade (having more ships, they also could boast that their vessels were of better quality, even if they were mostly unarmed), only decisive action to enact such protection could ensure that 'in a few years' the Dutch would not 'eat us quite out of them'.[7]

This desire to exert greater control over, and restrict access to, English markets is clearly on display in the Acts of Navigation. The legislation imposed an economic reorientation towards English trade through the creation of a 'national monopoly'[8] under which English long-distance trade, and its shipping capacity, could develop through the re-exporting of colonial staples. A secondary objective of the Acts, born probably from English admiration of and worry about the Dutch trading and shipping model, was the desire to create an entrepot system in London, similar to what existed in Amsterdam.[9] In

4 Israel (1989) 208.
5 Israel (1997) 349.
6 Ormrod (2015) 18.
7 Child (1698) 172.
8 Ormrod (2003) 36.
9 Ormrod (2003) 37.

practice, the Acts of Navigation required, first, that imported Asian, African, and American goods be shipped in vessels that were owned and operated by English subjects (the master and three-quarters of the ship's crew had to be English, although colonial subjects were also acceptable) and, second, that goods entering English ports come directly from their countries of origin. The Staple Act of 1663, intended to work in concert with the Acts of Navigation and a measure that also promoted the creation of an entrepot economy in London, stipulated that all European goods to be sold in English colonies be laden in England and then shipped directly to the colonies.[10] The strictures of this 'staggeringly ambitious'[11] attempt to limit the Dutch shipping industry were nearly impossible to enforce – particularly on the empire's peripheries, where there weren't enough officials to supervise all shipping and where more practical concerns, such as ensuring the arrival of those European products that could be essential to a colony's survival, could take precedence over a strict application of the law. Despite more stringent enforcement procedures put in place in 1673, and again in 1696, to discourage colonists from engaging in illicit trade, the Acts were difficult to implement.

One probable reason why these regulations seem not to have been appropriate for the newly developing Atlantic trade is that they were meant primarily to limit Dutch influence on England's Baltic and Norwegian trade. Only by the end of the seventeenth century – and, to a greater extent, the first half of the eighteenth – did the Atlantic trade become a significant factor in the English economy; only then did the profits from the trade become significant. As Ormrod points out, 'the contribution of the colonial periphery was limited to providing a flow of goods for re-export during a long period of import-led growth',[12] and the colonial export economy was mainly focused on providing European markets with staples such as Caribbean sugar or tobacco. However, while contemporaries were aware that the Acts of Navigation were important to the development of English trading capability, so much so that there was 'now more than double the quantity of Merchants and Shipping we had twenty Years past',[13] the situation was not ideal for those in the colonies. One of the colonists' chief objections to the Acts was that it would 'in time Ruin their Plantations, it they may not be permitted, at least, to carry their Sugars to the best Markets, and not be compelled to send all to, and receive all Commodities

10 Zahedieh (2010) 37.
11 Ormrod (2003) 32.
12 Ormrod (2015) 23.
13 Child (1698) 46.

from England'.[14] For planters and merchants involved in the Plantation Trade, the Dutch carrying trade was absolutely crucial for the success of their enterprises, since they brought essential cargoes and commercial options for colonies struggling under London's restrictive yoke. As is often the case on the peripheries of empire, practical and material concerns sometimes took precedence over strict adherence to commercial regulations. One thus finds examples of illegal exchanges persisting in English colonies, as well as a 'culture of cross-national cooperation in the Atlantic'.[15]

This is particularly significant when dealing with merchants whose access to the Dutch market was frequent and important – and suddenly and unilaterally interrupted by regulations imposed by English officials, to the detriment of colonial subjects. Indeed, in the early years after these trade restrictions took effect, colonial settlers expressed vocal opposition and sometimes refused to abide by the new rules, as is clearly expressed in a pamphlet written by Barbados residents and published in 1651 in The Hague. Its authors declared the new laws unreasonable and unfair, given that 'all the old Planters know how much they have ben houlding to the Dutch for their subsistence'.[16] They justified such resistance by insisting on the importance of the Dutch market and carrying trade for the successful settlement of the colonies, and pointed out the scarcity of commodities, and serious deficiencies in shipping, resulting from the new restrictions. A few decades later, as regulations became only more severe, the 'disjuncture between metropolitan aims and colonial practice'[17] was so pronounced that merchants needed to adopt a more flexible approach to the regulatory regime. Appearing to adhere to the law, they found ways to circumvent restrictions. For example, Barbados merchants sent a vessel, the *Experiment*, to Amsterdam by way of England, whose journey ostensibly adhered to the regulations (in the colonists' use of a British ship and its stopping at an English port). But in practice there are deviations that seem to indicate that the Dutch trade was still active, even if covered by a veneer of legality, and that merchants involved in colonial exports were still 'acting improvisationally in pursuit of personal and colonial profit, undermining the quest for orderly commerce found in imperial thinking'.[18]

14 Child (1698) 174.
15 Koot (2011) 3.
16 Barbados Council and Assembly (1651) 3.
17 Koot (2011) 88.
18 Koot (2011) 2.

3 The Case of the *Experiment*

3.1 *Samuel Hayne, the Curious Example of an Incorruptible Royal Officer*

The details of the case of the *Experiment* are known to us due mainly to an account written and published by Samuel Hayne, at the time a Riding Surveyor for his majesty's customs and Surveyor for the Act of Navigation in the counties of Devon and Cornwall. His background – both in service to Customs and as a merchant – was typical of the surveyors active in English outposts in the seventeenth century,[19] whose upbringing was often similar to those on the receiving end of their inspections. Born in 1645 or 1646, he was apprenticed by the age of sixteen to Joseph Ash, Esq, Collector for the Customs of Plymouth and Cornwall as Clerk Assistant. About seven years later, he was active in the Plantation Trade in America, but during the third Anglo-Dutch war he returned to his duty at Customs, both in the Prize office and in the Admiralty. He was afterwards active in commerce with France before the imposition of trade restrictions, which led to his return to service as a surveyor. In June 1680, he was commissioned as Riding Surveyor for the Customs and Counties of Devon and Cornwall as well as a Surveyor of the Act of Navigation.[20] Later in his career, after his stint in the southern counties, he was transferred to London, where he was directly employed by the Commissioners of Customs.

Samuel Hayne's career seems to indicate a particularly conscientious officer: there is evidence that he did not hesitate to take aim at anyone who violated customs regulations, irrespective of their status. For example, a few years after the conclusion of his conflict with the London Portuguese merchant community, he appears as a complainant in another affair, this time involving the contraband of large quantities of tobacco by employees of the Plymouth Custom house. Accusing his colleagues of enabling – and sometimes actively participating in – the smuggling of highly taxed (and easily diverted) goods through the port, he does not hesitate to expose their illegal behaviour to his superiors, who then indicted several of the wrongdoers on smuggling charges.[21] It should be noted that this behaviour was certainly not the norm for late-seventeenth-century customs officials, who were widely known to be easily corruptible. One commentator estimated in 1665 that 'The great and very many Frauds and Deceits used in deceiving the King in his Customes [amount to] almost as

19 Stephens (2012) 145.

20 Hayne (1685) 9.

21 Stephens (2012) 142–150.

much as two parties in three'.[22] Bookkeeping fraud, conflicts of interest, and actual criminal behaviour ran rampant, and the commissioners' limited resources proved insufficient to rein in customs officers, particularly when local merchants and notables encouraged them in their questionable practices.

3.2 *The Seizure of the* Experiment*: A Firsthand Account of Outport Customs Practices*

Evidence of Samuel Hayne's conflict with the Portuguese merchant community of London can be found in his forty-page abstract summarizing the affair, which he published in London in 1685. In this text he attempts to justify the actions he had taken five years before, providing a detailed explanation of their legal basis and recounting the series of events that led to his impounding of the ship and the confiscation of cargo owned by Jewish merchants residing in London – some of whom were denizens and had, therefore, enjoyed commercial privileges in the country (in particular, some were exempt from the Alien Tax). His main accusation is that, through what he calls the 'colouring' of goods, these merchants accorded with commercial privileges had defrauded the Crown via their claims on goods that did not belong to them.

According to Haynes's abstract, he first learned of a problem falling under his jurisdiction while in Cornwall in October 1680,[23] when he accidentally overheard talk that a large ship – the 300-ton *Experiment* – had been cleared at Falmouth 'without Unloading her whole Cargo' as was required by law and therefore had not acquitted itself of all its dues. The ship, loaded mainly with sugar, was making its way from Barbados to Amsterdam, and its cargo had been inspected and was cleared under the name of the ship's master, Henry Sutton, and an English merchant based in Falmouth, Bryan Rogers.

Hayne immediately set out for Falmouth and arrived after sundown – too late in the day to board the ship and survey its cargo. The following day, he was invited to dinner by a local notable, Sir Peter Killigrew, delaying his planned inspection of the ship. Killigrew, it turns out, had a vested interest in deferring the inspection, being the owner of the quay where the ship's inspection had occurred (and seeking to avoid the accusation that he had enabled customs fraud, which could result in loss of his licence to administer the only public quay where goods could legally be discharged). He used the dinner invitation to distract Hayne, keeping him occupied while the ship's master – informed of the customs officer's presence in town – was out 'hunting about for his men to get them on board, in order to set Sail immediately for Amsterdam'. Hayne,

22 Ashworth (2003) 158.
23 Hayne (1685) 15.

after realizing the deception, took immediate action to seize the *Experiment*: he 'laid a Stop on the Ship, put Wayters on board, &c. to secure her' and sent Thomas Enys, collector at Penryn, a request for assistance. Indeed, Hayne declared that there could not have been an illegal dispatch of such magnitude without the knowledge of 'all the officers' in Falmouth, and that no one there could be trusted to do their duty. The seizure imminent, Hayne was offered numerous unsuccessful bribes in exchange for letting the ship pass, including '50 Guineys, and the best Horse Sir Peter had'.[24]

Hayne's assumption that all officials in Falmouth were party to the fraud is plausible; provincial ports had earned a reputation as places where regulations could easily be ignored given appropriate incentives to look the other way. Historically, designating ports had fallen under the monarch's purview; designating the legality of specific spaces for the loading and unloading of merchandise was an important step in developing an administrative customs regime (an official port was supplied with 'the official seal along with the king's beam and official weights',[25] all the necessary accoutrements for dealing with merchandise on which customs was to be paid). Loading and unloading cargo outside these designated areas was considered a felony, punishable by up to three years' imprisonment. As a result, outports – provincial deep-water ports usually situated far from the capital and the seat of the government – were under the authority of London and subject to its supervision. These smaller ports, though having higher overhead costs relative to the revenue collected, amounted to a non-negligible source of revenue to the Crown: they account for thirty per cent of the total customs revenue (which does not account for smuggling and contraband) at the end of the seventeenth century.[26] They became more important during the eighteenth century and collected a greater amount of revenue,[27] in part due to the introduction by the Commissioners of Customs of more professional procedures and more inspections, aimed at making the Port of London's standards the norm in the rest of the kingdom. It was largely accepted that this greater degree of surveillance would also limit fraud and thus increase revenue.[28]

Indeed, those smaller ports, due to their geographical distance from the centre, were less strictly controlled and less rigidly organised than the port of London. A typical outport had just three patent officers: a customer, a controller,

24 Hayne (1685) 17.
25 Ashworth (2003) 151.
26 Stephens (2012) 4.
27 Ashworth (2003) 151.
28 Stephens (2012) 4.

and a searcher. Despite such meagre staffing such outports held authority over hundreds of miles of coastline as well as 'all the member ports and creeks that fell under its jurisdiction'.[29] Such a mandate was impossible to enforce – and smuggling, given the numerous hiding places and hidden ports in these coastal regions, could be a thriving business. Even when legal procedures were enforced, the distance to London and the centre of customs control presented problems: communication with the Commissioners was often difficult and the transportation of revenue to the Exchequer could be dangerous. In the absence of official directives, most outports had to use Bills of Exchange, paying cash to their towns' leading merchants in exchange for a bill that could be sent to the office of the receiver-general in London, who would then cash it with the merchant's correspondent.[30] Attempts to regularize port practices began at the end of the seventeenth century but, despite improvements, discrepancies persisted as late as the nineteenth century.

For those engaged in colonial trading, outports offered a lucrative alternative for merchants seeking to circumvent the regulations of the Acts of Navigation while maintaining the appearance of compliance. Merchants could ship cargo from the United Provinces to the Caribbean, or from English colonies to Amsterdam, with a brief stop at a convenient outport to acquire the appropriate certificates of English ownership or their equivalent (Jewish merchants often had patents of endenization that were also acceptable) and certificates from the customs house, before continuing the voyage to their port of destination. While the legalities of such activity were open for discussion, especially if one adopted a strict interpretation of the Navigation Acts, they were sufficiently common to have been accepted as justification in court when settling disputes. For example, when two vessels loaded in Amsterdam on behalf of Portuguese Jewish merchants, the *Matthew Francis* and the *Sarah and Mary*, make port in Barbados in 1668 loaded with European goods, the governor, Christopher Codrington, refused to seize the ships despite having advance knowledge of their arrival. Codrington argued that the shipment was legal, since England routinely allows 'shipps laden in Holland to touch and enter in some ports in England, from whence they Carry Certificates from the Custom house, upon which Lycence of Trade hath always been heretofore granted'.[31]

While such interruptions could be costly in both financial terms (English taxes were high) and time wasted (to satisfy the Acts' requirements, a ship had to be completely emptied and the goods warehoused while customs fees were

29 Ashworth (2003) 152.
30 Ashworth (2003) 152.
31 Koot (2011) 143.

calculated), the vessels that made it through were allowed legal access to all three markets. Furthermore, merchants with the appropriate contacts in the outport could, for a reasonable fee, unload only part of their cargo – as was done in the case of the *Experiment* – reducing both the duty paid and the time in port but adding an aspect of illegality to the whole transaction. Merchants could, as Hayne puts it, choose 'some Out-Port, and only Unloading part of the Cargo which lyes topmost, leaving the ground Tyre [tier]', which would allow them to 'conceal Goods of great value from the Eyes of any Officer',[32] and also to decrease their time in port. To pull this off, it was important to have trustworthy correspondents in all ports of call, so that the necessary bureaucratic tasks could be completed (and bribes paid, if needed to ensure that the vessel could leave without issue). Thus, according to Hayne, was the Jewish community in Barbados, with their familial and economic ties to England and Amsterdam,[33] so successful in importing manufactured goods from the Dutch republic to the colonies at lower prices than their competitors: they were able to 'Sell more Hollands there, than all the English merchants do'.[34] They were also willing to attempt to circumvent restrictions during return voyages, so that ships loaded with colonial staples could transport these items to entry points for the Dutch market. Having local contacts meant greater chances of success in all stages of the voyage.

3.3 *The Heart of the Affair: Identifying the Owners of the Seized Cargo, and Defending the Trading Privileges of a Religious Minority*

In the case of the *Experiment,* things did not proceed with the expected ease. Despite numerous attempts to persuade him to release the ship, Hayne persisted in its seizure and made haste with his investigation. To justify the seizure, Hayne provided the affidavit of five seamen who had given him an idea of the scale of the fraud: 'one hundred Butts and upwards of the said Sugars [...] were never Landed, taken out, or removed from the place they laid in the Ships Hold'. Armed with such knowledge, Hayne boarded the ship and found goods that had not been cleared through customs: three hogsheads of tobacco, and parcels of ginger, fustic, and lignum vitae. He also found illegal cargo hidden 'under her ground Tyre [tier]': three great copper guns, whose transportation and sale was forbidden. Hayne made one further discovery when he compared the cargo to what had been declared to customs: although Sutton and Rogers had entered the whole cargo under their own names, there were actually thirty-five

32 Hayne (1685) 27.
33 Samuel (1936).
34 Hayne (1685) 27.

different marks on the goods, indicating that they were probably owned by as many people. The five seamen offered a few names of Barbadian Jews who were among the owners: Aaron Barscoe, Abraham Barasse, Emanuel Rodrigo, and Lewis Dias. But they could name no others among the large group of Barbadian merchants who were attempting, nearly successfully, to unload commodities directly into Amsterdam, bypassing customs fees.

Once the goods and the ship had been seized, and Hayne made several more refusals to release them (no matter what persuasion was offered), he was forced to appear in London before the Commissioners of Customs, where the complaints filed against him had been serious enough to require his being escorted under guard to the hearings. At this stage, more information becomes available about the cargo's owners: an English solicitor, a Mr Hutchinson, speaking on behalf of several Jewish merchants based in London, argued that they indeed (and not the ship's master or the Falmouth merchant) owned the cargo, but since they held patents of indenization, there was no difference in the amount of duty that was due. It is interesting to note that the arguments made before the board of commissioners, both those of the accuser Hayne and of the solicitor defending the merchants' claims, relate solely to identity – more precisely, to the status of foreign-born merchants on English soil and what rights and trading privileges they might have acquired. This emphasis is somewhat surprising, because ownership and identity notwithstanding, there was an incontestable aspect of fraud at issue here: to avoid duties, an important part of the ship's cargo had not been unloaded on the public quay at Falmouth, as required by law. Whether the merchants were free to trade as English subjects or were compelled to pay the alien tax, the failure to fully unload the hold was a legal infraction.

However, the only aspect of the case of any interest to the commissioners concerned ownership, because ownership is what would have determined the rate of imposition on the shipment. Hayne, in particular, wanted proof that all the cargo was owned by merchants with trading privileges inscribed into their patents of endenization, because, as is stated in the Acts of Navigation, 'One English man may Custom Goods in another English Mans name, without prejudice; so may one Merchant Stranger Enter for another Merchant Stranger; but he that so enters Goods that the King loseth his Customs thereby forfeits the value of the Goods to the King and the like to the Merchant wronged'.[35] Therefore, if any of the goods could be proved to belong to a merchant who was not a denizen, then the seizure would be deemed justified. The Acts of Navigation, as they were published in 1671, imposed heavy duties on alien merchants and

35 *The Acts for Tonnage and Poundage. Shipping and Navigation.* (1671) 144–145.

instituted restrictions, and even more duties, on alien ships. All operations, from docking fees to customs, were more expensive for foreigners. Some duties, for fish imports for example, could be double what an English merchant paid. Since Portuguese Jewish merchants were thought, by and large, to belong to this category – having often been born outside England, possessing close ties to Amsterdam, and, in what is perhaps more damning in a society suspicious of religious minorities, being religious dissenters – it was natural for Hayne to question their claim.

Hutchinson the solicitor argued that the merchants involved with the shipment were denizens. To this end, he presented several patents granted to Jewish merchants in London, which were read to the commissioners. Two merchants named in the patents, Antonio Gomesera or Gomez Serra, as he appears in the State Papers, where his patent is registered on 23 December 1672,[36] and Antonio Lousada, who became a denizen in 1675, were partners and long-term London residents, where they had been active members of the city's Portuguese Jewish community. Their status as denizens was ambiguous – and at that time the handling of such patents could be contentious, and those with insufficient proof of 'belonging' could be economically disenfranchised.[37] In seventeenth-century England, naturalization was a difficult, expensive, and nearly impossible undertaking – primarily because it had to be granted by a vote of parliament. The only option for alien merchants who wished to establish themselves in the kingdom was, for those with sufficient means, to request a letter of endenization, a patent granted by the King to an individual (and sometimes his descendants and immediate family) granting him a certain number of rights and privileges. Sir William Blackstone, the English jurist and politician, wrote in the beginning of the eighteenth century that 'a denizen is a kind of middle state' between a native and a stranger, sharing some of the characteristics of each. A patent of endenization, since it originated directly from royal prerogative (the monarch granted it directly to an individual), was easily modified, including the imposition of restrictions. It was not difficult, for example, to protect royal revenue by forcing merchants to keep paying alien duty, which could be twice what native-born subjects paid. Especially in the second half of the seventeenth century, patents of denizens often contained a clause that specified whether or not the payment of alien duty was required: such language spelled out whether the individual should, for example, 'pay to us and to our heirs and successors customs and subsidy for his goods and merchandise at the rates which aliens pay or ought to pay'. The Acts of Navigation,

36 Shaw (1911) 108.
37 Snyder (2009) 51.

in turn, seem to imply that all denizens must pay alien duty in the absence of such a clause (certainly Hayne interpreted the text this way), stating that 'Aliens made denizens shall pay such Customs and other Duties as they did before'.[38] However, although restrictions could readily be added to letters of endenization, the opposite is also true: many merchants – certainly those with the requisite influence and means to negotiate such an arrangement – managed to have clauses added to their patents that gave them certain privileges, such as not paying alien duty.

Samuel Hayne had difficulty accepting the presence of such privileges: he maintains that a religious dissenter is necessarily a foreigner and therefore must pay alien duty. Furthermore, he believes that those merchants would otherwise enjoy an unfair advantage over Englishmen since, having many contacts in the Caribbean and in Amsterdam, they never pay double customs and can therefore sell their merchandise at prices twenty per cent cheaper than anyone else can. The commissioners rejected this argument in the case of the Portuguese merchants in London; the clause in their patent was accepted by the court. Such a result in favour of Jewish merchants was by no means a foregone conclusion, despite what Jessica Roitman calls a 'a complex and long-running assertion of their rights as subjects or citizens with metropolitan governments, colonial administrators, and non-Jewish settlers'.[39] While courts in England could – generally – be trusted to uphold the law and recognize patents of endenization, this was by no means true everywhere in the Atlantic world. In 1671, the well-known case of the Jewish merchant Rabba Couty shows that in a colonial context, following the law was often no guarantee of protection. Couty's ketch *The Tryall*, arriving in Jamaica from New York loaded with provisions, was seized on the basis that it was not an English ship and could therefore be considered a prize. Couty had documentation – a licence from the British governor of New York – that proved his status as an English subject, yet when presented with the licence the Admiralty Court nonetheless ruled that 'hee was no Denizen'.[40] The vessel and its cargo were condemned, and Couty had to sail back to New York to obtain further documentation about his status and guarantees that the vessel and the crew were English, so that he could petition the King to void the court's decision and have his vessel and his property returned to him. Investigating the affair, the Privy Council found that the ruling was not just and did not follow colonial policy since it was 'grounded on a presumption that the said Rabba Couty being not an Englishman, but a Jew

38 *The Acts for Tonnage and Poundage. Shipping and Navigation.* (1671) 144.
39 Roitman (2012) 55.
40 Snyder (2006) 152.

was for this cause to be accompted a Forreigner'.[41] Their final decision was that Couty had provided sufficient documentation to establish that he was 'an Inhabitant and free Cittyzen of your Majestyes Plantations'.[42] One finds further examples of disregard towards the legality of letters of endenization in Rhode Island, where in 1684 the seizure of a vessel and its cargo belonging to several Jewish merchants was justified by the claim that as aliens they were not permitted to trade under the Navigation Act. Their property was eventually returned – but they were forced to pay double duty, since their status as 'merchant strangers' was maintained by the court.[43]

3.4 *The Legal Conclusion of the Case of the* Experiment*: Quasi-Legal Commercial Practices Validated by the Courts*

In two of the cases described above – those of the Portuguese merchants in London, and of Couty in Jamaica – appeals to a higher court resulted in positive verdicts for the merchants. These show that the Jewish merchant community was perfectly at ease within the English judicial system, and that its members were able to obtain, by legal and, if Hayne is to be believed, non-legal means, favourable results through the courts. Indeed, while Hayne's testimony is obviously biased, the merchants' ability to mobilize their contacts both in London and in the outports of Falmouth and Penryn in the service of pressuring recalcitrant officers and protecting their profits seems indicative of close ties of mutual interest connecting highly placed port and customs officials. Their ability, as well, to mount a vigorous defence on different levels of the justice system – first in front of the Commissioners of Customs, later at an assizes court – shows a clear familiarity with the complex English system and a more than passing knowledge of their rights and privileges. The Portuguese merchants' skill in navigating the judicial system, and the presence of a network of political connections in England,[44] was well understood at the time: Hayne indicates that his unsuccessful defence of the *Experiment*'s seizure before the commissioners in London led to a vehement warning by his superiors that he cease pursuing the Jewish merchants. Indeed, they were recognized as dangerous adversaries, whose 'purses were too Heavy for' a simple customs officer to successfully contend with. To continue to fight would be to risk his wealth and freedom alike.

41 Snyder (2006) 152.
42 Snyder (2006) 152.
43 Snyder (2006) 153.
44 Fortune (1984) 64.

Such an outcome proved to be the case. After Hayne, against the recommendation of his superiors, refused to let the ship leave without a proper appraisal of all duties owed (and once more ordered the cargo inspected and the haul emptied), he promptly ended up in prison, accused by the ship's master of making spurious claims. The merchants sued him and anyone who helped him for damages ranging from 2,000 pounds to 11,565 pounds, as well as for the fees incurred by the extra time spent in port. While awaiting trial in prison, Hayne was again offered a number of bribes and other incentives to put a stop to the proceedings, declaring that 'they offered me 150 Guineys by Mr Hutchinson [...] if I [Hayne] would take it'[45] and allow the ship to leave immediately. In addition to the bribes, Hayne declared that he had been threatened – Sir Peter Killigrew, the notable involved when the ship was first allowed passage without paying all its dues, told Hayne 'That he would make [him] rot in Prison, that [he] must never expect to come out thence thill Death'.[46]

In a once again surprising example of strict adherence to his duty as an officer (one can imagine him receiving a substantial payout were the seizure to be upheld), Hayne refused all attempted bribes, and the whole matter was brought before a jury in the Launceston Assizes in Cornwall. Hayne's main accusations were reiterated at the trial, as he continued to base his claims on the idea that the merchants had violated the Acts of Navigation – more precisely, the Acts of Tonnage and Poundage and the Book of Rates – because they did not pay alien duty. However, he also added that a substantial part of the goods 'had not paid any Duty at all, either Jew or Gentile'.[47] Once more the Jewish merchants mounted a vigorous defence, involving the public reading of the patents for Gomesera and Lousada as well as testimony given by two of their servants – one Portuguese and one French – who swore that the entire cargo belonged to the two merchants, and certificates from the London Custom House. These efforts convinced a jury that the merchants were in the right. Faced with such an outcome, Hayne, who had spent over 600 pounds of his own money and was now at risk of imprisonment for debts as well as dismissal from his post at customs for dereliction of duty while in prison, had to bend to the merchants' will. As a contemporary declared, 'they [the Portuguese merchants] were resolved not to spare their Purses, and that he knew when that Frenchman and Jew [the two servants who testified at the trial] went down to Lancerston to manage the Tryal against [Hayne] there, they carried out 1000 Guineys along with them, and did not bring back five'.[48] In the end, Hayne

45 Hayne (1685) 26.
46 Hayne (1685) 28.
47 Hayne (1685) 27.
48 Hayne (1685) 28.

ended up accepting some small compensation to allow the ship to leave with all its cargo – even the three copper guns were illegally smuggled out – and, about a year after it dropped anchor at Falmouth, the *Experiment* was allowed to continue on its journey to Amsterdam.

4 The Differences between Imperial and Colonial Perceptions of Atlantic Trade and the Difficult Adaptation to the Strict Regulations of the Acts of Navigation

Quasi-legal strategies to maximize profits occurred regularly in colonial trading practices. In the end, none of the courts involved in the *Experiment* affair adhered to Hayne's strict interpretation of the Acts of Navigation – nor had any sought to implement such rigid control over colonial trading as he desired. It seems that the usual practices in force at the time were given an official seal of approval. Indeed, while the accusations focused primarily on the identity and status of the owners of the merchandise, the practices described were neither new nor unusual. Hayne claimed that the owners of the thirty-five different marks in the cargo were hiding behind the merchants, who possessed letters of endenization in order to escape having to pay double duty. Such a practice, which Hayne calls 'colouring goods', was common in England and in other Atlantic ports – one could almost say commonplace – but its legality was somewhat ambiguous. It consisted in registering a ship's entire cargo under the name of a single merchant – an individual who had trading privileges in the port and therefore paid the least in duties. Often this merchant was a local partner or correspondent of the cargo's actual owner (sometimes working on commission) and was charged with undertaking the necessary administrative tasks that would enable the voyage to continue. The name of the owner could change at each harbour, ensuring that only native duties were ever paid, which would therefore considerably reduce the total cost of transportation. While merchants usually chose to profit from their extensive international networks, this practice did fall into that quasi-legal category of trade that was common on the peripheries.[49]

All the accusations levied by Hayne – the colouring of goods, the choice of an English port to land in, their behaviour with customs officials – are examples of the day-to-day practices of trade in the British Atlantic colonies. They show how the restrictions imposed by the Navigation Acts were perceived and how they could be skirted by taking advantage of the 'openings for legal trade that

49 Koot (2011) 119.

the metropolitan restrictions provided',[50] especially considering the rather lax control exerted by royal officers in ports far from London. Indeed, some authors have insisted upon the importance of illicit commerce for the colonies' economic prosperity since 'agricultural production was unable to promote sustained economic health'.[51] In addition to participation in illegal trade in the Atlantic, the circumventing of English customs was a common practice. As late as in the 1720s, statements made before the Council of Trade and Plantations make reference to this problem: 'several vessels go from Barbados and the Leewards directly to Holland [...] and it is to be feared others of them found means to remit their effects in European commodities directly in ye colonies'.[52]

However, this is not exactly what was attempted in the *Experiment* episode: here the rules were acknowledged, but an attempt was made to maximize profits in spite of them. With the help of the ship's master and their London correspondents, the Caribbean merchants tried (with eventually success) to defraud English customs of several hundred pounds, according to Hayne's calculations: 'I sent for a Writ of Appraisement [...] the Kings Moyety amounted to 435 *l.* 10 *s.* 0 *d.* And on the Entry taken blind-fold by them he had not above 7 *l* 10 *s* 0 *d*'.[53] These merchants attempted to give all their actions a veneer of legality: they intentionally freighted their cargo in an English ship with an English master, giving instructions to dock at Falmouth to declare its cargo and pay any legally required dues while at the same time bribing officials to ensure that their vessel would not be barred or closely inspected. These efforts reveal an attempt to follow the letter of the law while skirting around certain aspects that might be damaging to trade. In effect, a façade of legality coexisted with several aspects of illegal trade. Caribbean shippers employed these strategies to 'avoid mercantilist restrictions and [to take advantage of] the difficulties authorities had in fully controlling colonial trade'.[54]

Successful implementation of these strategies required a well-established network of contacts and business partners. The Sephardic merchants who were among the group who organized the shipment of commodities to the Dutch market were therefore in an advantageous position to profit from Anglo-Dutch Trade in the Atlantic – and thus previously marginalized groups

50 Koot (2011) 118.

51 Fortune (1984) 129.

52 Rev. W. Gordon to the Council of Trade and Plantations, *Calendar of State Papers Colonial, America and West Indies*: Volume 32, 1720–1721. Ed. Cecil Headlam. London: His Majesty's Stationery Office, 1933. 21–36. British History Online. Web. 1 August 2019. http://www.british-history.ac.uk/cal-state-papers/colonial/america-west-indies/vol32/pp21-36.

53 Hayne (1685) 24.

54 Koot (2011) 118.

were now included in the colonial trade. With an established presence in Amsterdam, and a community in London that had been developing since the 1650s, these merchants now had trusted correspondents in all the important ports implicated in the exchange of goods.[55] The choice to use a British vessel and a British master to transport goods indicate an awareness of the need to adapt their practices – at least in part – to the new regulations that had been put in place by Parliament and the Crown. That the London merchants – in particular Antonio Lousada – had close family ties both to the Barbados merchants who were shipping the commodities and to merchants based in Amsterdam, such as Jacob and David Baruch Lousada, seems to reveal a form of collusion among the parties, first in planning the fraud, and then, after Hayne's intervention, in using all possible resources to protect the goods' shipment.

5 Maximizing Profits Despite Regulations: The Struggle of Colonial Traders to Adapt

However, although the fraud committed was significant, some part of the cargo in the *Experiment* bound for the Dutch market was legal, having been properly landed and all necessary duties paid. As Koot notes, it is 'not always possible to distinguish between legal, quasi-legal and illegal trade' between British colonies and the Dutch republic because the actors' decisions were not motivated by a straightforward desire to break the law; rather, 'what had been familiar and advantageous to them had been redefined as illegal by English officials'.[56] The restrictions put in place to protect British colonial interests from Dutch interference and allow for greater protection of the British colonial trade were, in 1680, still fairly recent. For colonists and merchants who relied on those open networks to find the most advantageous commercial opportunities, whether in England or in Amsterdam, they must also have seemed fairly arbitrary, taxing some products but not others, limiting legal shipping options to British vessels which were often insufficient to fulfil all colonial needs,[57] and instituting onerous bureaucratic duties. The mix of legal and illegal practices may have been an attempt to maintain access to the now restricted Dutch market, to sustain their grasp on the most advantageous trade routes while

55 Samuel (1936) 16–17.
56 Koot (2011) 119.
57 Reeves (1807) 10.

nodding to the new mercantile framework being put in place in what amounted to a 'begrudging adaptation to new regulations'.[58]

While there was also a clear economic incentive to participate in smuggling operations, and economic incentives must also have played a role in the choice to violate mercantile regulations, there is another aspect to the problem – one of necessity. In colonial locales, trading regulations meant that certain essential goods could be acquired only through illegal means, due to a lack of sufficient vessels to properly provision the islands. For colonists, it was not always easy as well to find British vessels to transport local products – ships were not always available in sufficient numbers to transport everything that had been produced. In such cases, rather than let products waste away in port, it was preferable to use Dutch vessels even though it was against the regulations to do so. Here, again, this practice falls into that 'quasi-legal' category that is difficult to determine clearly, and such activity was difficult to regulate at the time. The Acts of Navigation, in acknowledgement of the deficiencies in British shipping capabilities, allowed that 'where English Ships are not to be had, men may bring in or carry out their Merchandizes in strangers ships, but where English ships are to be had, then to freight Aliens Ships, forfeits their Goods and Merchandize, or the value thereof'.[59] The presence or lack of British vessels was difficult to measure, especially from the capital, so far removed from the reality of the colonies. Dutch vessels in the Caribbean thus fulfilled an important commercial need – and did so often at lower rates than the British. Jamaica's governor, for example, noted in 1682 that the Dutch 'sell European Goods 30 percent, cheaper than we [the English], and will paye deerer for American Goods'. Hayne remarked on the same phenomenon, complaining that English merchants could not possibly be competitive with their Dutch counterparts, since the latter didn't pay taxes in England on their return trip, and so could 'sell 20 per cent cheaper than the English'.[60] In the end, despite regulations that trickled down from the capital to the colonies, an important part of commercial practices seems to have been based on necessity and represented attempts to maintain access to the English market while fulfilling the bare minimum of regulatory compliance. Such perfunctory application of the rules certainly did not satisfy Hayne's precise interpretation of English commercial regulations.

58 Koot (2011) 120.

59 *The Acts for Tonnage and Poundage. Shipping and Navigation.* (1671) 133.

60 Hayne (1685) 12.

In his pamphlet, Hayne proposes a simple solution to this problem of semi-legal trade, a policy that would make it much easier to avoid fraud: the Crown should simplify matters and require that all Jewish merchants pay alien duty, irrespective of their legal status in the kingdom. The proposal effectively envisions the creation of a separate group of second-class citizens who possessed fewer rights than English-born subjects. For Hayne, this is the only way to protect the King's customs, which he felt to be threatened by the individualist and unfairly advantageous commercial practices of that group of merchants. According to him, such a decision could only be good for the kingdom and its merchants, and so Jewish merchants should be obliged to 'pay the Alien Duty, as by Law they ought to do; which will not only be many Thousands *per annum* advance to Your Majesty in Your Customs, but also be extream grateful to all Your Majesties fair dealing *English* merchants'.[61]

He assures his readers his concerns are primarily economic in nature (and not having to do, one assumes, with religion): he wishes above all else that the competitiveness of English merchants in the European market be ensured, so that they can 'be Enabled to Sell as Cheap as themselves [i.e., the Jewish merchants]'. Such a solution would also, Hayne assures his readers, promote the growth of English manufacturing that had been damaged by direct exchanges with Amsterdam, since 'most of their Cargoes for the Plantations [were] made up of the Growth, Product, and Manufacture of those parts, and none of English'.[62]

His views, at the time, were not unique in England – but they faced considerable opposition in the colonies, where more commercial freedom was always welcomed and was favourable to the development of the settlements. Any measures rendering the plantation trade non-profitable for Jewish merchants, because of abnormally high duties, would be perceived as hindrances to colonial development. As even Hayne admits, though not entirely, at the conclusion of his text: 'The Jews are a very Rich sort of People, their Trade is very great, they Imploy many Ships &c. And should that be cut off, abundance of People, both here and the *Plantations*, would soon feel the want of them. Moreover, the King would be much lessened in his Customs, by breaking off their Trade'.[63]

61 Hayne (1685) 33.

62 Hayne (1685) 34.

63 Hayne (1685) 37.

There was much debate in England and in the British Atlantic about the scope of the Acts of Navigation and whether their strict application was appropriate or even possible in a colonial setting. Such conflict between metropolitan and colonial concerns was commonplace – and unlikely to be resolved because of a single incident in a small English outport. However, the case related by Hayne offers an interesting and detailed account of the inner workings of the commercial activities conducted by merchants implicated in colonial trade. Faced with a regulatory system that was designed to restrict trade and exert a deleterious impact on profits (doubly so for members of religious minorities, who had to prove their right to participate in the colonial trade as equal actors), they instituted strategies that can be considered illegal or quasi-legal in order to maximize their profits and minimize their risks. Such strategies demonstrate complete familiarity with the judicial system in which they are active – a necessary skill in a society that often used the courts in the service of religious persecution, limiting the impact of privileges given to religious minorities. It also demonstrates how important it was for these merchants to mobilize correspondents and partners in order to react decisively to sudden complications, and to exert sufficient political capital to influence judicial procedures – even in the face of an overzealous customs official.

Bibliography

Printed Primary Sources

Barbados Council and Assembly, *A Declaration Set Forth by the Lord Lieutenant Generall the Gentlemen of the Councell & Assembly Occasioned from the View of a Printed Paper. Entituled. An Act Prohibiting Trade with the Barbados, Virginea, Bermudes and Antegoe* (The Hague 1651).

Calendar of State Papers Colonial, America and West Indies: Volume 32, 1720–1721. C. Headlam ed. (London 1933) 21–36. *British History Online.* Web. 1 August 2019. http://www.british-history.ac.uk/cal-state-papers/colonial/america-west-indies/vol32/pp21-36.

Child, J., *A New Discourse of Trade* (London 1698).

Hayne, S., *An Abstract of All the Statutes Made Concerning Aliens Trading in England Proving that the Jews Break Them All* (London 1685).

Reeves, J., *The Law of Shipping and Navigation: From the Time of Edward III to the End of the Year 1806* (London 1807).

Samuel, W.S., 'A Review of the Jewish Colonists in Barbados in the Year 1680', *Transactions of the Jewish Historical Society of England* 13 (1936) 1–111.

Shaw, W.A., *Denizations & Naturalizations of Aliens in England and Ireland (1603–1700)* vol. XVIII (Lymington 1911).

The Acts for Tonnage and Poundage. Shipping and Navigation. Prevention of Frauds in His Majesties Customs. And the Book of Rates, Together with an Abridgment of All the Statutes Now in Force, Relating to the Customs, Continued to 22 & 23 Car. 2. And Charta Mercatoria in Latin and English. Several Rules and Directions for Gauging of Ships, Casks of Wine, and Oyl and Measuring of Timber. Also the Fees of Officers, Fares of Commodities, Rates of Scavage, and Package, &c. Tables for Oyls, Linens, Silks, Tobacco and Wines, Calculated for the Duties Payable upon Them. To Which Is Added, an Index Alphabetically Digested. Collected for Public Use. (London 1671.)

Secondary Literature

Ashworth, W.J., *Customs and Excise: Trade, Production, and Consumption in England, 1640–1845* (Oxford 2003).

Farnell, J.E., 'The Navigation Act of 1651, the First Dutch War, and the London Merchant Community', *The Economic History Review* 16, no. 3 (1964) 439.

Fortune, S.A., *Merchants and Jews: The Struggle for British West Indian Commerce, 1650–1750* (Gainesville 1984).

Henriques, H.S.Q., *The Jews and English Law* (Clifton 1908).

Hyamson, A.M., *The Sephardim of England: A History of the Spanish and Portuguese Jewish Community, 1492–1951* (London: Methuen, 1951).

Israel, J.I., *Dutch Primacy in World Trade, 1585–1740* (Oxford 1989).

Israel, J.I., 'Jews of Dutch America' in P. Bernardini and N. Fiering eds, *The Jews and the Expansion of Europe to the West* (New York 2001).

Katz, D., *The Jews in the History of England, 1485–1850* (Oxford 1996).

Koot, C., *Empire at the Periphery: British Colonists, Anglo-Dutch Trade, and the Development of the British Atlantic, 1621–1713* (New York 2011).

Ormrod, D., *The Rise of Commercial Empires: England and the Netherlands in the Age of Mercantilism, 1650–1770* (Cambridge 2003).

Ormrod, D., 'From Seas to Ocean: Interpreting the Shift from the North Sea-Baltic World to the Atlantic, 1650–1800' in A.B. Leonard and D. Pretel eds. *The Caribbean and the Atlantic World Economy: Circuits of Trade, Money and Knowledge, 1650–1914* (New York 2015).

Roitman, J., 'Sephardic Journeys: Travel, Place, and Conceptions of Identity', *Jewish Culture and History* 11 nos. 1–2 (2009) 209–228.

Roitman, J., 'Creating Confusion in the Colonies: Jews, Citizenship, and the Dutch and British Atlantics', *Itinerario* 36, no. 2 (August 2012) 55–90.

Roth, C., *A History of the Jews in England* (Oxford 1964).

Snyder, H., 'English Markets, Jewish Merchants, and Atlantic Endeavours: Jews and the Making of British Transatlantic Commercial Culture, 1650–1800' in R.L. Kagan and

P.D. Morgan, *Atlantic Diasporas: Jews, Conversos, and Crypto-Jews in the Age of Mercantilism, 1500–1800* (Baltimore 2009) 50–74.

Snyder, H., 'Rules, Rights and Redemption: The Negotiation of Jewish Status in British Atlantic Port Towns, 1740–1831', *Jewish History* 20, no. 2 (June 2006) 147–170.

Stephens, W.B., *The Seventeenth-Century Customs Service Surveyed: William Culliford's Investigation of the Western Ports, 1682–84* (Burlington, VT 2012).

Zahedieh, N., *The Capital and the Colonies: London and the Atlantic Economy 1660–1700* (Cambridge 2010).

CHAPTER 15

When the War Came to Barbary: Dutch Traders and the Management of Their Entry into Conflict with Algiers, 1755–1757

Thierry Allain

1 Introduction

The war of 1755–1757 belongs to a very long cycle of conflicts between the Dutch Republic and Algiers. In the seventeenth century many wars were fought.[1] After each war, a treaty was negotiated. No fewer than ten such treaties between the two states were signed during the seventeenth century, followed by four in the first part of the eighteenth century.[2] There was a strong tradition of conflict management between the two powers. The war's outbreak in February 1755 occurred after a period of almost thirty years of peace. Indeed, the last Dutch-Algerian War had ended in 1726.[3] This chapter will discuss the legacy and resilience of armed conflict, which is relevant within the context of the decline of North African privateering in Mediterranean in the eighteenth century.[4] In the case of Algiers, some specialists have pointed out a decrease in the number of prizes taken in the mid-1750's.[5] Another special feature concerns the context of Dutch foreign policy. Seeking to avoid conflicts in the wake of a seventeenth century that had been pervaded by war, the Dutch Republic had tried to sustain a policy of peaceful neutrality since the end of the War of Spanish Succession.[6] Territorial integrity and trade protection remained the main issues of concern. Diplomacy and convoys replaced military interventions and naval warfare. Therefore, one might question the efficiency of a new foreign policy.

1 Krieken (2002) 25–30.
2 Calafat (2011) 187.
3 Ressel (2015).
4 Fontenay (2010) 243, 338.
5 Merouche (2007) 296–298.
6 Carter (1975), Stapelbroek (2011).

 | DOI:10.1163/9789004407992_017

The history of the relations between the Dutch Republic and the Barbary states has attracted considerable attention among historians, who have frequently addressed its legal aspects and capitulations.[7] Recent research has focused on the slave trade and the specific approach taken by the Dutch.[8] I would like to turn to a different topic. This paper aims at studying the intersection of diplomacy and trade within the specific context of an outbreak of war. To consider the management of entry into conflict, we have here a unique source of information: the judgement book of general average (*avarij-grosse*) compiled by the *Bank van Assurantien en Avarijen van Amsterdam*.[9] This unpublished primary source possesses obvious interest. In it the masters of ships described their routes and were required to explain their reactions to attacks by privateers. There is also a list of the merchants who had loaded products on board these ships. Records of twenty-four vessels are available that concern the Dutch-Algerian War of 1755–1757.[10] The usual reservations apply with regard to the credibility of testimonies, so it is useful and important to complement information gleaned from this source with evidence in consular and port archives and in business correspondence.[11]

The beginning of a conflict is difficult to manage at sea due to the slowness of communications and the necessary delay in outfitting a fleet. This is especially interesting in the Dutch case because there was no charter company for the Mediterranean.[12] The governing principle was one of free trade for Dutch and foreigners. Furthermore, the military effort was spread over five admiralties, which were sometimes unable to coordinate their actions.[13] From this perspective, it is possible to examine the choices of the private actors who, at this tumultuous moment of a conflict's beginning, had more latitude than usual. What was the traders' perception of the conflict? What choices did the masters of ships make in the heat of the moment? How were commercial interests formulated, being so far away from the fighting? Was it easy to establish dialogue between Dutch traders and the Dutch political authorities? To answer these

7 The capitulations were texts regulating the activities of European nations in Ottoman Empire. Groot (1978, 1985).

8 Panzac (2002), Kaiser (2008), Ressel (2013), Van Gelder (2015).

9 For an overview of this institution, see Go (2009) 95–117.

10 Stadsarchief Amsterdam (SAA), Schout en schepenen, Bank van Assurantien en Avarijen (BAA), register no. 2846 à 2847.

11 From the archival collections of: Nationaal Archief, Den Haag (NA), Archives Nationales de France, Paris (ANF), Centre des Archives Diplomatiques de Nantes (CADN), Archives Diplomatiques, La Courneuve (ADLC) and Archives de la Chambre de Commerce de Marseille (ACCIMP).

12 Groot (1981).

13 Bruijn (1993) 147–159.

questions, I will examine the content of this international crises but also the behaviour of the actors and the role played by their management of affairs.

2 The Course of the Conflict

The Regency was responsible for the outbreak of war on 20 February 1755. A few days later, Dutch consul Paraviciny wrote to the States-General that he had formally received notification of the change of circumstances.[14] In addition, the Dey told the consul that he had to leave Algiers. Within two months, Dutch merchant ships would be seized. Algiers reproached the Low Countries for not complying with the provisions of the treaty of 1726, that is to say, acting excessively slowly in their buybacks of captives and the payment of 50,000 guilders in the form of war materials.[15] This slowness accounted for considerable Algerian mistrust of the Dutch.[16] As far back as December 1715 the Algerians had made this sort of argument.[17] North African regencies commonly displayed such unpredictability and noncompliance with international treaties.[18] Therefore, the public perception of these regencies remained very negative in the Low Countries and elsewhere in Europe. Stories told by former captives fostered the image of untrustworthy enemies who showed little concern for international treaties.[19]

Algiers had long accused the Dutch of tolerating the sale of false 'Algerian passports' to the traders of Hamburg. As a result, the Algerians expressed a strong preference for the Danish flag. In fact, the political and economic environment surrounding the Regency is the most important element in explaining its geopolitical changeover. The domestic situation exerted significant influence on external issues. In the eighteenth century Algiers achieved a form of political stabilization, in particular the increasing number of deys who died in their beds instead of being assassinated.[20] But tax revenue decreased due to droughts and earthquakes and living conditions worsened for the population.

14 'Op den 20 dezes des namiddag een Moorse Chaous van wegens den Dey aan myn is koome zeggen dat ik binnen twee Maande myn van hier moest begeeven dewijl tot een vreedebreuk met Haar Hoog Mogende had geresolveert'. NA, Staten-Generaal, no. 6958, letter of 24 February 1755.

15 Krieken (2002) 152–157.

16 Panzac (1999) 95.

17 Ressel (2015) 239.

18 Panzac (1999) 29, 34–35.

19 Koopmans and Regtop (2002).

20 Wolf (1979) 289–296, Panzac (1999) 14.

Plague epidemics occurred in 1740 and 1752.[21] During that period, privateering remained an important part of Algiers's foreign policy.[22]

Discontent grew in Algiers and resulted in a palace coup in December 1754. Dey Muhammad Ibn Bukayr was murdered. Ali, the militia chief, became the leader of the state.[23] He was brutal and closely connected to the Algerian privateer's lobby. In his letter of 18 January 1755 to the States-General, Paraviciny, manifesting concern about this palace coup, mentioned 'a sort of fermentation'.[24] That meant the resumption of war. But the strategy taken by Algiers was avoidance of a general conflict with Europeans.[25] A war with France or Great Britain was not practicable due to the military strength of these major powers.[26] The Scandinavians, for their part, submitted to Algiers's demands. The Swedes agreed to deliver guns and ammunition to the Regency under the terms of the treaty of 1729 and even increased their supply. Their policy of active neutrality allowed them to augment their trade in the Mediterranean.[27] Thus the Dutch were now the easiest target, and accordingly the Regency broke the peace with the Netherlands. Algiers took the opportunity to declare war on Tuscany.

It seems that the two-month period was respected. On 22 March 1755, Paraviciny notified the States-General that he had just left Algiers for Toulon.[28] After the usual quarantine in the *lazaretto*, he left Toulon for Marseilles in April, then proceeded overland to Holland. Several Dutch ships remained in Mediterranean waters; there were no attacks through the end of April. Such was the conclusion of testimony provided by the captain Jan Nyps.[29] But at this stage there was every reason to fear the effects of the war on the Dutch trade. In the main ports, stakeholders were concerned about privateering. Some of their rivals, the French for instance, rejoiced at the prospect of such a threat to the

21 Grammont (2002) 228–230, 247.

22 Merouche (2007) 256–257.

23 Grammont (2002) 248.

24 'een soort van fermentatie'. NA, Staten-Generaal, no. 6958, letter of 18 January 1755.

25 Panzac (1999) 35.

26 Wolf (1979) 141, 309.

27 Müller (2004) 124–126, 144, 148–149; Andersen and Voth (2000) 10–15.

28 NA, Staten-Generaal, no. 6958, letter of 22 March 1755.

29 'Dat het voorsch schip tot Marseille belaeden zynde [...] in volkomen staat den 5 february deses jaars vandaar is vertrocken gedestineert na deese stadt. In't vervorderen van welke reyse zij tusschen Minorca, en Sardinien zyn belopen, door zware stormen [...] Dat zy den 4 Maart Gibraltar te zien kreegen, vervolgens door contrarie wind en stroom, weder zyn te rug gedreeven, en den 2 April door gebrek van verschwaeter en mondbehoeftens genoodzaakt geworden te Mallaga binnen te loopen, alwaar zij een Losgerugt hoorden van den Oorlog met Algiers [...]' SAA, BAA, no. 2846, f. 209.

Dutch trade. In the eighteenth century commercial jealousies sometimes played a key role in diplomatic relations. In March 1755 the Jewish trader Da Silva, based in Leghorn (Livorno) and in frequent contact with the Secretariat d'Etat in Versailles, described great consternation and concerns about trade on the part of his Dutch colleagues[30].

This concern was based on past experience. During the War of Austrian Succession, raids by British privateers against Dutch merchant ships had a devastating impact from 1745 onwards.[31] Even if its heyday in the Mediterranean had passed, Dutch shipowning remained vigorous in the eighteenth century.[32] The average number of Dutch ships per year was about 58.7 in 1741–1743.[33] But marked discrepancies existed, depending on period and destination. In 1754, Vice-Consul De Veer in Marseilles identified seventy-four Dutch ships entering the port, showing just how well integrated the Dutch were in the Mediterranean trade.[34] A neutral flag was a huge advantage for merchant shipping during periods of war, especially between France and Great Britain.[35] In 1755, Algiers privateers, eschewing the 'free ships free goods' rule, were planning to board any Dutch vessels they might encounter. Confidence in the Dutch flag could collapse and the insurance rates on shipping increase accordingly. During the war of 1715–1726 the losses were significant, according to various evaluations.[36] It cost several million guilders. The last five years were particularly bad, with 44 ships and no fewer than 241 captives taken.[37]

In 1755, Algerian privateers captured twelve vessels, though only three were from the Low Countries, one fewer than indicated in the alarmed reports of consul Paraviciny, who mentioned the transfer of four Dutch prizes to Algiers.[38] Caught off the Portuguese coast, the *Zes Zonen* and the *Phoenix* were brought back to Algiers on 29 April and 1 June, respectively. A French witness tells us that they were carrying millet and beans to Marseilles.[39] Thus each

30 ANF, Fonds Affaires Etrangères, BI, Consular correspondance Livourne, register no.744, f.43, 26 March 1755.

31 Allain (2017).

32 Israel (1989) 402–403.

33 De Vries and Van der Woude (1997) 381.

34 NA, Directie van den Levantschen Handel, Directie Amsterdam (DLHA), bundle 183, letter of 3 January 1755.

35 Carrière and Courdurié (1975).

36 Merouche (2007) 289, said 39 ships and 909 captives; Krieken (2002) 33, agreed with the number of ships but reduced the number of captives to 300.

37 Krieken (2002) 95–97.

38 NA, Staten-Generaal, 6958, letter of 28 April 1755.

39 CADN, Constantinople, Correspondance avec les Echelles, Série D Smyrne, carton no. 1, letter of the French trader B. Gilly of 19 June 1755.

vessels had a low value. Things were even more disappointing with the third Dutch prize. The *Maria Louiza* had left Venice to rally Vigo with a cargo of wheat by the end of February. Unaware that war had broken out, the ship was boarded off Ibiza. But it never arrived in Algiers because it was later released by a Spanish squadron.[40] After a fierce fight, Algerian ships were destroyed and almost all the privateers were killed. Thus the fourteen Dutch seamen taken would endure only a short period of captivity.

Overall, the war of 1755–1756 produced limited results for the Regency, except for the capture of two Neapolitan galleys.[41] The human and economic losses seem to have been very low for the Dutch, in striking contrast to the previous conflict with Algiers in 1715–1726. However, astonishingly, during the conflict several Dutch ships managed to arrive in Marseilles from North Africa. Some even sailed back and forth, such as the *Frederic*, commanded by Pieter Boysen. It was recorded being in Marseilles from Safi on 15 November 1755, laden with wool, copper, wax, and other products. On 4 August 1756 it was back, this time from Salé.[42]

The increase in vessels' turnaround times exerted a significant impact on the Dutch trade.[43] Sometimes the shippers operating in the Mediterranean would unload their cargo, which caused legal disputes. For example, the *De Jalousie* arrived in Marseilles in November 1754 and loaded cargo. But news of war encouraged the shippers to remove goods in the warehouses. Master Jan de Leeuw complained to the Admiralty Court, which dismissed the petition. His appeal to the Parliament of Provence was successful.[44] The inconvenience for the Dutch was, however, limited, in particular for loaders.

3 The Management of an International Crisis by a Neutral Power

In the judgement book of general average compiled by the *Bank van Assurantien en Avarijen van Amsterdam*, the shipmasters gave accounts of their navigations and were required to explain the choices they made when confronted with privateer attacks. The captains' statements show an extra degree of caution. Information was carefully collected in the ports and off the coast. During the earlier conflict, several shipmasters had considered it safe to sail with a

40 Krieken (2002) 112.
41 Merouche (2007) 296.
42 ACCIMP, Bureau de la Santé, Comptes de quarantaine, register 87, f.10.
43 SAA, BAA, 2847, f.135: the *De vrouw Elisabeth en Susanna* needed 388 days to voyage from Toulon to Amsterdam.
44 Ibidem, no. 2847, f. 167.

passport. For example, Adriaan Pooi, master of the *De Jacoba*, left Leghorn in November 1715. When caught by an Algerian corsair in the Balearic Islands, Pooi thought that his passport was in order. After being released by the corsair, he returned to Amsterdam in September 1718.[45] Checking information seemed to be crucial, as shown by the example of master Cornelis Klip, out of Smyrna on 12 February 1755 and collecting useful advices off the Spanish coast.[46]

The Dutch consular network – especially the posts of Barcelona, Napels, Malaga, Malta, Smyrna or Aleppo – seemed to be vital to a better understanding of the situation. A number of consuls were mobilized to intervene at the regional level in the service of the merchant's interests.[47] Several consuls showed leadership in crisis management, forbidding ships to depart without a convoy. For good reason, Dutch seamen feared being enslaved. Ransom payments had always been controversial in the Low Countries, which made the prospect of release all the more uncertain.[48] Some 909 Dutch people apprehended from 1714 to 1720 were freed on payment of, on average, 1,500 guilders.[49] It was a heavy responsibility that entailed a significant cost.

Usually Dutch merchant ships lacked sufficient guns and men to defend themselves against privateers with any chance of success.[50] Convoys, a very common means of protecting these ships, seemed to be a main feature of their trade in the Mediterranean.[51] The Dutch used dangerous commercial maritime routes, and corsairs could hide in the channels, archipelagoes and off headlands. In principle, convoys were mandatory for Dutch merchant ships from Holland to Leghorn or Malta. A resolution by the States-General required the Admiralties to provide military escorts.

But on the spur of the moment, shipmasters, who benefitted from a high degree of autonomy, had several options to choose from. In September 1755, two vessels joined a Swedish convoy from Malaga. At the beginning of January 1756, two other Dutch ships left Cadiz with an English escort. But on the advice given by several Dutch consuls, most of the vessels present in the Mediterranean in

45 SAA, BAA, 2821, f. 63.

46 'en den 8 April op de hoogte van Carthagena zy een Frans schip ontmoete die hun verdere onderrigtinge gaf wegens den oorlog met algiers waarop zy verder hunne reyze hebben vervolgt tot op de hoogte van Mallaga, alwaar zy den 12 dito, zyn binnen gekoomen, en aldaar dienzelve dagh van de Hollandse Consul en verdere coopluyden vaste verzeeckering wegens den oorlog kreegen, dewelke hun ook hebben geraden niet te vertrecken zonder convoij […]' (Ibidem, 2846, f. 277).

47 Allain (2018) 423–429.

48 Ressel (2012) 421–436.

49 Merouche (2007) 266.

50 Allain (2016) 106–107.

51 Israel (1989) 229.

1755 gathered in Malta, Malaga, or Gibraltar. Several vessels left Smyrna together, sometimes after a long wait.[52] The goal was to join the convoy under the protection of the fleet of Rear Admiral Boudaan. Indeed, in March 1756, thirty-four merchant ships gathered in the Bay of Cadiz. Assembling this large convoy took time, but it reached Holland without suffering any losses. The trend of gathering without waiting for a military escort continued in the second year of the war. Thus master Jacob Keetel left Smyrna with two other Dutch merchant ships on 11 February 1756, seeking to join a great convoy in Malta.[53]

Since the beginning of the seventeenth century, it had been commonplace for the States-General to deploy a naval force in the Mediterranean. From the 1630s onwards, the Dutch Republic and Algiers both regarded peace as useless and unprofitable. Michiel de Ruyter's military expeditions in 1655, 1661, and 1664 had severely degraded relations between the two powers.[54] The blockade and naval bombardment of Algiers were typical sorts of actions taken by Europeans during the second half of the seventeenth century. They were a response to aggressive Algerian privateering. But their results were limited. The last conflict of 1715–1726 had seen the dispatch of a squadron two years after the war's outbreak. But once again the results were disappointing. The experiment was not renewed before 1721. The enemy failed to fight a squadron of ships of the line.[55] After receiving strong criticism, the States-General decided to change their approach. Several frigates were built and, thanks to their speed and handling, were successfully sent to the Mediterranean from 1723 onwards.[56]

As regards the war of 1755–1757, the military response of the Dutch Republic was faster and more consistent this time. Public finances were probably in better shape than they had been at the end of the War of the Spanish Succession. In March 1755, the States-General approved a special budget of 674,000 guilders to equip a squadron of eight warships under the command of Jan Boudaan. It was based in Cadiz in August 1755. But the Algerians avoided battle, as they would with ensuing squadrons.[57] Logbooks provide details about the shipping. For example, the frigate *De Triton*, with twenty-four guns and under the command of Quirijn Dabenis, left Texel in October 1755 on a two-year mission. Privateers remained invisible to the Dutch.[58] Thus, a question arises with

52 A mass embarkation occurred from Smyrna on 19 October 1755. SAA, BAA, no. 2847, f. 27, 39, 47, 127, 148, and 156.

53 SAA, BAA, no. 2847, f. 262.

54 Krieken (2002) 25–30, 52–67.

55 Bruijn (1970) 26–27.

56 Bruijn (1993) 150–151.

57 Krieken (2002) 111–113.

58 NA, Admiraliteiten/Van der Velden, no. 3.

regard to the impact of this military presence far from home. The vessel *Blois* entered the Mediterranean in May 1757, cruising along the Italian coast and occasionally accompanying merchant ships to eastern Spain.[59]

From a military perspective, it was clear that the mere use of force was useless. The later blockade of Algiers by the Danes in 1770 was not really effective.[60] International law was never properly respected unless it was backed by force. A successful approach consisted in combining military pressure and negotiation. The issues of the ransom of slaves and privateering, among the major sticking points, remained unresolved.[61] The Dutch Republic had for a long time maintained diplomatic relations with the regencies. The 1612 capitulations with the Sublime Porte were amended by bilateral agreements with Algiers in 1616 and 1617.[62] Five years later, and after two stays in North Africa, a genuine treaty with the Regency was signed by Cornelis Pynacker in the name of the Dutch Republic. However, this law professor of Groningen had only modest diplomatic skills.

Principles such as 'free vessel free cargo', whose value was obvious to the Dutch, were established. This tenet was confirmed in the subsequent treaties of 1662 and 1679, although linked to the redemption of captives.[63] In 1679, Thomas Hees negotiated several favourable clauses regarding the freedom of entry for Dutch ships in Algiers and restrictions on inspections of merchant vessels by privateers.[64] In the eighteenth century, relations between the regencies and European states became peaceful. Numerous bilateral treaties were signed.[65] The North African regencies could then be regarded as sufficiently autonomous from the influence of the Sublime Porte.[66] But negotiations with Algiers were fraught with pitfalls and invariably there were misunderstandings about the interpretation of capitulations or treaties. Moreover, the Dey was uncontrollable, requiring active military pressure in order to secure international agreements. However, the States-General used Jewish traders present in North Africa. For example, the intervention of Juda Cohen was decisive in 1708: despite numerous setbacks, Cohen successfully gained the favour of the Dey.[67]

59 NA, Admiraliteiten, College te Amsterdam, no. 2389.
60 Andersen (2000) 243–250.
61 Groot (1978) 92–96, 125.
62 Krieken (2002) 19–22.
63 Ibidem, 61.
64 Groot (1985) 140–141.
65 Panzac (1999) 32–35.
66 Calafat (2011) 185–186.
67 Krieken (2002) 83–87.

Theoretically, the relations between the Dutch Republic and Algiers had been organized by the treaty of 8 September 1726, which marked a positive turning point and brought forth mutual concessions about old problems. For the first time, Algiers recognized the 'free vessel free cargo' principle and the Dutch, for their part, agreed to deliver weapons, ammunitions, and naval stores to offset the lack of prizes for Barbary corsairs.[68] But Algerian compliance remained problematic.[69] The interbellum period between 1726 and 1755 was turbulent, in partly due to the Dutch Republic's neutrality: the two powers no longer had common enemies. However, no one wanted a conflict. Moreover, the principle of the 'Algerian passport' also exerted a calming effect and made things easier.[70]

The outbreak of war in 1755 constituted a real break from the past. Habits adopted during the seventeenth century, such as implied understandings with Algiers against Spain, were no longer on the agenda for the Dutch Republic.[71] On the contrary: the States-General engaged in intensive diplomatic activity as soon as the war's outbreak became known in 1755. Both the British and the Spaniards were asked to support the Dutch Republic in the fight against Algiers's privateers. Therefore, these had been banned from the ports of Gibraltar and Mahon. Great Britain assured the Dutch of its support, as did the other trading nations, except for France. But the States-General failed to obtain an alliance with Madrid.

They did, however, receive diplomatic support from the Sublime Porte. The Sultan condemned the outbreak of war. The Dutch ambassador in Istanbul, Elbert de Hochepied, worked hard to obtain concrete measures and support from other European powers.[72] Despite a formal hearing with the vizier in Istanbul in August 1755, he could not achieve more than an exchange of letters between Istanbul and Algiers.[73] The diplomatic efforts of the Dutch Republic depended on the goodwill of its partners. During the Seven Years' War, the British government let its privateers operate in the Mediterranean, resulting in heavy Dutch losses in 1758.[74]

However, a new treaty was speedily signed between Algiers and the Dutch Republic, which is somewhat surprising when compared with previous agreements. Already in the spring of 1757, the Dey had showed himself to be obviously

68 Ibidem, 101–102.
69 Groot (1985) 144.
70 Krieken (2002) 107–109.
71 Groot (1985) 132.
72 NA, Staten-Generaal, no. 6958, letters from Pera of 17 May, 2 June, 18 June 1755.
73 *Ibidem*, letter from Pera of 1 September 1755.
74 Carter (1971) 103–128.

willing to negotiate a way out of war. He used the mediation of François Levett, a former Dutch consul in Tunis who was a prisoner in Algiers at that time.[75] A new treaty was signed on 24 November 1757 between Ali and Joost Sels. It was broadly in line with the agreements signed earlier by the Scandinavians and with the former treaty of 1726 between the Dutch and Algiers. The Dutch merchant ships' control procedures were lightened. Algiers was given a heavier tribute. It seems that the main objective of the conflict launched in February 1755 was to suck more money out of the Dutch Republic. Thus military pressure was a necessary evil that the Dutch had to accept, anchoring a squadron in front of the Barbary port starting on 7 November 1757. But relations were cordial; ships' guns fired off official salutes.[76]

4 Beyond Conflict Management

There is something peculiar about the so-called war of 1755–1757. A comparison with the previous conflicts is enlightening. The element of surprise was usually essential for Barbary corsairs.[77] The previous wars with Algiers had been bitter experiences for the Dutch. In 1686, the Dey granted the consul forty days to inform Dutch captains about the outbreak of war. But surprisingly, the attacks took place in the Bay of Biscay. Soon Algiers privateers had taken twenty-four ships.[78] In December 1715, the Dey simply notified the consul that his privateers were now allowed to capture Dutch merchant ships.[79] This war's outbreak caused heavy losses and probably fomented the boom of British trade in the Mediterranean.[80] Better organized through the Levant Company, and capable of defending themselves, the British increased their market share. But in 1755, the Dutch were fortunate to have Algiers waive surprise benefits. The start of military action in April meant a reduced campaign for the privateers.

The question arises concerning the Regency's actual power. It is difficult to estimate the size of the Algerian naval forces in the middle of the eighteenth century. According to French consular sources, Algiers would have had at its disposal a total of 21 ships and 260 guns. The spearhead of its maritime forces

75 Krieken (2002) 113–114.

76 NA, Admiraliteit, College te Amsterdam, no. 2391, logbook of *Damiaten*, 351 men and 68 guns; no. 2392, logbook of *Landskroon*, 250 men and 46 guns.

77 Fontenay (2010) 246.

78 Krieken (2002) 81.

79 Ibidem, 91–92.

80 Ressel (2015).

was formed by several xebecs, each bearing either twenty or thirty guns.[81] Historians familiar with Algerian records believe that the Regency could have boasted more numerous and better armed ships in the 1750s and 1760s.[82] State ownership and the use of captured enemy ships would have strengthened Algiers's military power.[83] However, it is certain that Algiers was less of a nuisance in 1755 than in 1715. Grain exports in North Africa were almost nonexistent in 1755–1756 due to weather conditions.[84] And a major earthquake struck Algiers in December 1755. Following another political putsch in July 1756, Algerians attacked Tunis.[85] Thus the foreign policy of the Regency was uncertain and fluctuating.

The States-General was well aware of this situation. In June 1755 the ambassador de Hochepied unambiguously described the weakness of the Algiers fleet.[86] After the departure of Paraviciny from Algiers, the States-General could count on other sources of information. The Dutch consuls in Tunis, Gibraltar, and Leghorn provided information about the course of the war.[87] The States-General was perfectly aware of the real threat of the war with the Regency because the Dutch information system in the Mediterranean worked extremely well. Consul Paraviciny periodically described political vagaries in Algiers during the winter of 1754.[88] The States-General was warned on 17 March 1755 about the outbreak of the war, leading to intense diplomatic activity. French diplomats seemed to be impressed with the States-General's speed of response. In a letter to Rouillé dated 15 April 1755, the French ambassador in Istanbul described the willingness of Dutch consul in Smyrna to prevent shipping losses.[89]

This attitude appears to mark a change of approach, in contrast to the relative inactivity marking the beginning of the last war in 1715–1720. Merchants

81 Devoux (1869) 401; Wolf (1979) 138–140, 294.

82 Merouche (2007) 270–272.

83 Wolf (1979) 143.

84 Merouche (2007) 262.

85 Grammont (2002) 249–251.

86 NA, Staten-Generaal, no. 6958, letter of 18 June 1755.

87 Ibidem, letters from Leghorn of 2 May 1755, from Tunis of 8 June 1755, from Gibraltar of 17 June 1755.

88 Ibidem, letters of Paraviciny from Algiers of 13 December 1754, 18 January and 15 February 1755.

89 'On mande, Monseigneur, par des lettres écrites de Smyrne à M. Peyssonel les 5 et 6 de ce mois, qu'il y était arrivé le 4 une tartane nolisée à Marseille par ordre des Etats Généraux pour informer le consul de Hollande établi dans cette échelle que la Régence d'Alger leur avait déclaré la guerre… Le consul de Hollande, dès le lendemain de l'arrivée de cette tartane, l'a fait repartir pour donner des avis aux capitaines des bâtiments hollandais et livournais qu'elle pourra rencontrer dans sa traversée'. ADLC, Correspondance Politique, Turquie, no. 128, f. 271–272.

had to impress upon the States-General the need to act. Several projects aimed at securing Dutch shipping in the Mediterranean failed due to their costs and constraints.[90] Although there was no clear and present danger on the part of the Regency, the States-General soon signed a new treaty. Privateering became a diplomatic tool for North African regencies in the eighteenth century. It was one of the means of pressure exerted in hopes of obtaining more money or ammunition from the Europeans. It was more profitable for them to pay tribute than to withstand commercial disturbances.[91]

Other factors must be taken into consideration as well. In the Dutch Republic, the political situation was very different in 1755 from what it had been forty years earlier in the 1710s. The Orangist restoration had occurred in 1747. The debate about neutrality was by then outdated. In 1754–1755, the threat of a resumption of hostilities between France and Great Britain was credible, indeed an imminent possibility. Both powers paid much attention to the neutrality of the Dutch Republic and the future of the barrier system.[92] But there was also a need for a quick settlement of the conflict with Algiers. For the Dutch, it became more difficult to impose compliance with treaties with France and Great Britain.

The balance of power within the Dutch political system also played a very important role here. Officially, the *Directie van Handel en Navigatie in Middelandsche Zee* (Directorate of Levant Trade) represented Dutch interests in the region. Not a chartered company, this body regulated Dutch trade and organized its protection. Although officially under the supervision of the States-General, it was a autonomous institution whose administration was in the hands of the major trading houses carrying out activities in the Mediterranean.[93] Some authors refer to lobbying conducted by influential groups of merchants. Such attempts at influence were particularly made by the directors in Amsterdam, who all had a stake in the Mediterranean trade. Aiming to protecting their commerce, they put pressure on the States-General to build up its military means.[94] In May 1755 it became mandatory for ships to incorporate a convoy. Several traders argued before the *Directie* about this system in November 1755 in order to protect the maritime route between Smyrna and Amsterdam.[95]

90 Wolf (1979) 310, Ressel (2015) 242–243.
91 Fontenay (2010) 338.
92 Carter (1975) 80–83.
93 Allain (2017) 168.
94 Brandon (2015) 114–123.
95 'Is er vergadering gecompareerd de heren Isacq Fremeaux, Leonard de Voogel, Jasper Bolte en Jacob de Roode, seggende dat sig hadde geflateerd dat er convooy naar Smirna

These four Dutch traders had access to government circles. They managed important and venerable trading houses and insisted on upholding a form of protectionism. Their reluctance towards convoying was typical. However, it is not certain that they would really have been influential. Over the course of the eighteenth century, Ottoman merchants penetrated Dutch trading networks. Their aim was to gain direct access to the Amsterdam market by short-circuiting Dutch trading houses.[96] They needed to protect Dutch shipowning. Some were powerful and managed international networks.[97] They defended the 'free vessel free cargo' principle.

Organizing a convoy was not easy due to the freedom exercised by Dutch trade and navigation in the Mediterranean. In theory, Dutch shipping had to respect a strict timetable and two annual convoys were to arrive in the Levant, respectively, in June and November. But in fact Dutch shipping benefitted from a more liberal approach.[98] In particular, the sailing schedule for Dutch ships voyaging from the Mediterranean back to Holland was deregulated in the eighteenth century.[99] This development was probably the result of Dutch participation in the coastal trade in the Mediterranean.[100] Constraints were greater for the ships concerned, evident in the example of *De witte Galeij* under the command of captain Joris Hendrik Pronk.[101] Besides, the dispersal of several Dutch merchant ships in the Mediterranean made the States-General's efforts at trade protection more complicated.

Fortunately, quite a few captains were able to rely on good experience in this maritime area.[102] And when the ship belonged to them, they exercised extra caution. So it was with Joris Ronnen and *De Snelle Galleij*. This master

soude geaccordeert syn, dog dat de heer de Roode een brief van syn schipper Pieter de Leeuw uyt Maltha had, die melde dat het Convoy met verder conde gaan als tot Milo, en dat dan ingevolge de ordres van de heer schout-by-nagt Boudaan testond na Maltha moest retourneren sonder scheepen van Smirna afgewagte, waardoor de scheepen van Smirna ingevaar soude syn, versoekende de raad en assistentie van het college hierwat daar en soud doen, waarop is gesegt, dat de consul Guerin van Maltha ons meld, dat het schip tot Serigo soude gaan, daar kruyssen, en de smirnse scheepen afwagten […]'. NA, DLHA, no. 14, 5 November 1755.

96 Kadi (2012) 170–187.

97 Ibidem, 215–220: for example, the Armenian family Massé, specialized in trade in wool: Alexander settled in Amsterdam in 1746 and became a citizen, whereas his brother Isaïe was drogman at the Dutch consulate in Smyrna.

98 Ibidem, 162–163.

99 Allain (2016) 104–107.

100 For an overview of this form of commercial shipping, see Buti (2005)

101 SAA, BAA, no. 2847, f. 69. This ship was going back and forth along Spanish coasts. Informed of the outbreak of war with Algiers, he had to wait in Salou, before going to Carthagena and then Malaga to join a military convoy.

102 Allain (2016) 108–112.

was familiar with the Mediterranean, as he often sailed between Amsterdam and Santa Cruz.[103] In March 1755, at the time of his departure from Salou, he got word of the outbreak of hostilities with Algiers. He did not hesitate to sail to Malaga and wait there for a convoy.[104]

Last but not least, the rivalry between Amsterdam and Rotterdam must not be overlooked. Since the end of the seventeenth century, the port of the Meuse had been refused the trusteeship of the Dutch Republic's main city. Specifically, the dispute concerned consular fees and the payment of fines imposed by the Ottomans.[105] Consul Paraviciny engaged in a thorough correspondence with the burgomasters of Amsterdam. On the one hand, the burgomasters received eighty-three letters from Algiers between 1733 and 1755. Paraviciny's last missive was sent from Marseilles at the end of April 1755. On the other hand, the consul received a copy of the deliberations of the city council.[106] Paraviciny had informed the burgomasters about the situation in Algiers, proliferating warnings about passports and inspection during the pre-war years.[107] Not surprisingly, he announced the war's outbreak to the Amsterdam city council the same day he delivered the news to the States-General.

It is interesting to note that the home port of the two Dutch ships brought to Algiers, the *Zes zonen* and the *Phoenix*, was Rotterdam. Loaded with wheat and beans, they were waylaid by privateers. They were probably outsiders, seeking to make a profit. They were punished for their lack of knowledge about the Mediterranean.[108] The commercial jealousy between Amsterdam and Rotterdam could paralyze aspects of Dutch foreign policy. Moreover, disagreements between Holland's commercial centres erupted shortly after the peace. The Amsterdam city council, starting on 17 November 1757, considered a project that envisioned a permanent fleet of six frigates for the Mediterranean. This proposal came from the States of Holland with the aim of holding Algiers at bay. After consulting the local chamber of the *Directie van Handel en Navigatie in Middelandse Zee*, the Amsterdam rejected the project on January 1758, deeming it too expensive as well as unfair for Dutch traders.[109]

103 SAA, BAA, 2835, f. 197 ; no. 2836, f. 105 ; no. 2837, f. 274 ; no. 2837, f. 278.

104 'Dat zy vervolgens missives dato 26 Maart van des affirmants correspondent uyt Barcelona tyding kreegen van den oorlog der Algerijnen tegens deese staat, waarom zy resolveerde ten beste en behoud van schip en laedingh om niet te vertrecken maar te blijven wagten op convoij [...]'. Ibidem, 2847 f. 19.

105 Allain (2018) 430–433.

106 SAA, Archives of Burgomasters, Diplomatic correspondance, bundle 248.

107 Ibidem, for example letter of 4 September 1754.

108 CADN, Constantinople, Smyrne, 1, letter of 19 June 1755.

109 SAA, Archief van de Vroedschap, Resoluties registers, no. 63.

5 Conclusion

This issue reveals the extreme volatility of international diplomacy, especially for neutral powers in the eighteenth century. The so-called Dutch-Algerian War of 1755–1757 reveals the problem with the foreign policy of a federal state that lacks an effective central authority. The Dutch Republic needed to resolve the conflict with Algiers quickly because of the serious threat of war between France and Great Britain. Due to the military weakness of the Regency, war was not a genuine concern for Dutch trade. But the better option was to pay an increased tribute to Algiers in return for peace. The quest for more pacified international relations within a context of a lawless international order seemed difficult. Thus the war of 1755–1757 was more important from a diplomatic viewpoint than from a strategic vantage.

Some aspects of the matter have received scant attention. The remote management of the entry into a conflict seems to have been very difficult due to the institutional structure governing the Dutch presence in the Mediterranean. Political lobbying by merchants played a key role, but sometimes there was an uncertain degree of efficiency due to the various interests involved. Despite the treaty of 1757, Algerian privateers continued to hinder Dutch shipping. A Dutch fleet mounted a punitive expedition off the coast of Algiers in April 1763; war broke out again in 1768 and 1793.[110]

Acknowledgements

The author is grateful to Caroline Wallis and Youenn Le Prat for their careful review of this chapter.

Bibliography

Allain, T., 'Des hommes entre Mer du nord et Méditerranée. Les équipages des navires de commerce d'Amsterdam vers la mer intérieure au XVIIIe siècle' in X. Daumalin, D. Faget and O. Raveux eds., *La mer en partage. Sociétés littorales et économies maritimes, XVIe–XXe siècle* (Aix-en-Provence 2016) 103–116.

Allain, T., 'International treaties versus "bonne prise". The case of the Dutch merchant ship De Vriendschap in the Mediterranean in 1745', *Comparative Legal History* 5 no. 1 (2017) 162–176.

110 Krieken (2002) 118.

Allain, T., 'Relations de pouvoirs et enjeux marchands autour du réseau consulaire néerlandais en Méditerranée (XVIIe–XVIIIe siècles)' in A. Bartoloméi et al. eds., *De l'utilité commerciale des consuls. L'institution consulaire et les marchands dans le monde méditerranéen XVIIe–XXe siècle* (Rome and Madrid 2018) 421–438.

Andersen D., 'La politique danoise face aux Etats barbaresques (1600–1845)' in G. Le Bouëdec and F. Chappé eds., *Pouvoirs et littoraux du XVe au XXe siècle* (Rennes 2000) 243–250.

Andersen, D., and H-J. Voth, 'The Grapes of War: Neutrality and Mediterranean Shipping under the Danish Flag, 1747–1807', *Scandinavian Economic History Review* 48 (2000) 5–23.

Asaert, G. et al. eds., *Maritieme Geschiedenis der Nederlanden* III (Bussum 1978).

Brandon P., *War, Capital, and the Dutch State 1588–1795* (Leiden and Boston 2015).

Buti, G., 'Aller en caravane: le cabotage lointain en Méditerranée, XVIIe et XVIIIe siècle', *Revue d'Histoire Moderne et Contemporaine*, 52 (2005) 9–22.

Bruijn J., *De Admiraliteit van Amsterdam in rustige jaren 1713–1751* (Amsterdam 1970).

Bruijn J., *The Dutch Navy of the Seventeenth and Eighteenth Centuries* (South Carolina 1993).

Calafat G., 'Ottoman North Africa and ius publicum europaeum. The case of the treaties of peace and trade (1600–1750)' in A. Alimento et al. eds., *War, Trade and Neutrality. Europe and the Mediterranean in the seventeenth and the eighteenth centuries* (Milan 2011) 171–187.

Carrière, M., and M. Courdurié, 'Les grandes heures de Livourne au XVIIIe siècle. L'exemple de la guerre de Sept Ans', *Revue Historique*, 254 (1975) 39–80.

Carter, A., *The Dutch Republic in Europe in the Seven Years War* (Miami 1971).

Carter, A., *Neutrality or Commitment. The evolution of Dutch foreign policy, 1667–1795* (London 1975).

Devoux, A., 'La marine de la Régence d'Alger', *Revue africaine* 77 (1869) 384–420.

Fontenay, M., *La Méditerranée entre la croix et le croissant. Navigation, commerce, course et piraterie, XVIe–XIXe siècle* (Paris 2010).

Gelder, M. van, 'The Republic's Renegades: Dutch Converts to Islam in Seventeenth-Century Diplomatic Relations with North Africa', *Journal of Early Modern History* 19 (2015) 175–198.

Go, S., *Marine Insurance in the Netherlands, 1600–1870. A comparative institutional approach* (Amsterdam 2009).

Grammont, H.D. de, *Histoire d'Alger sous la domination turque 1513–1830* (Paris 2002).

Groot, A. de, *The Ottoman Empire and the Dutch republic. A history of the Earliest Diplomatic Relations 1610–1630* (Leiden and Istanbul 1978).

Groot A. de, 'The Organization of Western European Trade in the Levant, 1500–1800', in L. Blussé and F.S. Gaastra eds., *Companies and Trade* (Leiden 1981) 231–241.

Groot, A. de, 'Ottoman North Africa and the Dutch Republic in the Seventeenth and Eighteenth Centuries', *Revue de l'Occident musulman et de la Méditerranée* 39 (1985) 131–147.

Israel J., *Dutch Primacy in World Trade, 1585–1740* (Oxford 1989).

Kadi, I.H., *Ottoman and Dutch Merchants in the Eighteenth Century. Competition and cooperation in Ankara, Izmir and Amsterdam* (Leiden and Boston 2012).

Kaiser, W., eds, *Le commerce des captifs. Les intermédiaires dans l'échange et le rachat des prisonniers en Méditerranée, XVe–XVIIIe siècle* (Rome 2008).

Koopmans J. and C. Regtop, 'Zeeschuimers en verachtelijke Barbaaren? Nederlandse nieuwsfragmenten over Barbarije in de achttiende eeuw', *Tijschrift voor Zeegeschiedenis* 21 (2002) 34–48.

Krieken, G. van, *Corsaires et marchands. Les relations entre Alger et les Pays-Bas 1604–1830* (Paris 2002).

Merouche, L., *Recherches sur l'Algérie à l'époque ottomane.* II *La course, mythes et réalités,* (Paris 2007).

Müller, L., *Consuls, Corsairs and Commerce. The Swedish Consular Service and Long-distance Shipping, 1720–1815* (Uppsala 2004).

Panzac, D., *Les corsaires barbaresques, la fin d'une épopée 1800–1820* (Paris 1999).

Panzac, D., 'Les esclaves et leurs rançons chez les barbaresques (fin XVIIIe–début XIXe siècle)', *Cahiers de la Méditerranée* 65 (2002) 99–118.

Ressel, M., *Zwischen Sklaven kassen und Turkenpassen. Nordeuropa und die Barbaresken in der Fruhen Neuzeit* (Berlin 2012).

Ressel, M., 'Venice and the redemption of Northern European slaves (seventeenth and eighteenth centuries)', *Cahiers de la Méditerranée* 88 (2013) 131–145.

Ressel, M., 'The Dutch-Algerian War and the Rise of British Shipping to Southern Europe (1715–1726)', *Cahiers de la Méditerranée* 90 (2015) 237–255.

Stapelbroek, K., 'The emergence of Dutch neutrality. Trade, treaty politics and the peace of the Republic', in A. Alimento et al. eds., *War, Trade and Neutrality. Europe and the Mediterranean in the seventeenth and the eighteenth centuries* (Milan 2011) 129–145.

Vries, J. de, and A. van der Woude, *The First Modern Economy. Success, Failure, and Perseverance of the Dutch Economy, 1500–1815* (Cambridge 1997).

Wolf, J., *The Barbary Coast. Algiers under the Turks 1500 to 1830* (New York 1979).

CHAPITRE 16

Les conflits permanents entre corsaires et neutres: L'exemple de la France et du Danemark au XVIIIe siècle

Pierrick Pourchasse

1 Introduction

Au début du XVIIIe siècle, il est théoriquement admis que les navires neutres ont le droit d'aller dans les ports des pays en guerre en suivant des règles bien précises concernant les cargaisons. Il est interdit de transporter certains produits mais la caractérisation des marchandises de contrebande est différente selon les pays. La France défend une définition étroite qui se réduit aux armes et aux munitions. L'Angleterre a une conception plus large qui, selon elle, inclut toutes les munitions navales et même l'avitaillement des navires de guerre (des navires chargés de bœuf salé danois sont ainsi déclarés bonnes prises au cours de la guerre de Sept Ans[1]), conception qui sera ensuite appliquée par la France. Au cours des conflits de la période révolutionnaire, l'Angleterre interdira même tout trafic de produits alimentaires notamment de céréales vers la France en raison d'une supposée illégalité du gouvernement de la nouvelle République. Le droit de transporter des produits appartenant à l'ennemi est également l'objet d'un désaccord entre neutres et belligérants. Pour les neutres, le pavillon couvre la marchandise (« free ships, free goods, unfree ships, unfree goods »). Pour la France, les traités autorisent la confiscation des biens appartenant à l'ennemi et le pavillon ne protège aucunement la cargaison. Le règlement établi par la France en 1744 stipule que si une partie d'une cargaison appartient à l'ennemi, celle-ci peut être confisquée mais le navire relâché. Ainsi les tribunaux autorisent la confiscation des propriétés de l'ennemi et le pavillon ne protège aucunement la cargaison[2].

Le but du Danemark au cours des conflits opposant la France à l'Angleterre est d'utiliser sa neutralité pour développer sa navigation et son commerce. L'activité maritime du royaume scandinave se développe considérablement et la période comprise entre la guerre de Sept Ans (1756–1763) et l'attaque de

1 Tuxen (1988) 217.
2 Schnakenbourg (2013) 181 et suiv.

 | DOI:10.1163/9789004407992_018

Copenhague par la flotte anglaise (1807), qualifiée de « florissante periode », est considérée comme l'âge d'or de la navigation danoise. Le Danemark bénéficie de traités avec les deux adversaires, l'Angleterre depuis 1670 et la France depuis 1742, traités qui lui garantissent une certaine protection en cas de prise. De plus, en utilisant de faux documents de transport, il est possible d'effectuer des trafics interdits par les belligérants. C'est une pratique courante et très bien maîtrisée par les neutres : ainsi, entre 1793 et 1795, 112 navires scandinaves passent le détroit du Sund en déclarant se rendre à Bilbao avec des cargaisons de céréales. Cependant, les archives de la province basque ne mentionnent aucune arrivée de grains du Nord au cours de ces années. Il est évident que la plupart des navires étaient destinés à la France qui souffre alors d'une grave crise frumentaire. Les Britanniques connaissent d'ailleurs ces trafics et font la chasse aux navires danois à destination de la péninsule ibérique.

Même si la France, dont la navigation est réduite dans les mers du Nord, est la principale bénéficiaire du trafic des neutres, cela n'évite pas que ces derniers soient une cible fréquente pour les corsaires français. Ainsi, comme au cours des conflits précédents et bien que la France ait proclamé le 16 avril 1793 sa volonté « de donner aux capitaines des bâtiments danois et suédois qui fréquentent les ports de la République française, l'assurance d'y trouver, pour eux et leurs équipages, le secours, l'assistance et la protection requises »[3], les autorités révolutionnaires prennent une position identique à celle de la Grande-Bretagne[4], et ne se préoccupent guère de protéger les droits revendiqués par les armateurs des pays neutres.

Les navires scandinaves peuvent naturellement effectuer des transports pour les ennemis de la France et, en conséquence, la Marine aussi bien que les corsaires leur font continuellement la chasse pour contrôler leurs trafics. Les prises sont nombreuses alors que l'aide des armateurs du Nord est nécessaire pour subvenir aux approvisionnements de la France. Les tensions entre les forces navales françaises et flottes neutres sont ainsi permanentes durant les conflits, entraînant violences envers les équipages et contestations auprès des tribunaux. Si les autorités françaises essaient de ne pas envenimer les relations diplomatiques avec les puissances scandinaves, les doutes sur la régularité des trafics conjuguées avec les exigences des corsaires conduisent souvent à des procédures très longues et très disputées.

---

3 Rigsarkivet, Copenhague, Department of Foreign Affairs, France, 2022, Représentation française 1776–1801, Proclamation du conseil exécutif provisoire du 16 avril 1793.

4 Rigsarkivet, Copenhague, Department of Foreign Affairs, France, 2046, Courrier du 12 mai 1793. « Il est clair que l'exemple des Anglais et des Espagnols qui, à ce qu'on prétend ici, s'emparent de tous les vaisseaux neutres chargés dans les ports de France a motivé cet injuste décret » (codé).

2 Comment justifier une prise

Lors des conflits, les navires neutres sont régulièrement visités par les belligérants en raison des trafics illicites dont ils sont coutumiers. En février 1793, un diplomate danois écrit : « La guerre ayant commencé, on doit s'attendre à ce que les corsaires français exerceront beaucoup de violences et d'injustices même envers les puissances neutres, ce qui donnera lieu à de fréquentes réclamations à faire au gouvernement »[5]. En effet, les autorités françaises se sont toujours méfiées des navires scandinaves. Les équipages du Nord, qui fréquentent les navires anglais dans les mers septentrionales, qui parlent des langues que la plupart des marins français trouvent identiques et qui sont de la religion honnie, sont des suspects potentiels. Le navire et l'équipage norvégien du *Diligencia* de Laurwigen, capitaine August Schielderup, sont « suspects parce qu'ils étaient habillés à l'anglaise et parlaient en partie cette langue »[6]. Cette méfiance transparaît dans de nombreux documents. En 1744, un avocat écrit au consul danois à Dunkerque, que le Conseil du roi « était dans une violente présomption que les nations neutres cherchent à favoriser les Anglais »[7]. Parfois des embargos sont imposés aux neutres comme en 1757 à Bordeaux pour « empêcher que la flotte anglaise qui est actuellement sur la côte de Saintonge ne soit pas à même de prendre des informations des navires qu'elle pourrait arrêter ni de se pourvoir des vivres dont elle pourrait avait besoin »[8]. Toujours à Bordeaux, le 31 juillet 1762, le consul danois Hanssen se plaint que l'embargo sur les navires étrangers dure depuis plus d'un mois et demi sur les ordres du commandant de quatre flûtes chargées pour le roi qui sont en attente de sortie, sans savoir quand celle-ci aura lieu.

Entre 15 et 18 navires « tant danois que norvégiens et nombre d'autres de différentes nations se trouvent dans le cas et sont détenus… fournissant des justes sujets de plaintes par le dépérissement de leurs cargaisons qui en résulte. Le négociant qui paie le vin et l'eau-de-vie avant de l'avoir reçue, reçoit au lieu du bon vin que l'on charge, que du vin gâté et des barriques à demi pleines ou entièrement vides, le rouge s'aigrit par les chaleurs excessives qu'il fait et le blanc vient en travail, fait sauter la barrique et perd en qualité…[9]»

---

5 Rigsarkivet, Copenhague, Department of Foreign Affairs, France, 2046, courrier du 15 février 1793.

6 Rigsarkivet Copenhague, Tyske Kancelli 298.

7 Archives Nationales de France (ANF), B1 477, Courrier du 14 octobre 1744.

8 Riksarkivet Stockholm, Gallica 417.

9 Rigsarkivet Copenhague, Tyske Kancelli 285, Courrier de Hanssen de Liliendahl du 31 juillet 1762.

Après un arraisonnement en mer, le corsaire cherche toujours à justifier sa prise et, s'il n'y a pas de réel motif, l'imagination ne manque pas pour trouver une raison plus ou moins défendable. Les corsaires affirment souvent que des papiers ont été jetés à la mer. L'action de faire disparaitre ses documents est une faute majeure :

> tout vaisseau pris de quelque nation qu'ils soient neutres ou alliés, desquels il sera constaté qu'il y a eu des papiers jetés à la mer ou autrement supprimés où distraits seront déclarés de bonne prise et qu'il soit besoin d'examiner quels étaient ces papiers, par qui ils ont été jetés et s'il en est resté suffisamment à bord pour justifier que le navire et son chargement appartiennent à des amis ou à des alliés[10].

Ainsi, curieusement, les corsaires voient très souvent les capitaines balancer leurs papiers à la mer. En 1779, le capitaine suédois Pierre Brandenbourg de Stockholm, effectuant une liaison entre Lisbonne et Gênes est accusé d'avoir « jeté ses papiers à la mer ce qui le fait déclarer bonne prise selon le règlement du 26 juillet 1778 »[11]. En 1759, une chaloupe corsaire voit *Le Soleil Levant* lancer des papiers et une bannière à la mer « que pour lors ils avaient ramé avec plus de force mais que tout avait disparu dans le moment »[12]. Ceci peut difficilement être prouvé et, dans ce cas, c'est la parole du capitaine neutre contre celle du corsaire. Parfois les navires pris arborent un pavillon ennemi avant de se faire prendre ce qui paraît totalement incompréhensible. Pour prouver leurs dires, les corsaires introduisent des pavillons et des documents divers dans les navires pris. En 1760, les corsaires du *Saint-Antoine de Padoue* dissimulent frauduleusement un passeport et pavillon anglais dans la soute du *Faucon* de Krageroe[13]. Très souvent il manque des papiers[14] ou ceux-ci sont incomplets. Les voyages maritimes sont souvent fort complexes et il est parfois bien difficile de déterminer la neutralité des marchandises. Ainsi pour le brigantin *Le Nicolas Christine* amené à Marseille en mars 1793, et porteur de 30 connaissements pour sa cargaison de retour vers Hambourg, l'avocat des corsaires réclame la preuve de propriété « par la lettre portant l'ordre d'acheter et d'envoyer les

10 Riksarkivet Stockholm, Gallica 418.

11 Riksarkivet, Stockholm, Gallica, 510, courrier de Fölsch du 3 mai 1779.

12 Rigsarkivet, Copenhague, Tyske Kancelli, 297, Akter og Dokumenter vedr. danske Skibe, opbragte i Frankrig 1758–60.

13 Ibidem.

14 Riksarkivet Stockholm, Gallica 417, Courrier d'Emmery (1758). Le navire suédois, *Le Rachel,* emmené à Boulogne est déclaré de bonne prise à cause d'absence du rôle d'équipage alors que ses marchandises appartiennent à des négociants de Hambourg.

marchandises, par la lettre en réponse assurant l'achat, par la lettre annonçant le chargement pour le compte du négociant d'Hambourg, par la facture desdites marchandises achetées pour le compte des négociants d'Hambourg et par la traite acquittée justifiant le paiement desdites marchandises »[15], ensemble documentaire quasiment impossible à collecter dans le délai imparti avant le jugement. Quand les documents du navire sont en règle les corsaires n'hésitent pas à les faire disparaître. *Le Comte de Gramont*, après avoir examiné les papiers du vaisseau *La Bourse de Copenhague* les déchire et les fait disparaître[16]. De son côté, *La Providence* a trop de papiers car « il en fut plus de 80 qui furent mises au rebut comme inutiles qui cependant étaient des lettres de mer et autres documents... pour la navigation »[17].

Les corsaires usent de tous les stratagèmes possibles pour que leurs prises soient déclarées recevables. *L'Anne-Marguerite* a des problèmes de jauge, ses documents indiquant 110 last alors qu'il est chargé de 120 last de marchandises. Le capitaine essaie d'expliquer que les mesures sont différentes entre Livourne et le Danemark mais les corsaires ne veulent rien savoir et font procéder à une expertise très précise du navire pour défendre leurs intérêts.

Les raisons les plus futiles donnent lieu à des procédures. Un document danois donne comme exemple la présence d'un seau de charbon anglais dans la cuisine ou d'une couverture d'origine britannique dans la chambre du capitaine[18]. On reproche au capitaine norvégien de la *Diligentia* de parler anglais, ce qui est le cas de nombreux maîtres de navires du Nord, et d'avoir séjourné en Angleterre, ce qui est véridique car le navire a été pris quelque temps auparavant par un corsaire britannique et a été amené dans un port outre-Manche.

Les preuves les plus couramment utilisées pour que les prises soient jugées bonnes sont l'origine anglaise du navire, la présence d'un membre d'équipage ou de produits anglais dans le navire. Les équipages du Nord sont généralement très cosmopolites, se reformant au gré des escales en raison des fréquentes désertions, et les marins britanniques naviguent régulièrement sur des navires scandinaves. Le capitaine du navire *La Providence* indique ainsi en 1755 à propos de corsaires français : « Ils ont mis en prison le mousse que j'avais puisqu'il est né en Angleterre. J'avais été obligé de le prendre à la place d'un autre danois qui s'était enfui à Londres »[19]. Le 27 février 1795, le vaisseau danois, *Le Dronningaard*, appartenant au sieur Pletinck domicilié à Fridericksnagore

15 Ibidem, Courrier de Tietjens de Marseille du 9 mars 1793.
16 Rigsarkivet, Copenhague, Tyske Kancelli 295, 1754–1762, courrier du 23 novembre 1757.
17 Ibidem.
18 Jespersen et Feldbæk (2002) 436.
19 Rigsarkivet, Copenhague, Tyske Kancelli 295, 1754–1762.

au Bengale et commandé par le capitaine Jacob Helleson, est arrêté par une escadre française à l'entrée de la Manche et amené à Brest alors qu'il effectue un voyage de Fridericksnagore-Copenhague. Sa prise est justifiée par le fait que le subrécargue, plusieurs matelots et quelques passagers sont d'origine britannique. Le transport de voyageurs de différentes nationalités ou de membres d'équipages étrangers est habituelle dans ces gros navires qui partent pour le longs voyages vers des destinations lointaines. Il n'y aura pas de suite à cette affaire car le navire se fait reprendre par une escadre anglaise au large de Brest et est amené à Falmouth[20].

Au cours de la période révolutionnaire, il n'y a même plus besoin de preuves pour justifier les prises et les services diplomatiques scandinaves ne savent plus à qui s'adresser pour porter des réclamations : « La capture des vaisseaux neutres nous jette dans un grand embarras [...] Les réclamer au conseil exécutif est absolument inutile parce qu'il ne peut soustraire aucune affaire aux cours de justice ordinaire et qu'il n'a aucune autorité sur les tribunaux. Dans beaucoup de ports, il n'y a pas de consuls pour donner aux vaisseaux arrêtés des avocats habiles pour les défendre »[21]. Ainsi sur une grande partie de la côte atlantique, le Danemark n'a plus de services consulaires pour s'occuper des vaisseaux pris par les Français :

> Toute la côte de Bretagne, le Poitou est entièrement abandonné et c'est cependant de cette côte que les armateurs français font leur croisière. Le consul de Nantes est à Hambourg [...]. Combien cela est nuisible aux affaires. Le Conseil royal verra avec déplaisir lorsqu'il me permet d'exposer qu'il y a entre autres à Rochefort, cinq vaisseaux danois dont on avait envoyé à Paris les papiers depuis trois mois et ces capitaines ne savaient point où en étaient leurs affaires lorsque cela est venu à ma connaissance[22].

Ces difficultés exaspèrent l'administration et les négociants scandinaves. Un diplomate danois écrit après la conduite à Lorient de trois vaisseaux : « il faut être sur les lieux pour se faire une vraie idée des horreurs et des injustices qui ont lieu ici et dans les autres parties de ce vaste et criminel pays. L'anarchie est à son comble... »[23]. Le négociant Hornbostel de Marseille est tout aussi furieux:

---

20 Rigsarkivet, Copenhague, Department of Foreign Affairs, France, 2053.

21 Rigsarkivet, Copenhague, Department of Foreign Affairs, France, 2046, Courrier du 25 mars 1793.

22 Ibidem, Courrier du 27 juillet 1794.

23 Ibidem, Courrier du 14 juillet 1793.

> Ce sont les équipages de corsaires qui jugent les prises car si les juges ne se prononcent pas en leur faveur, ils seraient bientôt pendus. Voyez donc ce qu'il en résulterait de faire des protestations, pour le moins seraient-elles inutiles. Notre vie et nos biens sont à la disposition de la prétendue Nation. Nous sommes donc résignés à être ruinés, heureux si on nous laisse la vie[24].

Certaines situations ne peuvent que provoquer une colère justifiée des armateurs scandinaves. Ainsi, en avril 1794, le navire norvégien *La Christiana Benedicta*, ayant chargé des fruits, des huiles et des confitures à Gênes pour Hambourg est pris par un navire de guerre français et amené à Port la Montagne (Toulon) où il est déchargé[25]. Son voyage de retour vers le Nord, qui n'est en aucune manière un trafic de contrebande, n'aura duré que quelques heures.

La reprise d'un navire saisi par un corsaire britannique fait l'objet d'une procédure particulière. Le Conseil des prises accorde le tiers de la valeur du navire et de la cargaison au corsaire « sauveur » même si le navire et la cargaison sont totalement neutres et ne courent aucun risque dans leur navigation. Le jugement est généralement très compliqué car quelques matelots ennemis ont été intégrés à l'équipage du navire saisi et les papiers ont, la plupart du temps, été dérobés par le corsaire[26]. Ainsi, en 1757 deux navires danois sont repris à des Anglais alors qu'ils effectuent deux transports neutres (Port Maurice-Copenhague et Hambourg-Lisbonne) et sont condamnés à payer le tiers de leurs cargaisons et de leurs navires. Les vaisseaux qui ravitaillent les arsenaux de la marine ne sont pas exempts de cette règle. En 1779, *Le Mercure*, navire suédois affrété par la maison française Raimbert de Saint-Pétersbourg, chargé de chanvres à destination de Brest est pris par un corsaire anglais puis repris par un français qui réclame le tiers de l'ensemble, navire et cargaison. Les services consulaires font remarquer aux autorités qu'il aurait mieux valu pour le navire qu'il ne se fasse pas reprendre car, en Angleterre, « le chanvre aurait été jugé bonne prise, le fret payé en entier et le navire racheté sur le champ »[27].

---

24 Ibidem, Courrier de Hornbostel de 1793.

25 Rigsarkivet, Copenhague, Kommercekollegiet, 1148, Journalsager, Courrier de Tietjens du 22 avril 1794.

26 ANF, B3 419, courrier du 12 mai 1747. La galiote suédoise *Le Saint Jean*, appartenant à un négociant de Stockholm, est affrétée en 1757 pour effectuer un transport de sucre entre Lisbonne et Le Havre. Pris par un anglais, le navire est ensuite repris par un corsaire malouin (*La Grande Biche*) qui déclare que c'est une bonne prise puisque le navire est sans papiers et vend la marchandise.

27 ANF, B3 419, courrier du 27 avril 1779.

Les prises peuvent parfois conduire a de graves problèmes diplomatiques. En 1757, le navire *Les Trois Princesses* de Copenhague est pris et amené à Brest alors qu'il transporte de la poudre, des canons et des cordages à Alger[28]. La cargaison représente le tribut versé par la monarchie danoise pour que ses navires ne soient pas attaqués par les corsaires barbaresques, selon les traités conclus entre les deux pays. En conséquence « selon des avis certains, ces barbares sont prêts à rompre la paix » si les différents produits n'arrivent pas au plus tôt. Les marchandises appartenant au roi du Danemark, le duc de Penthièvre, Louis de Bourbon, grand Amiral de France et gouverneur de Bretagne, s'interpose personnellement. Malgré cette intervention, l'affaire lente à se régler. Le corsaire réclame un jugement et une partie des cordages et des boulets a été utilisé pour les vaisseaux de roi. L'arsenal de Brest est obligé de fabriquer en urgence de nouveaux cordages mais ceux-ci sont de moins bonne qualité que ceux qui ont été prélevés et sont refusés par les officiers danois. Le consul de France à Alger est chargé de régler l'affaire en proposant, en contrepartie, une somme d'argent au dey. La brouille diplomatique se règle finalement à la satisfaction des autorités danoises mais le navire est repris par les Anglais dès sa sortie de Brest puis par les Espagnols sur sa route vers l'Afrique du Nord ce qui conduit à de nouvelles controverses sur les marchandises puisque celles-ci ont été fabriquées en France.

3 La violence envers les équipages

Lors des prises, les corsaires montrent très souvent, avant de savoir si la prise est bonne, une grande violence envers l'équipage. Un rapport de 1756 décrit le comportement des corsaires envers le capitaine de *La Providence*: « Depuis l'instant de la prise, il a maltraité le dit capitaine a exercé contre lui toutes sortes de duretés et en a agi avec lui avec tant inhumanité que les Turcs en agissent vis-à-vis de leurs esclaves »[29]. Le capitaine de *La Bourse de Copenhague*, navire chargé de sucre au départ de Lisbonne à destination de Hambourg, est encore plus malchanceux. Il est tout d'abord saisi par un câpre de Bristol :

> Le capitaine du corsaire le maltraita à tel point que l'ayant fait étendre à terre sur le pont dudit corsaire, il le menaça par trois fois l'épée nue à la main de le tuer s'il ne déclarait pas que la cargaison de son navire

28 Rigsarkivet, Copenhague, Tyske Kancelli, 296.

29 Rigsarkivet, Copenhague, Tyske Kancelli 295.

> appartenait à des Français… Le capitaine anglais ne pouvant pas venir à bout de son dessein lui jeta de fureur un vase à travers le visage.

Sur le chemin vers l'Angleterre, il est repris par des câpres de Bayonne :

> les deux corsaires s'en emparèrent, pillèrent le déclarant et son équipage, leur tirèrent les hardes qu'ils avaient dessus et enfoncèrent leurs coffres à coups de hache pour les piller, qu'on enleva un rouleau de tabac du Brésil avec trois ou quatre caisses de fruits qui furent transportés à bord du corsaire…[30]

Le capitaine du *Diligentia*, pris par un corsaire de Calais, est montré en spectacle dans toute la ville puis « enfermé dans une auberge sans pouvoir parler à personne et tout l'équipage mis en prison »[31] car il transporte du beurre anglais pour Rotterdam.

Les corsaires essaient de soudoyer les équipages pour les obliger à signer des documents favorables aux corsaires. Trois jeunes matelots du *Soleil Levant* certifient un document indiquant avoir vu leur capitaine jeter des papiers à la mer ainsi qu'un pavillon ennemi. Ne comprenant rien à ce qu'on leur demande, leurs signatures sont véritablement extorquées. Selon le capitaine de *La Providence*, les corsaires ont saoulé « deux personnes de mon équipage et les ont fait signer dans cet état quelques écrits dont ceux-ci n'avaient point de connaissance et les officiers du corsaire ont fait des menaces aux autres qui refusaient de faire la même chose »[32].

Le comportement des corsaires envers les navires neutres s'assimile à de la piraterie. La nourriture et les biens de valeur sont systématiquement pillés et l'équipage violenté comme nous l'avons vu pour *La Bourse de Copenhague*. Lors de la prise du navire *Les Trois Princesses*, un inventaire de 22 pages énumérant les biens abimés ou pillés est établi : « grande chaudière de cuivre avec sa couverture fracturée… 6 tonneaux de bonne bière perdue… pour le premier pilote pris et fracturé 1 veste de coton fin, 1 ditto de toile rayée des Indes… »[33] Parfois les corsaires proposent le versement d'une rançon afin de ne pas continuer l'affaire et aller devant le conseil des prises. Les armateurs, même si leurs navires sont en règle, préfèrent souvent ce type « d'accommodement » afin d'éviter les longueurs de la procédure et la détérioration du navire et des marchandises.

30 Ibidem, courrier du 25 mai 1757.
31 Rigsarkivet, Copenhague, Tyske Kancelli 298.
32 Rigsarkivet, Copenhague, Tyske Kancelli 295.
33 Rigsarkivet, Copenhague, Tyske Kancelli 297.

Ainsi, dès qu'ils prennent un navire, les corsaires considèrent naturellement qu'il devient leur propriété. Lors de la guerre de Sept ans le navire *Landschap van Eyderstadt* est pris alors qu'il doit livrer des huiles au Havre, c'est-à-dire pour un port français, et les corsaires agissent « comme si le navire et sa cargaison leur fut adjugée de bonne prise et la font décharger »[34].

Pendant, la période révolutionnaire, les autorités sont dans la totale incapacité de règlementer l'activité des corsaires et ne peuvent empêcher leurs exactions. Dès qu'ils prennent un navire, ces derniers considèrent qu'il leur appartient et qu'aucun jugement pourra les déposséder de leur prise[35]. En mai 1793, un courrier du consul du Danemark à Marseille décrit avec clairvoyance le problème de la course :

> Tout s'arrangera bien si les petits intéressés ne s'y opposaient pas et qui sont difficilement à débouter par les juges. Les matelots, par exemple, en s'engageant ont reçu une avance pour 3 mois de 300 livres en assignats qui font à présent 300 florins d'Hollande. Le terme des 3 mois est échu, l'argent est mangé, plusieurs n'ont pas fait des prises anglaises ou hollandaises qui se vendent de suite, exigent des captures où de ceux qui ont fait l'armement une autre paye. Ceux-ci ont une centaine d'hommes sur les bras ne savent trop comment faire. J'ai vu des scènes au tribunal où les matelots menaçaient leurs capitaines d'une manière épouvantable. Cela intimide les juges...[36]

Les autorités essaient de reprendre le contrôle d'une situation, où les corsaires sont finalement devenus de véritables pirates, et font parvenir une nouvelle proclamation dans les différents ports de la République pour protéger les navires neutres qui « enjoint à tous les commandants des bâtiments soit de la République, soit armés par des particuliers de ne les arrêter, ni contrarier dans leurs navigations pourvu qu'ils ne soient point chargés d'objets prohibés par les traités pour les puissances ennemies »[37]. Cependant, la situation n'évolue

34 Rigsarkivet, Copenhague, Tyske Kancelli 296.

35 Rigsarkivet, Copenhague, Kommercekollegiet, 1148, Journalsager : « Les corsaires et leurs intéressés montrent tant d'acharnement aux dites cargaisons qu'ils regardent depuis le commencement comme leur propriété et pour lesquelles ils n'ont rien fait que d'aller à leur rencontre avec des centaines d'hommes armés contre des bâtiments marchands qui ont 6 jusqu'à 10 matelots chacun d'équipage ». (courrier de Tietjens du 3 juin 1793).

36 Rigsarkivet, Copenhague, Department of Foreign Affairs, France, 2046, Courrier de Tietjens du 4 mai 1793.

37 Rigsarkivet, Copenhague, Department of Foreign Affairs, France, 2046, Courrier de Tietjens de Marseille du 4 mai 1793.

guère. Le consul de Marseille écrit en juin 1793 qu'il ne lui a pas été possible de faire relâcher un seul des cinq vaisseaux amenés dans sa ville.[38]

Même si la prise est jugée mauvaise, les marchandises et les navires sont souvent endommagés par les corsaires. En 1779, trois navires suédois chargés de poissons au départ de Falmouth en Angleterre à destination de Naples sont pris par des corsaires français et emmenés à Toulon. Les navires attendent le résultat du conseil des prises mais pendant les deux mois d'attente, « les harengs se sont totalement gâtés ». C'est une « véritable infection » dans le port. On est obligé de faire sortir les vaisseaux de l'arsenal car « les équipages se sont trouvés incommodés qu'il a fallu en envoyer plusieurs à l'hôpital ». Les magistrats de la ville sont obligés de louer des tartanes pour jeter le poisson en pleine mer mais « les ouvriers chargés de vider le navire se sont vus obligés de quitter l'ouvrage ». Finalement les corsaires sont condamnés aux frais, dommages et intérêts envers les capitaines suédois par le ministre[39].

Les équipages subissent des violences physiques et matérielles mais sont aussi dispersés un peu partout : certains matelots restent sur leur bâtiment, d'autres sont amenés sur le navire corsaire qui bien souvent les laissent dans le premier port venu suivant les aléas de la navigation. Comme il faut généralement attendre de longs mois le jugement, tous ces hommes repartent au gré des opportunités vers leur port d'attache ou vers les ports où ils pensent trouver des compatriotes.

4 Des procédures interminables

Les prises entraînent des contentieux interminables. La plupart des capitaines étrangers ne comprennent généralement pas le système juridique français et se défendent difficilement. Le consul de Marseille déclare « Comment veut-on que les capitaines puissent se défendre si on ne leur donne aucune communication des procédures que les capitaines corsaires font contre eux »[40]. Cette situation conduit à des discussions excessivement longues et les navires attendent de longs mois dans les ports en attente du jugement, comme le montre le tableau 16.1 concernant quelques prises amenées à Nice en 1794 et 1795.

38 Ibidem, Courrier du 3 juin 1793. « J'ai pour moi la conduite des Anglais et Espagnols qui ont laissé passer des navires danois et suédois chargés pour ici et pour l'arsenal de Toulon lesquels ils avaient arrêté quelques jours auparavant ».

39 Riksarkivet, Stockholm, Gallica, 510, courrier du 3 juin 1779. Les trois navires sont *Les Armes de Kalmar*, capitaine Jean Haverman, *L'Union*, capitaine Charles Moder et *La Marthe*, capitaine Auguste Degerstrom.

40 Rigsarkivet, Copenhague, Department of Foreign Affairs, France, 2046.

Prenons l'exemple de *La Bourse de Copenhague* pendant la guerre de Sept ans. Le navire, pris en mai 1757, est encore en rivière de Bayonne en janvier 1759, en attente d'une décision : « Les sucres coulent, dépérissent et perdent leur poids tandis que les tabacs « sèchent, se pourrissent et leur substance' s'évanouit ». Finalement, les corsaires vendent les marchandises « au cas où la prise serait bonne » en s'attribuant 12.445 livres de frais dont une confortable commission de 3.803 livres avec l'accord de l'Amirauté. En dernier lieu, la vente de la cargaison, arrangée par les corsaires ne produit que 3.000 livres. De son côté, le navire « a tellement vieilli et pourri sur cette rivière qu'on a été obligé de le vendre. Il a été acheté pour 6.050 livres, prix très modique mais bien payé pour ce qu'il vaut… » alors qu'il était estimé 20–25 000 livres à son arrivée à Bayonne. La décision royale arrive enfin le 11 septembre 1759 : les corsaires obtiennent le tiers de la prise. Ces derniers acceptent le jugement mais réclament « des frais pour la garde du navire, décharge, magasinage et vente des marchandises. Ces frais font un objet de 10.000 livres »[41].

Même si les décisions du pouvoir central à Paris sont favorables aux neutres, les corsaires ne s'avouent jamais vaincus et retardent systématiquement les bâtiments après les jugements. En avril 1793, trois navires danois sont amenés par des corsaires à Lorient. Tout d'abord, le tribunal de commerce invalide les trois prises mais, en raison du nouveau décret du 9 mai, le tribunal de district, où les corsaires ont fait appel, déclare le 12 juillet 1793 que les prises sont valables. Finalement, les services diplomatiques danois obtiennent des autorités parisiennes la libération des trois navires. Mais le 14 juillet, le chargé d'ambassade écrit :

> J'avais obtenu avec beaucoup de peine l'élargissement des vaisseaux danois richement chargés pour le compte d'Hambourg et d'Altona et détenus le plus injustement du monde à Lorient. Mr. Lebrun en m'envoyant la copie de l'arrêt du conseil exécutif me marquait que les ordres du ministre de la Marine pour la levée des scellés seraient incessamment envoyés à Lorient […]. J'apprends qu'ils ne l'ont pas été et on m'a assuré que les armateurs des corsaires ont déposé chez un notaire 200,000 livres pour obtenir, quant à ces prises, un décret favorable. Peut-être ne

41 Rigsarkivet, Copenhague, Tyske Kancelli 295, 1754–1762, courriers du 6 octobre 1759 et du 26 janvier 1760.

> réussiront-ils pas mais l'affaire est en attendant retardée et son issue donne des inquiétudes...[42]

En novembre 1793, le problème n'est toujours pas réglé.

L'arbitraire paraît en effet bien réel aux armateurs scandinaves car même les vaisseaux neutres à destination de la France sont parfois pris par les corsaires français. Ainsi, en août 1793, le navire *La Marguerite*, capitaine Morten Hansen de Copenhague, chargé de froment pour Bordeaux, est pris par un corsaire de Saint-Malo où il est déchargé, « la municipalité ayant un besoin urgent de grains »[43]. Le négociant bordelais von Hemert demande le règlement des marchandises, mais la municipalité malouine ne veut payer que 40 000 livres, c'est-à-dire ce qu'avait produit la vente de la cargaison, sans tenir compte des indemnités dues au capitaine. Il faut une décision du conseil exécutif provisoire du 11 mars 1794 pour que l'administration de la Marine verse un complément de 12 000 livres à Von Hemert, à charge pour elle d'obtenir le remboursement du solde à la municipalité de Saint-Malo[44]. Les situations sont parfois ubuesques. Ainsi, à Brest, les autorités du port exigent que les bâtiments pris par la Marine paient « un droit de tonnelage de 50 sous par tonneau », comme tous les autres navires étrangers[45].

Les règlements des différends entre la navigation neutre et les autorités françaises sont généralement compliqués à l'exemple des guerres révolutionnaires. La Convention sait qu'elle a besoin de l'aide des puissances scandinaves et ne veut pas que celles-ci passent dans le camp ennemi. En conséquence, pour ne pas trop les mécontenter, elle prend les mêmes dispositions que la Grande-Bretagne et décide, par le décret du 9 mai 1793, de faire l'acquisition des cargaisons de grains saisies, marchandises qui constituent la majeure partie des transports effectués par les flottes neutres en ces temps de guerre,

42 Rigsarkivet, Copenhague, Department of Foreign Affairs, France, 2046, courrier du 14 juillet 1793.

43 Rigsarkivet, Copenhague, Kommercekollegiet, 1817, Sager vedr. Danske skibes opringelse i franske farvande, Courrier de von Hemert de Bordeaux du 1er août 1793. MAE La Courneuve, Danemark, courrier du 20 pluviôse an II (8 février 1794). Depuis le 22 juin 1793, les autorités révolutionnaires, en raison du manque de marins pour la Marine de guerre, ont décrété un embargo sur la course qui n'est levé que le 23 messidor an III (10 août 1795). Apparemment quelques corsaires continuent à faire des prises au cours de l'été 1793.

44 Archives du Ministère des Affaires Etrangères (MAE) La Courneuve, Danemark, extrait des registres de délibération du conseil exécutif provisoire du 21 ventôse an II (11 mars 1794).

45 MAE, Suède, microfilm 7115, Lettre de Reinicke, consul de Suède au Havre du 23 mai 1794.

même si ces trafics paraissent douteux[46]. Cette solution permet de satisfaire tout le monde. Pour la France, elle permet d'obtenir des céréales, de les mettre immédiatement en vente et de faire chuter les tensions sur les marchés et, pour les neutres, les procédures sont allégées et il n'y a pas de contestations sur les marchandises qui sont immédiatement vendues. Ainsi, le chargé d'affaires du consulat du Danemark à Nantes, au sujet de deux navires qui viennent d'être saisis par la Marine française : « tout devra s'arranger à la satisfaction des parties »[47].

L'application du décret est cependant difficile comme l'indique un document daté du 2 ventôse an IV (21 février 1796)[48]. Tout d'abord, comme les armateurs prennent des destinations simulées quand ils viennent en France pour éviter la saisie par les Britanniques, « il arriva en conséquence que des blés achetés en Amérique ou dans le Nord, par un agent à Nantes ou Rouen ou de quelque autre ville, furent condamnés au Havre ou à Dunkerque. De là des réclamations sans fin, de la défiance et une stagnation totale du trafic »[49]. Ensuite, le gouvernement anglais « crut devoir se fonder sur la loi du 9 mai pour redoubler de sévérité envers les neutres … »[50]. Enfin, les navires scandinaves, ne pouvant plus naviguer sans être immédiatement saisis par l'un ou l'autre des belligérants, ce qui entraîne naturellement des pertes de temps considérables en raison des procédures,

> cessèrent d'envoyer pour leur compte des denrées en France de sorte qu'au bout de 8 mois, on ne vit plus dans nos ports que des cargaisons achetées d'avance par les agents de la Marine et la Commission de commerce. Après avoir donné une sorte de fonction au principe adopté par l'Angleterre, on mit un embargo sur nos corsaires ; dès lors tous les avantages étaient pour l'Angleterre et nous n'avions de commun avec elle que le dégoût et le mécontentement des neutres[51].

De plus, le décret du 9 mai 1793 a un autre inconvénient de taille : son coût exorbitant, alors même que les finances de la France sont limitées. En raison de tous ces problèmes, l'application de la loi est successivement confirmée puis

46 Décret du 9–12 mai 1793.

47 Rigsarkivet, Copenhague, Komercekollegiet, journalsager 1158, Courrier du 8 mai 1793.

48 ANF FII 63, Réflexions sur quelques inconvénients qui ont résulté de la loi du 9 mai 1793 touchant la navigation des neutres du 2 ventôse an IV (21 février 1796).

49 Ibidem.

50 Ibidem.

51 Ibidem.

rapportée ce qui conduit à des jugements arbitraires et à l'incompréhension des neutres.

Enfin, le décret du 9 mai prévoit :

> Dans tous les cas les navires neutres seront relâchés au moment où le déchargement des comestibles arrêtés ou des marchandises saisies aura été effectué. Une juste indemnité sera accordée, à raison de leur détention, par les tribunaux qui doivent reconnaître la validité des prises.

Dans la pratique, les prises de navires neutres conduisent à des multiples problèmes qui font naturellement monter les indemnités. Le 29 nivôse an II (18 janvier 1794), le représentant Lequinio indique auprès du port de Rochefort qu'il est « urgent de hâter » le départ du navire hambourgeois *La Dorothea-Maria* jugée comme mauvaise prise : « vous sentirez l'importance de l'expédier au plus tôt lorsque vous saurez que, jusqu'à l'entier payement de son fret, il lui est alloué vingt-cinq florins par jour »[52]. La cargaison a déjà été mise en magasin et une partie utilisée « pour la subsistance des ouvriers de ce port ». Les questions se multiplient : le capitaine peut-il prendre une cargaison de retour en eau-de-vie pour le Danemark pour diminuer les frais ? Quel est le cours du change pour le paiement de son fret ? Alors que le coût d'achat du chargement de 102 last de froment se monte à 5 272 florins, le montant de ses 82 jours d'indemnités (8 jours ont été déduits pour le déchargement) s'établit le 28 nivôse à 2 050 florins. Certains armateurs laissent volontairement courir les délais pour augmenter leurs indemnités. Ainsi, *L'Emilia Galotti* « reste en attendant tranquille à Toulon et grossit ses prétentions pour les jours qu'il consume sans rien faire »[53].

Une fois l'indemnité fixée en accord avec l'armateur, il faut qu'elle soit payée, ce qui nécessite encore beaucoup de mois, voire d'années.

> En général, tous les capitaines se plaignent avec raison de la lenteur que l'on met aux jugements de leurs affaires et au payement des indemnités qui leur ont été accordées. Plusieurs d'entre eux ont resté sur la rade de Brest pendant plus de deux mois, d'autres de 4 à 5 mois dans le port à attendre le payement de leur fret et accessoires et en particulier le capitaine Wallis, s'est plaint à mon vice-consul que le commandant de la Pomone l'ayant arrêté en mer, l'a forcé de quitter son navire et que, par-là, il

52 ANF, F11 435, courrier de Lequinio du 29 nivôse an II (18 janvier 1794).

53 Rigsarkivet, Copenhague, Kommercekollegiet, Journalsager, 1161, Courrier de Marseille du 25 octobre 1794.

a été à la veille de le perdre, n'étant entré au port de Brest que trois mois après son arrestation[54].

Bien souvent, les autorités qu'elles soient locales ou nationales n'ont pas les ressources pour régler les indemnités convenues et font traîner les paiements. En avril 1795, trois capitaines danois « n'ont pu jusqu'à présent être remboursés de leur fret et de leurs indemnités adjugées, et cela faute de numéraire és mains du payeur général de la marine, n'y en ayant point de disponible tant à Toulon qu'à Marseille »[55]. Le navire *La Minerve*, chargé de 110 last de froment entre Amsterdam et Carthagène, est pris le 5 janvier 1794 et amené à Brest. Le jugement de bonne prise du 6 mars 1794 établit que le fret et la cargaison doivent être réglés au capitaine « conformément à ses connaissements et à sa charte-partie »[56]. L'affaire n'est toujours pas terminée le 28 janvier 1802. De la même manière, Hendrick Hendricksen pris en l'an II au large d'Antibes alors qu'il transporte du vin, des cuirs et autres marchandises entre Porto et Gênes, doit justifier du non-paiement de sa créance aux autorités françaises en l'an X, soit huit ans après les faits[57].

Le tableau 16.2 qui présente deux états des réclamations liquidées de navires danois, malheureusement non daté, mais qui a sans doute été envoyé aux autorités françaises à la fin des années 1790 ou au début des années 1800, montre le coût très important des dédommagements dus aux armateurs des navires. D'une manière générale, si ces procédures d'indemnisation traînent en longueur, les montants demandés par les négociants scandinaves sont acceptés par les autorités révolutionnaires et sont finalement payées pour ne pas envenimer les relations diplomatiques avec des pays qui, s'ils ne sont pas alliés, ne sont pas non plus des ennemis.

6 Conclusion

Les prises, en temps de guerre donnent lieu à une véritable piraterie officielle organisée par les corsaires. Lorsqu'un navire neutre est saisi, les capitaines

54 MAE, Suède, microfilm 7115, Lettre de Reinicke, consul de Suède au Havre du 23 mai 1794.

55 Rigsarkivet, Copenhague, Kommercekollegiet, Journalsager, 1160, Courrier de Gênes du 7 avril 1795.

56 Rigsarkivet, Copenhague, Kommercekollegiet, 1817, Commission de la comptabilité intermédiaire du 8 pluviôse an X (28 janvier 1802).

57 Rigsarkivet, Copenhague, Kommercekollegiet, 1817, Commission de la comptabilité intermédiaire du 10 pluviôse an X (30 janvier 1802).

cherchent par tous les moyens à justifier leur prise et agissent comme si les bâtiments arraisonnés leur appartiennent. Les équipages sont maltraités et les pillages sont systématiques. Cependant, il est nécessaire de relativiser, ces cas restent malgré tout exceptionnels et le nombre de navires neutres qui ont de graves problèmes avec les corsaires est réduit comparativement à l'intense activité de leur navigation. De plus, les assurances peuvent couvrir les dommages subis et la flambée des tarifs des frets compense très largement ces désagréments. Le risque est calculé et les intérêts économiques des pays scandinaves ne sont guère lésés.

Le Danemark cherche à profiter des conflits entre la France et l'Angleterre pour développer ses activités maritimes. Pour ceci, il choisit de rester en bons termes avec la France, avec qui il est lié par un traité et qu'il approvisionne en produits du Nord. Il évite également de froisser la puissance économique britannique dont l'importante flotte alimente une grande partie la caisse de la douane du Sund, principale source de financement de la monarchie scandinave[58] mais qui a aussi besoin d'utiliser librement les mers du Nord de l'Europe. Satisfaire tout le monde signifie développer son commerce et sa navigation dans toute l'Europe, et donc enrichir le pays. Le consul de Trondheim a bien compris la situation du Danemark :

> pays neutre dont le prince a intérêt à faire respecter sa neutralité, également que de soutenir le commerce et la navigation des nations étrangères qui côtoient ses côtes et qui lui apportent et à ses sujets tant d'avantages, tant par les droits du Sund qu'elles payent que par l'argent considérable qu'elles répandent le long de la côte en pilotage et en approvisionnements[59].

Ainsi, la France tout comme l'Angleterre ont besoin d'être en bons termes avec le Danemark. S'il y a saisie de navires, les armateurs avec l'appui des autorités savent se défendre et profitent des avantages politiques du pays pour réclamer de confortables indemnités à leurs agresseurs.

58 ANF, B1 452, Mémoire sur un projet de commerce avec le Nord (1754). « Ce commerce de la Baltique paraît d'autant plus considérable qu'il est constant qu'il produit au roi de Danemark par année au moins 200.000 rxd argent de banque ce qui revient à un million cinquante mille livres de France ».

59 ANF, B3 418, Mémoire de Framery du 6 juillet 1779.

Appendices

TABLE 16.1 Navires amenés par des corsaires à Nice

Navire	Capitaine	Chargement	Saisie	Départ	Durée
La Dame Catherine de Norberg	Christian Leymand	78,1/2 last. Cuirs, blé, chanvre et cire Saint-Pétersbourg-Livourne	18 mai 1794	28 février 1795	254 jours
Emilie de Frunkeem	Hans Tonnesen	28 last Soies, étoffes et quincailleries Départ de Gênes	23 mai 1794	26 janvier 1795	216 jours
Le Prince Royal de Danemark d'Altona	Michel Lange	110 last. Marbre, raisins de Corinthe, huile, gingembre Livourne-Amsterdam	19 octobre 1794	26 janvier 1795	99 jours

SOURCE : RIGSARKIVET, COPENHAGUE, KOMMERCEKOLLEGIET, JOURNALSAGER, 1161, LISTE DE NAVIRES DU 5 MARS 1795

TABLE 16.2 État des réclamations liquidées

Navires	Capitaines	Montant liquidation		
		Livres	Sous	Deniers
La Dame Catherine	Ch Leyman	36086	12	
Le Neptune	Rickmers Peters	61360	5	
La Christiania	N. Abelste	75953	1	
La Belle Margarita	Auckes Reckers	44752	2	4
La Petronilla Cornelia	P. Willem de Jong	18790	8	11
L'Helène	Auguste Kock	12701		2
La Sophie	Rasmussen	1148		2
Le Neptune	C.P. Moller	12415	13	6
L'Enrum	Martin Langefeldt	18195	1	6
Le Hoop (*L'Espérance*)	B.S. Lon[a]	29959	9	3
La Louise	Penchaud	8893	11	11

TABLE 16.2 État des réclamations liquidées (*cont.*)

Navires	Capitaines	Montant liquidation		
		Livres	Sous	Deniers
La Minerve	Namen Jensen	22259	13	2
Le Petrus	L.F. Lorentzen	20697	18	6
Les trois Frères	Peter Hansen	7910	v	8
Le Triton	Henrichsen	56510	6	6
Les Deux Sœurs	Mads Schoustad	2403		
La Celeste	Sinclair	57624	12	7
Le Delphin	H Henrichsen	11805	5	
L'Emilie Galotti	Jurgen Nannings	68970	11	3
L'Espérance	And. Andresen	11111		9
L'Espérance	Carsten Kock	39395	3	8
L'Epreuve	A Nikelsen	120707	4	
Le Général Vouhult	J. Meinert Meinerz	43361	5	4
L'Expédit	Harwig Lund	258952	12	

a Montant liquidé d'après la loi du 24 frimaire an VI (14 décembre 1797) d'après la demande du fondé de pouvoir.

SOURCE : RIGSARKIVET, COPENHAGUE, KOMMERCEKOLLEGIET, 1817, DOCUMENTS NON DATÉS

TABLE 16.3 Navires danois pris au cours de la guerre de Sept-ans par les corsaires français

Date	Nom et origine	Transport	Corsaire	Port de conduite	Résultat et commentaires
24/01/1756	*Elisabeth* de Christiansand	Guernesey-Cork Eau-de-vie, thé et tabac	*L'Espérance* de Saint-Malo	Morlaix	Pas de passeport, Chartes parties simulées, anglais à bord Bonne prise. Affaire pas assez bonne pour un appel
18/04/1756	Brigantin du sr Beverhoudt			St Domingue	Pavillon et passeport anglais Bonne prise

TABLE 16.3 Navires danois pris au cours de la guerre de Sept-ans par les corsaires français (*cont.*)

Date	Nom et origine	Transport	Corsaire	Port de conduite	Résultat et commentaires
06/1756	« *Dorothée* » d'Altona	Gibraltar-Tetouan	Flotte de M. De la Galissonnière	Toulon	Présence à bord de 16 Turcs « dont quelques uns fort riches Algériens et autres sujets du roi de Maroc ». Navire pillé par les matelots de l'escadre Relâché
03/09/1756	*Le Mercure* de Copenhague	Navire de traite Ste Croix-Copenhague Sucre	*L'Espérance*	Espagne puis Bayonne	Navire pillé lors de la prise Mauvaise prise sans dommages à payer
07/10/1756	*Den Junge Tobias* de Flensbourg			La Spezia	Relâché
03/12/1756	*Le Neptune* de Christiansand			Marseille	Capitaine d'origine anglaise naturalisé danois (James Park) Navire construit dans les colonies anglaises Pavillon anglais à bord Confisqué
12/1756	*Le Prince* d'Altona	Exon (Anglet.) pour Gênes et Livourne Draperies et étoffes de laine	« *Le Grand Alexandre* »	Marseille	Capitaine d'origine hollandaise Confisqué avec la cargaison (marchandises pour compte anglais)
21/12/1756	*Catherine Jeanne* de Christiania			Marseille	Cargaison rendue aux propriétaires avec 1500 Livres de dommages et intérêts

TABLE 16.3 Navires danois pris au cours de la guerre de Sept-ans par les corsaires français (*cont.*)

Date	Nom et origine	Transport	Corsaire	Port de conduite	Résultat et commentaires
31/12/1756	*Le Soleil Levant* de Flensbourg	Gallipoli-Amsterdam Huile		Marseille	Obligé de suivre le corsaire « ce qui a beaucoup endommagé les mâts » Jugé mauvaise prise Dommages et intérêts
09/01/1757	*Anne Catherine* de Bergen		« *Le Colibri* », « *Le Soleil Levant* » et « *Bayard* »	Marseille	Jugée comme bonne prise Appel des propriétaires Le roi accorde une ordonnance de restitution
22/02/1757	*La Providence* d'Altona	Dublin-Livourne et Naples		Marseille	Confisqué avec la cargaison. L'interprète ne voulait pas traduire les pièces, selon lui inutiles, alors qu'elles étaient en défaveur du corsaire. Appel au Conseil Royal
05/03/1757	*Le Vieux Simeon* de Flensbourg			Morlaix	Relâché. Accommodement avec le corsaire.
05/03/1757	*Fredérique Sophie* de Porsgrund			Morlaix	Relâché. Accommodement avec le corsaire.
07/05/1757	*Lansskabet Egderstedt* d'Altona	Dép: Port Maurice Huile	*La Comtesse de Bentheim* de Saint-Malo	Cherbourg	Repris sur les Anglais Relâché mais doit payer 1/3 de la valeur du navire et de la cargaison Navire repris par les Anglais lors de leur descente sur Cherbourg

TABLE 16.3 Navires danois pris au cours de la guerre de Sept-ans par les corsaires français (*cont.*)

Date	Nom et origine	Transport	Corsaire	Port de conduite	Résultat et commentaires
06/05/1757	*La Bourse de Copenhague* d'Altona	Lisbonne-Hambourg Sucre	*Le Comte de Gramont* et le *Maréchal de Richelieu*	Bayonne	Repris sur les Anglais. Papiers en Angleterre Le tiers du navire et de la cargaison ont été confisqués Appel au Conseil Royal
10/06/1757	*Sainte Croix* de Ste Croix	Ste Croix-Møn Tafia et Coton	*La Princesse Soubise*	Morlaix	Navire repris par les Anglais Le capitaine (Robert Stapelton) supposé anglais est emprisonné
09/06/1757	*Marthe & Judith* de Christiansand	Guernesey-Hambourg Sucre, indigo café et tabac	Corsaires de Boulogne et Dunkerque	Ostende	Erreur dans le rôle d'équipage Navire confisqué avec sa cargaison
07/1757	*Les Trois Princesses* de Copenhague	Copenhague-Alger Munitions de guerre		Île de Ré puis Morlaix	Marchandises destinées à Alger (traité entre le Danemark et les Etats barbaresques) Le roi ordonne la restitution avec dédommagement
16/03/1758	*Kronprintz Christian* de Drontheim	Drogues et épiceries	*La Comtesse de la Serre*	Dunkerque	Navire acheté à Dublin Confisqué Appel de l'armateur
19/04/1758	*Helwig Catherine* d'Arendal	Poutres et planches	*Le Printemps*	Dunkerque	Accommodement et relâché
24/04/1758	*Elisabeth* d'Aabenraa	Planches et fer	*Le Printemps*	Dunkerque	Accommodement et relâché
	La Concorde de Christiania	Planches et bois de construction			Echoué sur la côte de Barfleur Confisqué par l'amirauté Relâché avec sa cargaison

TABLE 16.3 Navires danois pris au cours de la guerre de Sept-ans par les corsaires français (*cont.*)

Date	Nom et origine	Transport	Corsaire	Port de conduite	Résultat et commentaires
	Ida Catherine d'Aabenraa	Cuivre, fer, bois de charpente			Echoué Relâché
	La Nymphe de mer d'Altona	Cire jaune, draps, toiles			Echoué Relâché par ordre du roi
30/07/1759	*Le Soleil Levant* de Bergen	Stockfish	*Le St Jean Baptiste* et *La Vierge des Douleurs*	Port Mahon	Confisqué avec la cargaison
10/11/1759	*Le Jeune Tobie* de Flensbourg	Sucre, poivre, bois du Brésil, poisson salé et fer	« *Le St Antoine de Padoue* »	Port Mahon	Relâché avec la cargaison
23/01/1760	*Les Quatre frères* de Christiania	Oranges et fruits	*Le Danger* de Boulogne	Dunkerque	Relâché Confiscation des canons
30/03/1760	*La Concorde* de Bergen	Gibraltar-Livourne Sucre, café et indigo	*L'annonciation* de La Ciotat	Marseille	Relâché avec la cargaison Appel du corsaire. L'armateur décide s'accommoder avec le corsaire (600 livres de désistement)
08/06/1760	*Le Faucon* de Krageroe	Dest. : Ancône Sucre, poivre et étain	*Le St Antoine* de Padoue	Port Mahon	Prétexte prise : pilote côtier anglais à bord Les corsaires introduisent un pavillon et des papiers anglais à bord Relâché avec la cargaison sans dommages
10/07/1760	*La Demoiselle Anne* d'Altona	Dép. : Barcelone Eau-de-vie et mouchoirs de soie	*Le St Antoine de Padoue* et *La Brise*	Malaga	Chargement à Barcelone pour le compte d'une maison d'origine anglaise. Relâché avec 600 livres de dédommagement

TABLE 16.3 Navires danois pris au cours de la guerre de Sept-ans par les corsaires français (*cont.*)

Date	Nom et origine	Transport	Corsaire	Port de conduite	Résultat et commentaires
16/10/1760	*La Diligence* de Laurwigen	Waterford-Rotterdam Beurre	*L'Inpromptu* de Calais	Calais	Marchandises hollandaises Relâché sans dédommagement Appel de l'armateur
1760	*Dorothée Marguerite* de Bergen	Rogues et planches			Echoué Relâché
1760	*Anne Margrethe* de Flensbourg	Lisbonne-Gênes	*Les Droits de l'Homme* de Villefranche	Nice	
1761	*Providentia* de Bergen	Portugal-Guernesey Eau-de-vie	Corsaire de Nantes (Benoit)	Canaries	Le corsaire force le capitaine à lui expédier une lettre de change de 9000 livres
03/02/1761	*La Fortune* d'Aabenraa	Dép. : côte d'Afrique Blé	*La Vierge du Bon Chemin*	Mahon	Deux anglais à bord Confisqué avec les marchandises
08/03/1761	*Marguerite Dorothée* d'Eckernførde	Vin	*La Brave*	Mahon	Marchandises espagnoles Les corsaires prétendent que le vin est destiné à la garnison anglaise de Gibraltar Relâché sans dédommagement
03/06/1761	*Le St Johan* de Sønderborg	Alicante-Londres Barils et balles de soie	*La Victoire*	Mahon	Marchandises pour compte anglais et espagnol Relâché
12/10/1761	*Heldwig Catherine* d'Arendal	Angleterre-Hambourg Etain, sucre, café		Dunkerque	Accommodement entre les parties
1761	*Catherine Dorothée*			Mahon	Marchandises pour compte espagnol Relâché

TABLE 16.3 Navires danois pris au cours de la guerre de Sept-ans par les corsaires français (*cont.*)

Date	Nom et origine	Transport	Corsaire	Port de conduite	Résultat et commentaires
16/01/1762	*Le Soleil* d'Eckernførde	Soufre	*La Rigole*	Mahon	Navire relâché, cargaison confisquée
28/03/1762	*L'Union* de Christiansand	Plomb, alun	*La Vendangeuse*	Mahon	Relâché
30/06/1762	*La Constance* de Christiansand	Sucre et tafia	*César*	Bayonne	Relâché avec la cargaison et 500 livres de dédommagement
07/09/1761	*Anne Elisabeth* de Flensbourg	Blé	*L'Oiseau*	Marseille	

SOURCE : RIGSARKIVET, COPENHAGUE, ERHARD FRIIS' GESANDTSKABSARKIV, 295, 1754–1762, AKTER OG DOKUMENTER BVEDR. DANSKE SKIBE OPBRAGT I FRANKRIG

TABLE 16.4 Navires danois pris par les corsaires et les navires français en 1793

Date	Navire	Capitaine	Chargement	Informations
mars 1793	*Concorde* d'Apenrade	Peter Booy Simonsen	Vins et eau-de-vie Cette-Bremen	Pris par Le Général Courpon de Bordeaux Amené à La Rochelle Déclaré bonne prise
4 mars 1793	*Le Christian* de Bergen	Henrich Guisbert Ohman	Morue sèche, saumon salé et huile de poisson Bergen-Bilbao	
9 mars 1793	*Nicolas Christine* de Norborg	Thomas Thomssen	Raisin, Piment, coton… Navire ayant chargé « à la cueillette » (30 connaissements) Trieste-Hambourg	Pris par un corsaire de Marseille Amené à Marseille
16 mars 1793	*Bornholm* de Bornholm	Jacob Nicolai Wichman	Huile Gallipoli-St Petersbourg	Charte partie faite à Gênes à l'ordre de Wienholt, Tideman et Cie de Livourne Amené à Marseille

TABLE 16.4 Navires danois pris par les corsaires et les navires français en 1793 (*cont.*)

Date	Navire	Capitaine	Chargement	Informations
20 mars 1793	*Benedict van Eiben* d'Altona	Peter Jabobs	Div. marchandises Trieste-Hambourg	Amené à Marseille
9 avril 1793	*Union*	Pieter Taysen	Malaga-Stettin	Pris par L'Ambitieux de St Malo Amené à Lorient
10 avril 1793	*La Junon* de Brême	Herman Conrad Högeman	Riz Charlestown-Bremen	Pris par La Liberté de St Malo Amené à Lorient
11 avril 1793	*Gertrude Catherine* de Copenhague	Hausheimbrige	Sucre, café, indigo Cadix-Hambourg et Altona	Pris par Le Républicain de Nantes Amené à Lorient
21 avril 1793	*Fedessime* d'Arendal	Ole Evensen	Planches	Pris par la frégate La Tamise à 6 lieues de Portsmouth Amené à Roscoff
22 avril 1793	*Expédition* de Flekefjord	Peter Rafos	Morue, rogue, huile de poisson pour Bilbao	Pris par la frégate L'Insurgent Amené à Roscoff
24 avril 1793	*Dame Catherine* d'Altona		Vins, amandes et div. Marseille-Hambourg	Pris par Le Républicain de Nantes Amené à Lorient
Avril 1793	? de Flensbourg	Jordt	Vin et eau de vie Cette-Hollande	Amené à Dunkerque
Avril 1793	? de Flensbourg	Rasmussen	Vin et eau de vie Cette-Hollande	Amené à Dunkerque
Mai 1793	*Christian Severin* de Fahrsund	Gabriel Moswold	Chanvre et haricots Ancône-Barcelone	Amené à Marseille
Juin 1793	*Inge Louise*	Dirck Reinders	Tabac, coton, sucre... Lisbonne-Gênes	Amené à Marseille
27 juillet 1793	*Morgenrothe*	Jens Oluf Tanderup	Froment Flensbourg-Barcelone	Pris par la frégate Cléopatre Amené à Saint-Malo

TABLE 16.4 Navires danois pris par les corsaires et les navires français en 1793 (*cont.*)

Date	Navire	Capitaine	Chargement	Informations
Août 1793	? de Copenhague	Morten Hansen	Froment pour Von Hemert de Bordeaux	Pris par un corsaire de St Malo Amené à St Malo
26 nov. 1793	*Les Trois Frères*	Peter J. Clausen	Froment Amsterdam- San Sebastian	Pris par la frégate La Félicité Amené à Brest
31 déc. 1793	*Famke Margaretha* d'Altona	Giacomo Hansen Bruun	Orge Gênes pour Malaga, Cadix ou Lisbonne	Amené à Marseille Bonne Prise

SOURCE : LISTE TRÈS LOIN D'ÊTRE EXHAUSTIVE TIRÉE DE DIVERSES SOURCES NOTAMMENT : RIGSARKIVET, COPENHAGUE, KOMMERCEKOLLEGIET, 1817, SAGER VEDR. DANSKE SKIBES OPRINGELSE I FRANSKE FARVANDE

TABLE 16.5 Navires danois pris par les corsaires et les navires français en 1794–1795

Date	Navire	Capitaine	Chargement	Informations
janv.1794	*Die Junge Janus*	Christian Jorgensen	Copenhague-Carthagène	
février 1794	*Harmonie* Flensbourg	E Hanssen		Amené à Brest
5 janvier 1794	*Minerve*	Namen Jensen	Froment Amsterdam-Carhagène (110 last)	Pris par le Northumberland Amené à Brest Bonne prise
29 nivôse II 18 janv. 1794	*Dorothea Maria* Hambourg	Erdmann Sebalt	Froment Bremen-Bilbao	Pris par La Médée de Rochefort Amené à Rochefort Mauvaise prise
avril 1794	Trondheim	Peter H. Lunde	Stockfish pour Livourne	Amené à Toulon
avril 1794	*Christiana Benedicta* Bergen	Friedrich Hansen	Fruits, huiles, confitures Gênes-Hambourg	Amené à Toulon
21 avril 1794	*Le Krageroe* Tønsberg	Hans Peter Kinch	Tabac Nouvelle Angeterre.-Rotterdam	Pris par la frégate L'Insurgente Amené à Brest Bonne prise

TABLE 16.5 Navires danois pris par les corsaires et les navires français en 1794–1795 (*cont.*)

Date	Navire	Capitaine	Chargement	Informations
3 mai 1794	*Jonge Jean Gerard* St Thomas	Carl Gottfried Hintz	Amsterdam-Lisbonne	Amené à Brest
18 juin 1794	*Janus* Copenhague	Niels Holbaech	Froment	Pris par la corvette La Musette Amené à Nantes
15 juillet 1794	*Charlotte Marie* Altona	Johan Genry Axien	Salaisons	Pris par la goelette La Montagne Amené à Nantes
18 sept. 1794	*Delphin*	Hendrick Henrichsen	Vin, coton, cuirs etc… Porto-Gênes	Pris par la felouque Le Furet Amené à Villefranche puis Toulon (mauvaise prise)
7 oct. 1794	*La Jeune Helène*	Jeppe Hansen Holm		Main levée
14 oct. 1794	*Femsyskonde*	Laurentzen	Barcelone-Guernesey	Pris par la frégate La Précieuse Amené à Brest
3 janv. 1795	*La Dame Lucie* Flensbourg		Grains, cuirs, pelleteries, menus cordages et chandelles St Pétersbourg-Lisbonne	Pris par les frégates La Galatée et La Seine Amené à Dunkerque
27 fév. 1795	*Dronningaard* Friderichsnagore	Jacon Helleson	Friderichsnagore-Cop.	Amené à Brest mais repris par les Anglais
mars 1795	*Général von Huth* Altona	J.M Meinertz	Diverses marchandises Hambourg-Livourne	Amené à Marseille puis à Toulon
mars 1795	*Les Cinq Amis*	Jacob Jacobsen	Philadelphie-Livourne	Pris et relâché
mars 1795	Altona	Theunis Ericksen Munck	Lisbonne-Gênes	Connaissements suisses Relâché
Juillet 1795	*Emilia Galotti* Copenhague	Propriété de Lars Larssen	Bois Naples-Alicante	Amené à Toulon
Juillet 1795	Sønderborg	Koch	Sur lest Barcelone-Livourne	Amené à Marseille puis à Toulon

TABLE 16.5 Navires danois pris par les corsaires et les navires français en 1794–1795 (*cont.*)

Date	Navire	Capitaine	Chargement	Informations
Déc. 1795	*Peggy* de Ste Croix	Thomas Wattington	Esclaves	Pris par le corsaire Le Passepartout Amené au Cap Français Bonne prise (second d'origine espagnole)

Bibliographie

Crowhurst, P., *The French War on Trade: Privateering 1793–1815* (Aldershot 1989).

Jespersen, K. et Feldbæk, O., *Revanche og Neutralitet, Dansk Udenrigspolitiks Historie 2, 1648–1814* (Copenhague 2002).

Le Guelaff, F., *Armements en course et droit des prises maritimes* (Nancy 1999).

Schnakenbourg, E., *Entre la guerre et la paix. Neutralité et relations internationales XVIIe–XVIIIe siècles* (Rennes 2013).

Tuxen, O., « Principles and Priorities. The Danish View of Neutrality during the Colonial War of 1755–63 », *Scandinavian Journal of History*, 13, nos. 2–3 (1988) 207–232.

Index

The index includes names of persons. The names of modern historians have not been included. The pages 1–341 have been used for the index.

www.ingramcontent.com/pod-product-compliance
Lightning Source LLC
LaVergne TN
LVHW010639300926
849161LV00005B/991
* 9 7 8 9 0 0 4 3 8 0 6 3 9 *